RUSSELL B. STEVENS, Ph.D., University of Wisconsin, is Executive Secretary, National Research Council Division of Biology and Agriculture, National Academy of Sciences. Previously, Dr. Stevens was Professor of Botany and Chairman of the department, George Washington University, and on the faculty of the University of Tennessee, Auburn University, and the University of Louisville.

PLANT DISEASE

RUSSELL B. STEVENS

National Academy of Sciences
—National Research Council Division
of Biology and Agriculture

THE RONALD PRESS COMPANY · NEW YORK

Library of Congress Catalog Card Number: 73–77863
PRINTED IN THE UNITED STATES OF AMERICA

Preface

This student-oriented textbook for courses in plant pathology presents the basic dynamics of the subject against a backdrop of the agricultural system and the needs and problems of our society. The special emphasis of this book lies in what is sometimes called, rather loosely, the "principles" of plant pathology. What this means is that it strives to avoid becoming a catalog of diseases, their causes, characteristics, and cures. Rather, it looks upon plant disease as one complex of phenomena within the much larger complex of the biological sciences. It tries to portray plant pathology in such a way as to be understandable to the general biologist, yet in sufficient depth to be suitable for one who fully intends to specialize in that field. There is a conscious effort to look at the subject matter of plant pathology from the viewpoint of the nonspecialist— on the strong conviction that this is, at one and the same time, the best possible viewpoint from which the specialist should also commence his study.

Certain aspects of general agriculture are briefly treated. Long experience in teaching undergraduates has convinced me that it is risky indeed to assume that students generally are aware of what one might think must be self-evident items of background information.

Finally, throughout the book, I have striven to prepare the materials as though only students would see it. Clearly, one cannot lose sight of the student at any point without grave risk of introducing needless complexities. The biological sciences are quite difficult enough despite all that can be done; it would be most unfortunate to let nonessentials intrude. Technical terms have therefore been reduced to a minimum.

A review of the growth of the science and art of plant pathology is made substantially easier by the appearance, within the last decade or so, of a large amount of comprehensive and analytical literature. While this material is no substitute for first-hand familiarity with original re-

iii

search, the availability of review articles and monographs, properly used, greatly broadens and strengthens the student's early education. These and other important references are included in the citations at the end of this text.

To an extent substantially greater than the writer of an advanced treatise, the author of an introductory text must depend on materials provided by his colleagues in a number of specialties within the discipline. I am grateful to the many persons who supplied illustrations and supporting material, often at real inconvenience, and to those who so generously permitted me to quote passages from their published work.

RUSSELL B. STEVENS

Washington, D.C.
January, 1974

Contents

I

INTRODUCTION

1

Plant Pathology—
Art and Science

What does plant pathology include, what does it emphasize, and how do pathologists go about their business? Plant pathology is one of the life sciences, and deals for the most part with the highly complex interrelationships of two organisms—host and pathogen—in the phenomenon we identify as disease. To see its position clearly, one must look first at the fabric of the sciences as a framework on which to consider plant pathology in greater detail.

THE HIERARCHY OF THE SCIENCES

No science can fairly be called more difficult than another—any one of them can be pursued as far as the will and the mind suffice. Some are, however, more complicated than others in that they deal with more complex systems and with data that are more difficult to handle in quantitative terms.

Leaving aside the debate as to whether mathematics is or is not a science, few would argue the point that physics is the simplest of the sciences, dealing as it does with elementary particles, with the properties of the atom, with energy, with the characteristics of sound, light, mechanics, and so on. Mind you, we are not saying that physics is easy, in the usual connotation of that word—not easy then, but simple. Next in the ascending scale comes chemistry, because in the last analysis chemistry is involved with what happens when the atoms of the physicist are put together into combinations and these combinations in turn assembled with one another. Some have called physics the science of the atom; if this analogy holds then chemistry is the science of the molecule.

Biology takes as its sphere the problems of the cell and the organism, thus moving an enormous step beyond the complexity of the chemist and spanning

3

a very large sector of the total range of diversity in the physical world. At the
very top of biology, still measured by the complexity of the systems involved,
are those disciplines that must consider not only organisms as such but the interactions of diverse kinds of organisms and organisms as they occur in populations. It is here that plant pathology comes into focus.

DIVERSITY AND COMPLEXITY

What are the implications of the fact that plant pathology is among the
more complex specialties within what is the most complex general area of the
natural sciences? What meaning has this for the student who wishes to learn
about plant pathology and who may, in due time, wish to become a practicing
pathologist himself? It means at least these things: compromise, imprecision,
teamwork, challenge.

Compromise

Because plant pathology involves the interactions of diverse organisms, already at the upper levels of complexity, and the impact of the physical environment on these interactions, it cannot hope in the foreseeable future to
achieve the elegance of the physical sciences. We must settle for less and accept the compromises that are inherent in a situation where, most often, some
of the variables have not even been identified or, if identified, cannot be effectively controlled. Striving all the while to improve, the plant pathologist cannot simply wring his hands in dismay or postpone his investigations—he must
do the best he can, recognize the compromises that must be endured, and
push on with his work.

Imprecision

It has become almost a fetish with scientists these days to insist upon ever
more precise measurement of the data with which they deal. This is all to the
good provided it does not tempt them to abandon needed investigations in
which by their very nature the measurements will be imprecise. There is no
excuse for the plant pathologist to tolerate sloppy observations where it is
possible to achieve exactness, but many of the more important data of plant
pathology do not lend themselves to mathematical expression. The pathologist must be willing in these instances to settle for the degree of precision that
is attainable and to investigate whatever is of demonstrable importance

whether it is convenient to measure it or not. As someone at an earlier time has said, we can measure the size of fungus spores to the fraction of a micron and estimate the damage wrought by a disease epidemic only within a very wide margin of error. Yet who would argue that we should spend our lives measuring spores while the ravages of plant disease go unreported?

Teamwork

Plant pathology is within that category of sciences that can fairly be called synthetic. That is to say, a considerable fraction of the total substance of plant pathology is contributed more or less directly by other well-defined areas in biology—plant physiology, genetics, virology, mycology, soil microbiology, biochemistry, nematology—and from outside biology entirely—meteorology, soil science, and so on. In fact, the question has been asked whether there is anything to plant pathology other than what is brought to it from other disciplines. Most do feel that there is a valid claim for plant pathology as a science but recognize that it depends very importantly on related fields.

Another way of expressing the same point of view is simply to say that one cannot as a plant pathologist be nearly as learned in the subspecialties as he might like to be, nor as sophisticated as those who choose the subspecialty itself. The pathologist is perforce a less-than-ideal geneticist, plant physiologist, mycologist, or meteorologist, for he must be something of each and must still find time to put his knowledge and insights to work on the actual problems of disease in plants. This is an unavoidable compromise.

A wise and ready solution, or partial solution, is teamwork. By adroit management the combined efforts of several specialists can largely circumvent the barrier just noted. The plant pathologist can team with the biochemist, the mycologist, and the climatologist to work out solutions to a problem that no one of them could adequately handle on his own. Surely the fashions of the future will turn more and more to the cooperative work of several persons, building upon the special talents and experience of each.

Challenge

By far the most important and exciting aspect of the diversity and complexity of plant pathology is the challenge it affords for those engaged in it. It would be an inexcusable exaggeration to say that all of the questions in physics and chemistry have been answered. At the same time more and more physical scientists are finding their interest kindled by biological problems.

And surely the most intricate situations in biology are those that have a fundamentally ecological character, where the observed phenomena involve a number of interacting factors. In the decade of the 1960's molecular biology enjoyed a period of high popularity. Environmental biology, in its broadest sense, looks to be the fashion of the 1970's and will call for new insights, new energy, and new modes of attack. Plant pathology is not the least of the primarily environmental sectors of modern biological sciences.

In summary, then, it might be said that plant pathology by virtue of the questions that are its sphere of responsibility, rather than through any conspicuous inadequacies of plant pathologists, is a less mature science than is physics, or chemistry, or some of the simpler biologies. Brains, hard work, and a measure of luck will be needed in the years ahead to move plant pathology along in step with its sister sciences.

THE SIGNIFICANCE OF PLANT DISEASE

For so far as it is possible to see into the future, mankind will depend, as it always has, on the plant world for food and fiber and for a range of other essential materials. True, technology has made possible a whole host of products and processes that diversify the material resources of modern societies, but the crucial role of agriculture and forestry remains unchallenged.

Whatever else may be the implications of plant disease, its most direct impact is to reduce the quantity or quality of the materials derived from the agricultural lands, the ranges, and the forests. On balance this can never be other than detrimental to human welfare, although there can be circumstances where special groups will enjoy temporary gains. Just *how* harmful are plant diseases is a most complex and difficult question, the answers to which are many, depending on the crop, the place, the specific nature of the disease, and so on.

In a later chapter will be marshalled the several arguments concerning the economics of disease and disease control. Suffice it here to say that for the individual producer and for consumers as a group maximum production of agricultural materials with minimum disease loss is always to be preferred. The crux of the situation is to recognize that on the phenomenon of disease and on its detrimental effect on human welfare rests the entire fabric of plant pathology, from the most esoteric research to the most pedestrian applications.

Efforts have been made, of course, to estimate the toll taken by plant disease in terms of monetary losses, and in a few instances the human misery brought on by losses in essential food has been so great that it came to the attention of people generally. Doubtless the most publicized such event of all time was the potato blight epidemic of the middle nineteenth century. A considerable number of additional examples of catastrophic disease have been assembled by Klinkowski (1970), but the simple fact is that the year-in, year-out impact of plant disease on human welfare is imperfectly known and occurs in such a way as to be entirely missed by a very large segment of the human population. As the citizens of the technologically advanced nations become increasingly divorced from the agricultural enterprises that provide so large a fraction of their food and renewable resources, public awareness of the significance of plant disease is likely to dwindle to a point even below that which it enjoys at present.

Statistics aside, there can be no doubt of the central importance of plant disease in reducing the productivity of cultivated crops, rangelands, and forests (Figs. 1–1, 1–2). The difficult questions are those that relate to assessment

Fig. 1–1. Diagrammatic representation of yield reduction, based on 5-year average, caused by heavy infestation of potato fields by the golden nematode. (Spears, 1968)

of the relative costs of disease versus control measures, the choice of alternatives available in the wise management of resources, and the investment of time, energy, and funds in plant-pathological research and application.

THE STRUCTURE OF PLANT PATHOLOGY

For those who are most comfortable with a neatly arranged topical outline, attempts so to organize a study of plant pathology will prove more than a little frustrating. It simply cannot be done.

As an example of the difficulty, and without worrying about details, consider the question of how the environment affects the interplay of host and

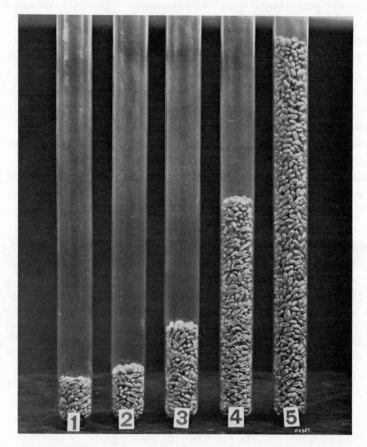

Fig. 1–2. Total yield of wheat from 36 plants infected with leaf rust in the seedling (1), jointing (2), booting (3), and flowering (4) stages, compared with yield from healthy plants (5). (Johnston and Miller, 1934)

pathogen in the production of disease—plant pathology has no more central issue than this. How can this be organized? If one focuses in turn on such obvious things as light, moisture, temperature, and air movement, then considerations of the effect on the host and on the pathogen become scattered into a number of separate subsections. Not only that, but the interrelations of light and temperature, or of temperature and humidity, or of air movement and precipitation, are lost.

Let the central concern be with environment-host relations, or environment-pathogen relations; then the effect of the two in combination is lost. Or suppose the choice be made to examine the development of disease from a chronological point of view. In such a case, the effects of each of the several environmental factors will be of necessity taken up over and over again at each step along the way. At some risk of belaboring the point the fact is that plant pathology is a multidimensional subject and that it cannot be handled except as such. Whatever line of attack one adopts will therefore have to be arbitrary to a degree and appropriate adjustments must be made in following through on it.

So far as this book is concerned, we have chosen to examine first the nature of the host plant, for it is the host plant that must occupy the central spot in our thinking; were we not primarily concerned with the fate of plants under disease or threat of disease, we would have at best only an academic interest in plant pathology. Next there is a catalogue and characterization of the agents and agencies that are responsible for the unfavorable effects that one observes upon the host plant.

Given a target, a cause, and an effect, it becomes crucially important to examine the complex mechanisms and interactions that come into play whenever the cause elicits the effect; this we call "host-pathogen interactions," constituting the bulk of the subject matter of plant pathology—the science— at the present time.

It is only, however, when the biological phenomena suggested above become generally present in substantial populations of host plants that society as such has cause for concern. This situation, which is called an epidemic, cannot be understood unless one has a fair grasp of the biology of disease in the individual plant, but to know the biology of disease is not of itself sufficient to handle the question of epidemics. It remains then to investigate what have been called the "public health" aspects of disease in plants, involving not only the phenomena of disease development but of disease control. In so doing one has repeatedly to return to the data of the individual plant but within a different context and with a new viewpoint.

Plant pathology is a public venture. The last look, then, is from society's point of view, with consideration given to the economic, cultural, even humanistic elements.

THE PUBLIC IMAGE OF PLANT PATHOLOGY

To many, science is largely unknown, the scientist a strange creature having but few of the motivations and responses of ordinary men. To others science is wrongly equated with technology, with the production of an ever increasing array of gadgets and machines. In either case there is scant feeling of identity between science and the public.

To this plant pathology is an exception. It is not one of the unknown sciences. True, the general impression that it consists of applying known remedies to treat familiar diseases may be far too narrow. It may be that the public has a distorted or outdated view. But most people do at least have an awareness of plant disease and of those professionally concerned with plant disease. This is as it should be, for plant pathology is a "practical" branch of learning in the best sense of that word. It must be ever mindful that it derives its support from public sources and exists in large measure for the more or less immediate furtherance of the public good. The age-old relationship of the physician to his patient has its partial counterpart in the public image of plant pathology. This fact both supports and complicates our efforts but it is a fact and as such must be reckoned with.

THE LITERATURE OF PLANT PATHOLOGY

Plant pathologists share with their colleagues in other branches of science a growing and general concern with the accelerating pace of research publication. The day when one individual could have at his command a respectable competence in all facets of his profession is gone forever. Indeed, the sheer mass of printed information goes far beyond what can be received, comprehended, and digested by a single mind, no matter how high its intellectual level. Regrettably, only very partial solutions are in sight.

As it stands, the literature of plant pathology falls into three general categories:

- Basic research reports, presenting for the first time the experimental and observational results obtained by investigators, singly or in teams, in some small sector of the field.
- Review papers and monographs, wherein a dedicated individual, customarily long-experienced in his specialty, attempts to distill from a large mass of research data the essential generalizations to which they seem to lead.
- Textbooks, general or specialized, whose chief aim must be to instruct the learner, to lead him toward his own comprehension of the subject matter.

For the beginner the second category of reference material will be the most rewarding in the long run. There are dangers, of course. One must particularly guard against the possibility that one reviewer's attitudes and analyses will be mistaken for generally proven and accepted fact. Alerted to this risk, one can read a scholarly monograph safely enough.

Textbooks must be relatively brief and generalized; research reports by themselves are too detailed, too scattered, and too specific. An effective route toward becoming informed about plant pathology is from the textbook to the secondary review literature, and through that eventually to the original papers.

PLANT PATHOLOGY IN PRACTICE

Research methods and techniques are not included as an explicit part of this examination of the art and science of plant pathology. But it should be realized that profound changes are taking place right now and that these changes will importantly affect what plant pathology will become in the foreseeable future. From a traditional cut-and-try approach, we have progressed to an era of controlled experimentation and to the application of the tools of molecular biology. In certain situations mathematical models are being introduced and in the near future pathologists will be testing the contributions of what has come to be called systems analysis. Pathology is, after all, one of a family of environmental biologies and will progress only so fast as we learn to deal effectively with large numbers of coincident variables.

It is inevitable that, with so many people involved and so many different individual diseases and phenomena to keep in order, plant pathologists have organized themselves into a fabric of societies through which to carry out their business. A detailed description of this is to be found in a paper by Chiarappa published in 1970, which includes not only the organizations themselves, but many of the committees and publications that developed out of them. Though it is fashionable to poke fun at the tendency of scientists to form ever more specialized associations and to invest substantial amounts of time in meetings of committees and boards, the fact remains that these are the mechanisms by which important work is done and decisions arrived at. We could scarcely do without them.

WHAT IS AGRICULTURE?

Plant pathology is an agricultural science; as an art it is applied to agriculture. It has an inescapable economic dimension without which it would be meaningless, save as an exercise in purely intellectual gratification.

To answer the question "What is agriculture?" is not easy. At least some thoughtful agricultural scientists have despaired of defining it by its boundaries, so to speak, and have fallen back on a definition based on focal interest.

Perhaps, in the long run, this is the better position. Agriculture, then, in this view, can be thought of as that human activity that centers on the management of renewable natural resources—biological environment—for the benefit of mankind. This concept would include the production of food, fiber, and specialty items from our cultivated, range, and forested lands, the proper use of soils and water in supporting that production, and the enhancement of the cultural and recreational aspects of the urban and rural landscape. From the special viewpoint of plant pathology, this very broad definition of agriculture would need to be restricted by omitting consideration of animals except as they directly affect the health and safety, as it were, of plants.

And why, at this juncture, should we be so concerned with reaching an understanding of the nature of agriculture? For the simple, if not obvious, reason that disease in plants is important—important enough to study, that is— only because in the last analysis it impinges on a segment of the total complex of agriculture. Unless man's welfare is affected, or potentially affected, the problem under consideration—whatever else may be the rationale of its importance—does not belong in plant pathology. Before, then, we turn to the host plant as such we must fit it into a proper context.

Historically

This is hardly the place to chronicle, even in general terms, the long and fascinating history of agriculture. But it is both interesting and important to note that some of our early assumptions about the manner of plant domestication are now being challenged by new discoveries at archeological digging sites and that some very interesting debates are developing about just what constellations of cultural and natural factors must be in effect before agriculture develops. Suffice it to say that, in both the Old and New Worlds, very many species and varieties were in fact brought into cultivation and that this occurred a very, very long time ago. One of the illustrious students of the problem, N. I. Vavilov (1949, 1950), has recognized some six centers of domestication, all in the rather mountainous regions of the south temperate and near-tropical latitudes of both hemispheres. Apparently, the ecological character of these areas led early man to adopt a sedentary life and to develop an agricultural society based on most of the very plants we use today.

Leppik (1969, 1970) has provided us with an updated version of the classic map of world gene centers developed by Vavilov prior to his death in 1943 (Fig. 1–3). It represents an extension and expansion of the number and geographic distribution of centers of origin, but adheres to the initial concepts much as Vavilov himself laid them down. From a standpoint of genetic resist-

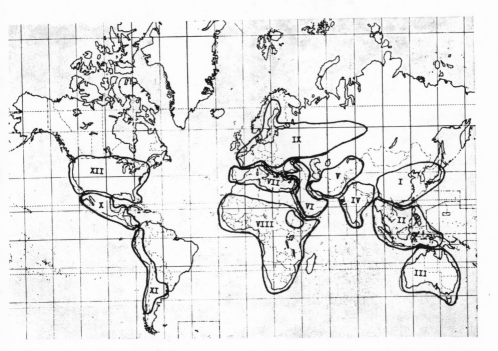

Fig. 1–3. Modified and updated map of world gene centers for cultivated plants, as originally developed by N. I. Vavilov. I. Chinese-Japanese; II. Indonesian-Indochinese; III. Australian; IV. Indostanian; V. Middle-Asian; VI. Near Eastern; VII. Mediterranean; VIII. African, including Ethiopian; IX. Euro-Siberian; X. Central American; XI. South American; XII. North American. (Leppik, 1969)

ance to disease, the central point in exploring the world centers is that to a considerable extent the cultivated plants of those regions exist along with a number of native related species. Not only this, but host and parasite have long been associated also, and it can be assumed that the individuals that have survived will have heightened measures of resistance. As the parasite itself produces new and often more virulent genetic races, a seesaw interaction between populations inevitably results—but at any given time the living host individuals can be expected to yield valuable genetic material for the plant breeder. It is, then, to the center of origin of the crop plant that the breeder goes in search of the resistant wild species that will provide useful new germ plasm (Figs. 1–4 and 1–5).

It should not be assumed from this that agriculture evolved as a uniform culture from a single site of origin—far from it. In the Americas, for example, it apparently arose in a number of separate localities and differed sharply

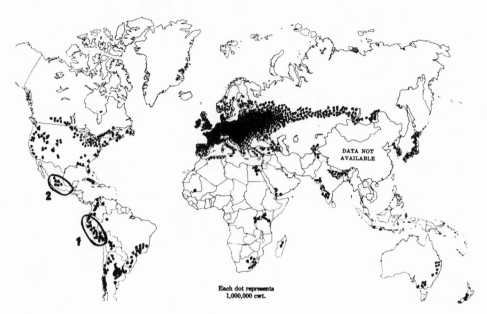

Fig. 1–4. Map showing present distribution of the cultivated potato and the locations of the origin of the host (1) and of the late-blight fungus (2). Disease-resistant wild species are found only in the region where the pathogen itself originated. (Leppik, 1970; by permission of *Annual Review of Phytopathology*)

from place to place as to the plant types on which the society rested. Whatever the origins of domesticated plants, most have long since been carried about by man's migrations and are now found wherever they will grow successfully; in short, their geographic limits are set by the ecological limits that they can withstand.

Today we have an agriculture of truly astonishing disparity and diversity. Without trying to examine the situation country by country or region by region it is nonetheless possible to identify several dimensions of difference.

- Intensity, by which we mean the relative amount of effort expended with a view to recovering the very maximum yield from the resources at hand—possibly Japan and certain areas of Southeast Asia, where populations are dense and labor cheap, are examples where this dimension is most striking.
- Efficiency and generally effective use of agricultural resources— wherein Northern Europe stands high in relation to most other regions.
- Mechanization, the application to agriculture of power other than that

of man and animals, and the development of agricultural technology—
the United States must surely take first rank here by a wide margin.

It is small wonder, then, that looking about the world one can find examples of virtually every conceivable kind of agriculture. Much of tropical agriculture is exceedingly primitive, with little intensity or efficiency, and almost
no mechanization. That of many densely populated parts of Asia is highly intense, but neither mechanized nor very efficient. United States efforts are
highly mechanized, reasonably efficient, and only locally intensive. Agriculture today must take into account all these regional differences if it is to
reflect accurately the present condition of man in relation to his environment.

In a Technological Society

To view agriculture as static could be seriously misleading. There is a time
dimension to be taken very much into account, for agriculture is changing, a
change that is taking place at disturbingly different rates from one country to

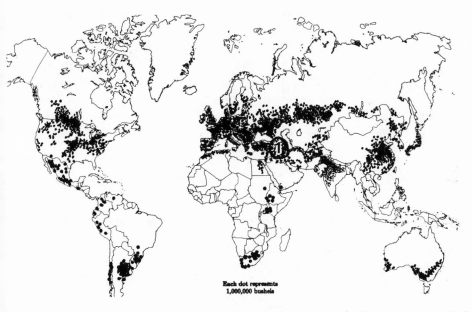

Each dot represents
1,000,000 bushels

Fig. 1–5. Map showing present distribution of major production of cultivated wheat and of
the stem rust fungus. The origin of both host and pathogen is indicated by the numeral (1),
the region where disease-resistant wild wheats are also to be found. (Leppik, 1970; by
permission of *Annual Review of Phytopathology*)

Table 1–1

Total Population and Numbers of Persons on Farms
(in millions)

Year	Population	Farm Population	
		Numbers	Percentage
1920	106	32	30
1930	123	31	24
1940	132	31	23
1950	152	23	16
1960	181	16	9

SOURCE: Barnes, 1964.

the next. In some of what have come to be called the "developing" nations, agriculture is highly primitive and shows little indication of change. In more sophisticated societies, having at the same time but limited industrial strength, agriculture is reasonably advanced and changing slowly. In highly technological, materially wealthy countries agriculture is changing so dramatically and so rapidly that even those personally involved do not fully realize and accept the implications thereof. A few at least of these implications merit more careful examination.

By almost any criterion one chooses, it is perfectly clear that the nature of agriculture has been changing in a rapid and significant way over the past several decades. Whether in terms of farm population in relation to total population, numbers of farms, size of farms, degree of mechanization, use of fertilizers, or consumption of pesticides (Tables 1–1, 1–2; Figs. 1–6 through 1–9), the picture is clear. These changes have important implications for disease losses and for disease control measures, as will be apparent almost immediately the situation is examined.

Table 1–2

Nitrogen Fertilizer Consumed in the United States
(in thousands of tons)

Year	Nitrogen Fertilizer	Nitrogen	
		Percentage	Tonnage
1940	9,360	4.8	449
1950	20,991	5.9	1,239
1955	22,194	8.7	1,792
1961	24,500	13.0	3,185

SOURCE: Barnes, 1964.

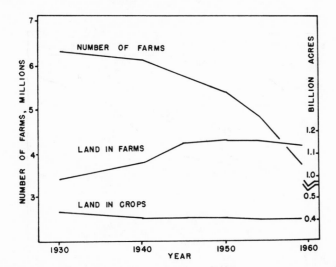

Fig. 1–6. Number of farms, and land in farms and crops in the United States, by year, 1930–60. (Barnes, 1964)

Shrinking Manpower. Firm statistics are somewhat hard to come by, so rapid is the transformation of American agricultural manpower. We are living in the midst of an incredible revolution without, perhaps for that very reason, being fully aware of it. Most dramatic of all is the plummeting of manpower required to produce basic agricultural commodities. Quite literally, this segment of our society has shrunken until it requires no more than one person in twenty to produce an abundance of production unmatched heretofore. Mechanization, genetically very highly productive crop varieties, major invest-

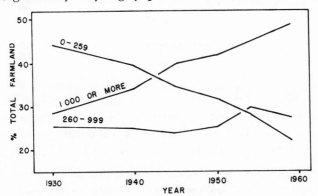

Fig. 1–7. Percentage of total farmland in the United States in farms of size up to 259 acres, 260–999 acres, and 1,000 or more acres, by year, 1930–60. (Barnes, 1964)

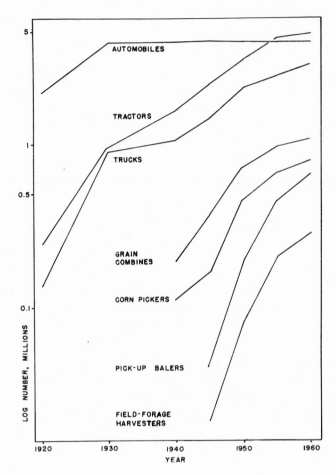

Fig. 1–8. Number of machines on farms in the United States, by year, 1920–60. (Barnes, 1964)

ments in agricultural chemicals, and so on, have transformed our farm economy from a small-scale enterprise carried on by most citizens into a highly technical, large-capital business managed by a skilled and experienced minority. There is not the slightest evidence that this trend will be reversed.

Expanding Ancillary Technologies. Along with the shrinkage in manpower required for agricultural production has come an expansion in agriculture-related industries and enterprises. Indeed, one can show that the total numbers of persons involved in agriculture, in the broad sense of that word, has not really decreased appreciably in recent years; workers have moved from production to other phases of the total effort.

Consumers now demand elaborate processing and packaging far beyond that of a generation or so ago. As the bulk of the population moves off the farms into the cities, transportation and storage requirements are greatly multiplied and marketing becomes much more complicated. An affluent society expects diversity, quality, and dependability to a degree not even dreamed of in earlier times. The role of skilled technical and managerial manpower in present-day American agriculture and agriculture-related enterprise is unique.

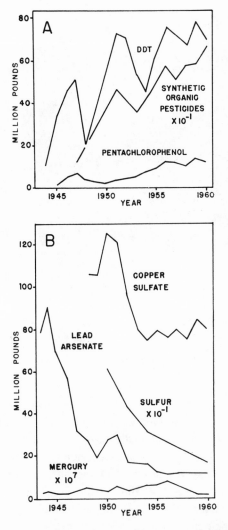

Fig. 1–9. Domestic consumption of (A) synthetic organic and (B) inorganic pesticides in the United States, by year, 1945–60. (Barnes, 1964)

Changes in Rural Living. In the United States during the decade of the 1950's, and markedly less so in the following decade, the changes that took place in the agricultural sector of the economy brought on severe stresses to the people who lived in rural areas. Technology had brought on remarkable gains in overall productivity and efficiency, but at heavy cost to parts of the populations affected. As the capacity of the agricultural industry increased it

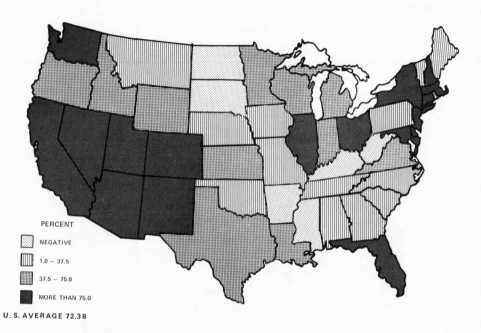

PERCENT

NEGATIVE

1.0 – 37.5

37.5 – 75.0

MORE THAN 75.0

U. S. AVERAGE 72.38

Fig. 1–10. Comparative success among states in creating employment, shown as that percentage of those added to the working-age group who gained employment, 1950–60. (Bishop, 1969)

tended to overbalance the more slowly growing demand, which led to decrease in the total number of producing units (see Bishop, 1969). More explicitly, technological and organizational changes brought on a major reduction in employment of rural people and a consequent mass migration from rural areas to the cities in search of better opportunity. As Figs. 1–10 and 1–11 show, the states varied greatly in their ability to provide employment opportunities, especially during the 1950's, although the picture became rather less bleak in the first half of the 1960's.

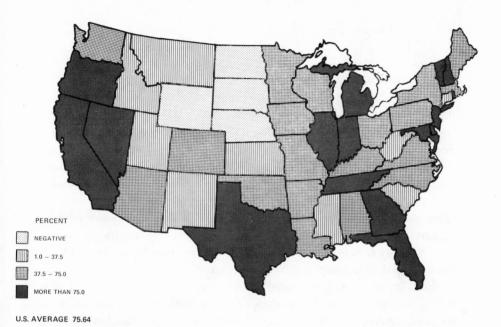

PERCENT

NEGATIVE

1.0 – 37.5

37.5 – 75.0

MORE THAN 75.0

U.S. AVERAGE 75.64

Fig. 1–11. Comparative success among states in creating employment, shown as that percentage of those added to the working-age group who gained employment, 1962–66. (Bishop, 1969)

Public policy is not, of course, primarily the concern of plant pathologists, but it is within the context of the economic and social conditions resulting from public policy that they must work, and it behooves them to remain reasonably aware of what these policies are.

Nontraditional Land Use.   We have defined agriculture in a most comprehensive way, quite beyond what might have been proposed a few years ago. More particularly, we defined it to include the management of resources for esthetic and recreational uses. No change in our rapidly evolving society is more striking than the shift toward automation and its consequent release of manpower from less skilled jobs—this at the very time agriculture is becoming almost entirely a big-business enterprise and while the total population is rising rapidly. All this leads to an unprecedented demand for land, much of it formerly in traditional agriculture, for a variety of essentially recreational purposes—campsites, golf courses, parks. To this should be added, probably, the very substantial amount of effort and attention devoted to the suburban dwellers' lawns and backyard gardens.

Unexploited Resources

The United States is an agricultural-surplus nation and by virtue of enormously expanded productivity and mechanization is supplying itself with abundant agricultural products on a stable cropland acreage and rapidly shrinking manpower force, while the world as a whole is in crisis. In very large portions of the globe, agricultural production is running far behind demand and the situation is rapidly worsening. In essence, we have at one and the same time a temperate zone agriculture that is highly mechanized and enormously productive in terms of manpower invested and a predominantly nontemperate zone agriculture that is so unproductive as to fall seriously below demand and where a large fraction of the available manpower is tied to primary production. Many feel that the great challenge at this juncture in human history is whether the needs of the have-not peoples can be met while there is yet time to avoid unreconcilable chaos.

Shorn of its countless smaller details, the problem resolves itself into finding a way to transpose the skills of the technological agriculture of the temperate zone and implant these skills on the very significantly different situations of the nontemperate zones. There are two such zones, the tropics and the arctic. Of the former, it need only be said that while we have long been acquainted with the environment and the people, past experience has served largely to prove that we cannot simply apply existing United States techniques to tropical problems; we do not yet have the basic information that will tell us what we should do.

One striking success that clearly indicates the measure of potential for future production has been dubbed the Green Revolution, and applies specifically to the development of high-yielding strains of rice and wheat in the Philippines and Mexico, respectively. While the word "miracle" has too often been applied to them, they are in fact highly responsive to fertilizers and water and, properly managed, produce four to five times the yield per acre. That there are attendant serious potential problems in disease control seems self-evident, and one can be very certain that the road to conversion of tropical agriculture from a subsistence to a market economy is a long and rocky one.

As for the arctic, it is provocative to speculate on what might be accomplished there (Anon., 1965a):

Take a map of the world. Pick out the 55th north latitude. This is the imaginary line which circles the globe just south of Moscow, the Scottish border, the southern portion of Hudson Bay and the southernmost part of Alaska's panhandle . . . North of that line, except primarily for Scandinavia, Scotland, and a few Soviet areas, there lies an endless emptiness stretching north and south, east and west across some 5,000,000 square miles of land.

Looking at this area more closely, and again leaving out the comparatively small area of Scandinavia, we find that over the livable portions of this immense land-mass there fly but three flags—American, Canadian, Russian. And in a world of escalating population, where more and more eyes are turning toward the earth's unpopulated areas, this joint possession of the unsettled North gives Russia many interests in common with America and Canada, whatever ideology may say. . . .

Therefore, might there not be great advantages to be reaped from an effort to develop the three lands concurrently? This could perhaps be done through some Northern Area Institute in which geologists, physicists, meteorologists, agriculturists, and many other natural scientists from America, Canada, and Russia could pool their discoveries and help correct each other's mistakes. . . .°

MAN AND HIS CROPS

If we accept the obvious truth that the welfare, indeed the very survival, of man depends in the last analysis on plants then it becomes important to discover just how productive or potentially productive they are. In this sense it is not without significance that the first of the great international scientific undertakings to have a biological emphasis, the International Biological Program, has as its central theme the productivity of the biological environment and man's adaptability thereto. In simpler terms this means a very major effort to answer objectively the question, "Just how much food and fiber do and can the plants of the earth produce?" The second and related question is "How can man best adapt, as a biological species, to this world of nature?" These are exceedingly difficult answers to come by, but none are more vital and it is gratifying to see that ecology is at long last leaving the ranks of a largely observational enterprise and coming to grips with the complexities of ecosystems. For the first time, ecology is "big science," with all of the demands for systems approach, for multidisciplinary research, for team action, and for multimillion dollar support. It is with issues of this magnitude that plant pathology at its very best comes to grips.

There is another almost philosophical issue that must be recognized early in an analysis of plant resources. None has stated it more cogently than Preston Cloud of the University of California at Santa Barbara, in an unpublished statement in 1965, when he said:

The foremost danger confronting man, in addition to his exponentially expanding population and the threat of nuclear war, is a deeply ingrained belief in some "natural" rate of economic and material growth that can and must continue into the infinite future but which, in plain truth, cannot do so.

What is needed, I think, is a critical assessment of these facts [about resources] in terms of their long-range implications for the future as related to global ecology, the aspirations of man, and the condition of society.

If the population could be stabilized, persuaded to discipline its rate of consumption, and taught to reduce wastage, much of the need for mineral resources in the future could be met by recycling already mined materials, and the necessary replacement substances could be extracted on a more rational basis over a longer period of time.

What, finally, about water supply, forests, agricultural lands, food and mineral production from the sea and atmosphere, the quality of the water we drink and the air we breathe, parks, wilderness areas, and wildlife?

As the now underdeveloped develop the problem will be exacerbated. For they will want a higher standard of living too, and they will have to grow faster than we to reach a comparable level. If, in the meantime, their resources have been plundered to increase our standard even beyond its present state of affluence, how will they feel toward us or toward those who follow us?

These questions are all intimately bound to the matter of population control, to the prevention of war, and to the ultimate welfare of man. They need sober reflection and thoughtful, honest answers.

Our estimates will, in the long run, almost certainly prove inexact. But the problem is there and it won't go away. Even the conquest of space won't make it go away. A choice must be made concerning the quality of life that future generations may lead; and this involves also the risks they will run of war, famine, pestilence, or psychological deterioration. To do nothing is equally to make a choice. And to do nothing beyond what has been done is inadequate. No measure of any society can be more telling than its ability to analyze its own ills, and to act with compassion and with good judgment as far as other parts of the world and the yet unborn are concerned.

Because he is a geologist by training, Dr. Cloud spoke much in terms of nonrenewable resources but the fundamental issues are the same: What can be done in the face of a frightening increase in demand to meet that demand and thus win time to attack the longer-range question of bringing that demand under some kind of effective control? These issues are examined in greater detail in the book *Resources and Man* (Cloud, 1969).

Why worry about these cosmic matters in a plant pathology text? For the very simple reason that one cannot consider what may be "wrong" with plants—the immediate concern of plant pathology—without an awareness of what is "right" about them. In other words, the first step is to see what the baseline of productivity in crop plants may be. Without this, assessments of damage are rather meaningless. And without a provisional assessment of damage, plant pathologists have but scant reason to move vigorously. Which is merely to reaffirm the fact that plant pathology has, quite properly, a strong economic base. Indeed, a nation such as the United States, plagued—if that be the term—for decades by crop surplusses, has seen those surplusses disappear almost overnight in the early 70's. Food, and the crops that produce it, is again a headline issue.

Optimum Productivity

It is remarkably difficult to discover what the productivity of a given crop plant would be if the environment were entirely favorable. In the first place, man has tended to plant his domesticated crops in a very large variety of places and to distribute them about the world at his own convenience. All too often, this has been done with little or no knowledge of or regard for the goodness of fit between the biological needs of the plant and the physical factors of the site. In the second place, the very multiplicity of environmental factors, their numerous interactions with each other, and the extent to which they fluctuate from one time to the next combine to make controlled experimental analysis both tedious and difficult.

In short, we simply do not know precisely how productive a thoroughly healthy plant would be, and although research is uncovering some answers, there remains much to be learned. One provocative example has been cited by Went (1957), who concedes at the outset that in seeking truly maximum production we should not discard prematurely the possibility, suggested from time to time, of altering the biochemistry of the plant. But he feels that the more promising move is to select for cultivation those plants already adapted to the environment in question or, one supposes, to achieve the same goal by selecting an environmental site to which a given crop is adapted. That this cannot be deduced from routine field trials is clearly shown by the following values for tomato yields in California:

Average field yields	20 tons/acre	(40 tons max.)
Average greenhouse yields	40 tons/acre	(80 tons max.)
Phytotron yields		(160 tons max.)

A "phytotron," for those to whom the term is unfamiliar, is a very elaborately controlled environmental chamber that permits adjustment of light, temperature, moisture, day length, and other factors so as to approach the ideal environment for a given kind of plant. More importantly, perhaps, the selected conditions can be maintained for indefinite periods of time and do not fluctuate widely, unlike the natural environment.

Went is careful to point out that because phytotrons are scarce and expensive and because much time and labor are involved in using them we have detailed data on only a few species of plants. He then summarizes the implications of this approach in five categories.

- "Maximum yields tell how far removed we are from ideal production in a given area and the improvements that are possible.

- "Optimal localities for production of particular crops are or can be established, though in many cases transport problems will favor local production under sub-optimal conditions.
- "Plants can be adjusted to specific climates within certain limits by breeding.
- "Local climate control may be feasible, if a very small number of factors (e.g., night temperature, temperature during the first two hours of daylight, or photoperiod) are involved.
- "Long-range weather forecasting, if established, might allow choice of best varieties in a particular year."

On the one hand we recognize that yields from crops as they are managed under routine farming conditions are far below that achievable under idealized environments such as can be experimentally attained in the controlled environmental chamber. On the other, it must be recognized that there are practical limits beyond which only substantial and fundamental changes in the plants themselves will permit us to go (Bonner, 1962). These upper limits are set by the efficiency with which the photosynthetic pigments can convert incident energy, assuming that all other factors such as water and carbon dioxide are nonlimiting.

Whereas forest and grassland is, by and large, in its "natural" environment, crop plants have been drastically challenged by being grown in habitats often quite unlike that to which they are best adapted. Nursery and greenhouse plots, seedbeds, and the like are usually spared the more extreme fluctuations of weather and soil conditions, but most ordinary field and horticultural crops are, once sown, left pretty much at the mercy of the elements. For the greater part of agriculture, for some time to come, this situation is as it must be—but it should be clearly recognized and reckoned with in trying to envision a truly healthy plant.

In summarizing its report on natural resources, a special committee of the National Academy of Sciences (Weiss, 1962) made this point, which underscores the foregoing discussion, in saying, "An imaginative attack on methods of raising world food and fiber production and further reducing losses and wastage would include investigation of agricultural environments and conditions beyond those that have received our principal attention."

Ecology and Crop Ecology

One very serious obstacle in the way of achieving the dependable knowledge of plants in relation to their environment that we badly need can be stated very simply: there are far too many mutually interacting factors to be taken easily into account. In the very readable report cited above (Weiss, 1962), this fact came out repeatedly and stood as a central theme in a series of "propositions" on the subject of renewable natural resources. Without trying to paint in all the shades and colors, two sentences from that report will suffice to make the point:

It is imperative that in dealing with problems of natural resources, whether in study or applications, one clearly recognize that viable ecological systems are composed of mixtures of heterogeneous member units and that this heterogeneity be fully taken into account as vital for the existence and equilibrium of each system. . . . the net-like character of the natural resource problem calls for the replacement of linear chain-reaction determinism by principles of thought and action which are based on the fact that in such network systems there can be many equivalent, multi-pathway, multiple-choice approaches to the same goals—in the present case, the common objective of optimization.

True, the above quotation deals with ecological systems in general, whereas we here are mainly concerned with the particular ecology of agricultural lands. To a degree, ecology as a recognized branch of biology tends very much to concentrate on natural as distinct from managed communities. The difficulty is compounded by the fact that surprisingly large numbers of agricultural biologists do not adequately recognize the ecological nature of their work. Much of the work of the plant pathologist is nothing more or less than ecology—of a rather special kind of plant community, of course, but none the less an ecological study. The imprecision we spoke of earlier stems as much as anything else from the very fact that plant pathology must continually operate within a complex, systems framework.

As ecology, bringing to bear the powerful tools of mathematics on the accumulating data, begins successfully to analyze natural ecosystems and to develop predictive models relating thereto, it is certainly to be hoped that attention will turn also to the ecology of croplands. There is scant doubt but that the returns from such an effort would be very much worthwhile.

II

ELEMENTS OF DISEASE

In the next three chapters will be presented the basic elements that are involved in what is called disease—and a great deal of uncertainty is covered by that one phrase, "what is called disease." For our purposes it will suffice simply to consider disease as any situation in which the structure and function of the plant with which the observer is concerned are to a greater or lesser extent unfavorably affected. This concept of disease is admittedly somewhat more catholic than is likely to please all plant pathologists. Even so it will be necessary arbitrarily to draw limitations about the concept as it is implemented in later discussions.

There are three fundamental elements involved in the situations that plant pathology must confront: the plant host; the infectious agent; and the physical environment. All three may interact simultaneously but they need not necessarily do so.

For example, extremes of low temperature in early winter following a comparatively warm period may result in substantial damage to crops or ornamentals. Pathogenic organisms if they appear in the lesions at all come in only belatedly as often unimportant secondary invaders. Interaction here is limited primarily to host and environment. Some might call this injury rather than disease, but to those who think of plant pathology primarily in its relation to man and his biological resources, it seems wise not to exclude environmentally induced difficulties from consideration along with the more widely recognized diseases caused by pathogenic organisms.

Whatever one's preferences in these matters, perhaps the truly important thing is to avoid a parochial argument over semantics and to avoid a too rigid insistence on form and protocol. When, for example, the sun is obscured by a cloud, photosynthesis rates in the leaf are reduced. Only the rank extremist would insist that these plants—or grass that has been cut by a mower—are diseased. Does this mean that the specialist in the "diseases" of plant materials in storage and transport should study only effects brought on by microorganisms and ignore, or rigidly compartmentalize, those maladies that result from undesirable atmospheric conditions in the warehouse or from unwise refrigeration practices? Of course not.

Plant pathology is concerned with whatever, alone or in combination, is wrong with the plant.

2

The Host

INTRODUCTION

At the very cornerstone of plant pathology lies the plant host. It is too easy to become so preoccupied with the *diseased* condition that one fails to recognize the crucial importance of the plant as such. In the last analysis, disease can be comprehended only in relation to the nondiseased plant. One simply must know the fundamental biology of the healthy plant before it is meaningful to consider the effects of environment or pathogenic organisms upon it.

THE BIOLOGY OF THE HOST PLANT

What, in the simplest terms, is this thing to which we give the name host? First and foremost, it is a living organism, with all of the delicate and complex attributes thus implied. This must never be lost sight of in the discussion to follow because it bears importantly on every facet of the story as it unfolds.

In one such emphasis on the basic biology of the host, George McNew some years ago (McNew, 1950) built a whole conceptual framework of disease and of disease control on what he cited as seven vital functions in the life of the plant centering on food relations. In his words, these are, chronologically:

- "Food is stored in the seed, roots, or modified stems where it maintains respiration of a bud or germ and supports growth after dormancy (correlates with diseases caused by destruction of stored foods and storage organs—i.e., soft rots and seed decays).
- "The stored foods are hydrolyzed into simple sugars and amino acids, and are transferred to the expanding germ or bud in the spring (correlates with diseases caused by destroying seedlings before food reserves are utilized for growth—i.e., damping-off and seedling blight diseases).

31

- "The new plant develops roots with limited food reserves that acquire water and nutrients from the soil (correlates with diseases caused by preventing uptake of solutes and water from the soil—i.e., root rots and girdling of underground stems).
- "The food reserves from the seed and solutes from the soil are used to inaugurate meristematic activity in the young plant. The process continues throughout the plant's development with cellular growth and differentiation predetermined by genetical factors. Food materials are secured from leaves rather than seeds after the seedling stage (correlates with diseases caused by instigation of abnormal meristematic activity and prevention of differentiation—i.e., galls, clubroot, and smuts).
- "As the seedling enlarges water must be transferred from roots to leaves if photosynthetic activity is to be sustained at efficient levels (correlates with diseases that prevent water movement through xylem in plants—i.e., wilt diseases).
- "The leaves combine water and carbon dioxide and fix photochemical energy in photosynthesis (correlates with diseases that prevent photosynthesis by destroying food manufacturing tissues; since many floral tissues and the stems are comparable to leaf tissue in morphological derivation, many of the leaf invaders cause floral blight and stem cankers as well as leaf blight, anthracnose, downy mildew, powdery mildew, and rusts).
- "The simple foods must be translocated from the leaves to meristems and storage organs where they promote growth, are used in reproduction, or are stored (correlates with diseases that interfere with translocation of food materials, either by injury to the phloem or by increasing the viscosity of phloem contents—i.e., viruses)."

Certain details in McNew's suggestions are rather too technical to consider at this point. Other implications must remain for a later discussion, but it is important to recognize that he was able to center his attention on the biology of the healthy plant and still come up with a framework that seemed reasonable for considering disease phenomena. Most people focus on the disease, but it does not have to be done that way.

More recently, Horsfall and Dimond (1959) selected six processes that they used as titles for key chapters in the first volume of their impressive treatise on plant pathology:

- Tissue is disintegrated.
- Growth is affected.
- Reproduction is affected.

- The host is starved.
- Water is deficient.
- Respiration is altered.

True, these processes are examined as disease processes, not those of healthy plants, but they could just as well have been represented as an abbreviated list of important biological phenomena: an organism develops a physical structure, it exchanges water and other materials with its environment, it requires a constant energy input from a basic food source, the machinery of its cells is driven by respiratory events, and it is perpetuated through time by self-reproduction.

Let us now turn to the healthy plant and review some of its structural, physiological, and ecological attributes.

Structure

With few exceptions the plants with which pathologists are concerned are vascular plants and the majority of these produce flowers, fruits, and seeds, i.e., are angiosperms. This fact alone greatly simplifies the problem of understanding the biology of the host for it removes from consideration a vast diversity of species that make up the plant kingdom.

Basically, a flowering plant is composed of a vertical axis with a number of lateral outgrowths—branches and leaves at the upper levels and secondary roots below ground (Fig. 2–1). The entire surface is covered with a single layer of cells, the epidermis, which may in older portions be replaced by cork. Thus all materials exchanged between the plant and its environment must move through this epidermal or cork barrier. How effective a barrier it actually is depends on local differences, for example, whether the stomates are open or closed, or the distribution and thickness of the acellular cuticle overlying the exterior walls of the epidermal cells. It must be recognized also that whenever new branch roots emerge, the outer surface is abruptly broken.

Beneath the epidermis lie thin-walled cells, more or less closely packed, making up the bulk of the younger tissues of leaf, root, and stem. These cells are metabolically active and have little if any structural features to prevent the inroads of attacking pathogens once the overlying barrier has been breached. The green cells of the leaf, the outermost layers of young stems, and the bulk of tissues in young roots are in this general category.

Finally, there is throughout the entire plant an intricate network of structural and conductive tissues that provides a degree of rigidity sufficient to maintain the organism upright and exposed to sunlight, and channels through

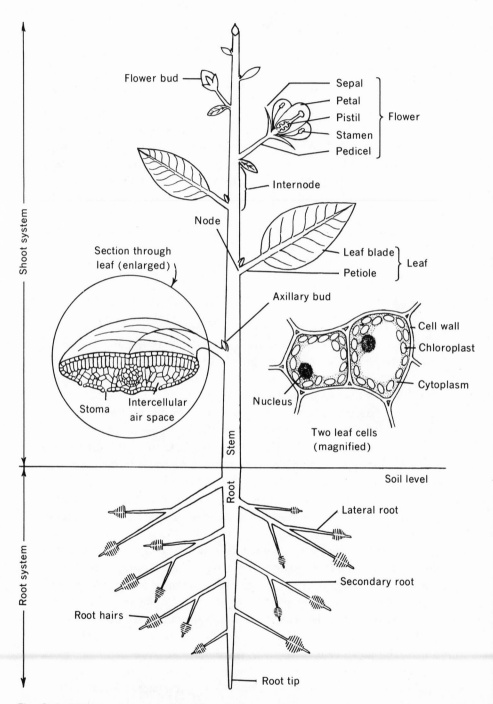

Fig. 2–1. Diagrammatic representation of the structure of a seed plant. (From F. D. Kern, *The Essentials of Plant Biology,* Harper & Row, 1947)

which water and elaborated foodstuffs may move with comparative freedom from one point to another.

No one even moderately familiar with botanical data will fail to recognize that, in detail, there is almost endless variation in the form and structure of flowering plants. But the basic plan is as stated—an upright, branching axis, enclosed in an epidermis, supported by an intricate internal conducting system, the remaining space filled with rather unspecialized, actively metabolizing cells. This is the prime target of the forces that bring about plant disease.

Physiology

Not only does the plant have form, it does something—it functions. Every living cell carries on throughout its existence an array of chemical transformations that we lump together in the term "metabolism." It would be a gross error, however, to think of the cell as nothing more than the microscopic site of a number of independent, unregulated enzymatic events proceeding in isolation. Far from it. While we know relatively little about the control mechanisms underlying metabolic phenomena, it is quite safe to say, in the current phrase, that cellular processes are "programmed" into a rather well-coordinated pattern. Relative rates vary, depending on a number of influences, only a few of which are presently known.

Imposed upon the chemical and physical phenomena that are common to cells generally are other often equally important processes that are unique to certain kinds of cells. Possibly the most dramatic of these special events is photosynthesis, a capacity only of chlorophyll-bearing tissues and hence mostly of the leaves and young stems. Others of less general occurrence might be various secretory activities—production of resins, gums, latex, essential oils—or the formation of alkaloids, pigments, and lipids.

Cells not only live, they grow. They grow by a process that involves increase in the total protoplasm, i.e., synthesis of additional nucleic acids, proteins, fats, and carbohydrates into that peculiar substance that, with water, makes up the physical entity of the cell. Having achieved an initial increase in protoplasm, rapid inward movement of water, coincident with extension of the enveloping cellulose wall, brings about a marked increase in cell volume. It is through this means that the dramatic growth of leaves and stems at time of germination, or the early spring response of perennial plants, becomes possible.

Probably because of its critical dependence upon inward and outward movement of materials, cells usually do not reach very impressive absolute dimensions. The largest are seldom more than a tiny fraction of a millimeter in the longest dimension and thus retain a very substantial surface-to-volume ratio. The size of the plant itself is therefore more a measure of the total number of cells than anything else. Growth, in the last analysis, is the sum of three distinct but related events: increase in size of individual cells, increase in number of cells, and perhaps to a lesser extent, increased spacing between cells.

So much for growth per se. Mere growth, however, would produce only a large, amorphous mass of indistinguishable cells—a far cry from the complex organism we recognize as a flowering plant. In other words, cells not only grow and multiply, they become specialized or differentiated. Here, incidentally, is one of the more puzzling problems in all of biology: by what mechanisms do cells with presumably identical heredity, derived from a single juvenile region at the stem tip or root tip, diversify into the array of highly specialized cells of mature tissue and, additionally, impart to the plant those consistent and intricate attributes of form that make each species morphologically distinct from all others? It may be some time before we have satisfactory answers to that question.

Still another fundamental process in plants is reproduction, in this case not of cells but of individuals. Indeed, the very term "flowering plant" carries with it the implication of reproduction, here by the formation under appropriate conditions of flowers and then fruits containing seeds—although propagation by vegetative means must not be overlooked.

Relation to the Environment

The host plant cannot meaningfully be dealt with in isolation. One must recognize not only that the environment is an ever present and important factor but that the interrelationships observed in the classroom, laboratory, and greenhouse are examples of more general phenomena. All too often the beginner falls into the error of assuming, subconsciously perhaps, that what happens to the experimental plant in the laboratory is not what would *really* happen to just ordinary plants outdoors. So when we talk of a plant and its environment, keep clearly in mind that there is no distinction between natural and artificial environments except perhaps the measure of control attainable. Molecules obey the laws of physics and chemistry wherever one observes them.

Requirements. Four categories of materials are necessary for the continued normal growth of the host plant. No one is "more important" than the others; without all four in adequate amounts the plant will certainly not prosper and may not even survive. These materials are: water, oxygen, carbon dioxide, and a conglomeration of substances often termed collectively mineral nutrients.

Water is the medium in which life on this planet exists. It constitutes the preponderance of the weight and volume of protoplasm and is the avenue of molecular movement within and between cells. In plants vast amounts of water pass, unchanged, through the vascular system to be lost as vapor through the stomates in the foliage.

Just as no cell can exist without water, so too it cannot without oxygen, for in a sense the cellular machinery is driven by the complex of events summarized in the term respiration, a process whereby energy in a form utilizable by the cell is derived from the available food materials. True, many of the individual steps in cellular respiration do not directly involve elemental oxygen, but the overall process cannot continue without it and there is consumption of oxygen with consequent release of carbon dioxide. Some confusion arises, from time to time, simply because photosynthesis, which releases oxygen, may under certain conditions proceed faster than respiration. If measurements of *net* oxygen–carbon dioxide balance are made, it looks superficially as though respiration had ceased entirely. Nothing could be further from the actual fact. Perhaps a good rule of thumb is to recognize that oxygen is required by all living cells in the absence of light and by all nongreen living cells whether in the light or dark—exceptions to this rule are chlorophyll-bearing cells in the light and only then when the photosynthetic rate exceeds respiration. Under these last circumstances carbon dioxide is consumed and oxygen in excess of that used in respiration is released.

Carbon dioxide is a raw material of photosynthesis and is thus virtually the sole source of carbon metabolism throughout the organic world. From the mineral nutrients come all of the elements other than carbon, hydrogen, and oxygen—the nitrogen, sulfur, phosphorus, potassium, calcium, and so on that enter in one way or another into the array of organic compounds involved in metabolism.

Quite aside from the substances essential for plant life to exist there are certain environmental conditions that must pertain—specifically, radiation within the visible light range as an indispensable factor in photosynthesis, and an ambient temperature that is neither so high nor so low as to be seriously harmful. We shall have more to say on that point later.

Mechanisms and Avenues of Exchange. The situation before us is, in summary then, this: a living, cellular organism, supported by an intricate conducting system and protected by an outer epidermal layer. This organism, to survive, must receive water from the soil, a large part of which is then promptly lost to the atmosphere. It must receive carbon dioxide and on occasion oxygen from the atmosphere. It must derive oxygen and mineral nutrients from the soil. We must therefore take a brief look at the means whereby materials enter and leave the plant.

Most water available to plants is present in the capillary spaces in soil. Whether it moves into the root system or remains in the soil depends upon opposing forces. On the one hand—tending to move water from soil to root— are osmotic forces derived from the lesser concentrations of solutes in soil water as compared to that in the vacuoles of the root cells. Much more important, in all likelihood, are the forces developed as water evaporates from the foliage. A combination of atmospheric pressure at the root surface and positive pull exerted at the site of water loss from the walls of leaf cells suffices to move water into roots with very considerable force, perhaps not so much from cell to cell as through the "free space" represented by the cellulose walls and intercellular spaces. Transport upward in root and stem is assumed to be in the xylem region of the conducting system.

On the other hand, cohesive forces between molecules of water in the soil and adhesive forces between water molecules and soil particle surfaces resist the movement of water into roots. When soil water is abundant, forces tending to move it into roots exceed those opposing and there is a flow into the roots. Assuming no further addition to the supply—as by rainfall—each succeeding increment of water moving into the root requires more force than that just ahead, until a point is reached at which no further water is available —it is then being held by the soil so strongly that it cannot continue to move into the plant.

Lastly, it will be obvious that the size and distribution of the soil particles greatly influence the nature of the capillary system and thus the plant-soil water relationships.

Provided the cuticle and epidermis are undamaged, loss of water by plants is almost wholly through the stomates. This loss is, despite widespread notions to the contrary, largely hazardous to the plant and occurs primarily because of the physical structure of the leaf. A diagrammatic view of the leaf of an ordinary plant (Fig. 2–2), such as tomato, will show that the inner atmosphere of the leaf is routinely saturated with water vapor derived from the wet cell walls of the mesophyll cells. Assuming that leaf and surrounding atmosphere are at the same temperature, water will diffuse outward through open stomates at all times when the outside air is not itself saturated. When leaf temperature exceeds that of the air, water will be lost even more rapidly, as the speed of the molecules increases and the capacity of the internal leaf atmosphere to hold moisture also increases.

Oxygen and carbon dioxide are intimately related in the metabolism of cells. In both photosynthesis and aerobic respiration, equivalent amounts of the one are evolved upon consumption of the other, e.g., for every molecule of oxygen used up in respiration by a root cell, one molecule of carbon dioxide is produced. Because root cells are not photosynthetic there is a constant inward movement of oxygen from soil to root and a reciprocal outward diffusion of carbon dioxide. Above ground, gas exchange is complicated by the fact that, in light, if photosynthesis exceeds respiration only carbon dioxide consumption and oxygen evolution are detectable.

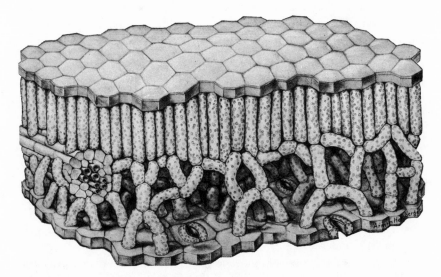

Fig. 2–2. Three-dimensional diagram of a portion of an unspecialized leaf blade. (From E. W. Sinnott and K. Wilson, *Botany*, revised 6th edition. Copyright © 1970, McGraw-Hill Book Company. Used with permission of McGraw-Hill Book Company)

Exchange of carbon dioxide and oxygen between foliage and atmosphere is by the same mechanisms and through the same channels as water vapor, i.e., gaseous diffusion through the stomates. Thus it is that the very structural peculiarities that permit access to these essential gases also subject the plant to what is very probably its greatest single hazard, loss of water. It cannot be otherwise.

In the soil, water and oxygen–carbon dioxide balance are inextricably interconnected. The above-ground atmosphere serves as the great reservoir from which oxygen diffuses into the soil and becomes dissolved in free water.

It is the reservoir toward which carbon dioxide diffuses outward. The speed with which this process occurs is directly affected by the porosity of the soil and by whether or not these pores are filled with water. As a rule, the more water in soil, the poorer is the oxygen supply; the drier the soil, the more abundant is the oxygen. Optimum conditions lie somewhere between the two extremes.

Granted that commercial fertilizer preparations may at times be applied to foliage, the fact remains that the avenue by which mineral nutrients commonly enter the plant is through the root system. Not all details are known but it appears that three processes account for the uptake of these many substances by roots—diffusion into regions of lesser concentration in the cell, energy-requiring active accumulation against a diffusion gradient, and direct ionic exchange between root surface and soil particles.

In summary, then, the living plant exists in a state of continuous interchange of water, oxygen, carbon dioxide, and mineral nutrients with its environment. Above ground, most exchange is by gaseous diffusion through pores in the otherwise largely impervious epidermal layer. Below ground, the entire root surface is involved in the inward movement of water, oxygen, and nutrients and the outward loss of carbon dioxide. The soil environment is further influenced by exchanges going on between it and the general atmosphere, and this in turn by the character of the soil.

It is only fair to recognize two limitations in the above statement:

- The analysis considers only the healthy plant, free of appreciable injury and not under attack by pathogenic organisms.
- It ignores the abundant evidence for exudation of various substances from the surfaces of the stem, leaf, and root. By contrast with the major exchanges discussed, these latter are of relatively little significance, but they do have important, if often obscure, implications for the host-pathogen relationship.

Extremes and Optima.   A word must now be said on environment and survival. Taking light as an example, there will be a level below which food accumulation fails to offset utilization and another point above which intensity is so high as to be harmful. In between there will be still another intensity that is maximally favorable. These three values are known, respectively, as minimum, maximum, and optimum. Much the same might be said for oxygen concentration, for available nitrogen level, for any other substance.

Two generalizations can be safely ventured at this point; they will be elaborated upon in Chapter 3.

- The welfare of the plant is more sharply affected by conditions lying toward either extreme than toward the optimum—one thinks of the ancient joke about the statistician who drowned in a river into which he had ventured with undue confidence because he knew it to have an average depth of two feet.
- In any situation involving multiple factors and processes, the overall operation can proceed only so fast as the least favorable element—the familiar concept of limiting factors.

What meaning has all this for the pathologist? For one thing, it relates directly to the rather esoteric concept of "ecological amplitude." This notion, in essence, recognizes that for every species of plant, wild or cultivated, there is a range of environmental conditions within which it can survive and grow satisfactorily. When any one or more of these conditions is exceeded, the species or variety loses its place in the community. A little reflection will show that this in turn determines the geographic limits within which a given host variety may be found; it cannot grow or be grown where it is too dry, too hot, too wet, or too cold.

VARIATIONS ON THE BASIC THEME

All living organisms are more like each other than they are like any nonliving objects. Yet no two living organisms are precisely the same. In the foregoing pages we have tried to cite some of the overriding generalizations that describe the typical seed plant and its relation to its environment. It is now time to have a look at some of the larger categories of variation among plants that will prove important when considering disease phenomena later on. Only a few dimensions will be noted here.

Life Span

By and large, plant pathology deals with cultivated crops rather than natural communities; forests and range lands are the obvious exceptions. Of the cultivated crops perhaps the greater part are annuals; they complete a full life cycle within a single growing season and cannot be induced to continue growth substantially longer than this. They are in the main small, rather succulent plants—one thinks of beans, tomatoes, cucumbers, wheat, and corn as examples—and grow in large numbers per unit area. At the opposite end of the spectrum are perennials, plants that, while they may indeed flower and fruit annually, persist for an indefinite period of time. Most persons tend to think of perennials as trees, and indeed many of them are, but so also are such plants as rhubarb, alfalfa, strawberries, the "brambles," most grasses, and a considerable array of ornamentals—"bulbs," flowering bushes, and shrubs. Because we manage them as we do, some perennials appear superficially to be annuals, but biologically the distinction is highly important.

Between the annuals and perennials come the biennials, such crops as carrots and beets that, if left undisturbed, will produce a fleshy storage organ in the first season, die back with the onset of cold weather, and quickly produce a flowering stalk in the second season.

Propagation

All mechanisms of plant multiplication are properly considered as either by seeds or vegetative propagation. The genetic implications of these two modes are profound, as will be noted in the discussion of plant breeding as a means of disease control (Chapter 14). For the most part seed-propagated crops, especially those that are not obligately self-pollinated, are genetically diverse within a given population; varieties of vegetatively propagated plants are, biologically, only subdivisions of a single plant and therefore genetically identical. Of common crops, the cereals and most vegetables, such field crops as tobacco and sugar beets, and annual ornamentals reproduce by seeds. Many fruit and nut crops, pasture grasses, and perennial ornamentals are vegetatively propagated.

Utilization

At least one more consideration must occur to the plant pathologist as he tries to map a meaningful approach to the host plant: that is, for what purpose is it grown, what good is it to man? A moment's reflection will show that the whole problem of the importance of disease, the feasibility of control, even the measure of control sought, is critically dependent upon the economic use and value of the plant or plant part involved.

Well at the top of the list of plant uses is that as food for man and animals. The details of this story are enormously varied, but at the same time reasonably well known to most and need not be recited here. Perhaps the commonest error is failure to comprehend the full extent to which the plant kingdom lies at the foundation of the entire food and energy complex.

Fiber, in the broadest sense of the word to include paper, lumber, and wood-based synthetics—in short, the utilization of cellulose—is second only to food. Beyond these two come a whole host of specialty products—perfumes and other essential oils, latex, resins, gums, pigments, tannin, waxes, drugs, insecticides, and so on. Each of these has its own history, its special techniques, its trade secrets and customs and, by implication, its own pathology.

Lastly, but importantly, is the role of plants as a means toward enhanced esthetic values—in common parlance the "ornamentals." Lawns, golf greens, shade trees, flowering shrubs, annuals and perennials of the dooryard, houseplants and cut flowers—all these have their own peculiar characteristics and their special values. The criteria of disease and disease control are not the same as for food and fiber plants, and the pathologist must learn to take this fact into consideration.

THE TARGET POPULATION

In the foregoing pages, we have tried to impress upon the reader the accelerating diversity of the agriculture within which the pathologist must work and to emphasize the great and growing diversity between the agricultures of the have and the have-not nations. We have tried to make a start toward realizing the challenge presented to present and future scientists by the vast tropical and arctic areas—a challenge thus far virtually unmet. In short, the plant pathologist starting out today must look far beyond the routine recognition and control of common diseases in orthodox crops. Even in the United States the range of target populations is appreciably greater than is often realized (Figs. 2–3, 2–4), particularly as the professional pathologist is forced by circumstances to concentrate on a relatively small area of the total fabric. One rough subdivision might be as follows.

Natural Communities

By natural communities, at least in this context, we mean economically or esthetically valuable tracts comprised of native species. For all practical purposes this means forest and range lands, although one must include some less extensive pasture lands and occasional areas of protected indigenous vegetation. As in all categories, there are marginal considerations. Who can distinguish fully, for example, between natural forests and planted woodland, between natural and seeded pastures, between native and landscaped communities? Clearly the trend in the United States is toward increasingly

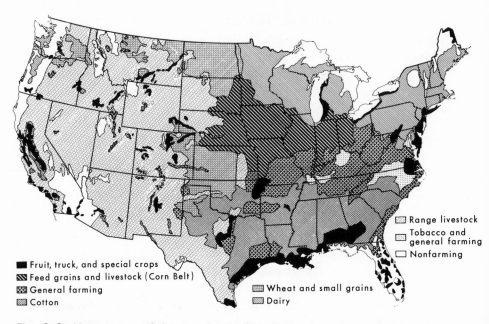

Fig. 2–3. Major types of farming in the United States, indicating diversity of target populations. (Mighell, 1958)

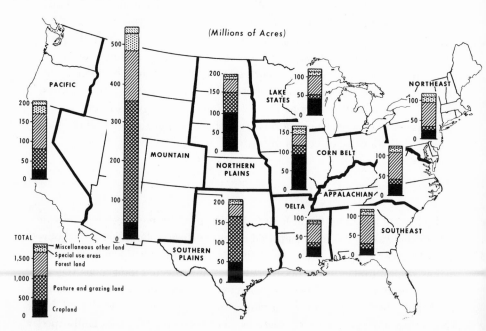

Fig. 2–4. Major uses of all land in the United States, by region, 1964. (Frey *et al.*, 1968)

carefully controlled management of what were once unmanaged forest and grassland resources.

Field and Forage Crops

A second obvious focus of agriculture is upon crops grown in large acreages and with relatively little continuous cultivation. One thinks particularly of seeded pastures, of small grains, and of such forage legumes as alfalfa. Again, the lines of demarcation are blurred, but in general field crops represent a somewhat lower investment of money and labor on a per acre basis than to those more intensively cultivated.

Cultivated and Orchard Crops

At first glance it may seem ill advised to put cultivated and orchard crops in a single category. By many standards perhaps they do not belong side by side, but in economic terms they have much in common. Both command a high value per acre; both require a substantial investment of time and labor; both justify, though for different reasons, expensive and complex disease control measures. As common examples of "cultivated" crops one might cite truck crops, small fruits, and perhaps tobacco, sweet corn, and sugar beets. By orchard crops we usually mean the tree fruits, nut crops, and perhaps such things as grapes, blueberries, hops, or the several bramble fruits—raspberries, blackberries, dewberries, and so on.

Specialties

Increasingly, technological societies are moving away from the traditional modes of agriculture toward new emphases. A few examples will serve to underscore this trend.

Ornamentals. Standards of value shift dramatically as soon as esthetic considerations take the place of more practical utilization. In a final chapter these issues will be more carefully examined, but it is not difficult to recognize the unique place held by ornamental flowers and shrubs, by city and suburban parks and lawns, by golf fairways and putting greens, athletic stadia and picnic sites. More and more attention is being directed toward the pathology of plants under these circumstances as their total number and diversity grow.

Backyard Agriculture.   A visit to the nearby hardware or garden store on a weekend spring morning will dramatize the tremendous upsurge of interest in what might be termed "backyard agriculture." Whatever misgivings there may be about the rationale and the economic wisdom of these efforts, the simple fact is that suburban America is going to have its fling at gardening and that it is already a very large enterprise. These are articulate and inquiring, if inexperienced and uninformed, people and they not only pose questions to the professional plant pathologist but they expect to receive answers. What is more, appropriate answers are not always to be had merely by quoting the practices of more orthodox agriculture.

Glasshouses and Nurseries.   A final category of target populations that is sufficiently distinct to merit consideration is to be found in nurseries, glasshouses, and in related highly intensified production of selected plant material. Not that all of these situations are necessarily identical. In the glasshouse, a specialized environment leads to unique disease problems; the opportunity to control this environment suggests possible corrective measures. As for commercial nurseries, whether they produce for orchard plantings or to sell ornamental trees and shrubs, the necessity frequently to meet rather exacting certification standards enhances the disease control requirements. Again, our changing society dictates a steady increase in the importance of these very specialized kinds of agriculture.

A LOOK AHEAD

For some interesting analyses of epidemics we might turn to J. E. van der Plank, who has written extensively on this subject and summarized his views in several convenient sources (1959, 1960, 1963) that are eminently worth careful study. The advantage of pausing here for a look ahead is mostly to underscore the importance of the host population in a concrete disease situation. Let two examples suffice—one in which the key is the biologic nature of the host plant per se, another where the critical issues lie in the way in which the host population is managed.

Annual Versus Perennial Crops

In true annuals, or in the annual growth of biennials or perennials, disease will be destructively important only if the speed of its development or the amount of damage caused by the initial invasion, or both, is relatively high.

There simply is not time enough, except in this way, for disease to reach significant proportions in view of the fact that it must, in effect, begin anew each season.

On the contrary, perennial plants have to be considered in a very different light, partly because they live very much longer and therefore cannot escape damage in the way annuals can, and partly because they are so often vegetatively propagated. There is some difference of opinion among pathologists as to the relative importance of the various factors, but most would agree to the following as demonstrable risks: sheer span of years that permits disease damage to accumulate; spread of inoculum through dissemination of propagative materials; genetic uniformity, leading, in susceptible lines, to augmented disease incidence.

Abundance and Distribution of Host

Assuming that the host variety in all cases was identical, what would be the importance of abundance and distribution? In a closely reasoned argument, van der Plank (1960) points out among other things that as susceptible host plants are increasingly crowded together, the "birth rate" of the pathogen increases more markedly than the "death rate," with the result that what he calls an epidemic point is reached. That this epidemic point varies from crop to crop is apparent from the following account, but the principle remains (see Horsfall and Dimond, 1960, p. 262 *et seq.*).

Take as examples three diseases of trees: rosette disease of peaches, swollen shoot of cacao, and tristeza disease of sweet oranges on sour orange rootstocks. All are caused by viruses that kill their hosts and die with them. Rosette virus ordinarily spreads slowly from peach to peach, and its birth rate is low. However, its death rate is high, because it quickly kills its peach host, which usually dies in the same season in which symptoms are first seen, and then dies too. Ordinarily, the death rate exceeds the birth rate, and the disease in peaches is self-eradicating although it occasionally flares up and affects a whole orchard. Swollen shoot of cacao has the same features as peach rosette, but not in quite such an extreme degree. It spreads slowly, but not quite so slowly; it kills quickly, but not quite so quickly, and infected trees may survive up to 2 years or longer. Tristeza disease has an abundant and efficient vector, *Toxoptera citricidus* (among others), which occurs in both winged and wingless forms, and infection spreads relatively fast through an orchard in which *T. citricidus* occurs. The disease kills sweet oranges on intolerant rootstocks but not very fast; the trees go into a decline that may last for several years. Compared, then, with peach rosette, citrus tristeza has a higher birth rate and a lower death rate.

The three diseases form an interesting series with regard to the epidemic point, which we define as the point in crowding plants together at which the birth rate of the pathogen exceeds the death rate. In peach rosette the epidemic point is usually imaginary; it is usually not reached even when peaches are in continuous orchard formation. The disease of peaches is usually sporadic and self-eliminating, and the virus persists only because it has other tolerant hosts such as the wild plum, from which it spreads to peaches. If epidemiology is the science of disease in populations, in peaches this behavior is epidemiological hypersensitivity, comparable in its effect on populations with ordinary hypersensitivity in its effect on the plant. Swollen shoot of cacao has a lower epidemic point, which was apparently reached in West Africa between the World Wars, when cacao production was expanding rapidly. Before then the disease in cacao had a long history of sporadic outbreaks; it was only afterwards that the epidemic began to rage. Tristeza seems to have a fairly low epidemic point in countries in which *Toxoptera citricidus* is present; in these countries the virus seems to pervade quickly all susceptible species of citrus, killing those trees which are on unsuitable rootstocks and saturating the rest.°

On the basis of his analysis, van der Plank strongly urges that by going still further in the direction of concentration, by increasing the size of fields and thus decreasing their number and proximity to each other, disease can be effectively reduced. This would appear to be true, for example, where inoculum comes in from native species or weeds on the periphery, or from adjoining fields of the same cultivated crop, or where juxtaposition of highly susceptible and resistant varieties permits inoculum to build up on the former to the point where it endangers the latter. For some diseases, particularly those where the movement of inoculum is for comparatively short distances and multiplication is slow, he is convinced that regional planning would markedly reduce disease losses.

These are but two rather simplified examples. Alerted to these sorts of relationships the reader should make other comparisons among the data in later chapters.

° From J. G. Horsfall and A. E. Dimond (eds.), *Plant Pathology: An Advanced Treatise* (New York: Academic Press, Inc.), vol. III, pp. 262–63, 267. Copyright © 1959–60, Academic Press, Inc.

3

Causal Factors: Nonparasitic

GENERAL CONSIDERATIONS

Overriding interest in plant pathology centers on the plant when there is something wrong with it. The "something" that may be "wrong" covers a wide range of ills and the burden of this chapter is to consider those aspects of plant disease that are the direct result of factors other than living organisms.

Over the years there has been debate on the preferred meaning of the word disease. Horsfall and Dimond (1959) make the dogmatic statement that disease is not a condition nor a pathogen and that it is not the same thing as injury—distinguishing in the last point between disease, wherein the action of the causal factor is prolonged, and injury when the causal factor acts suddenly. In their words, "disease results from continuous irritation and injury from transient irritation." To them, disease is a "malfunctioning process," that and nothing else.

Custom and the accidents of history have had much to do with what is customarily thought of as disease and therefore in the realm of plant pathology. Few would seriously argue that cows and lawnmowers are the proper concern of plant pathology and traditionally all aspects of direct damage by insects have been ceded to the economic entomologists. At the same time, Carter (1962) has identified a number of categories of what he calls "toxicogenic effects" of insects—effects other than direct feeding damage—that merge into the very sorts of symptoms that are familiar to plant pathologists:

- Local lesions at the insects' feeding point
- Local lesions with development of secondary symptoms
- Tissue malformations
- Symptoms indicating either limited or systemic translocation of the causal entity

Finally, again very possibly as an accident of history, the depredations of nematodes are accepted by most as the province of plant pathology, although as information accumulates the study of nematology is becoming more and more a matter for specialists.

Disease, so far as this text is concerned, will be considered in a somewhat larger context than that of Horsfall and Dimond. Here it turns out to be a concept of convenience, including all those entities that importantly affect unfavorably the growth, development, and functioning of a plant, and excluding arbitrarily some obvious categories such as insects, grazing animals, and most gross mechanical injuries. Actually, it would not be too far off the mark to define disease as anything that plant pathologists worry about.

Nonparasitic Diseases

Much of this chapter shares with ecology and plant physiology an emphasis on the environment in relation to the plant, except that it focuses on unfavorable conditions and their effects. Plant pathologists study the environment as it affects managed communities unfavorably and consider the abnormal physiology of plants. But once it is recognized that plant pathology extends to considerations of this kind, it is hardly possible to exaggerate the overall importance of the nonparasitic diseases. We do not know the precise toll, but it is entirely likely that it equals or exceeds that of disease caused by living organisms.

Environment and Parasitic Diseases

Before going into detail in the problem of nonparasitic diseases, it is well to look for just a moment at the relation of environment to parasitic disorders. There are several aspects of what must be, actually, a complex continuum:

- The role of environment in the interactions of host and pathogen (Chapter 8)
- The influence of weather upon the development and dynamics of disease epidemics (Chapter 11)
- The manipulation of the environment as a measure toward minimizing the impact of disease (Chapters 15 and 16)

In short, conditions external to the plant in question not only affect it directly but influence its response to attack by pathogenic organisms and may be capitalized upon by the agriculturist or forester in his efforts to avoid or control the inroads of pathogens.

WEATHER

Climate, or weather, are the terms usually given to the above-ground environment. If the immediate concern is long term and regional, the tendency is to talk about climate; it is climate that determines the geographic distribution of plants. If attention turns to local atmospheric conditions, particularly on a short-term basis, we speak of weather; it is weather, or at least extremes of weather, that causes many of the more conspicuous nonparasitic diseases of plants.

There is yet one more kind of "weather"—that in immediate proximity to the object under study. For most crop plants this environment, to which the name "microclimate" has been given, is usually confined to the atmosphere within no more than two or three feet from the ground. Generally, perhaps, microclimate is most critically important in its effect on the host-parasite relationship, but it is of significance as it directly impinges on the host alone. Above all, it is very important to recognize that the conditions of the microenvironment are not to be deduced simply by glancing at routine weather data. If accurate knowledge is to be gained, measurements must be made within the microclimate itself, an area of research that has been rather neglected until fairly recently.

Not only must a clear distinction be made between general climate, local weather, and microclimate, it is well also to avoid overuse of average or mean values. There are at least two reasons for this: (1) mean values give a far less complete picture of conditions than do actual readings; and more importantly, (2) it is usually the extremes that cause plant disorders, almost irrespective of the factor under consideration. It goes almost without saying, in this connection, that plants are importantly affected also by fluctuations in environmental factors, particularly if those fluctuations are pronounced.

Finally, it must be recognized that those elements that in the aggregate we think of as weather are hardly if ever independent of each other. Take, just as an example, radiant energy—the sum total of energy received from the sun. If in the visible wavelengths it is perceived as light, if of a longer wavelength it is perceived as heat. When light strikes a surface that is other than white, such as soil, energy is absorbed and the temperature of the mass rises. Energy then radiated from soil to atmosphere serves to increase air temperature.

So much, then, for a simple example of the interrelationships of light and temperature. But, to continue, an increase in air temperature, other things remaining unchanged, will decrease the relative humidity of the air, with obvious implications for the movement of water vapor from soil and plant into the surrounding medium. Thus light, temperature, and moisture—three of the most obvious elements in weather—are inextricably bound up with each other. A change in one directly affects the others.

It is inappropriate here to trace every last aspect of weather factors and their interrelationships, once the pattern is discerned. The following sections are thus to be regarded as representative of the kind of plant-environment interactions that may be encountered. So far as possible, the emphasis is on direct rather than indirect effects.

Temperature

Native vegetation taken as a whole occupies areas of extremely diverse temperatures. From the arctic winter to the equatorial noonday, temperatures may range over nearly 200° F; in almost every site some kind of plant life is to be found. Crop plants, as we usually think of them, are much more restricted in their distribution. Agriculture is primarily a temperate zone culture, with fringe extensions toward the arctic and tropics. And even within these limitations, very many of our common crop plants do not actually face the full rigors of the region in which they grow. By and large we try so to time the planting and harvest that extremes of low temperature are avoided.

It is sometimes not adequately appreciated that the success, even the geographical distribution, of the orchard crops are very much determined by temperature conditions. In a number of historic occasions, exceptional periods of freezing temperatures have wrought great havoc in this or that section of the United States—not the least was the 1933–34 episode in New England, which virtually eliminated the Baldwin as a commercial apple variety and killed or seriously injured millions and millions of trees. Several measures are available to counteract the effect of excessive cold (Gerber, 1970), although they are usually restricted to specialty situations where the crop is of high value and the threat is confronted at least often enough to make it economically sensible to take countermeasures.

By far the commonest, or at least best known, are measures to provide additional heat by oil burners. Gerber suggests that to be effective, such a system will require 35–40 burners per acre, consuming a gallon of fuel per hour and producing in the aggregate 2 to 5 million Btu's. Clearly this is an expensive system to maintain.

Overhead irrigation, while cheaper to maintain, has the disadvantage that it is not adjustable and that initial installation runs to $500 per acre. The biggest difficulty, however, is the fact that unless the amount of water put on the trees is sufficient to keep freezing of water at least 7 times that of evaporation, temperatures will be lowered rather than raised and serious trouble encountered. As a rule of thumb, conditions must be such that icicles form—a hazard in itself if the crop in question is a broad-leaved tree in foliage, such as citrus, leading to great risk from breakage of limbs and trunks.

In regions where there is intense low-level inversion, that is, where cold weather is accompanied by rapid warming aloft, as in southern California, the use of wind machines is especially promising. Most machines now in use require 8–10 horsepower per acre, i.e., an 85-horsepower machine, either electric or gasoline, will provide protection to as much as ten acres of orchard. Because the machine effects its protection by destroying the nocturnal inversion, they are not useful if winds exceed 3 to 5 miles per hour or if there the inversion itself is a weak one.

Most of the fund of knowledge of when and how to manage a given crop has developed by experience over the years. A few rules of thumb—the kind of thing to be found in small print on the back of seed packets (Fig. 3–1)—are useful, of course, but we simply do not yet fully know why different plants react differently to temperature regimes.

Take, for example, beans and peas—two closely related genera in the legume family. Peas may, and should, be planted very early in the spring. In Washington, D.C., the old-timers insist that the peas should be in the ground by "Washington's Birthday." If, as usually occurs, there are·subsequent frosts and snow it does no harm; seedlings seem wholly unaffected by it. Beans on the other hand must be planted only after all danger of frost is safely by. A single night falling below 32° F and every bean seedling in the garden will be killed. To say that peas are cold-tolerant and that beans are not is a long way from explaining why they are like this. Low temperature damage, then, is one of the commoner instances of the effects of unfavorable temperature. Not infrequently, the conspicuous effect of low temperatures at sowing time is not so much to injure or kill the seedlings as it is greatly to retard their germination, with consequent added risk of subsequent invasion by a number of different pathogenic organisms.

An attribute of plants that is clearly temperature related is dormancy. While most varieties of cultivated crops have been selected over many generations for nondormant seeds, there are still some that must go through a cold period before they will germinate dependably.

In plant pathology, dormancy as one encounters it in shrubs and other woody plants is probably the place where unfavorable effects are most likely to occur. This brings up another very important aspect of temperature—

namely, fluctuation. In a normal season, if there is any such thing, the temperature gradually diminishes as winter draws near and trees and shrubs go into dormancy—"harden off," as the vernacular has it. Come spring, the process is reversed. But suppose the fall is unseasonably warm and the hardening-off process does not occur? When this happens plants that would ordinarily survive the first really cold weather unscathed may be badly damaged. In Knoxville, Tennessee, for example, such a sequence of events took place in the late 1940's, to the extent that even English ivy was extensively killed and literally thousands of shrubs throughout the city lost.

LEAF LETTUCE — GRAND RAPIDS

High in Vitamin A. Average calories per portion 10. Approx. days to table size 42

Large, frilly, bright green leaves are tender and sweet. Upright plants grow quickly. Whole plants may be harvested, or you may pick only the outer leaves, allowing multiple harvests.

PLANTING DIRECTIONS

Plant as early in spring as soil can be made fine and loose and, thereafter, at intervals of 10 days or 2 weeks, as desired. Make rows 18 inches apart. Plant seeds thinly by

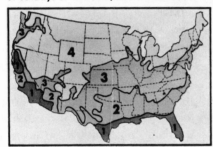

dropping slowly from corner of packet. Cover firmly with ½ inch of soil. When young plants have 2 or 3 leaves, thin to about 4 inches apart. As plants begin to crowd, thin and use.

Planting Depth ½" ▶ ▬▬▬▬▬

OUTDOOR PLANTING DATES

Zone 1 Jan.-March & Aug.-Dec.
Zone 2 Jan.-April & July-Sept.
Zone 3 March-April & July-Aug.
Zone 4 May-July

Seeds normally sprout in 14 to 21 days.

Fig. 3–1. Information as it appears on the back of a package of lettuce seeds as sold to the home gardener, showing a map of outdoor planting dates and table of intervals considered safe for these zones. (Courtesy of Ferry-Morse Seed Company)

Suppose again that after perennials have become fully dormant and have so remained for a few weeks or months there is an unseasonably warm spell for several days. By this time dormancy can be "broken," and new growth starts, only to be killed when the temperature again drops to levels that are normal for that time of year. Very often this accounts for the failure of ornamentals or fruit trees to develop fully when spring at last arrives—the buds, or a substantial fraction of them, have been killed in this manner.

In our preoccupation with the now well-established importance of photoperiod we often fail to recognize the possibility of thermoperiod. F. W. Went

(1957) has conducted a number of studies on, for example, the influence of day and night temperature rhythms upon the growth, flowering, and fruiting of some common food and ornamental plants. It begins to look as though at least a few of the puzzling disorders of plants may be explainable in these terms.

Temperature may be satisfactory for growth and survival and yet be unsatisfactory from man's special viewpoint. In the matter, for example, of tuber formation in potatoes an excess of photosynthesis over respiration is an obvious must. When, therefore, elevated temperature accelerates catabolic processes more markedly than anabolic ones—as of course it does—tuber formation is prevented or retarded and within the context of our definition the plant is diseased.

Light

Latitude and season determine regionally the intensity and duration of incident radiation. As one moves away from the equator the sun's rays strike the earth at an increasingly more acute angle, after therefore having passed through a longer and longer atmospheric path. Combined, these effects sharply reduce the total energy falling on a unit of soil surface. In the northern hemisphere, the intensity is minimal at the winter solstice, the time when the sun lies at its farthest point below the equator. Conversely, intensity is maximal at the summer solstice.

On balance, seasonal changes in solar radiation reaching the earth's surface determine the effective length and general characteristics of the growing season. More than any other one thing this in turn determines crop distribution —sets the geographic limits within which crops may be grown.

Within the regional limits, further marked effects are produced on a smaller scale and often highly irregularly by cloud cover and related atmospheric conditions. In a very restricted sense, but not less importantly, simple shading by other objects often affects light intensity falling on a given plant.

Variations in light quality depend upon the depth of the atmosphere through which the light travels, the amounts of water vapor and other materials in the air and upon whether or not the plant under consideration is overshadowed by adjoining individuals. Finally, besides intensity and quality, light duration is known to be highly significant in plant growth and response.

This is hardly the place to examine fully the vast literature on light in relation to plant physiology; a few somewhat random examples will have to suffice. Experienced gardeners know, often from unhappy experience, that tomato plants will produce luxuriant foliage but seldom set fruit if they are shaded by nearby trees. Plants adapted to one latitude will frequently fail utterly to flower if they are removed to a different photoperiod condition. Low light intensity very often leads to exaggerated stem length, interferes with leaf maturation, and reduces the concentration of both photosynthetic and non-photosynthetic pigments. Finally, the very structure of plants is controlled by light—most elementary biology students have been introduced to the fact of thick "sun" leaves and much thinner "shade" leaves from the very same plant. An often-cited commercial exploitation of this response is the production of large, thin-leaved "shade grown" tobacco in the Connecticut River valley.

Light is, in the final analysis, the environmental factor to which plants are most dramatically, most complexly, and most diversely responsive. Within broad limits there is an optimal intensity, quality, and duration for each species. Any appreciable departure from this optimum brings on detectable effects. A marked departure will produce significant damage, whether that departure be toward one extreme or the other.

Precipitation

Compared to light and temperature, precipitation as such probably has relatively little direct effect on plants, if one thinks of the falling of rain or snow from the atmosphere to the ground surface. Should rain descend with sufficient force it can damage the foliage of plants, and the destructive effect of hail is well known. Atmospheric moisture, which is quite distinct from precipitation, is important largely through its influence on water loss from foliage.

Precipitation as a reflection of climate and a determinant of soil moisture levels is a quite different matter indeed. More than any one single feature, certainly, availability of water in adequate amounts determines where crops may be grown and there is nothing else so likely to be the direct cause of crop failures in a given growing season.

There are many interrelations between light, temperature, and precipitation. Some are entirely obvious, others more obscure. The continuing problem in ecology is to recognize and reconcile three basic concepts:

- That environmental forces are acting simultaneously and continuously upon the plants of the community
- These forces are continuously interacting with and influencing each other in a host of different ways
- Despite this, the net effect of the total environment upon the whole plant is the sum of all the countless specific individual reactions

What the plant pathologist must strive for when confronted with a plant in a less than desirable state of health is constantly to keep in mind both the particular event and the net effect.

SOIL ENVIRONMENT

Matters become greatly complicated once attention shifts below ground. For this very reason the pathology of root systems, especially from pathogenic organisms, is very much less well known than are the diseases of stems, foliage, and reproductive structures. Accumulating evidence suggests that the magnitude of the problem is at least as great and that a carefully planned attack on the complexities of the soil environment has been launched none too soon. In the immediately following paragraphs attention centers on the nonparasitic causes of root maladies.

Water

Water, by all odds, dominates the soil environment as indeed it does the existence of all living things. We need to remind ourselves, further, that vascular plants receive from the soil amounts of water very much beyond that actually utilized in any of their life processes, water that escapes from the foliage as vapor through the mechanism of transpiration. First or last, all of this water comes from the atmosphere as some form of precipitation, during the growing seasons customarily as rain.

Mention was made earlier of the forces involved in the water relations of plants, especially forces that determine the availability of soil water to root systems. Our immediate concern is with the effects of imbalance in water supplies. Troubles due to inadequate moisture, with consequent reduction in growth rate, in photosynthesis and, when prolonged or extreme, in death, are probably commonest. Somewhat less often, excess water leads to damage as the intercellular spaces in tissues become filled and "water-logging" ensues.

Oxygen–Carbon Dioxide Balance

The very vastness of the atmosphere and the fluidity of the gaseous medium assure a remarkably constant level of carbon dioxide and oxygen. Small, local, and transitory changes do occur, but they do not seem to have much effect on the welfare of plants except perhaps in very closely confined space. The very intriguing question whether there is a long-term increase in total atmospheric carbon dioxide, with implications for climatic changes and human welfare, is not pertinent to the issue here under consideration.

Quite by contrast with the stability of the atmosphere, carbon dioxide–oxygen balance in the soil is very precarious. As a general rule, conditions that favor increased water supply lead to excess carbon dioxide and to oxygen deficiency—conversely, as the soil dries out the oxygen levels tend to become more favorable. The explanation for this is not hard to discover, because oxygen must move into the soil from the atmosphere above and is then in a position to be absorbed by the roots. Carbon dioxide, on the other hand, diffuses out from the root and will be dissipated to the atmosphere. Exchange of both gases would be maximal in a dry, sandy soil; in a wet clay soil in which all capillary spaces were filled with water, diffusion would be slowest. Under the latter conditions, or whenever fields are actually flooded for extended periods, plants will drown for precisely the same biological reason that land animals will drown if forced under water. One of the commonest instances of this is the destruction of seedlings in low-lying farmland, when spring rains maintain standing water over portions of the sown field. In suburban areas also, the purchasers of new homes are all too often painfully aware of the delayed effects brought on when a thoughtless contractor sees fit to raise the soil grade level about the base of mature trees already standing on the site. If so, "wooded lots" purchased as a premium become nothing more than patches of dead and dying trees in a year or so.

H. F. Bergman, who was for many years engaged in studying diseases of the cultivated cranberry, summarized (1959) the role of oxygen deficiency in the pathology of plants, including his own studies of the situation that arises when flooding waters are permitted to remain overlong on the cranberry vines.

Mineral Nutrients

By all odds the most obvious environmental effect of soil, other than moisture supply, has to do with mineral nutrients. Basically, this is a field of specialization that occupies the attention of plant physiologists. Any recent text in that specialty will furnish a wealth of information on the role of the various elements in plants, the investigative methods employed in plant nutrition research, and the diagnostic symptoms of the commoner diseases associated therewith. Only the barest outline needs to be included here.

It has long been known that nitrogen, phosphorus, potassium, sulfur, magnesium, and calcium are key elements in plant growth and for a shorter time that very low concentrations of iron, zinc, manganese, copper, boron, and molybdenum are necessary. Generally, each of these materials either constitutes an important constituent in the fabrication of biological compounds or is involved in intermediary metabolism, perhaps as a coenzyme or playing some other catalytic role. Without trying to catalogue all of the roles filled by individual nutrients, and all the details of symptomatology, it is still possible to distinguish three categories of nutrient-related maladjustments.

Deficiencies.   To the extent that a given essential element is inadequate, the plant will be adversely affected (Figs. 3–2, 3–3). Naturally, the absolute

Fig. 3–2. Effect of nutrient deficiency on plants: "drought spot" of McIntosh apples as a result of boron deficiency. (Woodbridge, 1950)

amount below which a detectable symptom appears will depend much on just which element is involved, but the principle remains the same. The crucial issue is, actually, the level of availability—if the element in question is present but unavailable, it is valueless to the plant.

Excesses.   A given element, particularly one of the micronutrients, may well be directly toxic if the available concentration is too high (Fig. 3–4). On

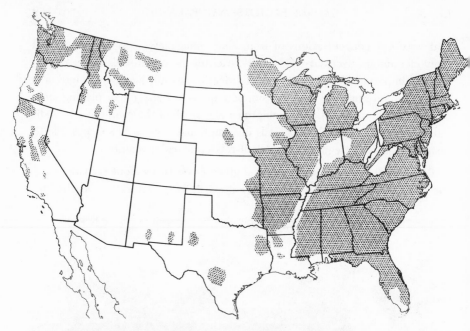

Fig. 3–3. Areas in United States where deficiencies of boron may exist. (Russel, 1957)

Fig. 3–4. Effect of excess minor elements on plants: boron toxicity symptoms on table beets grown with 200 pounds of borax per acre under conditions of high soil moisture. (Lorenz, 1942)

the other hand, if total dissolved materials in the soil water is so high that water tends to diffuse from, rather than into, the root cells of the plant—unless it be a species especially adapted to saline soils—it will be adversely affected and may even die of physiological drought even though in ostensibly moist soil.

Excesses of a given chemical in the soil may result locally from activities that are unrelated to the host plant directly affected. As an example of this, take the damage to roadside maples in New England that has been fairly clearly attributed to applications of salt in highway snow and ice control programs during the winter (Lacasse and Rich, 1964). Unlike white birch and white ash, maple apparently accumulates higher than normal sodium levels in leaves and twigs.

Imbalances. To a considerable extent, one mineral constituent in soil affects the uptake of others. Many details of the mechanism of ion uptake by root cells are as yet unresolved, but investigations clearly show that optimum conditions for plant growth demand a proper balance of available nutrients. If nothing else, where more than one element is involved in a complex system such as the growing plant, total rate cannot exceed that permitted by the least favorable factor—here it acts as a "limiting factor," as that term is usually used.

Other Soil Factors

Soil pH. Very high or very low pH values are directly harmful to most plants, although not all are suited to the same optimum (Fig. 3–5). Members of the heath family, for example, are favored by comparatively acid soils, perhaps because it is desirable as a medium for the action of mycorrhizal fungi, whereas many of the grasses do far better in more alkaline soils. Through its role in the solubility or insolubility of nutrient salts or its influence on ion uptake, pH may exert other important effects (Fig. 3–6).

Soil Temperature. Intensity and duration of incident light is the prime factor responsible for establishing soil temperature—as it is also of air temperature—although this effect can be modified by an insulating mulch. Under extreme conditions, soil temperature can rise or fall to a point where direct damage occurs. There are interesting data (Bonner and Galston, 1957) that suggest a relationship between high levels of nitrogen or low levels of potassium as accentuating low-temperature damage.

In recent years both private gardeners and commercial growers have evinced increasing interest in plastic film mulch as a means of sharply reducing evaporation losses. On a small scale this device proves highly effective, but used to cover extensive areas it would generate serious problems, particularly in how to avoid disastrous increases in soil temperature. The one seems inextricably bound to the other.

Soil Structure. "Structure" is used here rather imprecisely to mean the general physical nature of the soil. For most agricultural situations, aggregates and particles with diameters of ¼ mm or larger are preferable. Available supplies of water and oxygen tend to be favorable in soils of this nature, roots are seldom hindered, and seedlings can emerge without difficulty. In soils of

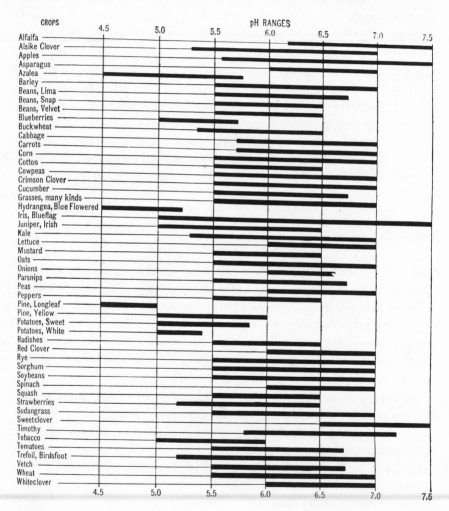

Fig. 3–5. Suitable pH ranges for various crops and ornamental plants. (Kellogg, 1957)

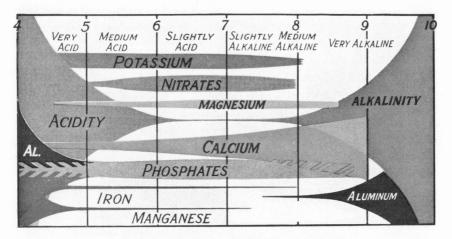

Fig. 3–6. Chart showing the relation of soil pH to the availability of plant nutrients to crops. (Virginia Polytechnic Institute, 1966; copyright by V.P.I.)

lighter texture, water supply becomes critical; heavy clay soils may be oxygen deficient or present physical barriers to root and seedling growth.

INJURIES

We turn now to what might be called for lack of a better term injuries. The distinction between disease and injury is arbitrary but useful. If plants fail to set fruit because of improper light intensity, it is difficult to think of them as injured, however much they may be disadvantaged. But if exposed portions of the developing fruits are killed by exposure during a day of strong sunlight it is easy to use the word. Injury, then, implies a sudden, acute response to unfavorable environment. In the long run it makes little difference what terms are employed; the plant pathologist will be summoned to help in any case by the anxious grower or home owner.

Injury by feeding insects is purposely omitted from this discussion, despite their recognized importance in the overall picture.

Weather Damage

Within the definition of injury adopted here, damage from low temperature is surely the most frequent. It usually shows up in the destruction of succulent new growth of seedlings or buds immediately after an unseasonable drop in temperature. How vulnerable the crop is depends greatly on its nature—citrus, in the United States at least, has been especially well publicized, but most varieties of cultivated plants will be damaged if temperature changes are sufficiently severe.

Occasionally the results of frost damage can be very striking (Figs. 3–7, 3–8). In mid-June 1963, for example, some hundreds of square miles of corn land in north central Illinois and in Indiana were subjected to a night temperature just below freezing. Driving along the highways a day later, the traveller could see in almost every field large areas of dead and discolored foliage —in every instance occupying the low-lying portions of the fields in clear

Fig. 3–7. Injury from low temperature: bark of trunk of Golden Delicious apple tree killed by freezing. (Groves, 1946)

Fig. 3–8. Cracking of Halehaven peaches caused by late frost. (Groves, 1946)

demonstration that a mere few feet of added elevation was quite enough to spell the difference between death and survival.

When high temperatures and cloudless skies follow a period of cool, moist weather the exposed parts of developing fruits are often killed. They look, when this happens, precisely as though they had been placed on a hot skillet —hence the common name "sunscald." Shortly, of course, the dead tissues will be invaded by weakly pathogenic fungi and give the misleading impression that the primary damage was biological in origin. When a similar sequence of weather kills portions of the foliage, it is usually called "sunburn," and is almost certainly related also to severe transpiration loss. Even woody stems are subject to high temperature damage, particularly in newly transplanted seedlings and on the exposed surfaces of recently pruned orchard trees.

In assessing temperature as the cause of injury to plants, two things must be kept in mind: (1) rising air temperatures greatly accelerate water loss through increased rates of diffusion and drop in relative humidity, and (2) absorption of light by leaf, stem, and fruit tissues, as well as soil, raises the temperature of these parts appreciably above that of the surrounding air. Both of these factors demonstrate that the conditions to which a plant is subjected may be considerably more severe than they appear to the casual observer.

Because light, except as it induces temperature extremes, is hardly likely to produce injury it will be omitted here. Air movement, on the other hand, is often destructive. If sufficiently strong, wind physically destroys the aerial portions of plants more or less directly proportional to its speed. By custom, perhaps, massive blowdowns resulting from sudden storms are not usually regarded as within the purview of plant pathologists. But air movement operates in at least two other ways to damage plants: (1) air flow largely from one direction, combined with water stress, will desiccate the buds on the exposed side sufficiently to produce a deformity in woody perennials sometimes known as "flagging," and (2) when loose sand is carried in the wind it often results in pronounced injury to seedlings, partly because there is rather more likelihood of bare soil being exposed to wind action in the early part of the growing season, before weeds have had a chance to develop, and partly because the tissues of recently emerged seedlings are particularly soft and vulnerable to sand-blasting damage.

Two more weather factors, hail and lightning, must be noted. The former is especially harmful to such large-leaved crops as rhubarb, cabbage, or sugar beets. When the actual appearance of the leaf, as well as its total photosynthetic area, is important, as it is in the case of many ornamentals and such crops as tobacco, the damage inflicted by hail is that much more serious. So

Fig. 3–9. Lightning injury: photograph of Burley tobacco taken 3 days after the plants were struck. (Valleau *et al.*, 1942)

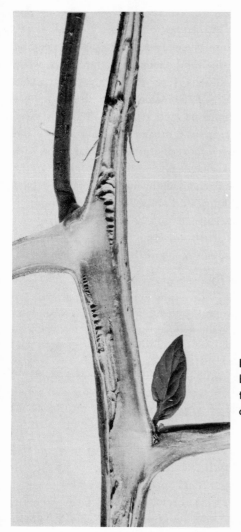

Fig. 3–10. Lightning injury: large branch of tomato cut longitudinally to show the destruction of localized areas of pith. (Whipple, 1941)

far as lightning is concerned, it most frequently injures large trees, but field crops are sometimes struck and if so the cause of damage is often difficult to diagnose and may well elude the novice pathologist (Figs. 3–9, 3–10). If there seems to be no other satisfactory explanation and if the pattern of injury seems to diminish outward from an apparent "ground zero" spot, there is at least a fair chance that lightning is the cause of the difficulty.

Chemical Injuries

Modern, temperate zone agriculture is highly technological, depending upon the regular use of a host of agricultural chemicals as fertilizers, weed killers, fungicides, soil fumigants, insecticides. It serves a highly industrialized society that in turn releases an array of volatile materials into the atmosphere from mines, manufacturing plants, smelters, and refineries. Many of these effluents have detectable effects on crops and ornamental plants, lawns and shade trees. The whole matter has been moved into the political arena with the eruption of a bitter controversy over pesticides, as they are dubbed in the popular press. There seems no escape from a lengthy and vituperative debate on the effect of chemicals on living things, and especially on man himself.

One wonders why the issue of pesticides has evoked so much feeling and why opposing views are so very far apart and firmly held. To this implied question there are no simple answers, but much of the difficulty lies in two foci:

- To a regrettable degree, the proponents and opponents of pesticide use do not have adequate information about the situation from several angles. They therefore tend to see the issue as simple and as resolvable in black-and-white terms. That is, the complexities are far greater than most who join the fray realize.
- Even more importantly, the truth lies mostly at neither end of the spectrum. Neither unfettered use nor total ban makes sense, but action must be based on a dispassionate weighing of benefits versus risks, including the benefits and risks of alternative measures.

Agricultural Chemicals. Even the most essential material may well be harmful if improperly used (Fig. 3–11). It takes but little contact with the amateur gardener to discover that many of them operate on the philosophy that if a little lime or commercial fertilizer is good, a lot will surely be even better. Too many well-meaning people consider their favorite plants as almost human, and tend, whatever the suspected indisposition, to respond by "feeding" their patients. Whether applied to foliage or soil, excess chemicals bring about such very high osmotic levels in the water surrounding the cells that they are quite literally desiccated and killed. The resulting "burning" of leaves, whole plants, patches of turf, and so on is a common occurrence after too enthusiastic application of lime or fertilizer.

Fungicides and insecticides used in improper concentrations, in incompatible combinations, at the wrong stage of plant development, or under inauspicious weather conditions will injure the very crops or ornamentals they are

Fig. 3–11. Effect of improper use of herbicides in vicinity of vulnerable crop plants: damage to leaves of cotton from 2,4–D. (Dunlap, 1948)

designed to protect. It will be apparent from Chapter 13, where development of new fungicidal chemicals is discussed, that much of the time and energy devoted to field testing of candidate substances is imposed by the need to minimize undesirable effects and to take careful note of those that cannot be avoided. Virtually all important agricultural chemicals must be sold with accompanying information on label or leaflet spelling out the precautions that must be taken. The whole problem becomes that much more troublesome when mixed cropping on very limited area is the rule, as it is with most amateur gardeners.

That plant pathologists must be constantly alert to the complexity of the situations with which they deal and receptive to the implications of what they see is highlighted by Ullstrup's (1969) observations on the relation of weather to the absorption of 2,4-D by field corn in Indiana and Illinois in 1968 and the relation of this in turn to the incidence of corn smut (Fig. 3–12). That the excessive absorption of the herbicide was due to weather is strongly indicated by the fact that only corn planted in late April and early May, and which was subsequently subjected to excessive rainfall and abnormally low temperatures, showed the effects of excess 2,4-D—the symptom itself was a "buggy-whip" fusion of the upper portion of the plant into a tube enclosing upper leaves and tassel. Even more interesting, possibly, was the fact that whereas

Fig. 3–12. Injury to corn by 2,4–D, producing the symptom known as "buggy whip," and its predisposing effect on the incidence of corn smut galls. *Top row:* Symptoms showing different degrees of fusion of the upper portion of the plant into a tube. *Bottom row:* Smut galls at the base of tubes. (Ullstrup, 1969)

ordinary plants showed perhaps 5% incidence of smut galls—a level that is characteristic of this disease generally—the "buggy-whip" plants showed the remarkable level of 85% smutting, usually located near the base of the tube. The precise explanation is unknown, but could very well be correlated with a prolongation of the embryonic state of the host cells as a result of the herbicide intake.

In the late 1960's, when concern for the effects of repeated pesticide use came to be expressed with special vigor and vehemence, it was common to relate these concerns to the development of resistant parasites, to the possibility of toxicity to humans, and to destruction of wildlife species held to be particularly desirable. But disease or damage does not always fall into common or fashionable patterns. Thus Dubey (1970) calls attention to a nitrogen-deficiency disease of sugarcane in southern Puerto Rico that clearly resulted from there having been as many as 19 applications of fungicides—maneb, zineb, and tribasic copper—to a preceding tomato crop. Apparently this virtual drenching of the soil, at least in less moist parts of the field, led to such disturbance to the normal soil flora as to upset the regular patterns of mineralization of soil nitrogen.

Atmospheric Pollutants. Most of the substances referred to in the foregoing section are applied as a spray, dust, or liquid to soil or foliage in such a way that it moves but little from the initial site of deposition. Even volatile soil fumigants are customarily enclosed by fabric sheets, a layer of water, or are deposited sufficiently below the soil surface to escape only slowly.

When chemicals are sprayed or dusted over large areas by aircraft, sensitive crops may very well be unintentionally hit and suffer injury. This is particularly likely to occur with highly effective, highly specific herbicides that are tailored, for example, to the control of broadleaved weeds in grasses and grain—when some of this material drifts onto a desired broadleaf crop, such as tomatoes or grapes, the results can be disastrous.

A very different category of atmospheric chemical injury includes a long list of effluents from manufacturing and related activities. Fluorine, for example, has been implicated in connection with aluminum smelters, phosphate processing plants, and certain atomic reactor installations. One of the most dramatic examples of sulfur dioxide damage is to be found in the Copperhill basin of extreme southeast Tennessee, where a hundred square miles or more of formerly lush southern Appalachian woodland lies in almost total devastation.

In the late 1960's, environmental quality in general and pollution in particular became household words throughout the United States and to an appreciable extent also in other parts of the world. This situation brought new recognition to work on damage to plants from atmospheric contaminants that had been done for a decade or more prior to that time, and stimulated an increased number of research publications, symposia, and journal articles. At about this time, also, a surge of interest in trying to monitor the environment as a way of establishing the direction and degree of change, especially undesirable change, led to search for dependable ways of assaying various components. The two interests converged in studies of the practicability of monitoring for such substances as sulfur dioxide, fluorides, and ozone by selecting especially sensitive host plants—ones that showed reasonably unequivocal symptoms—and using these as a bioassay device for detecting very low concentrations of a given material.

A summary of atmospheric pollutants (Deiler, 1970) shows the following, in very general terms:

Carbon monoxide	52%
Oxides of sulfur	18
Hydrocarbons	12
Particulate	10
Oxides of nitrogen	6
Other gases and vapors	2
	100%

Contributions to this total are judged to be about 60% from transportation, 19% from industry, 12% from generating plants, 6% from space heating, and the remainder from refuse disposal.

Only recently, as compared with other categories of plant pathogens, has it been recognized that contaminants in the atmosphere will bring about significant damage to plants (see Darley and Middleton, 1966). Much of the information on this situation has been tabulated (Table 3–1) in a 1970 bulletin of the National Air Pollution Control Administration (Hindawi, 1970).

Several of the more critical aspects of pollution damage to plants have been summarized in a symposium of the American Phytopathological Society, under the general chairmanship of Ellis F. Darley (1968). The symposium deals with such matters as sources of pollutants, effects of atmospheric dispersion, specific effects on various major plant groups, and mechanism of action of certain pollutants.

In generating public outcry nothing can match the atmospheric contamination of our metropolitan areas, perhaps especially those of the southern Pacific Coast. The effect of gaseous substances on plants has been a subject of study for a number of years and little doubt remains that they are harmful if in sufficient concentrations and for sufficient periods of time, although it is the threat to human health and comfort that occupies central attention. As populations increase and urban dwelling continues to predominate it is virtually certain that more attention will have to be devoted to industrial effluents and their effect on living things.

Mechanical Injuries

The question of mechanical injury needs little elaboration, except to point out that it is a common occurrence and needs to be considered along with everything else in making a diagnosis of unhealthy plants. Perhaps the most significant aspect of mechanical injury is found in the area of market pathology, which is to be discussed in the immediately following section.

POST-HARVEST PATHOLOGY

To an extent, it is inevitable that the pathology of agricultural produce in transit and storage has been dealt with rather independently of other aspects of the science of plant pathology, for several reasons:

- The persons who handle the crop after harvest are frequently not the same as those who have cared for it during the growing season.
- The conditions under which troubles develop are usually decidedly different from those that pertain in the field.
- The locale of the market pathologist has traditionally been urban-centered, that of his colleagues in other branches of pathology rural-centered.

Some evidence of closer cooperation is appearing now and it is to be hoped that it will continue. For the time being it will be advantageous to examine in greater detail the peculiar environment of post-harvest plant pathology.

Special Problems

Physical and Physiological Characteristics of Produce. If one excludes processed foods as being more properly the concern of other professions, the materials to be discussed here are generally classifiable as succulent plant fruits and vegetables; the mature seeds of plants, especially of grasses, legumes, and woody perennials; and fibers in the broad sense of that term.

Small grains, seeds, nuts, hay and other fodder, fibers, and wood products are by no means inert, but they are ordinarily so dry that even if the material in question is still alive respiration proceeds at a slow rate and physiological change is minimal; a very considerable fraction of plant material in this category is no longer living at all. Fresh tree fruits, small fruits, or vegetables, many edible root crops, and such specialty items as cut flowers, potted plants,

Pollutants	Source	Symptom
Ozone (O_3)	Photochemical reaction of hydrocarbon and nitrogen oxides from fuel combustion, refuse burning, and evaporation from petroleum products and organic solvents.	Fleck, stipple, bleaching, bleached spotting, pigmentation, growth suppression, and early abscission. Tips of conifer needles become brown and necrotic.
Peroxyacetyl nitrate (PAN)	Same sources as ozone.	Glazing, silvering, or bronzing on lower surface leaves.
Nitrogen dioxide (NO_2)	High-temperature combustion of coal, oil, gas, and gasoline in power plants and internal combustion engines.	Irregular, white or brown collapsed lesion on intercostal tissue and near leaf margin.
Sulfur dioxide (SO_2)	Coal, fuel oil, and petroleum.	Bleached spots, bleached areas between veins, bleached margin, chlorosis, growth suppression, early abscission, and reduction in yield.
Hydrogen fluoride (HF)	Phosphate rock processing, aluminum industry, iron smelting, brick and ceramic works, and fiber-glass manufacturing.	Tip and margin burn, chlorosis, dwarfing, leaf abscission, and lower yield.
Chlorine (Cl_2)	Leaks in chlorine storage tanks; hydrochloric acid mist.	Bleaching between veins, tip and margin burn, and leaf abscission.
Ethylene (C_2H_4)	Incomplete combustion of coal, gas, and oil for heating, and automobile and truck exhaust.	Sepal withering, leaf abnormalities; flower dropping, and failure of flower to open properly.

[a] Metric equivalent based on 25°C and 760 mm mercury.

[b] Chemical analysis often is not reliable for diagnosing chloride or sulfate accumulation in leaf tissue because undamaged plants often contain higher concentrations of these pollutants than are found in damaged plants.

SOURCE: Hindawi, 1970.

3-1

Vegetation Affected, Injury Thresholds, and Chemical Analyses

Type of Leaf Affected	Part of Leaf Affected	Injury Threshold [a]		Sustained Exposure	Chemical Analysis for Pollutants in Plants
		ppm	$\mu g/m^3$		
Old, progressing to young	Palisade	0.03	70	4 hours	None
Young	Spongy cells	0.01	250	6 hours	None
Middle-aged	Mesophyll cells	2.5	4700	4 hours	None
Middle-aged	Mesophyll cells	0.3	800	8 hours	b
Mature	Epidermis and mesophyll	0.1 (ppb)	0.2	5 weeks	Distillation and titration
Mature	Epidermis and mesophyll	0.10	300	2 hours	b
(Flower)	All	0.05	60	6 hours	None

and so on moving in commercial channels are comparatively much more biologically active. But even so they are in a condition distinct from that prevailing during the growing season.

By and large, harvested produce is mature or maturing—the apple lying in storage is a very different biological entity than it was when an unripe fruit still attached to the parent tree. As Ulrich (1958) says in introducing his review, "The physiology of harvested fruits is chiefly the physiology of ripening and senescence." The processes are a highly complex assemblage of enzymatic changes that might be summarized, again in Ulrich's words, as follows: "The end of life of a fruit is generally a slow agony, but it is often preceded by a period of great activity . . . Ripening is characterized by intense oxidations [the climacteric], by the appearance or increase of certain constituents such as pigments, volatiles, ethylene, sucrose, soluble pectins; and finally, by the decrease of other constituents such as organic acids, chlorophyll and auxins." [*]

Much plant produce is physically as well as physiologically different from the actively growing stage. It may tend to either of two extremes in texture— e.g., corn in storage is much harder and more resistant to damage than it was when unripe, but mature strawberries are highly fragile when contrasted to the same berries before ripening. The implications of these attributes are evident.

Special Environment.   Not only are plant products after harvest in a rather special physical and physiological condition, they are usually in an environment quite different from that at any earlier stage. As a rule they will be highly concentrated, highly homogeneous, and sharply confined to a limited volume. Compare, for example, a tomato plant and a tomato. In the first instance one deals with a plant during all stages of development from seed to maturity, with a diverse array of parts, occupying both soil and atmosphere, and subject to a fabric of changing environmental and microenvironmental factors. The tomato itself consists of nothing but the fruit portion of the plant. These fruits are in approximately the same stage of development. They are in very close proximity to many others like themselves and in a microenvironment within which the handler wishes ordinarily to reduce fluctuations. It exists, by contrast with that of the preharvest plant at least, in a controlled environment.

Small wonder that post-harvest pathology has developed rather apart from the rest; it operates in a distinct context and with its own special parameters.

[*] From R. Ulrich, Postharvest physiology of fruits, *Annual Review of Plant Physiology*, vol. 9 (1958).

Cost Factors. ". . . of all losses caused by plant diseases those which occur after harvest are the most costly, whether measured in monetary terms or in man hours. Even a crop like corn or potatoes which is harvested on a large scale by machinery has cost society measurably more in storage than in the field. By the time a crop, particularly a highly perishable crop, has reached a city consumer its cost has multiplied. The consumer's apple, for example, is the producer's apple plus the cost of picking, packing, shipping, storing and handling, as well as sales cost, allowance for spoilage, and profits." (Stevens and Stevens, 1952)

The foregoing statement, written a number of years ago, emphasizes a point that has immediate implications. Because the unit of produce is at its most expensive stage, an extraordinarily high level of control is regularly to be sought. At the same time, preventive measures that are themselves rather costly can be economically employed: the stakes are so high that a whole level of control effort above that of field pathology becomes not only advisable but imperative.

Methods and Problems of Storage and Transit

Virtually all biological processes are enzymatic. Any change in the external or internal conditions that affects enzyme action will have a corresponding effect on the biological processes they mediate. Thus in handling produce in storage and shipment, what the operator wants most is to influence one or more metabolic events. Sometimes he wishes to speed them, as perhaps in ripening; at other times to slow them down, as in senescence. But whichever the aim, it is achieved through the manipulation of the environment and its coincident effect on enzymatic events.

Throughout history, man has been obliged to conserve his food and fiber. In this time he has developed a very considerable array of techniques—some simple, others highly complex. By and large, all aim at the same objective, to slow down the rate of enzymatic events.

Low Moisture. Enzymes must operate within an aqueous medium. If materials are stored after the moisture levels are reduced below about 10–15% they will be largely unaffected by enzyme-controlled changes. Drying and dry storage, then, has doubtless been used from the very beginning of human societies as a preservation technique.

Low Temperature. Even when the substrate is moist, metabolic activity is sharply reduced at low temperature. The actual rate is relative, of course, approaching zero in frozen produce, but cooling is an effective storage measure even for those substances that cannot easily be frozen.

Controlled Atmosphere.   Respiration is but one of the very many events that occur in plant materials. On the other hand it is easily one of the more important. As a chemical event, it is subject to the same laws of mass action as any other transformation. When, therefore, oxygen levels in the atmosphere are high, respiration rates are high; when carbon dioxide is high, respiration is inhibited. The implications of this for those who manage storage operations are obvious.

There is a whole host of changes that occur in the complex processes of ripening and senescence. All will be affected by moisture and temperature, although so varied are the ends sought and so varied the assembly of responses from one kind of product to the next that each must be handled on the basis of accumulated information and research. It is not enough simply to keep everything "dry and cold"—desired top quality will be achieved in many cases only if the very special conditions appropriate to that particular item are provided. As will appear later, this effort often includes removal of various volatile materials from the atmosphere as well as oxygen–carbon dioxide balance and moisture control.

Special Handling.   Above and beyond the traditional measures just noted, occasional new techniques are introduced. One, which has thus far had a checkered history, is the use of ionizing radiations. The advantage of this method, if the drawbacks can be eliminated, is that once the enzymes have been inactivated, shelf storage at room temperatures or shipment in nonrefrigerated vehicles at appreciable cost reductions becomes possible.

Special packaging and handling methods are very important in offsetting the hazards of dealing with crops that are in their most fragile condition. A truckload of ripe grain is one thing; a load of ripe peaches quite another—although the latter is a not uncommon sight along rural highways at harvest time. Much can, and is, being done to minimize mechanical injuries—the important thing is simply to recognize packaging and handling as one of several crucial issues in post-harvest pathology.

Disease Problems

To this point we have tried to call attention to the peculiar nature of the "host" in post-harvest situations, and to emphasize in a very general way the fundamentals of product storage and preservation. A complete survey of the individual problems that arise within this context would be inappropriate to a beginning text. At the same time there are a few broad categories that can be brought into focus and that encompass the preponderance of situations encountered.

Storage Atmosphere. The relation of oxygen–carbon dioxide concentration to ripening and senescence has been touched upon; it is a relationship that can be capitalized upon in produce handling. For some fresh fruits and vegetables, however, there are limits beyond which increased carbon dioxide/oxygen ratios will produce distinct injury, usually to the internal tissues—most probably as a result of asphyxiation.

No measure of the change in agricultural practices over the past several decades is more dramatic than is the development of highly sophisticated produce storage facilities and techniques. As Hunter (1965) describes one such facility, the Mountain Orchard Cooperative of Aspers, Pennsylvania, the picture emerges of a storage complex of eleven rooms with a capacity of 28,000 bushels each, and one smaller, totalling some 325,000. To this are added a peach hydrocooling facility, peach and apple packing lines, and other mechanized handling facilities. Storage rooms are carefully constructed so as to be gas-tight, with the result that shortly after sealing a filled room, oxygen concentrations fall by about 1% a day from an initial 21% to a final 2–3%. From then on oxygen is added to keep respiration rates at the desired level. Along with this, carbon dioxide must be removed so that concentrations do not rise above about 5%. Temperature must be kept just above that at which low-temperature injury would develop. To make all this possible, automated gas analyzers and temperature sensors are an essential part of the system. The ultimate, which he notes has already been instituted in one Swiss plant, is automation of the gas content and temperature regulation as well as the sensing apparatus.

By far the most intensively studied of the specific diseases associated with storage atmosphere is "scald" of apples and pears. Curiously enough, an effective control has long been available despite the fact that the cause is still subject to debate—namely, to surround the fruit with mineral-oil-impregnated paper and thus remove the volatile materials emanating from the fruit itself. The precise nature of the substance that causes the damage remains in doubt, although ethylene has been repeatedly cited as responsible.

Humidity, along with carbon dioxide–oxygen balance and volatile substances, represents a third major attribute of storage atmosphere. In those instances where the stored produce is rather inert—such as grains, dry seeds, fiber, or wood—a minimum humidity level is almost always desirable. Fresh fruits and vegetables must on the other hand be protected from excessive dehydration, to the extent feasible, by packagings and coatings and by moistening the surrounding atmosphere.

Temperature. More troubles arise from unfavorable temperatures than from any other single cause, although the relationships are not particularly simple. Outright freezing will seriously damage all succulent materials, often to the point where they are economically worthless. Temperatures that are not so extreme but nonetheless either appreciably above or below optimum ("optimum" is almost literally at a unique level for each commodity) will very often have highly undesirable effects upon the appearance, texture, flavor, and color of perishable items. Some symptoms of temperature change are sufficiently well recognized to have been given names; others are still more than a little obscure.

Besides its direct effect, a too-high temperature aggravates the impact of other nonparasitic maladies. Respiration rates increase, and with it all sorts of undesirable effects. Volatile emanations are more likely to produce appreciable damage at elevated temperature, dehydration is accelerated, and so on.

Refrigeration, particularly of perishable fresh fruits, is so thoroughly a part of everyday thinking that it is with some surprise that one encounters suggestions that appear contrary to that approach. Couey and Follstad (1966), however, have found that moist air at about 44°C for 40 to 60 minutes, followed by refrigeration, is highly effective against two very troublesome softrot ogranisms, *Botrytis* and *Rhizopus*. Surprisingly, perhaps, the pasteurization does not seem to affect flavor or texture adversely.

Handling and Related Problems.   The temperature and composition of the surrounding atmosphere are far and away the most important elements in determining how well plant products can be maintained in storage and shipment. There are a few ancillary considerations, one of them the question of how carefully soft produce is handled. Physical injury is a constant hazard. Some measure of the situation is expressed in the following paragraph from a summary by Bratley and Wiant (1950).

Market produce usually passes through the hands of a considerable number of individuals before it is finally purchased by the consumer. The handling of western-grown lettuce will serve to illustrate the point. The heads are cut and thrown into racks mounted on trailers or placed in field crates which are hauled from the field to the packing house. In the packing house each head is subjected to several separate handlings while being graded, trimmed and packed. The packed crates are lidded and hand-trucked into railroad refrigerator cars, where they are stacked and top-iced. At destination the receiver may inspect the lettuce and divert it to another market or may have the car unloaded and the lettuce trucked to his store. From there it is sold in small lots and delivered by truck to the retailer. It is unpacked, trimmed and displayed by the retailer, and, if not sold promptly, it is retrimmed and rearranged for further display. In view of all this handling, it is not surprising that considerable spoilage is frequently encountered in shipments of this commodity, and of others as well.

A consideration of post-harvest disease problems ought, also, to take note of chemical injury, much of which comes about through the accidental association of sensitive produce with residues left in the container, truck, or warehouse, or by the peculiar interaction of plant products with some component of the packaging or packing material. It may also derive from unwise use of fumigants, either in the wrong amount, at the wrong time, or of the wrong kind.

Classification of Post-Harvest Diseases

Bratley and Wiant (1950) furnish us with an especially cogent view of generally accepted classification of market diseases, based on long familiarity with the subject. In so doing they point out that etiology, or cause, has been little emphasized, chief attention being paid to whether the disease originates before or after harvest and upon whether subsequent development is slow or rapid. The implications of this view for both control programs and for the legal aspects of the situation are substantial.

Nonparasitic Versus Infectious Diseases

Up to this point, the discussion of post-harvest pathology has avoided the subject of infectious diseases because they are a secondary aspect of the overall problem. Most of the serious maladies of an infectious nature either originate in the field or if originating after harvest are caused by weak parasites whose success is due to the physical and physiological condition of the host tissues. Conscious omission of biological decay and deterioration of foodstuffs, fiber, wood, plastics, metals, and other material from detailed consideration in this chapter is in no sense intended to minimize its importance, scientific, economic, or social.

CONTROL OF NONPARASITIC DISEASES

Control of infectious disease, and by implication the control of pathogens associated in post-harvest disorders, is considered in Chapters 12 through 16. There is besides this an impressive amount of factual data relevant to control of nonparasitic diseases, but it does not really need to be detailed here. A moment's reflection will show that the cause-effect relationship in nonparasitic disease is very direct. If the disease is caused by too intense sunlight, the effective control must be to interpose a screen, whether it be an elaborate shading device, a simple fabric, or the plant's own foliage. If oxygen is deficient in the soil, the latter must be better drained; if available water too low, the area must be irrigated or the structure improved. If frost threatens, measures must be developed to avoid the danger; if seedlings are in danger of sand blasting, they must be protected.

Once the cause is discovered, the cure is obvious. It may not be feasible, true enough, but it is obvious and direct. Generally, what the grower strives for is really amelioration of the environment—to move the offending factor from an extreme toward the optimum. It is safe to say that control of nonparasitic disease may at times be very difficult, or even impossible, but that it is almost never either complicated or puzzling, once the cause is known.

For that matter, to a surprising extent infectious post-harvest diseases are best handled by the very same measures as characterize most nonparasitic diseases—by manipulation of the environment. There are several bases for this:

- Parasitic diseases are generally severe only when one or more factors of the environment is unfavorable to the stored produce, per se.
- Within very broad limits, the two disease control measures most widely employed against field diseases—chemicals and resistant varieties—are inapplicable to the market. So far as edible products are concerned, most chemical control cannot be safely applied. And plant breeding, where it is successful as in the development of firmer fruit or of varieties less susceptible to pre-harvest infection, falls into the category of orthodox disease control measures.

In the continuing search for improvements in the control of post-harvest diseases, it is necessary not only to concern oneself with the effectiveness of

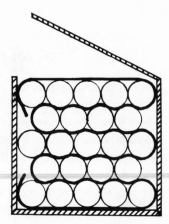

Fig. 3–13. Diagram of a produce container shown in cross section with strip winding between successive layers of fruit. (Gutter, 1967)

the method but with the economics of its implementation. And as the cost of hand labor increases, almost any device that will reduce the amount of that component in the system is worth serious consideration. At times the change is modest indeed, but if effective, amply repays the cost and trouble of the investigation. Gutter (1967) suggests just such a minor technological shift in the control of citrus fruit rots with biphenyl, one of the more effective antifungal compounds in general use. In this case, instead of individually wrapping each fruit, as is the usual practice, he has devised a strip winding (see Fig. 3–13) that effectively contacts each fruit, yet avoids the cost of wrapping and the inconvenience of subsequent unwrapping for display purposes.

4

Causal Factors:
Pathogenic Organisms

THE BIOLOGY OF INFECTIOUS DISEASE

No one would seriously argue that noninfectious diseases are simple, but for the most part they do show a clear-cut cause-and-effect relationship between two elements—host and environment. However destructive they may be, they take a secondary position in plant pathology where the undeniable central focus lies in the impact of pathogenic organisms. Here the problems are highly complex, and here lies the host–environment–pathogenic organism interaction with which plant pathologists are preoccupied.

The Biology of the Host

Historically, attention has been so centered on the pathogenic organism that the host, as a biologically active component of the interaction, has been rather neglected. Chapter 2 includes some of the more important attributes of the host as it is encountered in field, forest, garden, or greenhouse. The essential thing to keep in mind is that the host is itself a living thing, responsive to the external and internal environment and to the impact of the pathogen, an interrelationship examined in Chapters 5 through 7.

The Biology of the Pathogen

The present chapter is devoted to a look at the basic biology of the living organisms that are responsible for undesirable reactions on the part of the host.

In dealing with infectious disease we will not distinguish between parasitism as a biological phenomenon and pathogenesis caused by living organisms, although they need not be identical. Thus the terms "pathogenic organism," "infectious agent," and "parasite" will connote the same thing, for the central issue is the disease that results from the activities of one organism in relation to another. Parasitism, in the strict sense, is but one of a set of relationships.

The Biology of Disease

Disease, when incited by a living organism—that is, infectious disease— presents a situation in which neither participant can be considered in exactly the same light after they come into contact as they could have been prior to that time. Much of phytopathology lies right here in the biology of disease.

Diversity of Pathogens

Because the organisms causing disease in plants range over almost the complete spectrum of biological forms, there is merit in a quick look into the nature of the infectious agents themselves. They will be seen to be exceptionally diverse, both from one group to the next and within a single group. The student already familiar with the subject will need this material only as reference. Considerations of the environment as it affects the pathogenic organism will be postponed to a later chapter.

THE VIRUSES

The Nature of Viruses

Considered collectively, viruses are substantially more diverse than are those associated with plant hosts only; the latter will be examined here. They are, to a unique degree, understandable more on the basis of what they do than what they are.

Little is to be gained by prolonging the old argument as to whether viruses are or are not alive. They consist basically of genetic material enclosed in a protective protein sheath and have, so far as anyone has as yet been able to determine, no metabolism of their own. Needing help, in a sense, they gain control of the cellular machinery of the host and divert it to the manufacture of more virus.

Plant viruses are composed, apparently without exception,° of a ribose nu-

° Recent work by T. O. Diener (1971) and colleagues shows that one of the common "virus" diseases of the potato, i.e., spindle tuber, is caused by an entity that is not only free ribonucleic acid, but of such low molecular weight as to be incapable of self-replication. For this he proposes to replace the term "virus" with "viroid," and suggests that they must depend on mechanisms already operative in the host cell for their replication.

cleic acid of very high molecular weight and a protein with perhaps a half-
million amino acid units. Within these limits there is a great deal of variety, of
course. Much of the research that has been done on plant viruses has employed biochemical and biophysical techniques in an effort to discover the
precise attributes of these very large molecules, in the hope that the information so gained would provide a clue to behavior in the host cell and in turn to
pathogenic activity. In this search electron microscopy has played a very important role, augmented by X-ray diffraction, by density gradient centrifuga-
tion, various filtration techniques, and so on. In the fourth edition of his monograph, Bawden (1964) quotes Schachman and Williams in an especially
effective and perceptive commentary on the complications encountered in investigations of this kind.

. . . [the words size and shape] are always circumscribed in their meaning by consideration of the ways in which they are measured. Thus, the X-ray crystallographer determines the size of a virus as it exists in a unit cell of a crystal; the hydrodynamicist
determines the effective size of the particle as it plows its way through a solution; the
electron microscopist finds its shape and size, when dry, by direct photography. If
virus particles were hard objects, like marbles, these distinctions among methods
would be irrelevant, but a virus particle may be more like a sponge with water bound
both internally and externally. It has amphoteric properties which may confer upon it
different effective diameters, depending upon concentration and the ionic environment. We should not be surprised if we find that the same virus particles apparently
have different sizes and shapes in the hands of different experimenters, all of whom
have performed their work correctly. (H. K. Schachman and R. C. Williams. 1959. In
The Viruses 1:223. Academic Press, New York)

Whatever the discrepancies in detail, plant viruses are commonly recognized as "spherical"—a better term is isodiametric—and "rod shaped." Most
if not all in the first category are properly considered polyhedral bodies, in the
range of 20–60 mμ. The rod-shaped ones can be subdivided (after Bawden)
into short rods (18 $\times$ 36–60 mμ) like alfalfa mosaic; the rigid rods characteristic of tobacco mosaic virus (18 $\times$ 300 mμ); and very long flexible rods, nar-
rower and much longer than is tobacco mosaic virus (TMV)—up to 1250 mμ
in beet yellows.

No protein or protein-like substance, perhaps, has had so much concentrated study as has the virus of tobacco mosaic. As an outcome of much highly
sophisticated research work, a probable structure has emerged that has been
widely represented in the literature (see Fig. 4–1). Here it will be seen that
the "rod" has, actually, a hollow core about which is wound a flat coil of nucleic acid and on which in turn are affixed a number of tightly fitted protein
sub-units. In much the same way, although less well established at the present
time, the protein of isodiametric viruses seems to be arranged about a central

O   100 Å

Fig. 4–1. Diagram showing structural relationships of nucleic acid and protein in a short segment of tobacco mosaic virus. A spiral of nucleic acid, containing three nucleotides per protein subunit, lies inside a protein framework. (Courtesy of A. Klug; from F. C. Bawden, 1964)

nucleic acid core. If present indications prove correct, the structure of the alfalfa mosaic virus is more or less intermediate between these two—it seems to have the overall shape of the rod-shaped viruses but to have closed ends and a fine structure reminiscent of polyhedral forms (see Fig. 4–2).

Lest the above mislead one to make a too-optimistic assessment of the state of knowledge, it must be recognized that only a relatively few viruses have been sufficiently purified and examined to yield convincing data on size, shape, and morphology. Many are as yet known solely for their disease-inducing effect on the host plant.

There is probably no area of plant pathology where the electron microscope has been of more crucial value than in the study of virus structure, al-

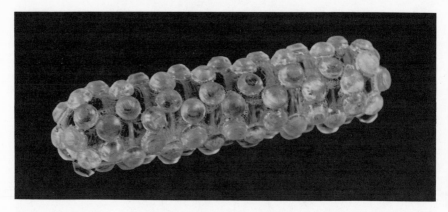

Fig. 4–2. Model of alfalfa mosaic virus, a form structurally intermediate between the rod-shaped and the isodiametric viruses. (Courtesy of A. Gibbs; from F. C. Bawden, 1964)

though it has been used very much in working out the fine structure of many aspects of the host and parasite relationship. In a general way, studies of plant viruses with the electron microscope have concentrated on preparations that are removed from the host cell, but it is entirely possible to discern particles within the cells of diseased plants. Sometimes, provided the technique is applied skillfully, the pictures obtained are clear even to the unsophisticated observer. Kamei *et al.* (1969), for example, have obtained electron micrographs of the turnip mosaic virus in *Brassica perviridis* that reveal much about the nature of the virus particle as it is to be found within the host cell (see Fig. 4–3).

It is illustrative of the nature of viruses that they can be dealt with in some measure as though they were chemicals in the more orthodox sense of that term and in some measure only as they are manifested in the host plant as a set of symptoms. For example, a physical mixture of two viruses—which incidentally very often produces a more severe effect upon the host than either one would separately—can sometimes be separated by the addition of selected chemical compounds (Fig. 4–4). If dilute silver nitrate is added to an inoculum containing both cucumber mosaic and potato ring spot virus, plants inoculated with the resulting material will show only cucumber mosaic symptoms. If on the other hand dilute lithium carbonate is used, the symptoms will be those typical of potato ring spot. In this case the selective action takes place *in vitro* and seems to have little to do with the phenomena of host and virus interaction.

When the relationships of two viruses such as tobacco etch and tobacco mosaic are studied by reference to the hosts on which they can establish

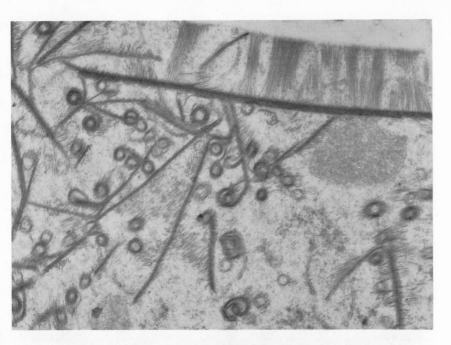

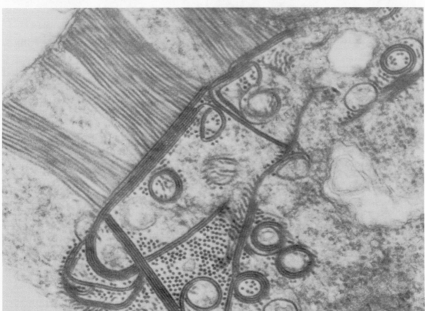

Fig. 4–3. *Top:* General view of turnip mosaic virus as it appears in the cells under electron microscopy. *Bottom:* Bands and rings shown above resolved into several lines at higher magnification, showing virus particles cut parallel, perpendicularly, and obliquely to their long axes. (Kamei *et al.,* 1969)

Fig. 4–4. Separation of two viruses by treating a mixture of the two with selected chemicals prior to inoculation. *First column:* Uninoculated controls. *Second column:* Plants inoculated with a mixture of cucumber mosaic and potato ring spot. *Third column:* Plants inoculated with a mixture that was first treated with dilute silver nitrate, and showing symptoms typical of cucumber mosaic virus only. *Fourth column:* Plants inoculated with a mixture treated with dilute lithium carbonate and showing symptoms of potato ring-spot virus only. (Allington, 1938)

themselves, it appears that there are definite taxonomic relationships between the susceptible species. The accompanying figure (Fig. 4–5) emphasizes that susceptibility or resistance to either or both of these viruses tends to occur consistently within a given family, although there are minor deviations from this pattern.

No evidence of the resemblance between viruses and other pathogenic entities was more convincing than the demonstration that they underwent the same kinds of genetic changes that living organisms generally show. That this is so has been shown in a wide variety of situations, including of course the mutation of common strains of viruses into a number of related but different forms (Fig. 4–6). As techniques for handling viruses, particularly bacterial vi-

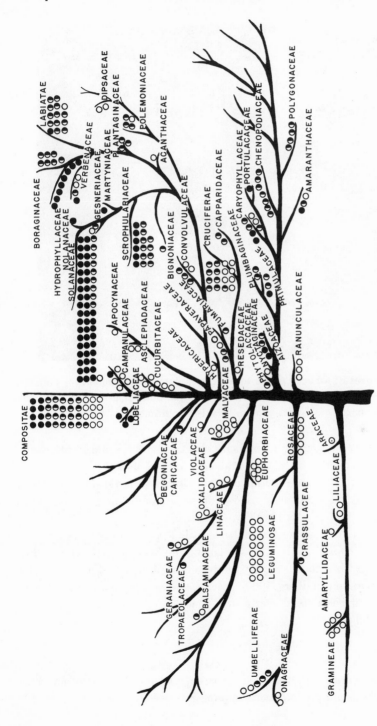

Fig. 4-5. Chart showing taxonomic relationships of plants susceptible to tobacco etch and tobacco mosaic virus. *White circles: Susceptible to neither. Black circles: Susceptible to both. Half-black circles: Susceptible to tobacco mosaic virus but not to tobacco etch.* (Holmes, 1946)

Fig. 4–6. Leaves of tobacco plants showing symptoms of six genetically different strains of tobacco mosaic virus. Symbols indicate the particular name by which the mutant strain is commonly designated. (Stanley and Knight, 1941)

ruses, have become ever more and more elaborate and precise, an increasing number of discoveries in fundamental mechanisms of genetic events have been made on the basis of experiments with viruses. In the realm of practical plant pathology, virus variability shows up as one more complication in the overall campaign to produce healthy crops.

Virus diseases of fungi, or transmissible maladies that strongly suggest that viruses are the causal agents, still rank among the biological curiosities. They have been described thus far in the cultivated mushroom and in a species of *Helminthosporium* (Lindberg, 1969), at least, and may be more widely recognized in the future as more investigators come to recognize that they are indeed a possibility.

Transmission

Given the entity just described—a large nucleoprotein molecule—how does it survive, multiply, produce symptoms?

Save under very special circumstances, as in the case of deep-frozen preparations, most viruses seem not to survive for very long outside of a compatible
host cell. The striking exception is the virus of tobacco mosaic, which may remain in the dry state for many years without losing its biological integrity.

Plant viruses do not have any mechanism for getting from one host individual to another except through an external agent. Experimentally, virus may be
transmitted by grafting, by dodder bridges (Fig. 4–7), by applying fresh extracts of diseased plants to the surfaces of healthy plants, or through a biological agent. Natural propagation is almost always by vegetative means, through
the seed, as a result of insect feeding activity or, when "soil borne," through
the activities of nematodes or such fungi as *Olpidium*. Lest there be misun-
derstanding here, it must be emphasized at the outset that by no means are all
viruses transmissible by each of the different mechanisms. Indeed, for each
virus the actual mode of transmission must be carefully examined. It is critical
that the virus be somehow transmitted from the old to the new site and introduced into the cells of susceptible tissue. Details of its survival will vary from
virus to virus, but in all cases there must be an avenue of transmittal and
entry.

Fig. 4–7. Experimental use of dodder as a way of transmitting viruses that cannot
be transmitted conveniently by more orthodox means. (Johnson, 1941)

The mechanics of transmission through grafts or by vegetative propagation are more or less self-evident and consist of a mass transfer of virus-bearing tissues to the new site. From that point on virus movement is a matter of extension into new regions of the host. When dodder is used as a biological bridge it permits virus movement between species that are so taxonomically distinct that ordinary graft unions will not form successfully.

Transmission through the seed is not very common, but it is characteristic of a number of legume viruses. Here the decisive factor seems to be whether the virus can or cannot invade embryonic tissues of the seed. If so, the virus appears in the emerging seedling; if not, it does not persist into the next host generation.

Transmission through juice is mostly, although perhaps not exclusively, an experimental means of virus disease propagation. In essence the procedure involves rubbing a fresh extract of juice from a diseased host onto the surface, usually a leaf surface, of a healthy plant, after first inflicting numerous small injuries—or rather, insuring that there will be numerous small injuries during rubbing—by preliminary dusting of the area with carborundum. In practice the technique is not so complicated as it may at first appear. All kinds of variables affect the outcome.

- Viruses in plant juice are variously affected by the temperature and pH of the medium.
- A number of enzymes or other components of the crude extract may well partially or wholly inactivate the virus.
- Concentration of virus in diseased plants on the one hand, and that required for successful invasion of the inoculated plant on the other, will differ greatly from situation to situation.
- Likelihood of success can be enhanced by preconditioning the plants to be inoculated—holding them under low light intensity and at elevated temperature—by adding phosphate to the juice extract, and by minimizing the elapsed time for transferring juice to the new host.

Under very special circumstances it has been suggested (Bawden, 1964) that the extract be first fractionated in phenol, thus separating the protein and nucleic acid components, and inoculating with the phenol phase only. Even so, it must be acknowledged that a number of plant viruses have thus far resisted all efforts to transmit them through mechanical means.

In nature, transmission from plant to plant is most often by insect feeding activity. Extensive research has revealed much about host-virus-insect relationships and there are several useful and reliable generalizations to be made. In the first place, the preponderance of known insect transmission is by aphids or leafhoppers and virtually all by sucking insects of one sort or another. Just as major wounds inflicted in mechanical transmission are largely ineffective in successfully implanting the virus, so are the biting or chewing insects poor agents of virus inoculation. The invaded cell must, after all, be intact if the virus is to multiply within it.

One pattern of virus transmission, characteristic of many aphid-borne types, involves feeding insects that become infective within a very short time after beginning to take materials from the diseased host (Fig. 4–8) but remain so only rather briefly. These viruses, often termed for this reason "nonpersistent," are usually also transmissible by mechanical means. The obvious supposition is that the virus is carried as a contaminant of the mouthparts. It is a curious fact, repeatedly observed, that transmission of nonpersistent viruses is most effectively accomplished if previously fasted insects are allowed to feed

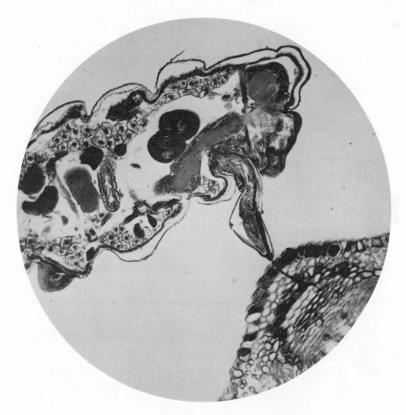

Fig. 4–8. Photomicrograph of an aphid feeding on a leaf as it appears in cross section; penetration of the mouthparts into the phloem is clearly evident. (Wedderburn, 1948)

for brief periods. That many of the viruses falling into this category are concentrated in epidermal cells of the host offers a plausible clue to the phenomenon (Bawden, 1964, p. 136).

By contrast with nonpersistent viruses, which in the aggregate show substantial variation in persistence, specificity, and related characteristics, the persistent viruses comprise a rather uniform group. Viruses of this kind are characteristically carried by leafhoppers—a few are carried by aphids—and are not passed along to the recipient host until an appreciable time after the insect has initially taken it up. Once infectivity is established, however, it continues for some time. Moreover, the very viruses that require as much as several days to become transmissible have been shown in a few well-established cases to multiply in the insect vector. Not surprisingly, in view of this, persistent viruses prove to have much more pronounced vector specificity than do the nonpersistent forms.

Intermediate between the nonpersistent viruses and the persistent ones are several types—especially curly top of sugar beet and maize streak—that have an incubation period of a few hours, do not seem to multiply in the vector, and are highly stable. It is commonly surmised that the period prior to infectivity here is that interval necessary for the virus to penetrate the gut wall and return to the salivary glands, whereas the long incubation period of a virus like aster yellows is imposed by the need for actual multiplication in the host.[*]

It is probably significant that nonpersistent viruses are located, or at least recovered by the insect from, superficial host tissues, whereas persistent types are to be found deep within the tissues, in the phloem.

Thrips, mealybugs, white flies, chewing insects, mites, and nematodes have all been implicated in one or more instances of biological transmission, although they constitute only a fraction of the total. Doubtless as we know more about them they will come to be recognized as more important than they now seem.

As research on plant virus transmission continues, more and more vector species are recognized and a wider and wider biological diversity is included in the overall list. At the same time (see Holmes, 1968) there are helpful generalizations:

Despite occasional but unconfirmed reports, no leafhopper-transmitted virus has ever been transmitted by any other type of arthropod vector. . . . A considerable degree of specificity for other types of insect, nematode, and fungus vectors also exists. Viruses known to be transmitted by aphids, whiteflies, thrips, mealybugs, psyllids, lace bugs, mites, or fungi are not, in general, known to be transmitted by other vector types. . . . If exceptions can be discovered, they may be so few as to establish the gen-

[*] Note that aster yellows may be a mycoplasma rather than a virus (Table 4–1).

eral rule that vector type is constant enough to guide us in formulating a natural classification of viruses.°

While the vector-virus relationship is often very specific and precise indeed, there are also many instances of multiple transmittal. Chances are that
the commonest examples of this capability are to be found among the insects,
a few species of which can transmit impressive numbers of viruses. But there
are instances also among nematode vectors, as demonstrated by Fulton (1967)
in a paper on dual transmission of tobacco ringspot virus and tomato ringspot
virus by *Xiphinema americanum*. Each virus can be acquired by the vector in
a brief feeding period, either from a doubly infected host or from two separate hosts, can be retained up to several months by the vector in the absence
of a susceptible host, and can be transmitted either singly or together during a
short feeding period.

Infection and Multiplication

If it is to survive, virus must be moved from diseased to healthy host plants.
If the agent for this movement is an insect there seems little doubt that the
virus is carried directly into the tissues of the host by the feeding activities of
the vector.

What happens in mechanically transmitted viruses is not nearly so self-evident. In fact, surprisingly little is known about the phenomenon, in spite of
extensive research effort aimed at elucidating it. The situation is summarized
by Siegel and Zaitlin (1964) in a review of the available information. Virus
particles—probably singly—have the capacity, within a limited period of
time at least, to establish a center of infection at a given site. Some of the centers, in turn, eventually become visible as lesions having the particular characteristics of the virus-host association involved.

To accomplish invasion it is obvious that the initial particle, however introduced, must multiply. Here much of our current knowledge of virus behavior
is based on supposition; painstaking biochemical and biophysical investigations are going on to discover more concrete evidence of what goes on. The
generally accepted view now is that the nucleic acid central core of the invading virus escapes from its protein shell and becomes affiliated, as it were,
with the genetic apparatus of the host cell. As a result, more nucleic acid
identical with that of the virus is manufactured, along with proteins of the
kind that enveloped the nucleic acid of the original virus particle. The two
components are then fabricated into additional whole virus. It is quite clear

° From F. O. Holmes, Trends in the development of plant virology, *Annual Review of Plant
Phytopathology*, vol. 6 (1968), p. 42.

from controlled experiments, however, that nucleic acid alone is entirely effective as an invading component.

Virus Movement

The very existence of a lesion large enough to be seen indicates that virus must spread from one cell to another. That many viruses become systemic in their hosts, and fairly rapidly so, proves that movement may not necessarily be confined to a cell-to-cell path but may instead involve vascular tissue. In view of the overall size of the virus, or even of its infective nucleic acid, rapid movement from cell to cell is rather surprising. Indeed it is hard to see how any pathway other than the plasmodesmata can satisfy the conditions inherent in movement of these macromolecules. As for long-distance movement, which can be rather rapid, most of the evidence points to the phloem as the more likely route—a few instances of movement in the xylem are on record.

Probably because it enhances the likelihood that virus material gets into vascular tissue, long-distance movement in plants wherein surrounding cells are susceptible is appreciably more successful than it is in plants where the tissue adjoining the vascular tissue is immune. It may be this factor that determines, in the final analysis, whether a given host shows systemic involvement or merely local lesions.

MYCOPLASMA-LIKE PATHOGENS

In recent years it has become evident that a considerable number of plant diseases long thought to be due to viruses—the so-called yellows diseases— are actually caused by agents that resemble the group of human and animal pathogens known as *Mycoplasma*. Terms such as PPLO (pleuropneumonia-like organisms) and PLT (psittacosis-lymphogranuloma-trachoma group) have also been applied. In retrospect it is not especially surprising that these pathogens were thought to be viruses. They are sensitive to heat, they pass through filters—although more slowly—of the same general porosity, they are infectious in much the same way, they are often insect-transmitted. If present indications are borne out, it seems very likely indeed that a considerable number of plant diseases will end up in the category of mycoplasma-like maladies (see Table 4–1, from Whitcomb and Davis, 1970).

A consistent characteristic of these diseases is their response to therapy with the tetracycline family of antibiotics and the appearance, in the phloem of affected hosts, of pleomorphic bodies.

Table 4–1

Some Plant Diseases Whose Causative Agents May Be Mycoplasma-Like Organisms

Disease	Distribution
Aster yellows	U. S., Far East, Europe
Mulberry dwarf	Far East
Potato witches' broom	Far East
Paulownia witches' broom	Far East
Clover phyllody	Europe, Canada
Tomato big bud	U. S., Australia, Europe
Potato stolbur	Europe
Parastolbur	Europe
Corn stunt	U. S.
Sugarcane whiteleaf	Taiwan
Rice yellow dwarf	Philippines, Far East
Legume little leaf	Australia
Clover dwarf	Europe
Apple proliferation	Europe
Oat sterile dwarf	Europe
Western X-disease	U. S.
Peach X-disease	U. S.
Alfalfa witches' broom	U. S., Europe
Cranberry false blossom	U. S.
Sandalwood spike	India, Far East
Flavescence dorée	Europe
Strawberry green petal	Europe
Peach yellows	U. S.
Little peach	U. S.
Cherry buckskin	U. S.
Cotton virescence	Europe
Crimean yellows	Soviet Union
Eggplant little leaf	Europe
Papaya bunchy top	Puerto Rico
Witches' broom of groundnut	Java, Far East
Clover stolbur	Europe
Blueberry stunt	U. S.
Tobacco yellow dwarf	Australia
Yellow wilt of sugar beet	Argentina
Little cherry	U. S.
Rubus stunt	Netherlands
Mal azul	Portugal
Sweet potato witches' broom	Japan and Taiwan
Witches' broom of legumes	Japan and Taiwan
Cryptotaenia japonica witches' broom	Japan

SOURCE: Whitcomb and Davis, 1970.

Maramorosch *et al.* (1970) have summarized much of the available information in this area. A study of electron micrographs (Fig. 4–9) clearly reveals structures substantially larger and more morphologically complex than the viruses.

Plant pathology is no exception to the generalization that once a new avenue of thought has been opened, discoveries are made with appreciable speed even though the material being examined may itself be long familiar to investigators. Hibino and Schneider (1970) provide evidence that the pear decline disease falls in this category, and report mycoplasma-like bodies in the sieve tubes of the swollen brown veins of old leaves.

With almost every new number of the major journals in plant pathology one finds still another suggestion that mycoplasma-like organisms are responsible for some of the diseases long assumed to be caused by viruses. At times (see Casper *et al.*, 1970) the situation is complicated by the presence of what appear to be combinations of the two types of organisms. They found, for example, in *Opuntia tuna* with witches'-broom, not only a mycoplasma-like organism but as many as three viruses; all had been detected not only by visible symptoms but through electron microscopy.

Another disease now strongly suspected of being caused by a mycoplasma is the white leaf disease of sugarcane (see Lin *et al.*, 1970). The evidence presented is like that for other instances in the same category: effectiveness of tetracycline antibiotics in reducing the severity of the disease, and isolation in culture followed by transmission to new host individuals.

But Gillaspie (1970) puts in a word of caution in reporting his work on ratoon stunting disease of sugarcane, and concludes that on the strength of evidence available, the etiological agent is a virus and not a mycoplasma. It seems clear from his examination of the effect of tetracycline that a mycoplasma is very unlikely to be the cause—in a sense, we are cautioned not to assume that all diseases of questionable etiology are mycoplasmal.

BACTERIA

Bacteria, although they may well seem simple by contrast with most other cellular organisms, are enormously larger and more complicated than viruses. The real distinction between bacteria and viruses is that the former have a metabolism—that is, enzyme systems—all their own and with it the independence that characterizes it.

In the following discussion, attention centers on the bacteria that are implicated in plant disease, including storage rots; it does not purport to be a complete analysis of the biology of bacteria.

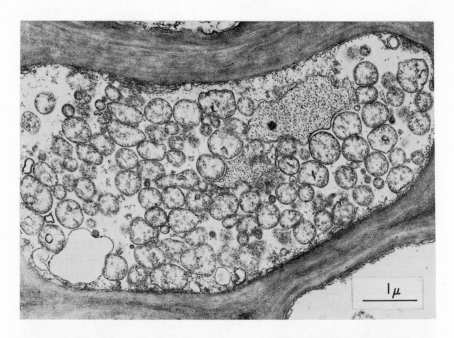

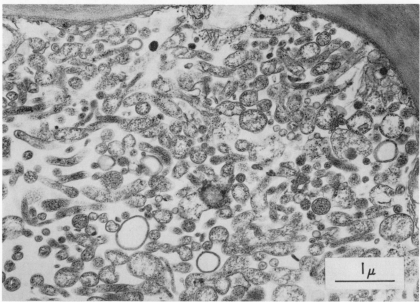

Fig. 4–9. Photomicrograph of phloem cells of a *Nicotiana rustica* plant infected with aster yellows, showing mycoplasma-like bodies. These are mostly spherical in the upper micrograph and in large part filamentous in the lower micrograph; these may well be stages in the development of the organism. (Maramorosch *et al.*, 1970)

Bacterial Morphology

Bacteria are so small as to be invisible to the unaided eye—at best a few microns in the longest dimension. Viewed under an ordinary microscope, little but the outline of the cell is discernible. Very often the observer sees myriads of tiny, nearly colorless, rod shaped bodies, perhaps in apparent motion, but nothing more. More important, perhaps, samples taken from very different sources and hence presumably of distinct kinds, will not be separable on the basis of visual characteristics. In short, almost nothing can be told with certainty about bacteria simply by looking at them. They are too tiny and too morphologically homogeneous to be very rewarding to this kind of scrutiny.

As in the case of viruses and the mycoplasma-like pathogens, bacteria are detected on or in plants mostly by the effects they bring about. In a few cases the sheer mass of cells becomes so great—as in the vascular wilt diseases and some phases of the fireblight disease of orchard crops (Fig. 4–10)—that they are visible to the unaided eye. Fireblight is generally credited, incidentally,

Fig. 4–10. *Left:* Cankered limb of diseased orchard tree showing exuding masses of fireblight bacteria, which are then carried about by insects or splashing raindrops. (Whetzel and Stewart, 1909) *Right:* Advanced blight on tree trunk, showing streaks of bacterial ooze. (Courtesy of T. van der Zwet)

with being the first disease shown to be caused by a bacterium and the first in which insect transmission was demonstrated, although Bittancourt (1945) disputes this claim.

A first step in most studies is to isolate the organisms in pure culture. This must be done by diluting the sample in a series of tubes of sterile water or media and then streaking it out on the surface of a solid nutrient substrate—if the initial population in the sample is not too great it may be plated out directly. Subsequent incubation permits the growth of a very large number of individual colonies. By this means and by subsequent culturing the investigator is assured, provided his technique is adequate, of having a single species of bacterium with which to work.

At this point, three avenues are open to further effort: (1) special light microscopy, such as darkfield or phase contrast; (2) electron microscopy, which permits enormously increased magnification; and (3) the application of one or more of a great array of cytological stains. Traditionally, staining has been used more extensively than any other method, for the simple reason that it is inexpensive and convenient. Special stains have been developed to detect this or that component of the cell—lipids, nucleic acids, flagella, capsule, and so on. It is no exaggeration to say that the bacteriologist would be almost completely lost without recourse to staining techniques. In the last few years, the spectacular capacity of the electron microscope has been exploited and much has been added to our knowledge of bacterial morphology.

On the basis of accumulated evidence, the cells of bacteria appear to be enclosed by a membrane and to contain a mass of cytoplasm presumably very like that to be found in other organisms, plus chromosomal material. There are no conspicuous vacuoles, nor plastids, and the nuclear component is not organized into the discrete, readily observable structure that is so characteristic of all other plants and animals. Much of the evidence for the conclusion that bacteria have functional nuclei is derived from experimental rather than observational data. For that matter, work with bacteria has contributed greatly to the current explosive advances in our knowledge of the relation of nucleic acid structure to genetic coding systems. There is no longer any reasonable doubt as to the presence of an effective nuclear and genetic mechanism in bacteria, conforming in all fundamental attributes to that found in other groups.

Bacterial Physiology

Because the morphology of bacteria affords so little basis for distinguishing species and is in almost every way so unrewarding to routine observation, attention long since turned to their physiology. Identification, beyond the very crudest observations of colony type, cell size, and shape, and possession of a motile phase as seen in young broth cultures, is dependent upon two kinds of data:

- Biochemical reactions on a selection of standardized media, which is in reality an identification of certain selected enzyme systems
- Serological response to various known immune sera

To this list might well be added, for plant-pathogenic forms, capacity to produce characteristic symptoms (Fig. 4–11) on susceptible host plants.

Thus the bacteria, like the viruses, are judged more on the basis of what they do than what they look like. And they do very remarkable things. Considered as a whole, bacteria occupy a vast array of ecological niches, endure extremes of temperature, of moisture, of pH, of oxygen availability, and so on. They are responsible for most of the transformations in what we have come to call the nitrogen cycle, for many degradations in the carbon cycle, for a great array of economically valuable processes in industrial chemistry and food processing, and for a goodly portion of infectious human and animal disease.

Virtually every level of complexity exists somewhere in the bacteria, so far as nutritional requirements are concerned. At one extreme are those able to grow successfully on very simple substrates—that is, bacteria that possess sufficiently complex metabolic systems as to make all needed conversions from inorganic substances. At the other are extremely fastidious organisms that require very elaborate media: these species clearly lack enzymes by which the simpler materials can be utilized. Plant-pathogenic forms lie somewhere intermediate between the two extremes.

It must not be overlooked that the extremely high surface-to-volume ratio of the minute cells of bacteria facilitates, where external conditions permit, a correspondingly high rate of food utilization and therefore of growth. Since for all practical purposes growth consists of the enlargement of newly formed daughter cells to a point where they too can divide, and since reproduction is merely the vegetative division of one cell into two, there is an immediate, direct relationship between the three—food utilization, growth, and reproduction. Under ideal circumstances these events occur with almost explosive speed; it is only the complete dependence of bacteria on favorable temperature, water supply, and food that keeps them in most situations within acceptable bounds.

Cell division in bacteria is preceded by a precise mechanism of division of

Fig. 4–11. Response of host tissue to invasion by the crown gall bacterium. *Above:* Galls on apple following inoculation after 12, 10, and 8 weeks (*left to right*) (Riker and Hildebrand, 1934). *Left:* Gall tissue in aseptic culture after 6 weeks' incubation on agar medium. (Hildebrandt, Riker, and Duggar, 1945)

the nuclear material; all studies of genetic constancy attest to this. Once the nucleus has divided, the entire cell is cut into two approximately equal halves by the formation of a transverse septum and a constriction of the exterior wall. Whether the daughter cells actually separate or instead remain in a more or less firmly organized filament or mass varies from one species to the next. Cell differentiation, except at a most primitive level, does not show up in bacteria.

Movement

Many species of bacteria are immotile. If they change positions at all it is because they are swept along by air or water currents, splashed by rain, or carried as a surface contaminant on a moving substratum. In a very special sense, of course, the accumulating mass of cells within a colony may serve to move the periphery for a short distance.

The cells of some species possess, for part if not all of their existence, flagellae that produce active swimming motion in a liquid medium. There is no evidence of directed movement other than perhaps along a chemical concentration gradient, but at least the cells are capable of self-propulsion. This attribute, alone, may often be decisive when it comes to invasion of the host by pathogenic forms.

In later chapters it will seem that the data on bacterial plant diseases are appreciably less comprehensive than those on diseases induced by viruses and fungi. The simple fact is that by their very nature bacteria are not really very successful plant pathogens. As a rule they do not enter the plant host very effectively, do not always spread through the host very rapidly, and are transported to new host individuals rather inefficiently. Perhaps only in the special case of storage rots do they rank high in relation to most other plant pathogens.

THE FUNGI

In Alexopoulos' (1962) excellent textbook of mycology we find fungi described as "nucleated, spore-bearing, achlorophyllous organisms which generally reproduce sexually and asexually, and whose usually filamentous, branched somatic structures are typically surrounded by cell walls containing cellulose or chitin, or both." In other words, the bulk of the organisms usually thought of as fungi differ from those commonly regarded as bacteria by having achieved a significantly more elaborate morphological diversity. As will be noted, this attribute influences very markedly their biological effectiveness in the causation of plant disease.

Morphology of Fungi

Whole textbooks have been written on the morphology of the fungi— whole monographs on a single group or genus. Only the very barest outlines are appropriate to the present discussion. What is most important is to get a reasonably clear picture of how much more complex are the fungi than the bacteria, yet how much less elaborate than the vascular plants.

Characteristically, the vegetative portion of a fungus is an irregular mass of filaments. At one extreme there is no semblance of further differentiation, at the other the filaments are organized into a rough approximation of tissues, but not nearly so elaborately as the cells of seed plants. Virtually every fungus cell has the capacity to survive under favorable conditions and in turn to grow into a new thallus. While certain large groups of the morphologically simpler fungi have no crosswalls in their hyphae, the bulk of the species do, although they not infrequently have more than one nucleus per cell.

In establishing taxonomic relationships among fungi, in contrast to higher plants, much attention is given to their cultural and physiological characteristics. Genetic similarities, as evidenced by cross-fertility in sexual reproduction, serve as a further very useful key to the closeness of relationship between two apparently similar or identical isolates.

It has long been known that the filamentous fungi have a capacity for hyphal fusion that has the effect of bringing two morphologically distinct individuals together and to bring the nuclei and cytoplasm of these two into direct contact. And when the organism in question is known primarily in the mycelial condition only—as is the case in *Rhizoctonia solani*—it proves necessary to utilize the phenomenon of anastomosis as a clue to genetic similarity. Parmeter *et al.* (1969), in tests involving well over a hundred isolates, were able to allocate most to one of four compatibility groups on the basis of this test. But even among the members of a given anastomosis group the actual amount of nuclear exchange across the bridge varied substantially.

Fungus nuclei are small by comparison with those of higher plants. In many species they have been observed to move from one cell to the next through perforations in the crosswalls. There is little doubt as to their identity or that they function in an orthodox way, although there is debate over the exact patterns of nuclear division in the somatic nuclei of certain species. Perhaps this uncertainty is simply because they are so very small. The surrounding cytoplasm of a fungus cell tends to be more vacuolate than that of bacteria and frequently contains oil or other substances in droplets of size visible to the ordinary microscope.

To make advances in knowledge of relationships between host and pathogenic organisms, beyond a certain point, new technologies must be brought to bear. The more recent literature of plant pathology reflects increasing use of electron microscopy to detect structural details that are wholly impossible of resolution with traditional light microscopes. Bracker (1968) has used this technique to make a detailed study of the physical relationships between the haustorium of the powdery mildew fungus, *Erysiphe graminis*, and its barley host.

Much is already known of the gross structure of the haustorium, and of its more conspicuous variations from one species to the next. What Bracker was concerned with in his examinations were the fine details, for which the term ultrastructure has become the common term. In very general terms—the details can best be provided by a careful reading of the entire paper—the haustorium resembles a fungal cell, the wall of which extends through the host cell to the external mycelium. It, the haustorium, is separated from the host protoplasm by a distinct sheath of an apparently amorphous material. Many of the positional relationships appear on the accompanying diagram (Fig. 4–12A) and electron micrographs (Fig. 4–12B). A still different aspect of haustoria appears when micrographs of whole haustoria are examined (Fig. 4–12C).

Finally, fungi are characterized by producing a large number of different kinds of spores, many of which are highly significant in the multiplication of the species. In the identification of fungi, the nature of spores and the manner of their production are every bit as important as are physiological characteristics in identifying bacteria. To suggest the converse of a point made earlier,

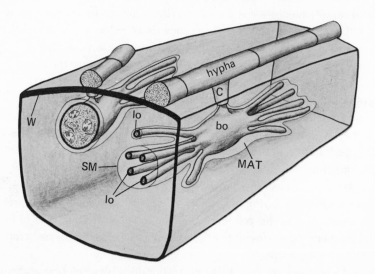

Fig. 4–12A. Cutaway three-dimensional diagram of an epidermal cell with two haustoria of powdery mildew: *bo*—haustorial body; *C*—collar; *lo*—haustorial lobe; *MAT*—sheath matrix; *SM*—sheath membrane; *W*—host wall. (Bracker, 1968)

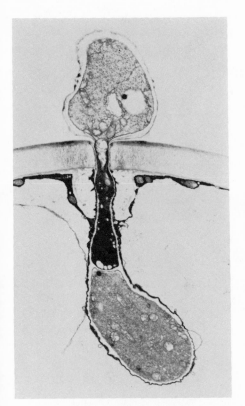

Fig. 4–12B. Three electron micrographs, in increasing magnification, of the penetration site of powdery mildew on the epidermal cell of a wheat leaf. The cytoplasm of the haustorial neck is very dense, with a perforate septum separating it from the haustorial body. At the top of each micrograph appears the appressorium, beneath it the host cell wall, and below that a collar surrounding the haustorial neck just after it penetrates. At greatest magnification (*below*), the cuticle of the host wall can be seen pushed down into the hole caused by the invasion of the hypha. (Courtesy of C. E. Bracker)

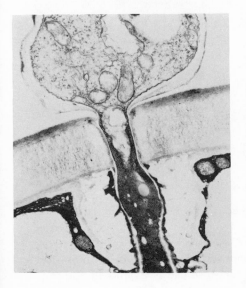

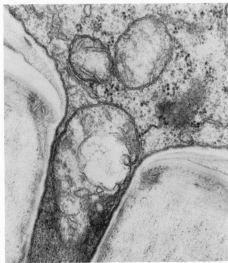

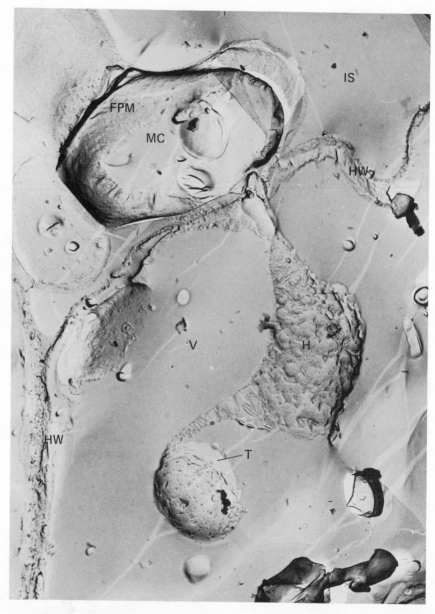

Fig. 4–12C. Micrograph of frozen-etched whole haustorium of flax rust in mesophyll: *H*—haustorium, covered by invaginated host plasma membrane; *HW*—host cell wall; *V*—host vacuole; *MC*—haustorial mother cell; *IS*—intercellular space; *T*—piece of host tonoplast that was not fractured away; *FPM*—fungal plasma membrane. (Courtesy of L. J. Littlefield and C. E. Bracker)

fungi are sufficiently distinctive morphologically that the systematist can base his work more on what they look like than on what they do.

Fungus Physiology

To a considerable degree the metabolism of fungi is like that of the bacteria. They are nutritionally dependent organisms. They vary greatly as to how dependent they are upon already synthesized organic compounds in the substrate. Some can grow well enough on minimal medium, others do not have enzyme systems that permit them to make the necessary transformations. They vary greatly, also, on whether they colonize living or nonliving matter—some are confined to nonliving organic matter, others act as weak parasites, still others are mostly to be found on living hosts, and a last group, the obligate parasites, cannot grow anywhere except on living hosts. These last develop very intimate contact with the host cells through specialized structures known as haustoria, which seem to contain a preponderance of the mitochondria in the fungal cell from which they extend, strongly suggesting that haustoria are chiefly responsible for nutrient absorption by the invading hyphae.

Fungi elaborate a number of extracellular enzymes that permit them successfully to attack such diverse materials as cellulose, simple carbohydrates, lignin, and cutin. Pathogenic forms also produce toxins, just as bacteria do. Like bacteria also, fungi are useful in a number of industrially important processes.

Many details of fungus physiology, as it relates to host-pathogen interaction, will appear from time to time in the next few chapters, as appropriate to the context of the discussion.

Growth and Reproduction

Growth in the fungi is hardly different from that of other groups of organisms. Most cells are capable of forming additional protoplasm, of receiving water and thus increasing in volume. In due time nuclear division occurs and the daughter cells are separated by the formation of a crosswall. As one observes growth in a colony it appears to be mostly on the periphery because it is here that the youngest cells are to be found—at the tips of radiating hyphae. Rate of growth, as would be expected, depends upon nutrient supply, moisture, temperature, and the accumulation, in confined media at least, of staling products. As a general rule fungi are favored by a more acid environment than are bacteria, a fact that has important implications for the microbial biology of the soil environment.

It is in connection with reproduction in fungi, both asexual and sexual, that one comes face to face with the full measure of their complexity and diversity. A concise summary can be found in Hawker's little monograph (1957) or in any general introductory mycology text. The primary achievement of asexual reproduction is to increase the number of individuals, to provide ready means for dissemination of the species and, at least much of the time, to effect survival over a period of unfavorable environment. While asexual reproduction is at times nothing more than fragmentation of the thallus, it is much more commonly accomplished by specialized spores.

There is an almost endless variety of spore types and patterns of spore production in the asexual reproduction of fungi. For the most part they are produced inside a specialized structure, the sporangium—as for example in a number of the lower fungi—or are borne at the ends of specialized hyphae and termed conidia. In the latter instance, especially, spore type varies all the way from thin-walled, fragile cells to thick-walled objects highly resistant to the vicissitudes of the environment; they range from very tiny to comparatively large, from colorless to heavily pigmented, from one- to many-celled, from one to several nucleate, spherical to needle-shaped, smooth-walled to ornate, with or without appendages.

Asexual reproduction is especially important in the Fungi Imperfecti—a group of fungi very important in plant pathology that are not known to produce spores by any other means. Of necessity, therefore, classification of the Fungi Imperfecti depends almost entirely on the manner of spore production and the characteristics of the spores. Traditionally, the basis of separation has been first upon the overall nature of the fruiting body and within that upon the shape, pigmentation, and number of cells in the conidia—an admittedly wholly artificial classification. Alternatively, it has been suggested that a more natural classification would put primary emphasis on the structure of the spore-bearing hyphae and the mechanism of spore formation (Alexopoulos, 1962, p. 390).

For those fungi having a sexual phase, virtually all major taxonomic groupings and subgroupings are based thereon. In very general terms, three large groups of fungi can be distinguished that are of first importance in plant pathology—more definitive characterizations will appear as appropriate later on:

• Phycomycetes—aseptate filamentous fungi that reproduce sexually by fusion of a relatively large female gamete with small male cells (e.g.

Pythium) or by fusion of similar gametes (e.g. *Rhizopus*)

- Ascomycetes—fungi in which, following gametic union, there is a more or less extended period during which the two nuclei continue in a "dikaryon" condition prior to fusion, and in which spores are regularly formed within a sac or ascus
- Basidiomycetes—fungi that differ from the Ascomycetes most conspicuously by virtue of forming their sexual spores on the outside of a specialized hypha termed a basidium.

In the main, asexual reproduction in phytopathogenic fungi is associated with the active phase of the disease. Following initial invasion of the host and a period of growth at its expense, pathogens usually produce very large numbers of asexual spores of whatever type is characteristic of the species. Very often these spores are capable of promptly initiating new lesions on susceptible host tissue and in so doing are by all odds the chief means of epidemic spread during the growing season. The sexual phase of fungus reproduction, to the contrary, is more often associated with the onset of senescence in the host and with the close of the growing season. Thus sexual fruiting bodies and their associated spores may be more a means whereby the pathogen survives from one host generation to the next, or through unfavorable environmental stresses, than as a primary means of dissemination. Other wholly unrelated devices for survival in fungi take the form of sclerotia (hard masses derived from vegetative hyphae), chlamydospores (thickwalled asexual resting spores), and so on.

Isolation of Fungi

Because fungi can be identified far more than can the bacteria on the basis of morphological characters does not mean that they need not be studied also in pure culture. Far from it—partly for convenience, partly because various manipulations that are carried out most readily in the laboratory are essential to a full knowledge of the fungi in question, and partly because physiological and pathogenic characteristics must usually be determined with laboratory isolates. In any event, a wide array of laboratory techniques have been developed for handling fungi in the laboratory and are available in standard reference works. Beyond these routine methods, special situations call for special manipulations.

It has been known for a substantial length of time that fungi—in the case here noted, *Ceratocystis*—are often intimately associated with one or more insect genera. The problem is likely to be to find a means of selectively isolating the pathogenic forms from the numerous saprophytes that regularly contaminate the bodies of the insects. As one approach, Moller and DeVay (1968) tried an adaptation of Yarwood's technique with considerable success. Their approach was to prepare 2-cm-long disks of fresh carrot tissue, thoroughly washed in running water, and then again sliced into two roughly equal halves. On the inner surface of one of the paired discs, a small cavity was gouged out as a site for placing the suspected insect vector. Pieces containing the "caged" insects were kept at about 25°C for 4 days in high relative humidity, after which they were opened and examined, although the fungus frequently grew through the vascular tissue of the carrot and appeared on the outer surfaces. Identifications could easily be confirmed by examination of perithecia and spores.

Although they cannot fairly be classed as major scientific discoveries, one cannot help but admire those imaginative solutions to problems of technique that make experimentation feasible. As an intriguing example of this, take Shaw's (1967) observation that the oospores of certain species of *Phytophthora*, which under ordinary conditions do not germinate readily, and which have been observed to germinate in the feces of the land snail, could be conveniently handled by feeding cultures directly to these animals. Cultures of *P. cactorum*, for instance, were grown on sucrose-asparagine agar with certain supplements and then, after oospores were abundantly present, placed in beakers of water harboring *Planorbarius corneus*. These snails then grazed on the fungal mat and produced feces consisting almost entirely of oospores, which could then be surface sterilized and cultured in large numbers.

FLOWERING PLANTS

In the mid-1950's there appeared in several counties in North and South Carolina a new pest, called "witchweed," soon identified as the flowering plant *Striga asiatica*, that attracted widespread attention among United States plant pathologists. This parasitic species, imported by some means or other from its overseas home, proved to be a serious threat to corn, sorghum, and sugar cane, affixing itself to the root system and thereby causing appreciable damage. The very abundant tiny seeds, easily carried about from place to place, and capable of lying dormant for several years until stimulated to germinate by the secretions of a potential host root, serve as a very efficient means of propagation. The years since its first appearance have been spent in a vigorous campaign to limit its geographic spread, with reasonable success. But the point here is that the very excitement shown by pathologists is a measure of how little attention is ordinarily given to flowering plants as pathogenic organisms. Had the outbreak been of just another virus, fungus, or nematode, chances are very good that no such flurry of notoriety would have developed.

As of 1973, there was reason to hope that the infestation of witchweed in the southeastern United States was losing out, starting in 1957; in 1958 there were 2,184 newly infested farms, 2,167 in 1959, 1,885 in 1960, 1,587 in 1961, 971 in 1962, 831 in 1963, and 693 in 1964. No new counties were found to be infested in 1964 to add to the 34 in North and South Carolina already infested (Anon., 1965b). Surveys, quarantines, and eradication programs have been launched against the parasite, but chief reliance was placed on 2,4-D as a weedkiller before seeds are formed. Because the latter are formed in very large numbers, are individually minute, and may lie dormant for a long time until stimulated to germinate by proximity to a host root, there is little that can be done unless seed formation can be prevented. Of course, if the host plant stimulant could be isolated and then synthesized in substantial quantities, it might be possible to treat seed-infested soil and thus induce seeds to germinate in the absence of a satisfactory host.

Vascular plants as pathogens do not usually represent major problems to the plant pathologist as they directly affect host plants of economic or esthetic value, despite the fact that there are a considerable number of different kinds on a number of species. In temperate United States there are only three that occur widely—leafy mistletoe, dodder, and the dwarf mistletoes. While one can find taxonomic studies on these forms, they are but briefly treated in most pathology texts.

Leafy mistletoes—species of *Phoradendron*—are more curiosities than anything else. They may be seen, especially in winter, as bushy green clusters usually high in deciduous woodland trees. Not infrequently, once an infestation has been established, it will intensify to a point where an acre or more will be conspicuously affected. The plant itself is a dioecious, broadleafed evergreen, bearing clusters of the familiar whitish berries that, because they have a sticky substance surrounding the seed, adhere to the surface of the host once they come in contact with it. Most dissemination seems to be through the agency of birds. After seed germination, a modified root penetrates the tissues of the host and, as time goes on, develops a very firm connection between host and parasite. Most of the photosynthate available to the mistletoe is formed within its own green tissues; water and dissolved nutrients are procured from the host. It has been supposed for some years, and is now supported by direct measurements, that the sap pressure of mistletoes is less than that of the host. Scholander and others (1965) report this difference to be as much as minus-10 to minus-20 atmospheres.

The dwarf mistletoes of the Western evergreen forests are even more intriguing than the leafy forms of the East. A useful introductory treatment of the dwarf mistletoes was published by Kuijt in 1955, another by Hawksworth and Wiens (1970). As the name suggests, they are appreciably smaller than *Phoradendron*, do not have nearly so well differentiated leaves, and contain little if any chlorophyll. This all ties in with the fact that they are much more dependent, nutritionally, on the host plant and do correspondingly greater damage. Kuijt goes so far as to say: "Economically the damage done by these parasites to many forest trees, especially in Western North America, exceeds that of almost any other single cause, with the possible exception of heart-rotting fungi."

Most of the damage is apparently done by mistletoe-induced growth abnormalities in the host, resulting in swellings and clusters of more or less parallel twigs or small branches often called "witches' brooms" (Fig. 4–13). Seed production, lumber quality, growth and general vigor are adversely affected and the host becomes increasingly liable to invasion by insects and fungi.

Unlike *Phoradendron*, species of *Arceuthobium* have an explosive mechanism in the fruits that suffices to propel the sticky seeds for a considerable distance and, aided by the wind, effectively disseminates the plant to new hosts and new sites. This exceptionally effective seed dispersal mechanism is summarized by Hinds *et al.* (1963). Apparently, when the fruit is ripe, hydrostatic pressure in a layer of cells surrounding the seed increases to a high level, such that when the fruit breaks away from the pedicel the outer layers contract rapidly and throw the seed upwards. Initial velocities of nearly 1400 centimeters per second are achieved, and horizontal distances of up to 66 feet attained in certain species. Very-high-speed photography makes it possible to see precisely what happens in the first few fractions of a second after expulsion (Fig. 4–14).

Last of the common native plant genera that are significantly destructive to crop plants is *Cuscuta*, or dodder. It is a large genus found on many species of wild plants as well as cultivated crops. A member of the morning-glory family, dodder is a nearly leafless, nearly chlorophyll-free, slender twining vine, attached to its host by modified roots and deriving most of its elaborated food and water therefrom. In heavy infestations, as for example in lespedeza fields of the Tennessee valley, the entire aspect from a distance may be the yellow of dodder rather than the normal green of the healthy host. Growth and productivity are sharply reduced and economic damage is appreciable.

Fig. 4–13. Mature ponderosa pine in the Grand Canyon National Park, Arizona, showing the effects of infestation with dwarf mistletoe. (Photograph by Division of Forest Pathology, USDA, courtesy of L. S. Gill)

Fig. 4–14. Seed expulsion in the dwarf mistletoe. *Top:* Seed out of sight to left. *Middle:* Seed with viscous sheath intact. *Bottom:* Seed in flight 3–4 cm from fruit. (U.S. Forest Service Photo, from Hinds *et al.*, 1963)

Dissemination of dodders is more casual than that of either of the mistle-toes. Seed are produced in great abundance and are then carried along as a contaminant of the crop seed. If the sizes are very nearly the same, as they often are, separation is impracticable; whenever the crop is sown, dodder will be sown also. Initially, dodder seed germinate and seedlings are established much as they are in free-living plants, but the tip of the seedling stem soon evidences an exaggerated spiral growth that, if it contacts a solid object, re-sults in its twining tightly about that object. If, in turn, the contacted surface is a potential host plant, organic connections are rapidly established and the lower portion of the dodder plant atrophies and loses contact with the soil. Subsequent growth is entirely as a nearly complete parasite on the host.

Anyone interested in tropical America will profit from reference to Well-man's paper (1964) in which he lists the important phanerogamic parasites and brings out at least two provocative points:

- The development of hyperparasitism series extending to as many as four levels—two fungi growing on a species of parasitic vascular plant that is in turn colonizing a second parasitic vascular plant and that one in turn on an original host.
- The occurrence, within the single family Loranthaceae, of seven distin-guishable levels of parasitism, from "independent," through short-lived associations, to permanent attachments wherein the vegetative growth of the parasite is submerged within the host tissues.

Possibly the most significant single statement in his paper, however, is the following:

In phytopathology, parasitism is commonly accepted as a special habit of trouble-some, unwanted microscopic organisms. So much attention is given to diseases caused by viruses, bacteria, fungi and nematodes that there is scant time for or interest in par-asitism by phanerogams. . . . intimate host-parasite relations and even the general biology of most of the phanerogamic parasites in the neotropics have not been stud-ied.°

NEMATODES

By all odds the most recent arrival to prominence on the plant-pathological scene is the nematodes. The story of nematology is a bit like that of virology in that it is an area of greatly expanded and accelerated interest in recent years. The details are substantially different. One must suppose that while virus disease symptoms would have been very early recognized, a reasonably

---

° From F. L. Wellman, Parasitism among neotropical phanerogams, *Annual Review of Phyto-pathology*, vol. 2 (1964), p. 43.

clear understanding of the nature of viruses had to await the development of sophisticated biochemical and biophysical methods for studying protein structure and nucleic acids. Nematodes as biological organisms, to the contrary, have been known and studied for a century or more and many of the finer details of their morphology carefully documented. What was missing was an inkling of the extent and diversity of the damage wrought on the root systems of plants by these minute worms. Study of viruses was delayed because agriculturists knew of the symptoms but were ignorant of the nature of viruses; plant nematology suffered because zoologists knew much about nematodes but failed to identify them as the causal factor behind pathogenic conditions in crop plants and ornamentals. A generation ago the specialists in plant nematology could quite literally be ticked off on the fingers of one hand—today it is one of the more fashionable and actively pursued branches of plant pathology.

The literature of nematology suitable for the student has been greatly augmented by publication of a monograph by Sasser and Jenkins (1960) that was developed from a series of lectures and laboratory exercises used in a Southern Regional Graduate Summer Session in Nematology in 1959.

General Characteristics of Nematodes

Nematodes are animals—roundworms, in common terminology. Plant-parasitic forms and those in soil are but one component of a very large assemblage of related families and genera. Any introductory or advanced text in zoology will include descriptive morphological information on nematodes (see Fig. 4–15).

All nematodes have bodies that are elongate, round in cross section, and unsegmented. The species with which plant pathologists are concerned are so small as to be visible only with difficulty, if at all, to the unaided eye. The outer wall of the body is covered by a flexible, rather tough cuticle and is provided with a layer of muscles that produce the characteristic undulating or snake-like movement of the animal. Within the body is a digestive system, reproductive organs producing sperms and eggs, a primitive nervous system, and excretory organs. Finer points of nematode taxonomy depend often upon highly esoteric details of anatomy. The total number of species is very great. For practical separation of root-attacking forms from free-living species a great deal of significance is given to the occurrence and detailed structure of the stylet, a spearlike device in the buccal cavity by which initial penetration of the root surface is effected.

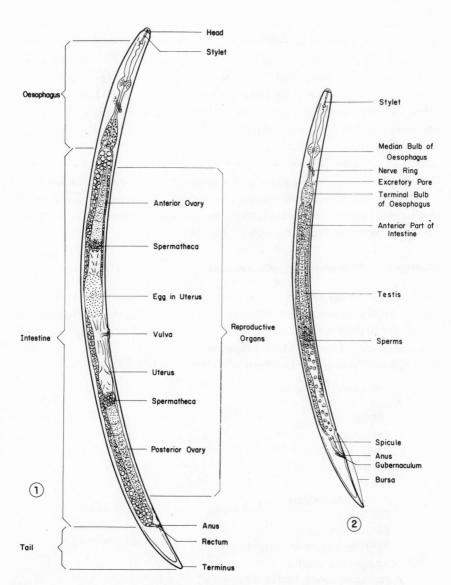

Fig. 4–15. Diagram of plant-parasitic nematode, showing a number of character-istic structures. (Taylor, 1967)

Reproduction

Functionally, nematodes fall into one of several reproductive groups. In what are usually termed bisexual species, roughly equal numbers of either sex are found in the population and eggs must be fertilized before they will develop further. In hermaphroditic species, self-fertilization occurs, a circumstance in which both sperm and egg are produced in the same individual and fertilized there. Specimens producing both eggs and sperm, more often than not, resemble females; males, if they occur at all, are uncommon and probably nonfunctional.

A third category, parthenogenic species, are characterized by the maturation of eggs without fertilization. Males in this group are entirely lacking.

Whatever the circumstances prior to embryonic development, subsequent cleavage and differentiation leads to the production of larvae. These, in turn, grow into adults, probably through a series of four moults.

Ecology and Host Relations

In a lengthy contribution to the monograph cited above (Sasser and Jenkins, 1960), Winslow calls attention to some useful highlights in the relation of nematodes to their host plants, points that it will be well to have in mind before undertaking Part III, which follows shortly.

Winslow's "ecological classification" (1960) is as follows:

Nematodes not zooparasitic
  Aquatic
    Marine
    Brackish
    Freshwater
  Amphibious
  Terrestrial
    Particulate feeders
    Predators
    Parasites of fungi
    Parasites of higher plants
Zooparasitic nematodes
  Parasites of invertebrates
  Parasites of vertebrates

Within the category that is of most immediate interest to the plant pathologist—parasites of higher plants—Winslow makes the following subdivisions. The broad outlines are instructive.

Parasites of aerial parts (Fig. 4–16)—buds, leaves and stems, flowers and
　　seed; ranging from ectoparasitism to endoparasitism
Parasites of underground parts
　　Ectoparasites—not normally penetrating root tissues
　　　　Migrating species
　　　　Sedentary species
　　Semi endoparasites—usually feed with anterior part of body in host
　　　　Migratory species
　　　　Sedentary species
　　Endoparasites—feed with entire body inside host tissue. Here is found
　　　　the best-known of all nematodes, the "root-knot" nematode, so
　　　　named for its stimulation of a pronounced hypertrophy of invaded
　　　　tissue.

Fig. 4–16. Photograph showing effect of the wheat nematode on the kernels of
the invaded plant, compared with a healthy kernel to the left.

The interrelations of nematodes and their hosts are highly varied and complex, but they can be grouped into a relatively small number of categories as
to manner of feeding, cell response, and so on (see Dropkin, 1969). All species
of nematodes attacking plants are possessed of a stylet that can be used to
penetrate the host cell wall, glands near the esophagus, and a sort of pump
that lies behind the stylet. Most species remove cell contents or bring about
lysis of the cell; a few stimulate the host to one or another of several growth
responses. The accompanying series of diagrams (Fig. 4–17), taken from
Dropkin's paper, illustrates the range of interactions that can be found among

I. No visible destructive effect

Cyclosis continues during prolonged feeding; dome of granules forms at stylet tip.

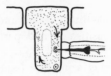

II. Immediate removal of cell contents

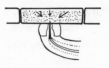

III. Delayed removal of cell contents

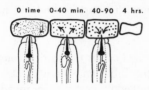

0 time   0-40 min.   40-90   4 hrs.

Penetration - cyclosis stops
Injection - cytoplasm becomes granular
Ingestion - granulation increases
Withdrawal - cell shrinks

IV. Progressive penetration

V. Cell lysis

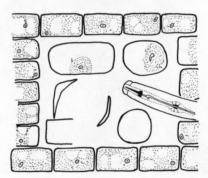

Cells near nematode enlarge and separate; cytoplasm withdraws, walls collapse; cavities form in tissues.

VI. Nurse cells of Tylenchulus

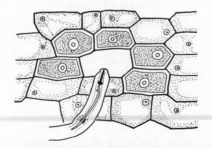

Nuclei and nucleoli enlarge, cytoplasm becomes dense, walls thicken, vacuole disappears.

VII. Syncytium of Nacobbus

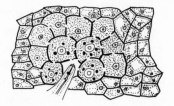

Cells hypertrophy; nucleus and nucleolus enlarge, divide
amitotically; cytoplasm becomes dense; starch accumulates,
walls dissolve in part but also thicken, cells retain identity.

VIII. Syncytium of Heterodera

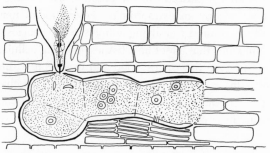

Nuclei enlarge; cell walls dissolve, but not completely;
cytoplasm merges into one unit; nuclei disintegrate;
cytoplasm becomes dense and granular; wall thickens.

IX. Giant cells of Meloidogyne

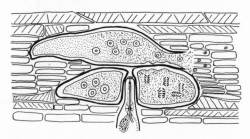

Nuclei enlarge, become polyploid, undergo synchronous
mitoses; cytoplasm becomes granular; new cells incorporated
by cell-wall dissolution; walls of syncytium thicken; cells of
pericycle divide repeatedly.

Fig. 4–17. Diagrams showing range of interactions between nematodes and their
host plants. (Dropkin, 1969)

the many phytopathogenic species. For those instances where the change is no more than of immediately attacked cells, one has no difficulty in postulating mechanisms that would bring about such changes—mechanical penetration, toxic effects on cells, physical removal of contents, and so on. When there are growth responses, it seems almost inevitable that the attacking nematode in an as yet unknown way alters the metabolism of the host much as viruses are known to do on a different size scale.

Physiology

Excluding the animal parasites in the phylum, which have evolved to the point where they occupy an extraordinary environment, nematodes reflect the basic physiology of most free-living animals. Some species secrete biologically active compounds that affect host tissues, eliciting cellular and tissue responses, but in the main they ingest food and process it within the digestive system. Like most living organisms they are sensitive to pH changes, temperature, oxygen tension, moisture levels, osmotic pressures. Many can enter a dormant stage and in so doing successfully withstand an unfavorable environment.

III

HOST-PATHOGEN INTERACTIONS

To this point attention has focused on the host, on inanimate causes of disorders in the host, or on pathogenic organisms that in one way or another bring about ill effects. It is now necessary to examine closely what happens when two organisms—a living host and living pathogen—come into direct contact with each other. This interaction is often complex—so complex that many needed answers are still to be sought despite the fact that data already in hand are formidable. Four dimensions are involved—host, pathogenic organism, environment, and time. Disease, as it is observed in nature or in the laboratory, is the net effect of all the many individual reactions among these four components.

It is characteristic of disease development, as it is of virtually all complex events, that to a large extent each phase is dependent upon the completion at some minimal level of the next preceding phase. From this stems the concept of "limiting factors," which says that the total process cannot proceed at a rate faster than that set by the least favorable component. If that component be for any reason blocked, the whole process collapses. Host, pathogenic organism, environment, and time—all must be present or disease is clearly impossible. How *much* disease depends upon how favorable—in the aggregate—these variables are. Whether we can identify it or not, there will be a limiting factor in every disease situation, although in a given instance it may permit development at such a rapid rate as to be of no practical consequence.

The presentation to follow emphasizes first of all chronology. Pathogenic organism and host come into contact, the latter is then in some way entered by the pathogen, and in due course extends through the tissues of the host.

Thus the problem is considered in a series of four chapters. The first, Chapter 5, is restricted in so far as practicable to the events immediately related to entry, per se. The second, Chapter 6, aims at an elucidation of the structural or morphologic aspects of interaction after successful entry has been accomplished—in a sense it focusses on the visible, tangible results of successful establishment of pathogen within the host. Chapter 7 centers on the metabolic bases, the biochemical mechanisms, that lie behind the observed effects on structure. Influence of environment will be handled in Chapter 8.

Two elements pervade the whole: (1) the effect of environment and (2) manifestations of host resistance. Considerations of the latter are inserted wherever they seem most pertinent throughout Chapters 5, 6, and 7, so close is the connection between attributes of the pathogen affecting entry and establishment and those of the host.

PREDISPOSITION

To be entirely consistent with a chronological approach, it is appropriate to consider first those circumstances prior to contact between the interacting individuals—host and pathogenic organism—that may affect the outcome of that contact. Here a reasonably satisfactory distinction can be made between those factors that diminish the likelihood that the two will come into contact in a significant way and those factors that influence the outcome of the contact once made.

In the first case, one usually hears the term "disease escape" used, which usually refers to instances in which a given host plant, otherwise liable to invasion, is not in fact subjected to attack because host and pathogen do not coincide in both space and time. Chapter 15, on cultural control of disease, includes a discussion of how disease escape phenomena may be capitalized upon through adroit management. Gäumann (1950) singles out three categories of escape mechanisms:

- Noncoincidence of the inoculum with the susceptible phase of the host, which is obviously maximized when each event is of limited duration and when they occur other than simultaneously.
- Situations where the portal of entry is the flower and where the duration of the flowering period, either of individual plant or of the field population of plants, is limited.
- Situations where the growth habit of the host is such that the microclimate is materially affected in ways that are not conducive to invasion and establishment of the pathogen and to subsequent development of the disease.

With characteristic clarity and imagination, Yarwood (1959) has summarized most aspects of predisposition and its implications, first pointing out the uncertainty that has dogged every attempt sharply to delimit the concept from related ones. Not surprisingly, he settles for an operational definition and considers predisposition to be any circumstance whereby the host is rendered either more or less vulnerable to pathogen attack (infrequently, to noninfectious disease) as a consequence of some antecedent event other than the basic genetic character of the plant. He extends this concept to include changes in susceptibility that are correlated with age of host, season of the year, or time of day, but concentrates particularly on what he chooses to call "environmental predisposition"—the aspect most commonly called to mind by the term itself. Thus temperature, light, atmospheric humidity, and pressure have been shown in a number of instances to influence the eventual outcome of an encounter between host and pathogen.

No situation better emphasizes the difficulty of clearly delimiting predisposition from most other aspects of pathology than does mineral nutrition. Repeatedly, one hears the generalization expressed that increased nitrogen levels enhance susceptibility, that increased potassium tends to reduce it, and that phosphorus may in one instance increase and in the next instance reduce resistance. The real difficulty here lies in the fact that unless predisposition can be clearly distinguished from other kinds of effects, experimental data are likely to be unconvincing or at best no more than a correlation. In Yarwood's view, predisposition can be shown effectively only when groups of presumably healthy plants are subjected to conditions differing in one important variable, the entire lot then returned to a situation where all are subject to the same conditions, and are then inoculated or otherwise challenged by the pathogenic organism being studied. If, when so tested, plants of the two groups show significantly different levels of disease, predisposition can safely be assumed. The difficulty in many cases is that not all of the criteria are met, as for example when different nutrient levels are maintained not only prior to, but continuing through, the disease phase. If so managed, it becomes wholly impossible to rule out the effects of the factor being tested on the pathogen itself, or on host-pathogen interaction, and the case for predisposition is thereby greatly weakened.

A number of factors may be thought of that are primarily predisposing agencies. Among these are the existence of damaged sites or wounds on the host, the enhanced likelihood of invasion by a given pathogen that results when there are earlier lesions produced by an earlier invasion, and so on.

As Yarwood (1959) phrased it:

It is a disturbing commentary on our knowledge of plant pathology that most known cases of predisposition, especially those involving treatments that offer promise of increased crop productivity, usually result in increases in susceptibility. The many hopes in the past of growing plants in such a way that they will resist disease, have mostly proved illusory.

Most recorded predisposing treatments have increased the susceptibility of plants which were genetically somewhat resistant. There are fewer cases where predisposing treatments have greatly increased resistance of plants which were genetically rather susceptible, yet these are what is needed in order to apply predisposition to control.°

Because plants are, quite literally, of different ages in different portions of the same individual it is difficult to make simple tests of the relationship between age and susceptibility. In an effort to improve the standardization of experimental techniques, Schein (1965) studied the susceptibility of bean leaves to bean rust and to tobacco mosaic virus and found that while the unfolding leaves were markedly resistant to both pathogens there was an increase in susceptibility up to the point where the leaves were 20 to 40% expanded. From that point on susceptibility decreased until it was again very low in the fully expanded leaves. By carefully controlling the inoculum dose Schein sought to eliminate this variable from the experiment.

Differences in age of even a relatively few days, if it occurs during the seedling stage particularly, can bring about striking differences in the susceptibility of the host, as indicated in the accompanying figure showing the effects of the blue mold fungus (Fig. III–1).

Among the numerous factors that have been investigated as predisposing host plants to disease, substantial attention had been devoted to heat in one context or another. Various investigators have shown that heat predisposes the host plant to invasion and pathological damage by the pathogenic organism. By submerging the roots and hypocotyls of soybean plants, Chamberlain and Gerdemann (1966) were able to heat-treat the hosts at temperatures of 42 to 45°C for one hour without undue direct damage. Under these conditions, heat predisposed a highly resistant variety, Harosoy 63, to the point were it was as susceptible as the common susceptible variety, Harosoy; not only this, but the latter could be rendered even more susceptible than normal. Perhaps more striking, however, is their discovery that after treatment with heat in this fashion, soybeans became susceptible to two nonpathogens of soybeans, although not to a number of others tried. Three days after heat treatment normal resistance was recovered (Fig. III–2).

We commonly recognize the fact that plants are capable of adapting to low temperatures and that the extent to which they are injured depends very

° From J. G. Horsfall and A. E. Dimond (eds.), *Plant Pathology: An Advanced Treatise* (New York: Academic Press, Inc.), vol. I, p. 546. Copyright © 1959–60, Academic Press, Inc.

Fig. III–1. Relation of age to susceptibility of tobacco seedlings to infection by blue mold. *Left: Nicotiana rustica,* front inoculated at 14 days, rear at 35 days. *Center: N. maritima,* inoculated at 14 and 35 days. *Right: N. exigua,* an immune species, inoculated at 14 and 35 days. (Clayton, 1945)

much on the conditions leading up to the time of extreme cold. Less attention has been given to heat tolerance, although damage from high temperatures is a widely encountered phenomenon. Experiments by Yarwood (1964) on bean leaves provides evidence that the conditions leading to the critical temperature have appreciable effect on how severe the reaction is. If, under the conditions of his experiment, there is a preliminary heat treatment about 24 hours earlier, then what he calls the challenge heat (about 120 seconds at 50°C) is less damaging. If, on the other hand, the challenge heat is preceded by a conditioning heat one hour earlier, damage is intensified. The age of the bean plants, predisposition early in the morning, a dark period during predisposition, or high soil moisture also affect the outcome, mostly to make it more severe.

When the relation between a diseased host and a presumed pathogen is obscure or when the incidence of disease is more than ordinarily irregular, one can suspect that complicating factors are confusing the picture. As an example of this, McGuire and Cooper (1965) investigated the collar rot of peanut in North Carolina and found that it seems to be related to predisposition by heat, especially on light sandy soils, and that it tends to be worse when the peanut crop follows a cotton crop than when it follows corn—in the latter

Fig. III–2. Effect of heat treatment on the reaction of soybeans to *Phytophthora cactorum. Left to right:* Column 1—unheated, no inoculation. Column 2—heated, no inoculation (slightly stunted). Column 3—unheated, inoculated. Column 4—heated, inoculated. (Chamberlain and Gerdemann, 1966)

case because cotton provides a very favorable site for the overwintering of large amounts of inoculum.

C. E. Yarwood, who has long been interested in every aspect of the question of predisposition, has provided us with an attractively simple example (see Fig. III–3) of interacting factors in the case of Pinto beans and cowpeas subjected to inoculation with conidia of powdery mildew (*Sphaerotheca fuliginea*) taken from cucumber. These two legumes are normally highly resistant or immune, but when infected by rust, heated, abraded, or pressed, susceptibility is substantially enhanced. The predisposing effect of rust infection, especially when the rust is killed by heat prior to mildew inoculation, is very great. As for the other factors, Yarwood reports a typical experiment as follows: number of lesions on three square inches on an untreated leaf—0; as one heated 20 seconds at 50°C—11; pressed—25; abraded—12; heated and pressed—29; heated and abraded—17; pressed and abraded—24; heated, abraded, and pressed—40.

Additional attributes of the complex of factors involved in predisposition are indicated in the following two examples, but they by no means exhaust the known ramifications of this phenomenon.

Much as the Dutch elm disease has been studied, surprises continue to crop up when a biological interaction so complex as that of host, insect vector, and fungus pathogen are involved. In 1963 (see Hart *et al.*, 1967) in the city of Detroit, an unusually high incidence of the disease was traced to areas that had been trimmed in July, August, and September of the preceding year, only those streets showing a departure from what might have been expected for past experience. It is by no means certain just why—several possibilities were noted—but the net effect was to make the lower trunks of the recently trimmed trees attractive to the smaller European elm bark beetle as a site for constructing brood galleries. During the formation of the galleries, of course, the beetle acts as an effective vector of the causal fungus.

It has repeatedly been recognized that certain crop sequences result in

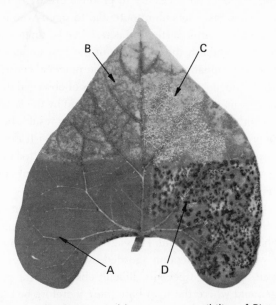

Fig. III–3. Effect of rust infection and heat on susceptibility of Pinto bean leaf to powdery mildew. The right half was inoculated with rust and the upper half dipped in water at 50°C for 64 seconds, after which the entire surface was dusted with spores of mildew. *A*—Necrotic mildew colony in untreated quadrant of leaf. *B*—Heat injury in upper left quadrant. *C*—Luxuriant mildew development where rust has been killed by heat in upper right quadrant. *D*—Scattered colonies of luxuriant mildew. (Yarwood, 1965)

marked yield reductions in the second crop in the sequence, a situation for which a number of explanations have been proffered and for many of which there is a respectable amount of evidence. Doubtless the mechanism of action is not the same in every case and that at times a combination of factors is present. Carley and Watson (1967), in studies of a number of crop residues on root development in clover, radish, and wheat, conclude that toxic substances were responsible for the direct damage observed in the roots. This, in turn, retards nutrient and water absorption by the root system and renders the plant more than ordinarily vulnerable to the diseases common in the soil.

INOCULUM POTENTIAL

While the general sense of the term "inoculum potential," or if one prefers, "numerical threshold," is fairly well agreed upon, the concept has been rather differently treated by various writers. In crude terms it refers to the size of the dose of inoculum necessary to produce disease in the host.

One point of view takes inoculum potential to signify the minimum number of infective units—virus particles, bacterial cells, fungus spores—necessary successfully to establish the pathogen in the host under conditions that permit invasion. As Gäumann (1950) points out, practical considerations force the investigator to judge "infection" on the basis of observed disease, whereas the former need by no means be inevitably followed by the latter. Debate also persists over whether a threshold greater than one results because there is need for some group or synergistic property, or whether it is a simple matter of statistical probability that the necessary requirements for invasion will coincide at the particular site of a given infective unit. Current opinion seems to favor the latter view.

S. D. Garrett (1959) takes a different tack in his interpretation of inoculum potential as being mostly determined by the food resources that the inoculum has and must have to be successful. His view was developed in relation to root disease fungi, where the protection afforded by the cork layer on the outside of the host tissues poses an especially difficult obstacle to the pre-invasion life of the pathogen and where the food base must therefore be especially abundant. Garrett argues for a wider application of the notion when he points out that each fungus spore, on the leaf surface for example, has its own energy content and that variations from spore to spore will determine in the last analysis which ones can and which ones cannot infect.

"Numerical threshold" may, in many instances, be no more or less than the number of infective units necessary to insure that at least one possesses sufficient "inoculum potential" to succeed. To this degree, the two concepts outlined above are one and the same.

That the intensity of inoculum varies from one season to another, and in direct relation to a biological attribute of the pathogen, is well shown in McOnie's observations on ascospores of *Guignardia citricarpa* (see Fig. III–4). By means of spore trapping, bagging the fruit, and spray experiments, he showed that initial fruit infection coincides with earliest heavy discharge of ascospores. Perithecia, which are present throughout the year on citrus leaf litter, discharge by far the most ascospores in the summer months, as would be expected; infection seems not to be correlated with other possible routes of invasion.

BIOLOGY OF HOST-PATHOGEN INTERACTIONS

Part III simply assumes that pathogenic organism and host are in initial contact with each other, leaving for a later consideration just how they reached that state. The central concern is with what happens between a host unit and a pathogen unit, under the impact of environment.

Most attempts to develop generalizations from the wealth of detail about host-pathogen interactions have related to such topics as the evolution of the parasitic mode of life (e.g. Yarwood, 1956). In so doing, great emphasis is often placed on the importance of distinguishing between parasitism and pathogenicity. Without challenging the validity of such a distinction, it is still difficult to see why the principal emphasis of the plant pathologist must not necessarily be on pathogenic effects—parasitism, as such, is but one of a number of considerations. Hence the term host-pathogen interaction—implying a pathogenic organism in this context—seems far more appropriate than host-parasite interaction.

In Chapter 2, McNew's thesis that the host plant passes through six identifiable major phases in its life history was briefly summarized. He then went on to suggest that as one moved up through the list—utilization of food reserves, development of new shoots, formation of roots, transport of water and nutrients, food manufacture in leaves, transport of photosynthate—there is a marked change in the nature of the pathogens that most commonly affect these processes and events. That is, at the early phases, facultative saprophytes are more common and that the situation changes until in the last phases the obligate parasites are conspicuous. He sees this progression as evidence of an increasingly precise balance between host and pathogenic organism and a general reduction in the tendency of the latter toward general invasion and destruction of cells.

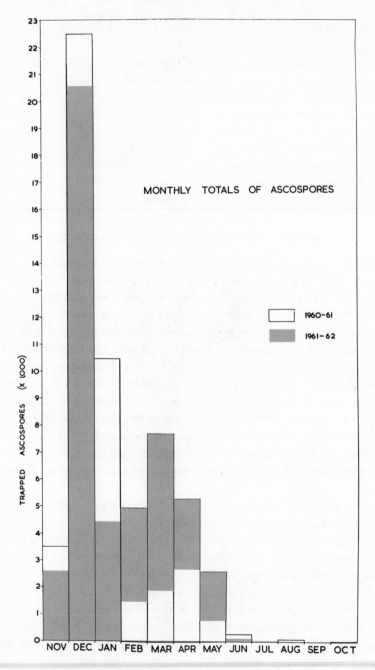

Fig. III–4. Graph of totals of discharged ascospores of *Guignardia citricarpa* showing variation in intensity of inoculum from one season to the next. (McOnie, 1964)

In a still further exploration of the situation, McNew develops certain postulates as to the relation of the six growth phases and the observed effects of climate and mineral nutrition on disease development—and relationships between these same phases and the mode of disease control most likely to prove effective.

Whether one is convinced by the arguments or not, McNew's proposals have considerable merit in that they strive to derive generalization from the mass of detailed data and provide a framework upon which to build a workable theory.

5

Entry of Pathogen

If the interaction of host and pathogen ceased upon entry, the observer would seldom even be aware of it, much less be concerned from the standpoint of pathology, although it is now widely accepted that microorganisms do penetrate some hosts that they do not then exploit. The significant entry remains, however, the one that leads to establishment and spread.

AVENUES AND MECHANISMS OF ENTRY

Pathogenic organisms gain entry to the host in a variety of ways. For some, success depends upon the intervention of another organism or upon there being a breach in the normal defenses of the host—in other words, they are passively involved in the event. Others can invade their host species by virtue of one or more active steps. In either case, the actual mechanism of entry can be either predominantly a physical or predominantly a chemical one. The key seems to be the biological nature of the pathogenic organism itself and only secondarily, perhaps, the nature of the host. Some modes of entry are just not available to a given kind of pathogen.

Viruses

Viruses cannot, so far as is known, enter the cells of a host plant unaided, nor can they multiply except within the living protoplasms of the host. Physical wounding of the host must therefore precede penetration of the pathogen.

For convenience as much as anything, viruses are often classified as "mechanically transmitted" or "insect transmitted," although this fails to take into account all of the known mechanisms—e.g., virus transmission by animals other than insects or by dodder. Even so, it must be obvious that viruses, unless they remain in the plant tissues and are moved about in this way—by grafting, vegetative propagation, in seeds, or pollen—must be got into new sites through wounds. An abbreviated catalog of wounding phenomena would include: mechanical transmission of plant extracts by rubbing, feeding activities of chewing and sucking insects and of mites, puncturing of host tissues by nematodes, the inroads of the parsitic dodders, and the invasion of the host by several species of soil-inhabiting Phycomycetes.

Much research on viruses has dealt with mechanisms of sap transmission and of insect inoculation. Most attempts to transmit viruses by "sap inoculation" involve rubbing the surface of the leaf with brush or cloth pad dipped in viruliferous leaf extract, augmented by some such abrasive as carborundum dust. Of the factors that tend to enhance the likelihood that inoculation will be successful, pretreatment under elevated temperatures, reduction of light intensity, and inclusion of phosphate ions in the "abrasion medium" have been established. Mechanical pressure, even without evident wounding, has been shown to have an observable effect.

Two avenues of entry have been most frequently cited as the likely route for sap transmission, leaf hairs and the plasmodesmata of epidermal cells. As investigation continues, the former seems less and less likely to be correct; viruses must therefore be presumed to move through protoplasmic strands in plasmodesmata exposed by physical removal of the cuticle during abrasion.

Whatever the precise nature of the infective site, there is an important time relation to be considered. Inoculation coincident with abrasion is in most cases much more effective than when an interval, even a very brief one, intervenes. Siegel and Zaitlin (1964), in their analysis of the events surrounding virus entry, hold to the view that a single particle is sufficient to establish an "infective center" at an "infectible site." If, indeed, plasmodesmata in the outer wall (ectodesmata) are the sites of virus entry, then something altogether akin to pinocytosis seems a likely mechanism (Maundry, 1963).

The full story of virus transmission by insects is a very long and complicated one, involving many fascinating and subtle relationships between the two biological entities. So far as initial entry is concerned, the two major categories have been noted in Chapter 4—those insects that carry virus mostly as a contaminant on the surface of mouthparts and those in which the virus moves through a regular route within the body of the insect, appearing in due time in the saliva that is injected into the cells of the host. Virus is introduced into a wound produced by the insect—into a crude injury caused by chewing, into superfiical punctures of the epidermal and mesophyll cells, or into the underlying phloem. Placement of virus protein by sucking insects is naturally far more precise than it is by those that feed by chewing.

In support of the specificity of leafhopper vectors of plant viruses, Bennett (1967) notes that of 109 species, 94 transmit only one virus, and only one transmits as many as 4 viruses. Along the same line, of 51 viruses listed, 33 are transmitted by only one vector and only 4 by 5 or more vectors. These viruses are much more characteristic of vascular tissue—usually phloem—than of parenchyma and, therefore, rarely induce mottling. They are difficult to transmit mechanically and are not seed-borne.

Not the least intriguing are the rather imperfectly known "soil-borne" viruses (Cadman, 1963). To some extent, at least, they can be divided into two groups depending upon the vector responsible for their transmission. The first are transmitted by ectoparasitic nematodes that harbor the virus in their bodies—the virus-vector relationship is highly specific in at least some instances—and transmit in the act of puncturing host tissue with their styli. The second group is introduced into the host through the activities of soil chytrids, especially *Olpidium brassicae,* which intermediate host also provides a reservoir for the virus during periods when the vascular plant host is not available.

A study by Campbell and Grogan (1964) of mechanisms of transmission of the virus of lettuce big-vein by the fungus *Olpidium brassicae* has clearly shown that zoospores of this organism are capable of acquiring the virus from roots of the host and transmitting it, presumably internally carried in the zoospore cell, to new hosts.

The concept of "soil-borne" viruses was arrived at before there was much if any clear understanding of how they were able to survive and move from one host to another. As noted, a number of organisms have since been implicated as vectors for the soil-borne plant viruses, among them several species of fungi. One of the more specialized associations is that between the wheat mosaic virus and the plasmodiophoraceous organism, *Polymyxa graminis.* Rao (1968) has worked out the host-parasite relationships of this microorganism on the wheat host and established correlations that persuade him of the vector role played by it.

Bacteria

Whereas bacteria loom very large among the causal agents of infectious disease in man, they are of decidedly secondary importance in plant pathology. The situation regarding fungi is exactly the reverse—the fungal diseases of man are wholly insignificant beside those that afflict agricultural crops, forests, and ornamental plantings. The paramount, if not the sole, reason for this difference lies in the sheer unsuitability of the bacterial cell for penetrating the initial barriers to entry of the plant host.

Many species of bacteria can move by virtue of hairlike flagellae on the cell surface, but for obvious reasons they cannot force their way through the unbroken epidermis of the host any more than a man can swim to the side of a pool and push out a section of the rim. Neither bacterial cell nor human body, unanchored, provides appreciable inertia and whatever force might be generated serves only to move them away from the contacted surface.

Natural openings—stomates, lenticels, hydathodes, nectaries—or wounds produced by environmental factors, by man, by insects, or by other animals are essential if bacteria are to get within the host. A liquid medium is also necessary except in those cases wherein wounding and transmission are simultaneous, as for example potato ring rot, where contaminated cutting knives are responsible for carrying the pathogen.

While a common portal of entry for pathogenic bacteria is through the stomates of leaf and young stems, Lewis and Goodman (1965) in a study of the fireblight of apple find that the pathogen can enter the upper surface of the leaf even though there are no stomates at all. In this case the entry is effected through trichomes, through hydathodes, and through the lenticels of the young stem. Once in, the cells move rapidly and at least in the stem, travel by way of the phloem.

It is generally assumed that nematodes are instrumental in facilitating the entry of plant pathogens into the roots of host plants, but direct evidence is not especially abundant. Libman and colleagues (1964) have made controlled experiments with three species of nematodes and demonstrated that *Meloidogyne hapla* and *Helicotylenchus nannus* increased the incidence and severity of wilt, whereas *Rotylenchus* had no significant effect—the pathogen in all cases was the bacterium responsible for a wilt of tomatoes, *Pseudomonas solonacearum*. A limited incidence, up to 10%, occurred in the absence of the nematodes and was attributed to entry through wounds at the site of secondary root emergence (Fig. 5–1).

Not surprisingly, insects are importantly involved as agents of bacterial pathogen entry. As an illustration of the way in which science actually progresses—by contrast with the way that students are too frequently taught that it progresses—we might follow the trend of interest in bacterial diseases of plants with special reference to insect transmission.

Burrill is generally credited with first showing that plant disease could be caused by bacteria, although the date is variously cited as 1878, 1881, and the intervening period. Some ten years later Waite uncovered the role of honey bees as transmitting agents of the fireblight of pears and apples—the very same disease that Burrill had worked with. These two "firsts" are routinely cited in every text on the subject, although there is at least one piece of evi-

Fig. 5–1. Relation of wounding to invasion of tomatoes by the nematode *Helicotylenchus nannus:* B + W—bacteria plus rootwounding; B + N—bacteria plus nematodes; B—bacteria only; N—nematodes only (Libman *et al.,* 1964)

dence to the contrary: A. A. Bitancourt (1945) has commented that the work of Draenert in Brazil in 1869 on gummosis of sugar cane should be recognized as the first on a bacterial disease of a plant.

Then again, one of the more legendary debates in the annals of plant pathology was that which raged in the late 1800's between Erwin F. Smith and the German Alfred Fischer over whether or not bacteria could cause disease —Smith championing the view that bacteria are phytopathogenic. It is a significant commentary on the generally high level of scientific discourse that this particular one is notorious more for its acrimony than for its factual content. In any event, Smith's polemics won the day and there has been no serious doubt on the matter since that time. And on the general question of insect transmission of bacteria, Carter in 1962 could preface his book on insects in relation to plant disease by showing the sharp contrast between emphasis on viruses and on bacteria: "Insect transmission of phytopathogenic bacteria has received little attention during recent years . . ."

All this is by way of emphasizing the role of fashion, of chance, of subjective judgment, in the process of science.

Actual transmission of bacteria is not infrequently a matter of direct contamination of the insect body. When, as in the case of fireblight, the feeding or other behavioral activities of the insect are clearly related to the point of entry, the relationship is more precise. Bacteria may, for example, survive in the intestinal tract and be thus introduced in feeding activities; this seems to be true of a number of bacterial pathogens whose overwintering depends upon survival within the bodies of the vector. Oviposition may, if the egg or ovipositor carries bacterial cells on the surface, effectively insure entry of the pathogen.

In but relatively few cases does there seem to be a highly specific "symbiotic" relationship between insect and bacterial plant pathogen—most insect-symbiont associations are what Carter calls "host bound" in that the organism does not ordinarily leave the body of the host and is not therefore important in plant pathology. In one instance, however, the olive fly serves as a very effective vector of the olive-knot disease bacteria by harboring them continuously, not only throughout the life of the insect but from generation to generation through the egg. In this species, sacs at the lower end of the intestinal and reproductive systems assure that deposited eggs are contaminated; similar diverticula of the esophagus serve to sequester the organisms during metamorphosis and insure their continuation to the adult phases. In this particular instance, the larvae initially become infected when bacteria deposited on the egg at time of laying enter through the micropyle and invade the developing embryo.

Fungi

The fungi, more than either bacteria or viruses, have interesting and diverse characteristics so far as host penetration is concerned. They, more than any other group, have been the center of attention as causal agents of plant disease. In part, this greater interest derives from the fact that they were the earliest noted back in the days when the infectious nature of disease was first being established. But it is far more than sheer chance that has led to their preeminence for so many years—by any reasonable criteria, fungi continue to rank in the forefront of etiologic agents.

Fungi are by far the most conspicuous of the plant pathogens. Many species are readily discernible without the elaborate instruments needed for virological studies or the high magnifications needed to observe bacteria. Unlike the nematodes, fungi to a large extent attack the aerial parts of plants and thus came early to the attention of farmers and pathologists alike.

In the aggregate, the fungi are exceedingly diverse, although the great majority of plant-pathogenic forms are filamentous, a factor that proves to be of crucial importance when it comes to penetration, as will be noted below.

Spore Germination. By no means all fungus inoculum consists of spores, but a very large fraction of it does. Spores, both sexual and asexual, are the characteristic reproductive and disseminating elements in the fungi and, at least in above-ground situations, are the chief entities that initiate a new disease lesion. More than any other one mechanism, they serve as a means whereby the pathogen survives periods of unfavorable circumstances—unfavorable in the sense either that there is no readily available host in a vulnerable condition or that the environmental conditions are not conducive to growth and reproduction.

Assume, then, that there is a fungus spore lying on or affixed to the surface of the host. It makes no particular difference at this point whether the spore be large or small, hyaline or colored, single- or multinucleate, single- or multicelled, vegetatively or sexually produced—unless it germinates nothing further of significance will occur. For the most part, depending on species and circumstances, a hypha or germ tube is produced, or motile cells are released (several highly specialized events occur in certain species). Motile cells, once formed, will in turn settle down and produce germ tubes very like those formed directly from spores.

In most species, spores absorb water and swell appreciably before germination itself actually takes place, although there are exceptions. Then, if the spore is mature and not in a dormant phase, the cytologically visible events of germination ensue. Swarmspores may, for example, be cut out from the cytoplasm of the spore itself and, after a period of mobility within the spore wall, burst through the outer wall and escape. More commonly, spores germinate by forming a filament. These filaments, or germ tubes, emerge randomly in some species; in others they arise from specific sites in the spore wall known as germ pores. As the germ tube grows, cytoplasm and nuclei flow into the developing filament.

There is a world of data on the internal and external conditions that influence spore germination. But exceptions to rules are many and there is much that remains unknown. Spores generally are influenced by humidity, temperature, light, pH, and by the nutrients or other constituents in the medium. But by no means all species find their optimal circumstances for germination within a single set of conditions. Virtually all require fairly high moisture levels, with the conspicuous exception of the powdery mildews where the water content of the spores themselves may be well above average. Within what might be fairly regarded as "moderate" temperatures, optimum levels for spore germination vary considerably from group to group—the levels in turn usually correlate well with the ecological requirements of the disease complex itself. Most spores require an external source of oxygen and a pH in the 4.5–6.5 range. Light does not, as a rule, markedly affect the process.

There remain two additional important aspects that are related to the process of spore germination:

- Nutrients or otherwise stimulating substances in the surrounding medium, which have obvious implications for the significance of materials that may move into surface moisture from underlying host tissue.
- Movement of materials through spore walls and membranes, which is of immediate concern to the study of fungicide toxicity.

Whatever may be the ethical and practical considerations of biological warfare agents against man, animals, or crops, there can be little question that research carried on in this general area has been very productive indeed in leading to a better understanding of the phenomena of plant disease. The point, very likely, is that the approach of the researcher is directly contrary to that of plant pathologists in general; he is interested in seeing how bad an outbreak can be induced, not how a natural epidemic can be lessened. In so doing, he may well hit upon new insights into the biology of disease that are useful in agriculture generally. Several aspects of experimental initiation of stem rust epidemics with uredospores, including the matter of storage under conditions of maximum retention of viability, have been reported by Bromfield (1967). Reducing spore moisture to about 10% and storing at 4°C will keep most spore collections viable for one to two years; if vacuum dried and stored in the absence of both oxygen and water vapor they will last five years; in liquid nitrogen they will remain almost indefinitely, but require certain special techniques to restore germination percentages when brought back to ambient temperatures. But, as Bromfield notes, germination is a necessary but not sufficient condition—for adequately predicting field infection it is also necessary to know the degree of susceptibility of the host at the particular growth stage tested, and the conditions of temperature, light, and duration of leaf wetness during penetration and prepenetration phases of infection.

Entry Through Wounds. Whether the fungus inoculum is a conidium, a zoospore, or a vegetative filament, penetration of the host is almost without exception accomplished by hyphae. The least definitive mode of entry is probably through various kinds of breaks or wounds in the outer surfaces—

least definitive in two senses: (1) relatively few "wound-parasites" are restricted to this pathway alone, and (2) the relationship of pathogen to host on a cellular basis is very much less specific than in most other modes of entry. Thus wounds ranging all the way from the minutest lesions to major physical damage are utilized, often by fungus species that are entirely capable of entering through more specialized avenues as well as species that are entirely dependent upon injury sites.

Wounds result from a very large number of contingencies—frost cracking, fire, lightning, cultivation and handling injuries, ice and snow breakage, and the prior (or simultaneous) activities of another organism, particularly the nematodes and insects. For that matter a lesion produced by one pathogenic organism, if so capitalized upon, can be considered the wound through which a subsequent one enters the plant.

Setting aside for the moment the role of insects in dissemination, overwintering, diploidization ("fertilization"), and other phenomena related to the total biology of the pathogenic fungi, insects assist fungi to penetrate the host almost exclusively by their feeding and egg-laying activities. To this extent, the portal of entry is a wound. In some instances the interrelationships of fungus and insect are very precise and complex; at the other extreme fungus pathogens simply utilize an existing lesion produced at an earlier time by insect or nematode. Either way, the contribution of the vector is to breach the outer defenses of the host and, often, to deliver inoculum to a vulnerable site behind those defenses.

Natural Openings.   Of the natural openings in plants, stomates are by far the most abundant, although hydathodes are a not insignificant avenue for some fungi. Penetration through stomates, whether by a species that can successfully enter closed stomates or one that can negotiate only open ones, is characteristically preceded by a swelling of the germ tube in such a way that the opening is obscured. Subsequently an infection hypha forms beneath the adherent swelling (appressorium). Evidence is rather convincing that the appressorium is just what it appears to be—an adherent body that provides the essential inertia against which the developing hypha pushes as it moves downward through the stomatal opening. Without such an anchoring device, certainly, elongation of the invading filament would serve only to push the germ tube away from the surface of the leaf or stem.

Studies of stomatal penetration by the pathogens of wheat stem rust and leaf rust (Yirgou and Caldwell, 1963) seem to indicate clearly that the crucial factor is not the direct stimulus of light nor, as has been thought for some time, is it a question of whether or not the stomates are open. The observed fact is that stem rust, *Puccinia graminis*, penetrates well in light but not in darkness, whereas the leaf rust pathogen, *P. recondita*, is effective under either condition. When atmospheric carbon dioxide is removed from the system experimentally, penetration by stem rust fungi is markedly enhanced, whereas an overload of CO_2 of 5% or so will nearly suppress penetration even under light conditions. The leaf rust pathogen is unaffected, suggesting that the observed effect of light on stem rust penetration is due to changes in carbon dioxide concentration as photosynthesis is accelerated or retarded.

Intact Surfaces. In special instances—e.g., stigmas and nectaries of flowers or root hairs—the walls of the outermost cells do not have a cuticle and thus interpose no more hindrance to fungal entry than do the parenchyma tissues underneath normal epidermis. Over most of the host tissues a noncellular cuticle of greater or lesser thickness overlies the epidermis and must be successfully penetrated by the invading pathogen before any further steps toward establishing itself can take place.

The visible mechanism of penetration is approximately that described above for stomatal entry—formation of an appressorium and infection peg. Despite the small size of the elements involved, the exceedingly small cross-sectional diameter of the peg permits it to exert very high pressures indeed. There seems little question but that the physical force generated by growth is quite enough to account for entry through intact surfaces. It is a very different matter to determine whether physical forces are the only ones involved, or whether chemical factors contribute to the process; opinions have swung back and forth over the years. The more recent view ascribes *initial* penetration mostly to physical events.

Studies of infection processes in poplar by Marks *et al.* (1965) have provided detailed accounts of the action of appressoria and infection peg, as shown in the accompanying figure (Fig. 5-2). The special advantage of this particular host-pathogen interaction is that the fungus can penetrate young leaves, but not mature ones—hence successful and unsuccessful attempts can be compared under very nearly identical conditions. In this case, at least, the outcome seems to depend almost entirely, if not entirely, on whether the physical force of the infection peg is sufficient to accomplish penetration; there is virtually no evidence in the very earliest stages of chemical dissolution of the host cuticle.

Whatever the means of getting through cuticle and cell wall, the hyphae emerge just below the point of entry, reestablish the normal hyphal dimensions, and continue to invade the host. As an exception to the above, the large rhizomorphs of soil-inhabiting root pathogens can often establish themselves on cork-covered host tissues by physical force.

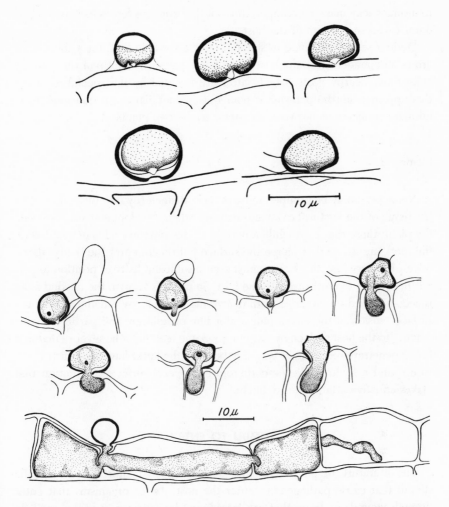

Fig. 5–2. Diagrams of direct penetration of poplar leaves by the fungus *Colletotrichum gloeosporioides. Top:* Abortive penetration attempts on a mature leaf. *Bottom:* Penetration and infection of a young leaf. (Marks *et al.,* 1965)

Flowering Plants

There are relatively few flowering plants that are of importance as plant pathogens, and as a consequence little attention has been centered upon them. Seeds, of course, constitute the initial inoculum. In the case of mistletoes, the seeds become affixed to the surface of the host by virtue of the surrounding sticky mass, whereupon the root that emerges forces its way into the outer cortex and xylem of the host.

Dodder seeds germinate in soil and form a seedling that, for a short time, grows independently of any host plant. Soon, however, the tip of the seedling coils about nearby hosts, which latter are invaded by the specialized roots that appear from the parasite at points of contact. These, in due time, form intimate connections between the stems of the two plants.

Nematodes

Nematodes may be grouped more or less satisfactorily into those that enter the tissue of the host as larvae and continue their development wholly inside the plant, those that feed while a portion of the anterior end is embedded (in the root), and those that pierce the surface but do not enter the tissues themselves. In every case the worms must secure sufficient fixity of position to permit the stylets to be thrust into the host. So far as is known, the needed fixity is accomplished by either or both of two maneuvers—by bracing against the surface tension of the enveloping water film or adjacent soil particles, or by holding to the host surface by the mouth. Some feel that whenever nematodes fail to penetrate root hairs it is simply because the latter have too sharp a curvature and a hydrophylic (and therefore slippery) surface, a situation that makes effective attachment unlikely.

STIMULI TO ENTRY

The literature of plant pathology shows repeated effort to identify the stimuli that cause pathogens to enter the host. As for organisms that enter through wounds or those that are introduced by a vector, it seems unlikely that there is any directional activity on the part of the invader. But when one considers the behavior of spores and germ tubes on the surface of an uninjured leaf or young stem—germination, formation of germ tube, and penetration through stomate or intact epidermis—it is equally difficult not to feel that there must be a definite, directional response. The issues are not yet fully resolved, but it seems likely that in some cases diffusable materials enter the surface liquids and hasten spore germination. It seems also that contact stimuli account for the formation of appressoria and infection pegs. Whether chemical stimuli or humidity gradients are also involved is less certain.

By various techniques, as by exposing host tissues enclosed in membrane bags to populations of motile fungus spores or nematodes, it has become clear that in at least some cases diffusable materials escape into the soil fluid and produce a gradient to which the organisms respond directionally.

There seems little question but that motile spores of soil fungi are specifically attracted to the roots of host plants, although the mechanisms are not all known and surely vary from one host-pathogen association to the next. In studies of *Pythium* infection of bentgrass, Kraft *et al.* (1967) not only followed the cytology of invasion, but observed that the zoospores tended to aggregate only on the region of root tip maturation, provided the roots were uninjured. If, on the other hand, physical injury had occurred or been intentionally in-

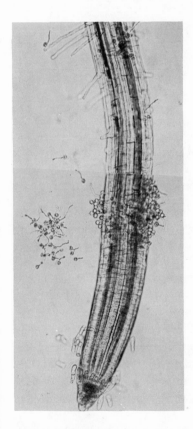 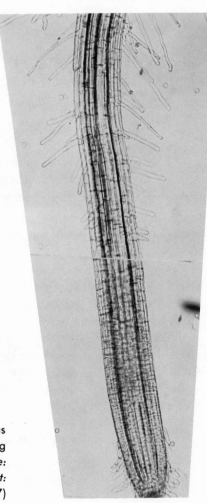

Fig. 5–3. Zoospores of the fungus *Pythium aphanidermatum* on young root of bentgrass seedlings. *Above:* Amassing at puncture injury. *Right:* Unwounded root. (Kraft *et al.*, 1967)

flicted, zoospores could be induced to mass at the site of injury on either the zone of elongation or of differentiation (Fig. 5–3).

An understanding of the relationship between host and pathogenic organism develops gradually as the result of accumulating data and observations. On the question of the behavior of directional response of motile cells and of growing fungus hyphae, Klisiewicz and Johnson (1968) have noted in studies of *Phytophthora* root rot of safflower that the zoospores encyst at random on undamaged tissue but tend to aggregate about wounds. Not only this, but when the encysted spores subsequently germinate the germ tubes are again directionally random on an unbroken surface, whereas they grow selectively toward a wound whenever one is present (Fig. 5–4).

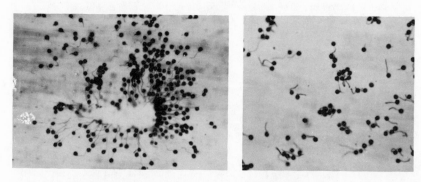

Fig. 5–4. Germination and growth of encysted zoospores of the fungus *Phytophthora drechsleri* on sunflower hypocotyls. *Left:* On injured surface. *Right:* On uninjured surface. (Klisiewicz and Johnson, 1968)

Generally, the apparent attraction of free-swimming motile spores to the surface of host roots has been thought to be in response to a chemical stimulus. While this may very well be true, the possibility of another stimulus has been raised by experiments on weak electric currents, carried out by Troutman and Wills (1964). Observations of motile spores in small glass observation cells indicate that they always moved toward a negative electrode, that they tended to collect in certain areas of the root surface in response to weak electric currents, and that the attachment of spores by their flagellae is effected by electrostatic forces (Fig. 5–5).

HOST RESISTANCE

The resistance-vulnerability-virulence problem can be handled in a variety of ways, none entirely satisfactory. The approach in this volume will be on a chronological basis. Thus we will consider here the interaction of host and pathogenic organism at the initial entry phase. Then in Chapters 6 and 7 will be found the predominantly morphologic and physiologic aspects, respectively, of the postentry establishment and extension of the developing association.

As for resistance of plants to penetration by pathogenic organisms, there are several specifics worth noting. In the first place, there is evidence that on occasion exudates from underlying epidermal cells have the effect of inhibiting spore germination or that diffusates otherwise act against the pathogen; the classic instance of smudge-resistant pink onions (Walker, 1923) is one of the better-known cases of this (Fig. 5–6).

Varieties of plants with a dense growth of hairs on the surface or whose leaves and fruit are covered with a conspicuous waxy bloom will have a functional kind of resistance by virtue of the fact that droplets of water form only with difficulty on the surface of the epidermis. This in turn reduces the likelihood of successful fungus or bacterial invasion.

One could argue that resistance to wounding itself is a form of resistance to entry; certainly this is the net effect. The more generally accepted view is that rapid formation of a suberized layer over surfaces exposed by injury, or a comparable reaction, is a specific feature of resistance to entry through these channels. In the same sense, unsuberized lenticels are penetrated by wound pathogens with little or no difficulty; suberized lenticels form an effective barrier.

As for stomates, it can be shown that significant differences exist between species and between varieties within a species. When, for example, the guard cells are so structured that a continuous water channel through the aperture is unlikely to form, bacterial entry will be much hindered. Or, again, in instances where fungus germ tubes cannot enter closed stomates, a functional kind of resistance is conveyed to those host species or varieties in which stomates are not open during periods favorable to spore germination.

Lastly, plants show marked differences in resistance to direct penetration, related to at least the following features: (1) the nature of the cuticle; (2) the type of epidermal cell walls; and (3) infrequently, possession of a hypodermis. So far as is presently known, pathogenic fungi do not usually have enzymes capable of hydrolyzing cuticle, although it must be assumed that a substantial number of saprophytes do. The very thickness of the cuticle is an important factor in resistance, as is the presence of minute splits or discontinuities. By the same token a thicker-than-average cell wall affords appreciable resistance, especially if the food reserves of the invading germ tube are marginal—a de-

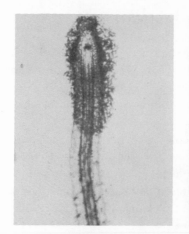
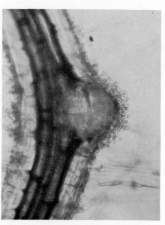
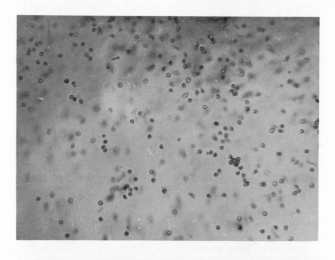
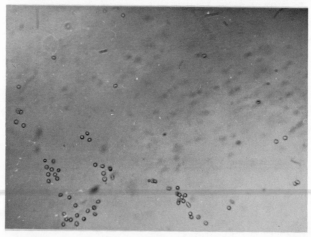

154

Fig. 5–5. Electrotaxis of the motile spores of the fungus *Phytophthora parasitica.*
Facing page—Top left: Mass of spores at root cap. *Top right:* Spores at wounded
area formed by eruption of small lateral root. *Middle:* Spores accumulating at
negative electrode. *Bottom:* Reduced number of spores after electrode shown in
middle photo became positive as a result of reversing the polarity of the system.
(Troutman and Wills, 1964)

---

fense that will only be supplemented if there is a hypodermis with thickened
cell walls.

If insects and nematodes are going to be resisted at all, it must be in the
entry phase. Presumably, characteristics of the host surface that are inhospitable to the insect—e.g., dense hairs (Fig. 5–7)—could be construed as a form
of resistance, as could the formation of cork layers or other physical barriers.
In the main, however, what resistance there is, as shown by greater preference for one host variety or another, seems almost always to be a chemical or
physiological interaction. At one extreme are plants that contain a compound

Fig. 5–6. Development of smudge on the fleshy scale of a yellow variety of onion,
in which the protective fungicidal effect of soluble substances in the dry outer
scales has failed because this layer split and exposed the vulnerable fleshy scale
underneath. (Hatfield *et al.*, 1948)

Fig. 5–7. Resistance to leafhopper resulting from hairiness of leaves, petioles, and stems. (Monteith and Hollowell, 1929)

distasteful to the insect or nematodes and are therefore directly repellent. At the other extreme are cases where *de facto* resistance to nematodes results from the fact that the host lacks a diffusate needed as a hatching factor in promoting larval emergence.

6

Symptom Expression

The present chapter emphasizes the more structural and morphological aspects of disease development, leaving to Chapter 7 most of the primarily physiological interactions. After all, once entry to the host has been accomplished, the critical issue is whether the invader extends itself through the host—how rapidly it does so, and with what effect. Behind the grosser and more readily visible effects of penetration and spread lie the biochemical phenomena of host-pathogen interactions. "Symptom expression," as here used, refers to those conspicuous changes that follow successful invasion.

Symptoms in themselves are of little interest, except as they signal the complex of events that results from the interaction of pathogen with host. They are the sum of pathogen impact and host response; they are not by any means directly translatable into degree of damage. Indeed, one of the most difficult aspects of assessing the seriousness of disease is to establish the correlation between a particular symptom and the amount of real damage it represents.

ESTABLISHMENT AND SPREAD

Gäumann (1950) phrases a number of questions that address themselves to what he calls the stages of disease: infection, incubation, disease proper, healing, and rehabilitation. Infection, to him, is subdivided into six areas:

- How does the pathogen reach the interior of the host?
- Under what external conditions does an infection occur?
- How long does the infection require to establish itself?
- What number of pathogens is necessary for an infection to "take"?
- By what route does the pathogen reach the interior of the host?
- How is the occupation of the host affected by the pathogen?

157

It is with the last of the above questions that we are now concerned. Characteristically, Gäumann in turn dissects the problem into five further questions:

- How does the pathogen proceed to colonize the host?
- By what route does the pathogen spread in the host?
- How long does it take the pathogen to spread in the host?
- How far does the pathogen spread in the host?
- Where does the pathogen go in the host?

Sites and Pathways of Invasion

With two exceptions—wound parasites and those pathogens that produce exotoxins that provide a constantly advancing zone of damaged cells and tissues—invading organisms utilize more or less specific pathways and occupy rather precise sites in the host.

At the one extreme are highly selective or highly specialized organisms, confined to very limited areas. Some occupy single cells but more characteristically they are to be found only in green parenchyma, or only in cambium, or only in phloem. Or they may be strictly on the surface, or subcuticular, or subepidermal. Again, a given pathogen may be identified with given portions of the plant—with anthers, ovaries, petals, leaves, or vascular tissue.

At the other extreme are pathogens that seem to be able to establish a beachhead indiscriminately, the site determined by the pure chance of initial contact, or that seem to be destructive to so many kinds of cells and tissues that no specificity can be detected. One aspect of the latter is the kind of involvement that has been dubbed "systemic"—meaning that the extent of the invasion is so great that most or all of the host individual is implicated. Systemic infections do not necessarily show systemic symptoms.

Pathogens not only occupy different sites in the host, they also invade via different pathways and spread by different mechanisms. To some extent proliferation of invaded cells contributes to spread, but by and large the means of extension are two: either the pathogen actively pervades the host or some element of the pathogen is passively carried about. In the first instance, spread may be from cell to cell by penetration of intervening walls, through plasmodesmata or pits, or by way of the intercellular materials. At times the vascular tissue provides a channel by which pathogens grow into previously noninvaded parts of the host. Rates of advance in these instances depend primarily on rates of pathogen growth.

Passive movement of pathogens occurs in the vascular tissues of the host and is therefore dependent mostly on the flow of substances in them. Bacteria and fungus spores, and virus particles, are often moved in this manner.

Electron microscopy (see Esau, 1967) has been very useful in making possible more precise information on the position of viruses within cells, the distribution of virus through the various tissues of the plant, pathways of movement, and sites and modes of entry. Suffice it to say here that there are few generalizations that may be made to hold for all viruses—from one virus to the next the differences are striking. But viruses do not, for the most part, successfully invade meristematic tissues and most, but not all, are unable to invade and multiply in nonliving tissues—several have been clearly shown to be characteristic of xylem cells, although presumably they do not actually multiply there.

The Nature of Symptoms

There is no unequivocal definition of symptoms, but the term conveniently refers to those readily demonstrated evidences of a diseased condition that appear after the establishment of the pathogen. Some distinguish between symptoms and signs, the latter term being used to designate such evidence of a pathogen as does not directly involve the host. Fungus spores appearing on the surface of a lesion would be an example of a "sign" of disease. Symptoms and signs, in the aggregate, are pretty much the means whereby the plant pathologist recognizes and distinguishes diseases in the field, just as the practicing physician diagnoses illness by weighing the evidence from a combination, a syndrome, of individual symptoms.

In the very early stages of involvement, at least, there are no symptoms in the usual sense of the word. As reactions set in, symptoms begin to appear. But under certain circumstances the evidence is misleading. In the X-virus of potato, for example, symptoms are so subtle that only inoculation of a more grossly affected species will clearly establish the presence of the virus.

Even more intriguing is the apparent recovery of a diseased host. The tobacco virus known as "streak," for instance, will when inoculated into a healthy plant induce marked symptoms, but new growth at the stem tips will appear as if it were completely healthy. Juice from this new tissue proves highly infectious to uninoculated plants, showing that the virus is still very much present.

A rather comparable circumstance is reflected in those situations where general involvement appears as a localized group of symptoms. The blossom-infection smuts, to cite one case, permeate the embryo of the developing seed and the greater part of the plant itself, yet by far the most conspicuous evidence (symptom) is the mass of black teliospores that are formed in place of the seeds at maturity. The antithesis of this situation, in many ways, would be a disease like *Fusarium* wilt of tomato, where the pathogen is confined mostly to the vascular system but where the obvious symptom is a wilting of the entire plant.

The plant pathologist must, when confronted with a new disease complex, be alert to the danger of assigning too quickly the cause thereof to an obviously likely source. This point is very nicely brought out by Nault *et al.* (1967) in their study of kernel red streak in the Midwest. The symptoms of the disease strongly suggest a virus etiology; indeed, early trials showed that a virus could be transmitted from diseased to healthy corn plants, a virus that later proved to be a strain of the wheat streak mosaic virus. More detailed and careful studies, using inbreds of either high or low resistance to this virus, proved that it was not in fact the causal agent of the disease. Interestingly enough, however, it was the vector of the wheat streak mosaic virus, the wheat curl mite, that proved to be the culprit. This insect, when placed on healthy corn and when the insects themselves were known to be virus-free, brought on typical symptoms of kernel red streak. Or when correlations were sought between numbers of mites and degrees of symptoms, they were strongly positive. Indications are that the phytotoxin is carried in the saliva of the insect.

The important relationship between symptom expression and environmental factors will be considered in Chapter 7.

Role of Pathogenic Organism

Fungi are able to penetrate and spread more effectively and in more diverse ways than are bacteria or viruses, although the latter rank high among plant pathogens in importance, abundance, and diversity. There is a general tendency to play down bacteria, nematodes, and vascular plants.

So far as bacteria are concerned, establishment and evocation of symptoms depend mostly on the production of diffusable metabolites that progressively break down the soft tissues and permit enlargement of the lesion. Spread within the host, at least for nonmotile forms, is either by passive transport or by accumulation of bacterial mass. In either case it is not possible to breach physical barriers and one or more of the natural channels must be utilized.

Nematodes, to the extent that they enter the host—many of the root-inhabiting species are ectoparasites—do so by active movement of the animal's body as it feeds on and invades tissues. They are, of course, very large in comparison with the individual cells of the host.

Dodder and the mistletoes, broomrape, witchweed, and other flowering plants are another major step up the size scale from the nematodes. Modified root systems extend into the host tissues and, when they establish themselves on perennial species, are further buried by the radial growth of the host.

That two pathogenic entities can produce a combined effect greater than either by itself has been established in a number of instances—perhaps the double-virus disease known as tomato streak is as well known as any, but there are others. When the two pathogens are biologically rather distant from each other the situation is even more intriguing. Nitzany (1966) has provided

Fig. 6–1. Bacterial wilt of sweet corn, showing early streaking of the foliage, followed by severe wilting and death. (Courtesy of Benjamin Koehler)

an interesting case in studies of cucumber wilt in Israel, where he finds the symptoms very much more pronounced when virus-infested plants are grown on contaminated soil—the virus in this case is cucumber mosaic and the soil pathogen a species of *Pythium*. The effect can be achieved either by inoculating cucumbers with virus, provided they are growing in *Pythium*-infested soil or by the reverse approach, adding *Pythium*-infested soil to plots of cucumbers bearing the virus.

MORPHOLOGICAL CONSEQUENCES OF INVASION

The impact of invading pathogens is not a matter of structural *or* functional manifestations; it is a complexly interwoven pattern of both. Of these, the predominantly morphological are singled out for attention here. In one sense the morphological consequences of invasion might be thought of as the visible or gross symptoms of disease, whereas the physiological effects are the less obvious ones.

Just where to place that broad category of symptoms commonly called wilting is rather a question. The visible effect is clearly morphological in the sense that the structure of the plant is markedly altered, but there need be no immediate change in the tissues and to a large extent the mechanisms leading to wilting are more physiological than morphological. In the bacterial wilt of sweet corn, for example, the first symptoms are a streaking of the leaves and only after the disease is well along do the plants visibly wilt (Fig. 6–1). In this case, of course, and unlike the wilting that results from a transient inadequacy of water, the wilt is irreversible.

Necrosis

The first symptom to catch attention is the destruction of tissues by the less delicately adjusted types of pathogens, in contrast to the obligate parasites, where the characteristic host-pathogen interaction is most often of the non-necrotic type.

Tissue breakdown depends on the detailed nature of the particular tissue in question. Plants contain an impressive array of highly specialized cells arranged in complex patterns—from young, thin-walled, undifferentiated parenchyma to thick-walled, lignified, nonliving fibers. At the same time, one has to take into account the ubiquity, diversity, and specificity of enzymes—those substances that mediate virtually every event in the machinery of the cell, usually through a series of sequential biological transformations.

At the onset of symptom expression, then, the host presents a chemically and physically diverse array of tissues, cells, and cell constituents. The pathogen is served by an impressive arsenal of enzymes and enzyme complexes. If necrosis is to take place, it depends on whether the pathogen possesses, in active form, the enzymes necessary to bring it about.

What processes and events, in the aggregate, constitute necrosis? At least the following must be taken into account:

- Degradation of pectic substances of the cell wall and middle lamella, leading to loss of coherence in soft tissues as cells become detached from adjoining cells
- Hydrolysis of cellulose, resulting in destruction of the cell wall proper and penetration of cells by other than physical means
- Decomposition of lignin in hard tissues, by a comparatively few species of wood rot fungi
- Destruction of the living protoplasm contents of the cells

By no means all pathogens possess the enzyme armament to perform all of these feats. Most bacteria and fungi responsible for soft rots and for necrotic lesions of root, stem, and leaf almost certainly secrete enzymes capable of breaking down the pectic, and very often the cellulosic, components of cell walls. Most act through toxin-like substances to kill the cells themselves and, presumably, additional enzyme systems are brought into play in the utilization of cell contents.

Traditionally, wood rot fungi have been classed, on the basis of symptoms, into "white rots" (those having most pronounced effect on lignin) and "brown rots" (those showing affinity for cellulose). It now appears that the distinction is overly simple and that a greater variability than this actually pertains, though the major distinction remains.

Necrotic lesions are characteristic of bacteria and fungi, but not of the other major categories of plant-pathogenic organisms, unless one includes the familiar "hypersensitive" reaction that is so prominently a feature of certain host-virus associations. Where tissue degeneration does occur following the attack of insects or nematodes it is usually attributable to a bacterium or fungus carried as a contaminant, so to speak, of the active agent, or to its having utilized the inroads of the animal as a portal through which to gain access.

Growth Effects

In marked contrast to the crude impact of pathogens that bring about necrosis are the organisms whose most conspicuous effect is to alter the growth of the host. Because biologists know so much less than they would like to about growth and morphogenesis in normal, healthy plants the effect of pathogens is all the more difficult and challenging.

Some of the events related to growth in plants are reasonably well understood. There is a great deal of data on nuclear and cell division, on cell enlargement, on fabrication of cell wall and protoplasm, and on the array of events that is often summed up as "cell differentiation." What is not at all clear is the mechanism by which the many isolated phenomena are programmed into an integrated series of steps, resulting in an organism with a consistent and recognizable pattern—a characteristic form. It is the forces and events responsible for morphogenesis that are largely unknown.

Until imaginative new insights are developed, there are few ways to probe the complexities of morphogenesis, but one can think of three that do provide useful data:

- Intensive study of comparatively very simple organisms, such as the cellular slime molds, in the hope that the systems operative at this level will be easier to decipher
- Observation of the effect of imposed stresses, i.e., the recovery and repair responses to injuries inflicted by the investigator
- Study of abnormalities in plants, as clues to what is normal growth

Growth effects of pathogens lie within the second and third categories above. As a consequence they have significance above and beyond the immediate consideration of disease damage. They can, hopefully, contribute to an eventual understanding of growth phenomena, per se. One of the aspects of growth and differentiation that seems to be consistent, so far as present observations go, is the extent to which the process becomes increasingly irreversible as time passes. That is, the farther along a given process has moved along a particular developmental pathway, the more unlikely and difficult it is to switch to an alternative mode.

Mechanisms of Growth Effects.   Within limits one can generalize as to the mechanisms leading to growth effects produced by pathogen invasion. Normal plants, free of pathogens, will respond to stimuli and will develop in their characteristic way as a result of the net effect of biologically active substances variously called hormones, growth regulators, and so on. Much good work has been done on this aspect of plant physiology, although a considerable number of unanswered questions remain. Enough data are at hand to say that while some of these growth regulators—e.g., the auxins—play several different roles, for the most part compounds of this kind are highly specific. Not only are they specific, but there are an impressive number of different ones already isolated or identified. The actual growth response of the plant is usually the result of the complementary, or mutually antagonistic, action of two or more such substances.

Although the mechanisms do not necessarily operate alone, and though much yet remains to be discovered, pathogens can be seen to affect the host in at least the following ways:

- By influencing the amounts of naturally occurring growth regulators in the host plant
- By changing the nature of the host cells' response to the concentration of growth substances present
- By forming extraneous compounds that, when released into the host, produce effects similar to those of naturally occurring substances

It would be illogical to consider changes that occur because of inadequate food or water—e.g., stunting that results from pathogenic destruction of the chlorophyll-bearing tissues—as a growth response in the present context.

Kinds of Effects.   A. C. Braun (1959), long a student of abnormal growth patterns in plants, has published a number of papers dealing with these matters, especially with the plant-pathological aspects of growth. He distinguishes first those changes that he calls "harmonious"—wherein the familiar form of the host is retained, while growth is either accelerated or depressed—and those he terms "amorphous"—derived from substantial qualitative changes in the host cells and tissues and the resumption of undifferentiated growth.

In the first category one encounters a number of the better known symptoms of disease, including the gibberellin effect—excessive stem elongation—on rice seedlings attacked by *Fusarium*, epinastic response of leaves, leaf curls, the formation of adventitious roots and witches-brooms, and modifications of flowers and fruiting structures.

In dealing with amorphous growth changes, Braun makes a distinction that is analogous to the physicians' use of the terms benign and malignant in human medicine. On the one hand—as evidenced by the galls resulting from insect activity or the invasion of the root-knot nematode or clubroot fungus—are the self-limiting types of overgrowths that, for some reason or other, do not progress beyond a given point. On the other hand are cancer-like growths that seem to have no self-limiting mechanisms. By far the best known and most intensively studied of this latter category of diseases is bacterial crown gall, which has the capacity to continue growth after tissues are freed of the causal bacterium. It may be that the affected cells take on the synthesis of hormones related to cell enlargement and cell differentiation in markedly increased amounts. A rather less well-known, virus-induced neoplasm is caused by Black's wound tumor virus, which seems to result when a susceptible, viruliferous host is subject to wounding.

STRUCTURAL RESISTANCE

While the concept of structural resistance as here used focuses on primarily morphological attributes of the host, it excludes the matter of disease escape, even though some instances of the latter are morphological in the sense that they depend on growth habit, duration of the susceptible phase, or like matters.

Resistance to penetration depends on those characteristics that tend to prevent invasion at the very outset, and rely on the structure of the epidermis and stomates. Resistance to encroachment beyond that point depends on a rather more complex array of factors, some of which are routinely present in the host, others elicited in direct response to the invasion of the pathogenic organism. The terms static and dynamic have been used to express this distinction.

Static Factors

Most attributes that can fairly be classified as static factors have to do with the nature of the cell wall. Both thickness and resistance to mechanical forces are important, augmented by the deposition of lignin in at least a substantial number of cases. As a generalized instance of differences between tissues that are almost wholly attributable to differences in the nature of the cell walls, one might cite the strikingly greater susceptibility of sapwood than of heartwood to invasion by fungi. Another example is the delimiting role of sclerenchymatous tissue in the stems and leaves of rust-infected cereals. Here, both macroscopically and microscopically, the pathogen can be clearly seen to be confined to the parenchyma tissues, with the result that the shape of the pustules is determined quite precisely on just this basis.

It can hardly be argued, however, that the physical nature of the host, alone, is very often crucial in determining whether or not an invading pathogen will become established and spread effectively. It is those changes that result from a more or less specific reaction to the pathogen that are more likely to be meaningful.

Induced Morphologic Resistance

The more striking instances of structural resistance are usually those that develop out of a reaction to invasion. Most are not clearly distinct from "physiological" effects, but do have at least a few clearly visible attributes. They may be considered under two subheadings: (1) demarcations, and (2) cell wall reactions.

In the first category, the crux of the response lies in the formation of a barrier in advance of the extending pathogen, a layer of suberized cells through which it does not successfully advance, or a deposit of wound gum capable of walling off the attack. The cork layer, particularly in stem tissues, forms the kind of canker characteristic of anthracnose diseases, of the chestnut blight, and others. In leaves, if accompanied by the formation of an abscission layer, the result is a "shot-hole" syndrome—small portions of necrotic tissue drop from the leaf and leave it perforated as by a shotgun blast. By contrast, abscission of the entire leaf follows after the apparently modest damage caused by such other leaf pathogens as *Septoria*.

A number of hosts, rather than forming cork layers, are prone to react by secreting rather large quantities of gummy substances; this material by itself has the capacity to impede, to a very considerable degree, further advance by the pathogen.

Less widely known because less conspicuous are the responses of cell walls to individual fungus hyphae. In this case the wall, rather than suffering penetration, increases in thickness, often forming an encasement over the surface of the hypha that may extend as an elongated protuberance within the cell. At times cellulose is the predominant constituent; at other times callose, suberin, or even lignin is present in significant amounts. Whatever the composition, there seems to be little doubt of the effectiveness, at times, of this resistance mechanism.

It is far easier to show that a given host plant is susceptible or resistant to a given pathogenic organism than to discover the mechanism of that response. We do have a number of particular studies that suggest answers to the question (see Beckman, 1966). In the case of vascular wilts, for example, there is evidence to suggest that the difference between a resistant and susceptible variety depends upon the extent to which the mobile inoculum is screened out of the transpiration stream, aided by gel formation and, eventually, the development of tyloses. Beckman goes on to propose a scheme of biochemical interactions between host and parasite that are diagrammed in the accompanying figure (Fig. 6–2).

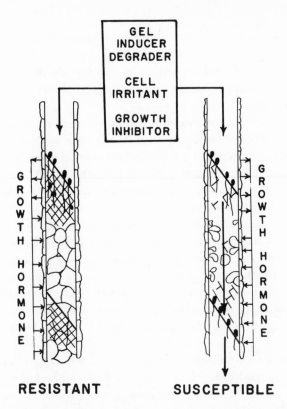

Fig. 6–2. Diagram representing one scheme of interacting metabolites of host and parasite that act to produce a resistant or a susceptible reaction. (Beckman, 1966)

Not infrequently, age of a host plant or stage of maturity of a plant part will greatly influence its susceptibility to invasion by a pathogenic organism. Papaya, for example, characteristically shows lesions of anthracnose only after the fruit are ripening, immature fruit being largely immune to invasion. In studying this phenomenon, Stanghellini and Aragaki (1966) found that the resistance of immature fruit was correlated with the capacity of the wounded fruit to form a lignified periderm. If the fruit were immature, but detached from the plant, or if it were mature, the ability to form periderm was apparently not present. Unwounded fruit, even though inoculated and even though the inoculum had developed and formed appressoria, failed to show signs of infection; whether callose deposits in the vicinity of the appressoria were significant has not yet been determined in their studies.

HYPERSENSITIVITY

There are few more striking developments following pathogen invasion than the sudden appearance of localized necrotic lesions that have the effect of precluding more extensive damage (Fig. 6–3). From a practical standpoint this hypersensitivity has been utilized as a most valuable form of disease resistance, much sought after by plant breeders for incorporation into new horticultural varieties of crop plants.

One of the well-documented instances of hypersensitivity is the reaction of a wild species of *Nicotiana* (*N. glutinosa*) to the highly infectious tobacco mosaic virus. In host varieties that are susceptible to this virus symptoms are characteristically systemic and productivity of the plant is sharply reduced. When the gene from *N. glutinosa* is incorporated into cultivated tobacco, inoculation with the virus results in at most a few scattered necrotic spots appearing in the vicinity of the inoculation several days later. No further encroachment of the virus takes place. From an experimental point of view, the formation of local lesions has also proven to be a very valuable bioassay technique that has been put to use in a wide array of different situations.

Viruses and fungi are especially likely to elicit hypersensitive reactions, although a few bacteria and even insects have been cited in the literature. If the response were only to obligate pathogens—rusts, powdery mildews, and

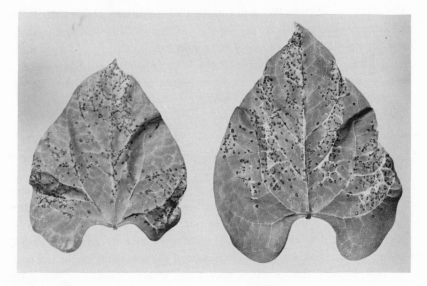

Fig. 6–3. Local lesions produced by hypersensitive reaction of bean leaves to southern bean mosaic virus. (Zaumeyer and Thomas, 1948)

viruses—it would be almost too easy to conclude that the cessation of pathogen growth was strictly the result of nutritional stress. After all, obligately
parasitic organisms by definition do not grow in killed tissues. But other
pathogens, particularly fungi that grow readily on artificial media, and hence
presumably on necrotic tissue, also cause hypersensitive reactions. The phenomenon seems to be substantially more complicated than just an enhanced
sensitivity leading to death of host cells and starvation of the pathogen.

Certain conspicuous attributes of hypersensitivity are reasonably well established:

- Visible events are dramatic and rapid.
- The phenomenon is not restricted to obligate parasites and is not nec-
  essarily a purely nutritional relationship.
- There is a characteristic early loss of turgor, probably linked to loss of
  cell membrane selectivity.
- It is associated with a measurable rise in respiratory rate.

To K. O. Müller, who has devised a simple but elegant experimental technique and who has published extensively on the topic, one of the key phases
of the hypersensitive response is the elaboration by the host of an antitoxic
substance for which he has coined the term "phytoalexin." If his evidence
stands the test of time, hypersensitivity becomes a precise, mostly biochemical reaction between closely interrelated organisms.

The relation between the concentration of substances elaborated by the
host that are antagonistic to pathogenic microorganisms—generally phytoalexins, though there is a diversity of compounds involved—and host resistance to disease is often not direct. Bell (1969), in studying the formation of
gossypol-related substances produced in cotton when invaded by the wilt
pathogen, *Verticillium albo-atrum*, found that both virulent and nonvirulent
strains induced the host to react in this way. Rather, resistance seemed to depend on the speed with which a concentration sufficient to be wholly fungis-
tatic was formed at the invasion site. If this occurred promptly, invasion was
halted, but if the build-up was delayed, then the parasite can move to new
sites and accomplish a highly successful involvement with the host. The nonvirulent pathogen and resistant host, then, are measures of speed of reaction
rather than total amount of phytoalexin produced.

The very fact that environmental conditions markedly affect the hypersensitive reaction stands as further evidence of the specificity of the phenomenon. Temperature change alone may bring about a complete shift from
local to systemic symptoms in, say, a virus disease, or cause a marked shift
in the reaction of established test varieties of wheat to the stem rust fungus.

7

Physiology of Host-Pathogen Interaction

In the 1960's, the pendulum of biology swung very much to the side of molecular biology—a modern euphemism for biochemistry—and with that trend came increased interest in and awareness of the metabolic events that lie behind biological phenomena of all kinds. The physiology of disease is no exception; disease symptoms are but the outward manifestation of the changes and interactions at molecular levels. When two organisms—host and pathogen—come into the close association characteristic of disease it is not even certain that their respective metabolisms remain unchanged; it could well be that there are new considerations that are unique to the diseased state.

It must be recognized at the outset that the association of pathogen and host that results in disease is very much the exception, not the rule. Viruses, bacteria and fungi, and nematodes do not attack plants ubiquitously and it is not just a stroke of luck when hosts are encountered that do not fall victim. Because disease is "bad luck" and health is good fortune—and because there seem to be an almost overwhelming number of diseases about which to be on guard—it is well nigh impossible to realize that most plants, most of the time, do *not* react to most microorganisms. The key, or keys, to pathogenicity when finally discovered will lie in that rare set of circumstances that leads to disease. The resistant host is not a special case, it is the norm. The diseased individual is the one that is peculiar.

One can but speculate on where the missing keys lie. Some feel that it is to be found in the critical stage of invasion and establishment—that this is the point of greatest hazard for the invader. Because no clearly superior thesis has been developed thus far, it deserves to be adopted tentatively until such time as more evidence is available.

PHYSIOLOGY OF PARASITISM

Embodied in the phrase "physiology of parasitism" are the fundamental reactions between host and pathogenic organism that lead to demonstrable disease. It has at least three aspects.

Entry and Establishment

The biology of the pathogen is directly related to its mode of entry. Viruses must rely on certain modes of entry. Bacteria, being different from viruses, enter by different avenues and by different means. Thus each kind of pathogen has strengths and vulnerabilities, operates within certain limitations set by its characteristics. What, then, are some of the biochemical events that characterize the host-pathogen relationship?

Prior to penetration there are some undoubted interactions between host and pathogen, especially in the fungi, which are most studied and best known. The influences of the host are many. Spore germination, for example, is sometimes stimulated by host exudates, although in the case of soil-inhabiting fungi this phenomenon seems better explained as removal of a soil-induced fungistasis than as a direct stimulation. Conversely, spore germination may be inhibited by resistant host varieties. Not only germination, but directional response of swimming zoospores, can be shown to result from a chemotropic mechanism, as seems also to be true of pathogenic nematodes.

As between soil and airborne fungi, Flentje (1959) points out what may be a very significant difference in the behavior of infection hyphae. The directional growth of these hyphae, and particularly the morphologic changes that give rise to appressoria or appressoria-like structures, seems to be mediated by a host-derived exudate in the soil environment, but to be induced by physical (i.e. contact) stimuli on the above-ground host surface. He postulates that each pattern has important survival value for the pathogen concerned. In the first instance pathogens would tend to develop appressoria only when in contact with a host surface rather than with any of what must be a very large array of other surfaces encountered. Airborne pathogens, on the contrary, destined as they are to encounter only a single site, stand the best chance of survival if they form appressoria and attempt entry in every instance of contact.

Still another insight into the mechanisms that seem to account for the action of soil organic amendments on the microflora is provided by Owens et al. (1969) in their investigation of a number of plant volatiles that have the effect of stimulating the respiration and growth of microorganisms. In a number of cases the effect is to produce a rise in the respiration rate, followed by an increase in numbers of both bacteria and fungi. Compounds such as acetaldehyde, isobutylaldehyde, methanol, and ethanol were identified among the active substances; of the assemblage, acetaldehyde was particularly effective. Not infrequently, a particular volatile brought about more pronounced respiratory and growth changes in one group of microorganisms than another. Not only were competing species stimulated to grow more rapidly, but several of the substances tested also had the effect of bringing pathogenic species out of dormancy. Whether direct application of the more effective chemicals has the potential of being used in practical disease control is unsettled at this juncture.

Most responses of potential pathogens are less precise than that just noted. Germinating seeds, for example, leak substantial amounts of carbohydrates, amino acids, etc., into the soil, with attendant effects on spores and hyphal growth. Various nutrients and inorganic substances have been shown to affect appressorium formation in foliage-attacking fungi, although much remains to be done on this problem.

As for viruses, they too seem to escape from root systems. The nature of viruses being what it is, it took quite some time before the reality of transmission in soil was fully recognized—we now know that several important plant viruses are harbored and moved from plant to plant in soil by vectors of one or more groups. What is even less well known than the transmission of viruses in soil is that they are released from roots in appreciable amounts wholly independent of the vector itself (see P. R. Smith *et al.*, 1969). The tobacco necrosis virus, for example, moves into the soil from roots and can then be transmitted by the zoospores of the vector, *Olpidium*. But so, apparently, can other viruses be released from systemically infected hosts—cucumber necrosis, petunia asteroid mosaic, tomato bushy stunt, tobacco mosaic, and southern bean mosaic. Release, in at least some of these instances, will occur in the absence of living organisms in the soil, suggesting that it is not the result of injury. On the other hand, there is little or no reason to believe that the viruses escape from living cells. More likely they move into the soil with the decay or dissolution of cells sloughed off in the normal maturation of the root. In moist soil viruses persist for several weeks, whereas in dry soils they cannot be detected after much shorter periods. In any event, soil-inhabiting vectors seem capable of recovering virus from soils long after their detection by more direct methods has ceased to be successful. It is probably worth noting that viruses need not be among the potentially soil-borne group to be released—witness the southern bean mosaic virus as a case in point.

In many ways the events leading up to penetration by fungi are more puzzling than is penetration itself. On the basis of present evidence the latter entails a fairly straightforward physical puncturing of the cuticle, plus enzymatic dissolution of the cellulosic and pectic components of the cell wall. By contrast, many uncertainties remain as to what happens, at the molecular level, that leads to directional response of bacteria, fungi, and nematodes to host surfaces and to the formation of appressoria and infection pegs.

Obligate Parasitism

The relationship that exists between host and pathogenic organism under conditions of obligate parasitism is very striking. Obligate parasites are those organisms—viruses, some fungi and nematodes—that no one has as yet been able to culture under conditions other than on living susceptible host varieties. So far as viruses are concerned, there seems to be general agreement that their synthesis requires the machinery of the host cell and that the virus itself has not the necessary enzymes to replicate itself in a nonliving environment—certainly not in the absence of enzyme systems from outside sources. As for nematodes, it is very difficult to be certain. Until fairly recently relatively little attention has been devoted to these forms, despite a marked upsurge in interest and activity. The preponderance of effort has been in the areas of symptomatology, disease control, pathogen morphology, and systematics. It will take much further effort before pure culture techniques are well established, although preliminary reports are already to be found in the literature.

Obligately parasitic fungi are well known, much studied, and economically important. Not infrequently pathogens long accepted as obligate parasites—on the basis that they could not be grown in culture—have been eventually so grown successfully and hence dropped from the list (e.g. the late blight of potato pathogen). It is therefore in many ways a rather artificial distinction. Thus far, three important groups of fungus pathogens, the rusts, the downy mildews, and the powdery mildews have mostly defied efforts to grow them other than on the host, although there are indications of success from time to time.

The rust fungi have been for many years symbolic of the inability of investigators to grow obligate parasites in culture, but when the trick was finally turned, the success was virtually complete. Williams *et al.* (1967) were not only able to show vegetative growth, but far more remarkable, induced cultures of stem rust of wheat to produce numbers of spores (see Fig. 7–1) and to demonstrate the pathogenicity of both mycelia and spores.

As the years go by, more and more of the fungi that have traditionally been considered obligate parasites are shown to be amenable to growth in artificial culture. The late blight organism, *Phytophthora infestans*, is now routinely carried in the laboratory, whereas once it was regarded as impossible to do so. But, as noted above, the most dramatic success was the publication in 1966 of the culture of wheat rust uredospores in the laboratory (see Scott and Maclean, 1969).

In the early 1950's Cutter had done extensive experiments with the apple rust fungus in an effort to induce the mycelium to grow in tissue culture and on artificial media, but although he seems to have been occasionally successful, later workers were unable to duplicate his work. It remained for Williams and his colleagues, in Australia, to achieve successful growth of stem rust cultures from uredospores, after many others had tried and failed. At the same time it is by no means wholly clear why they succeeded where their predecessors failed, although they apparently laid great stress on avoiding contamination, thereby making it possible to hold the inoculated media for extensive periods of time. That the resulting colonies are indeed the pathogen is clearly demonstrated not only by the fact that they developed typical spores of the species, but that material taken from the cultures is capable of inducing pustules on inoculated host plants. From these inoculated plants one can, in turn, establish a second axenic culture.

Scott and Maclean do not profess to know precisely why the rusts behave as they do in their saprophytic phase, but surmise that part of the complex genetic control characteristic of the parasitic phase is lost. In their terms: "One could thus expect infection to be associated with successive repression of those parts of the sporeling genome not required for parasitic growth [after the metabolic syntheses necessary for spore germination, germ tube elongation, and differentiation have been accomplished] . . . We suggest that a different expression of the fungal genome is necessary for saprophytic growth to occur . . . The many varied forms of growth observed in axenic cultures (e.g., sectoring, nuclear content, aberrantly produced spores, the extent of vegetative growth, and the occurrence of staling) can all be explained by loss of some of the metabolic control associated with parasitic growth."

Obligate parasites produce a minimum of morphologic change in the host, a fact that has been considered by many as evidence of a highly evolved state of parasitism. The pathogen seems to be in close balance with the host, and to produce symptoms that are less drastic, on the whole, than those produced by organisms that indiscriminately destroy large segments of the invaded plants.

Obligate parasites have, also, a more precise histological and cytological relation to their hosts than do other microorganisms. A most striking feature is the formation of haustoria, which are invaginations of the host cell with which

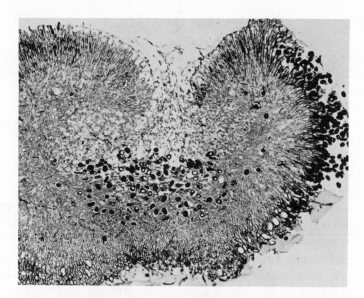

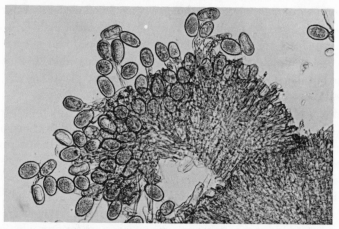

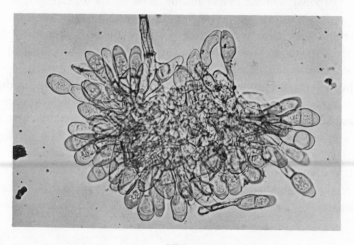

the pathogen seems to establish an exceedingly intimate, though indirect, connection. Haustoria do not form *in vitro* except to a very limited and insignificant degree, and it has been repeatedly postulated that this is the chief reason why fungi of this type cannot be cultured. Additional evidence of the importance of haustoria shows up in electron micrographs of these structures that show mitochondria literally packed into the haustorial swellings. From what we know of the role of mitochondria in respiratory activity this evidence strongly suggests that the haustoria are very active metabolically.

Allen (1959), among others, has discussed the details of interaction between obligate parasites and their hosts. Three major events can be identified: increased respiration, mobilization of materials and an accumulation at the site of the lesion, and shifts in the pathways of carbohydrate utilization. No entirely satisfactory way of separating the metabolism of the host from that of the pathogen has been found although techniques that remove the predominantly superficial mycelium—of the powdery mildews in this case—or that measure uptake of radioactively tagged materials, will uncover very useful clues.

It seems clear that the respiration of the host itself is materially stepped up and that this change, with an accompanying increase in synthetic activity, occurs well before the period of maximum development of the pathogen itself. Materials tend therefore to accumulate in the immediate vicinity of the lesion or "infection court" as the combined effect of redistribution and accelerated synthesis.

Much of the relationship between pathogenic organisms and host remains to be discovered and, of course, it may differ appreciably from one association to the next. But it seems generally true that the changes intensify as the pathogen extends itself and that the welfare of the pathogen is enhanced thereby. This last is at least indicated by observations that maleic hydrazide, which tends to break down rust resistance, has some of the same metabolic effect on inoculated plants as is observed in actual disease studies.

Also associated with obligate parasitism is an accumulation of auxins and a shift to direct oxidative utilization of carbohydrate. In Allen's opinion, the latter represents a shift of host metabolism toward pathways more like those that are utilized by the pathogen. This could be yet another measure of the increasing closeness of fit in the evolution of this very special kind of host-

---

Fig. 7–1. The rust *Puccinia graminis tritici* in pure culture. *Top of facing page:* Section through stroma showing original inoculum in center and spore-forming layer surrounding it. *Middle:* Uredospores formed in culture. *Bottom:* Teliospores formed in culture. (Williams *et al.,* 1967)

pathogen interaction. In any event it is not difficult to convince oneself that these changes, by which the pathogen takes advantage of regulating mechanisms inherent in the host, are of direct value to the nutrition of the pathogen.

Enzymes and Toxins

There remains one more facet of host-pathogen interaction that deserves comment—the role of enzymes and toxins. To do so is to recognize a field of research activity that has captured the interest of increasing numbers of investigators. Significant results are hard to come by, scattered, and often equivocal, but this is the kind of gradual advance that is rather the norm in scientific endeavor.

"Toxin," as the term is used in plant pathology, covers a substantial array of substances. It is almost as though it signified any pathogen metabolite that seems detrimental to the host plant. As a practical matter the term here is operationally limited to those pathogen metabolites that are harmful to the host in its interaction with the pathogen and that are not identifiable as enzymes. As diverse as enzymes may be, the "toxin" category is even more of a catch-all group and includes substances with only the remotest affiliation to each other.

One group of toxins—those eliciting primarily growth responses in the host, and hence presumed to be of an auxin-like nature—have already been commented upon. We are more immediately concerned here with the impact of substances associated with facultative parasites and especially with wilting, chlorosis, death of cells, tissue browning—common and conspicuous symptoms of familiar diseases.

The very names that many toxins bear attest to how little we know of them: lycomarasmin, piricularin, fusaric acid, diaporthin. Each of these terms is no more than a modification of the name of pathogen or host with which it has been associated. Very often a chemically uncharacterized substance is initially isolated, perhaps from culture filtrate, and experiments performed with the crude extract. Small wonder that for some we have only the most general picture of their composition and mode of action. Despite all this, useful characteristics can be identified and distinctions established, certain mechanisms suggested, and a few difficulties pointed out.

Characteristics of Toxins.   Many toxins seem to be organic compounds, often acids or substances that yield acids upon hydrolysis—some contain nitrogen, others are nitrogen-free, a few may actually be proteins. Still others are glucosans and related compounds.

There are rather striking differences between those substances whose action is general, in the sense that it affects more or less uniformly a substantial number of host species or varieties tested, and those that are highly selective; the latter have been called "host-specific" and are distinctly less common. By far the best known is the toxin produced by *Helminthosporium victoriae*, causal agent of the Victoria blight of oats, which is damaging only to varieties carrying this single-gene susceptibility. Extensive studies have shown that this substance is formed by linkage of a peptide fraction and an amine. The suggestion is made (Braun and Pringle, 1959) that toxicity can be attributed to the amine fraction (victoxinine), the specific enhancement of the effect due to the peptide fraction, possibly by its role in increasing the ease with which the linked compound enters the cells.

Mechanisms of Action of Toxins.   One of the most thoroughly studied effects of toxins is that associated with wilt diseases, certain general aspects of which are noted in a later section. The immediate question at this point is to examine in what way or ways the effect comes about. Setting aside for the moment the distinct possibility of enzymatic degradation of cell wall materials, it appears that substances of the lycomarismin, fusaric acid type act by chelating such metallic ions as iron and copper. Others—the high-molecular-weight glucosans—may well exact their toll by physically slowing passage of water through the xylem tissues.

A second action of toxins, or so it seems, is to speed senescence and thus to render the host more than ordinarily susceptible to the attack of pathogenic fungi. A third is to affect adversely the selectivity of the plasma membrane.

Finally, in the case of the toxin of the tobacco wildfire bacterium, a clear-cut mechanism of action has been elucidated. Here the toxin is shown to be a structural analog of one of the essential amino acids, methionine, and hence to act as an antimetabolite.

The foregoing listings by no means represent the full range of toxic mechanisms. The simple truth is that for most of the effects there is as yet no fully satisfactory information. And as earlier noted, growth-regulating compounds, and those substances such as ethylene whose effects seem to be brought about through the growth regulator pathway, are expressly excluded. The discussion omits also the interactions of obligate parasites and hosts that lead to respiratory acceleration.

Difficulties in Research on Toxins.   There is an obvious and continuing problem in trying to isolate toxic materials in sufficient quantity to examine them conveniently, to so purify the crude extracts that precise analysis becomes possible, and then to carry out the often tedious step-by-step characterization of the substance.

A second difficulty is to correlate toxic compounds as recovered from the culture filtrates of bacteria and fungi with substances presumed to be acting in the host plant. In relatively few instances has it been possible to extract the toxin from the host tissues and then, by reintroduction, to duplicate the disease syndrome. Failure to do so cannot be accepted as proof that the substance in question is not the causal agent. It may have become bound to some reactive site, may be so labile as to have been altered during processing, or may be effective in concentrations other than that at which the host was challenged. By and large, one could say that to isolate and reintroduce a substance successfully is strong positive evidence of a causal relationship, but that failure has scarcely any weight on the negative side.

Enzymes

Although too often overlooked, in our preoccupation with the host-pathogen interaction, the simple fact is that most microorganisms cannot attack most crop plants—or vascular plants in general, for that matter. It is not the phenomenon of resistance, then, but the phenomenon of susceptibility that is the more nearly unique. The question naturally arises just what is the key to the ability of microorganisms to succeed on a given host. To this Albersheim et al. (1969) suggest that in a large number of cases it is an interaction between the pathogen and the carbohydrates of the host that, in turn, determines whether the pathogen can or cannot produce the enzymes needed to degrade the cell walls themselves. In support of this view they offer the argument that every instance thus far examined demonstrates that the pathogen can produce enzymes that attack the polysaccharides of cell walls, and that the variety these enzymes show is very great indeed.

Two general categories of enzymes are involved in the impact of pathogenic organisms on host plants: the cellulases and those acting on pectic compounds. In the past, attention has tended to focus on the latter, perhaps because the initial effects are rather more dramatic. If one takes into account not only the middle lamella but the pectic components of the cell wall proper, there are a number of chemically different substances to be dealt with: pectates of calcium and magnesium, pectin itself, pectic acid, protopectin, and so on. There are, predictably, specific enzymes with the capacity to transform these substances in one way or another.

To generalize, this family of enzymes serves to macerate tissues by destruction of the cell wall lamellae and very likely also to break down the pectic matrix of the walls themselves. Tissue so affected becomes disorganized and the cells die. It is still not entirely clear whether pectic enzymes are directly responsible for cell death or whether death results primarily from the destruction of tissue coherence. In either case, there is no doubt as to the causal role of enzymes in the steps leading to this eventuality.

Tissue damage is quite the most striking effect of pectic enzymes. They have been implicated, additionally, in some aspects of vascular wilt diseases. According to this latter view, hydrolysis of cell wall materials not only releases large-molecule polymers into the xylem fluids and thus inhibits flow, but weakens pit membranes and promotes tylosis formation, a frequent concomitant of wilt-affected plants. Tissue browning, which so often accompanies wilting, appears to result from the oxidation of phenolic compounds in the host cells.

There is relatively little to be said about cellulases, although, being highly adaptive, they are known to be formed by some pathogenic fungi. A good bit of the difficulty lies in the question of trying successfully to correlate the results of laboratory studies on, say, cotton fiber with the observed results of pathogens on cell walls. At present, efforts to achieve clearcut results in studies of host-pathogen interactions in this area leave much to be desired.

Brown (1965) has provided an instructive overview of the way research progresses in his account of the work on enzymes in relation to the effect of pathogenic microorganisms on host tissue. Here he shows how rather crude extracts from pathogen cultures were first shown to have a macerating and lethal effect on host cells, how increasingly precise analytical techniques made it possible to separate the enzyme complex into more and more specific entities and, by so doing, how the effect of a given substance on a particular component of the cell and cell wall could be identified. He reminds us, too, of the far greater sensitivity of host tissue—at least of the potato tuber used for much of his experimental work—to enzymes when in a fully turgid condition. On the basis of available evidence, it appears that the host tissue in a nonturgid condition contains some sort of inactivating substance that is not effective in turgid cells.

PATHOLOGY OF PROCESSES

It is now appropriate to return to the question of symptoms and to look at several types that are most conspicuous for their effect on fundamental processes in the plant host. There are two that take precedence—food manufacture and water economy. Some authors add a fifth—reproduction—which is more or less intermediate between the histologically and the physiologically oriented effects.

Food Manufacture and Utilization

In a review of pathogenic effects on the food relations of plants Sempio (1959) has listed the following categories of injury:

- Impairment of synthesis in photosynthetic tissues
- Accelerated respiration and inhibition of carbohydrate resynthesis
- Disarranged equilibrium in the host
- Action of antimetabolites or toxins
- Alteration of cell permeability
- Impairment of transport
- Deleterious effects on mineral uptake

In looking at any of these more explicitly, it must be kept in mind that the nondiseased plant in its metabolism does show a wonderfully orchestrated balance of a very large number of individual events. In a very general but important way disease is disease because it upsets these balances to the detriment of the plant.

Photosynthesis. The obvious aspect of this situation is the reduction in photosynthesis that stems from destruction of chlorophyll, death of portions of green tissue or leaf or stem, and premature defoliation of plants. Any one of these, and not infrequently the additive effect of two or more, can easily be seen as the result of invasion by a pathogen. Annuals and perennials alike fall victim to diseases that bring about massive reductions in total photosynthetic tissue. Even when the damage is repaired, so to speak, by newly formed foliage, it must be done at the cost of reduced food production, lessened leaf surface presented to the sun for the interval required to recoup the loss, and at the expense of accumulated reserves.

Above and beyond the direct destruction of chlorophyll, the efficiency of the process is often impaired and a complementary situation results: less green tissue, and less efficient production by that which remains. Very naturally, these latter relations are mostly brought on by the action of obligately parasitic or closely comparable pathogens.

There seems to be a direct relationship between the sugar content of host tissue and the vulnerability of that tissue to invasion by a pathogenic organism in at least several cases. One such is summarized by Lukens (1970) in a study of the so-called "melting out" of Kentucky bluegrass, caused by the fungus *Helminthosporium vagans*. Trials show that leaf sugar content is lower and disease more severe in turf that is cut at a height of one inch than in comparable turf cut at two inches. Not only this, but shading has the effect of reducing leaf sugars and increasing disease incidence and severity. The initially therapeutic effect of glucose sprays seems to confirm the fact that melting-out is a low-sugar disease. Lukens speculates that a high content of reducing sugars in the host may be required to inhibit the macerating enzymes of the pathogen, or to synthesize fungitoxic compounds in host tissue.

Distribution of Materials. An almost immediate effect of invasion by pathogens is an increase in respiratory rate in the vicinity of the lesion and a mobilization and accumulation of metabolites in the area. By what means does this occur, and what is the local and general impact of the event?

At least one of the mechanisms seems to be a change, usually toward greater ease of movement, in the plasma membrane of the host cells. When this is accompanied, as it so often is, by marked differences in the diffusion pressure deficit of host and pathogen cells, there is not only accelerated movement to the site of invasion, but greater facility in the uptake of materials by the cells of the invader.

So far as carbohydrates are concerned, therefore, one has a situation where local production, though initially high, is reduced, where material from surrounding areas is moved in at abnormally rapid rates, where uptake by the host is facilitated, and where a speeded respiratory apparatus raises the level of utilization. Small wonder then that those portions of the host plant that derive their food supplies from tissues other than themselves—i.e., roots, stems, and fruits, as contrasted to foliage—face critical shortages.

Imbalances and Secondary Effects. Suppose that roots are inadequately supplied with food, especially of carbohydrate. Obviously they will grow slowly, if at all, and both water and mineral nutrient uptake will suffer accordingly. This in turn impoverishes amino acid and protein formation and other anabolic events of the whole plant. Developments are thus cumulative, each event very likely to generate other undesirable events, and so on.

Metabolic imbalances may also occur by the appropriation of the protein-forming machinery of the cell by an invading virus, although this is by no means the only irregularity in nitrogen metabolism. When for any reason amino acids, to choose an example, are in short supply locally, carbohydrate accumulation may result, which affords a convincing explanation of the occurrence of isolated starch grains in the immediate vicinity of disease lesions.

In the midst of all this, fairly abrupt fluctuations in respiratory rates are taking place in both pathogen and host, concurrently with an undesirable—for the host in any rate—"uncoupling" of the oxidative from the later stages of glycolysis, thus in effect wasting a substantial amount of energy.

Transport. It is no accident that a considerable array of virus diseases have in their descriptive names the term "phloem necrosis," for many are tissue-specific and produce dramatic damage to the phloem at a point in the life cycle. No more striking example is known than the virus disease of the American elm that was responsible, over the midcentury decades, for the destruction of hundreds of thousands of these trees in the Central Atlantic and especially the midwestern states. Death of the afflicted trees occurs in a single season, by the total starvation of the root system. Other pathogens than viruses, including notably the fungi, are responsible for interrupting transport of elaborated foods.

Less directly, perhaps, any hindrance to the flow of nutrients from root to foliage is properly considered as adversely affecting the overall metabolic well-being of the host. The more immediate effect, that on water supply, will be considered in the next section.

Food and Reproduction. Nutrition is importantly related to flower and fruit formation. Although the former is primarily a light-mediated response, an adequate and balanced supply of carbohydrate and nitrogen-containing materials is essential, as are the other mineral nutrients involved in so many enzymatic events. By the same token any imbalances or inadequacies will seriously affect flower initiation, fruit set, and fruit maturation.

Water Economy

For all living organisms food and water are the *sine qua non* of continued existence. An impoverished water supply surely brings about a prompter death than any other single cause. Plants, at least the mesophytic types represented by most common crop plants, are especially vulnerable because of their unavoidable transpirational loss.

When the focus of interest lies in the host-pathogen relationship as expressed in symptoms affecting the water economy of plants, the problem divides itself into three aspects—effects on water loss, on water movement, and on water uptake. Besides these there are certain general effects of water deficiency that can arise by any one or more of the three avenues just noted. Growth, as achieved by cell enlargement, for example, is critically dependent upon adequate water supplies. When water is insufficiently available, plants are visibly stunted even though they may not otherwise be seriously damaged. Rather less directly, perhaps, photosynthesis rates are reduced at early stages in water-deficit situations; part but presumably not all of the reduction is attributable to the immediate effect of turgor loss upon the position of guard cells.

Water, indeed, is so completely and exclusively the medium within which the metabolic machinery of the living cell operates that deficiencies lead inevitably to unfavorable shifts in enzyme production and activity, in the physical characteristics of protoplasm, in the turgor of cells, and so on. Water levels and water movement influence concentrations of many cell components, the uptake, movement, and accumulation of nutrient materials, elaboration of cell metabolites, and a host of activities in the plant. How, then, do pathogens bring about unfavorable conditions of the water economy?

Effects on Transpiration Loss.　In the healthy plant most water moving into the plant is lost as vapor through the stomates; nominal amounts transpire through the epidermal layers directly. Pathogens, particularly fungi, will sharply increase "cuticular" transpiration if they breach this layer in one way or another—through cracks, by damage to epidermal layers, as a result of local necrosis, and so on. For a number of diseases, water loss is aggravated by changes that result in greater permeability of the cell membranes under the impact of pathogen metabolites. Part of the explanation of the impact of the "wilt" pathogens is to be found at this point. Finally, any pathogen that damages stomatal action will endanger a most vital control mechanism in plants.

Effects on Water Movement.　Botanists have argued for many years about the forces responsible for the movement of water in stems, particularly for upward movement in the stems of very tall trees. The most generally held view is that loss of water in the exposed surfaces of mesophyll cells sets up a transpiration pull sufficient to overcome the effects of gravity, the internal friction of the conducting vessels and the forces tending to hold the water in the soil, and that the pathway of water movement in stems is in the vessels and tracheids of the more recently formed xylem. In moving from root surfaces to vascular tissue, water is presumed to go through "free space," the aggregate of intercellular space and the cellulose walls, which latter offer very much less resistance than would a cell-to-cell transfer.

In this context, two rather general kinds of adverse effects can be identified. Physical interruption of water flow can be achieved by the sheer accumulation of pathogen substance in the vessels—bacterial mass or fungal filaments—or it can be accomplished by the development of tyloses to such an extent that the channels are occluded. A second mechanism is more indirect. Here enzymes produced by the pathogen stimulate the formation of polysaccharides or bring about the hydrolysis of pectic substances, or trigger the formation of gums and other viscous compounds. These and related events have the effect of sharply altering the rate of flow and thus producing water stresses in the foliage.

Fig. 7–2. Wilting in red clover induced by the fungus *Fusarium. Facing page: (Top)* Cuttings after 48 hours in distilled water, culture filtrate subsequently heated, and unheated filtrate (*left to right*). (*Middle*) Cuttings in continuous light in sterile filtrate, cuttings in continuous darkness in *Fusarium* filtrate, and cuttings held in continuous light and *Fusarium* filtrate (*left to right*). (*Bottom*) Cuttings in sterile filtrate (*far left*) and in filtrates from six different isolates of the fungus. *Above:* Dye distribution in three unwilted (*left*) and two wilted (*right*) stems of red clover after cut ends were placed in eosin solution. Failure of dye to move up in wilted stems indicates obstruction of vessels, as result of being placed in unheated *Fusarium* filtrate. (Chi and Hanson, 1964)

The mechanism by which *Fusarium* brings about wilt in red clover, like that in tomato, appears to involve plugging of the vascular elements by a substance that can also be induced by commercial pectinase preparations. Chi and Hanson, in careful experiments with this disease (1964), showed that culture filtrates of several species would bring about wilt of cut stems and that the passage of materials up the stem could be demonstrated by placing them in eosin solutions (see Fig. 7–2). A comparison with material collected in the field showed close correlation with experimentally induced wilting.

Much has been written on "wilt toxins," as distinct from the physical blockage that was for so long assumed to explain the observed symptoms. At least one of the avenues through which pathogens cause the wilting syndrome associated with "vascular wilts" is by a deleterious effect, evidenced by necrosis, on xylem elements and probably more importantly by destroying the selective permeability and hence the osmotic properties of the leaf cells.

In a quite different sense water movement is interrupted by growth abnormalities. In the case of crown gall, for example, water-conducting tissues are poorly developed and disorganized. The same is true of root-knot nematode infestations of the root system.

Effects on Water Uptake.   Most pathogens responsible for reduction of water absorption do so through outright destruction of root tissues. Bacteria, fungi, nematodes, insects—any organism with the capacity to enter and establish itself in young roots—is likely to damage greater or lesser areas of absorptive tissue. In at least a few cases, physiological effects on root growth, on rate of suberization, and on the selectivity of the plasma membrane have important implications for the efficiency and effectiveness of the root as an avenue of entry for water.

Other Processes

Considering reproduction as a distinct process, clearly disease affects it unfavorably. Abnormal growth responses are not infrequently found associated with reproductive organs, as is the case in the big-bud virus of tomato and the fungus responsible for plum pockets. Perhaps the most precise relationships of pathogen associations are those that are confined to reproductive organs or that develop an important phase of their life cycles on flowers or fruits. Among these are the "flower-infection" smuts of small grains, the anther smuts, the flower-blighting bacterial and fungal pathogens, many storage diseases, and those that are seed-borne.

Respiratory changes occur widely in infected plants. These changes include basic increases in rate that accompany rises in temperature, alterations in the concentrations and distribution of enzymes and substrates, and significant rerouting of the pathways of carbohydrate metabolism.

BIOCHEMICAL RESISTANCE

We are concerned here with those biochemical phenomena that seem to characterize host-pathogen interaction as it pertains to host resistance. Use of the term "biochemical" resistance is arbitrary; it refers to those phenomena that are not primarily morphologic or histologic and that do not fall into the category of hypersensitivity. To an extent it includes those instances of host resistance assumed to be "biochemical" or "physiological" because no clearly visible event can be discerned, yet where there is obvious hindrance to the rapid invasion and establishment of the pathogen. "Biochemical resistance" is at once the most basic, most pervasive, and yet most elusive of the mechanisms by which the host wards off or counteracts the inroads of pathogenic organisms.

Much has been accomplished in the decades between 1950 and 1970 in gradually unraveling the complex biochemical events that hold the key to the phenomena of disease in plants. Much remains to be done, most of which must be hammered out by careful examination of comparatively simple phenomena under experimental conditions that make the results intelligible. Only after many fragments of information have been accumulated does a convincing general statement become possible.

One continuing difficulty is to find suitable experimental models, models where the complications do not too greatly obscure the results. In just such an instance, Lovrekovich *et al.* (1968) have examined the peroxidase activity of tobacco leaves as it relates to resistance of the host to the wildfire bacterium, *Pseudomonas tabaci*. They were testing the general assumption that increased levels of peroxidase activity was positively correlated with increased resistance, and found support for this thesis. When heat-killed cells were injected into the host, peroxidase activity did increase and resistance increased. Cell-free extracts of the bacterium and solutions of commercial peroxidase likewise led to increased resistance to the disease.

Possible Mechanisms

Of possible and probable mechanisms of biochemical resistance, several are identifiable. In the first instance are pH and osmotic effects. Generally, the pH of host tissue is rather more acid than is favorable to bacteria and in special instances the pH of tissues drops so low through accumulation of organic acids as to be inhospitable even to fungi. As for osmotic values, it is generally accepted that the diffusion pressure deficit (DPD) of pathogen cells must exceed that of the host if necessary transfers are to occur. By this token any circumstance that tends to increase the DPD of host cells—or any host variety with characteristically high DPD—would make for greater resistance.

An obvious aspect of resistance, not easily demonstrated *in vivo*, relates to simple availability of nutrients. If, for example, the host lacks an essential nutrient—be it a food constituent, growth factor, vitamin, co-enzyme, or other substance—then obviously it will be a less than satisfactory substrate and will be in that measure resistant. Admittedly, most attempts to demonstrate this phenomenon have been made with extracts of host tissue, but the technical difficulty of carrying out experiments directly with the host-pathogen complex does not, per se, affect the likelihood that resistance phenomena of this kind do in fact occur.

A third possibility lies in the area of toxins and antitoxins. There is some evidence to suggest, for example, that where a major weapon of the invading organism—in the wilt fungi for example—is a toxin, host resistance consists in part of the presence, either beforehand or in response to attack, of an antitoxin. On the other side of the coin, it may very well be that the abrupt inhibition of invading hyphae results from the elaboration of materials in the host protoplasm that are directly toxic to the invader. Susceptibility would in the first instance be either a sensitivity to pathogen toxins or failure to elaborate an antitoxin. Susceptibility in the second instance would stem from failure to elaborate substances directly harmful to the attacking pathogen. It might be argued that the specificity in the host-pathogen interaction here lies in eliciting—or in failure to elicit—the response rather than in the biochemistry of the reaction itself.

The fourth and last category might be termed the immune reaction. Here are included the immune-like "protection" phenomena in plant virus studies, the formulation of antibiotic substances—dubbed "phytoalexins" by Müller—the production of bacterial agglutinins and lysins, and so on. Research in this general sector has been hampered by the very natural tendency to equate findings in the disease-resistance mechanisms in vertebrates, particularly those of human medicine, to plant pathology. We are now reasonably certain that the correlations can hardly be very close, but much remains to be done.

The Question of Induced Resistance

In large measure the events that occur in plants generally cited as evidence of resistance are elicited by the invasion of a pathogen or by wounding, or both. The capacity so to react is what really spells the difference between a host variety that is resistant and one that is susceptible to a given pathogen. Results obtained by measuring the effects of tissue extraction can be highly misleading, as can experiments that do not distinguish fully between the response of the host to wounding and its direct reaction to the pathogen. These circumstances make all the more satisfying the ingenious efforts of Müller in employing the intact, sterile inner surfaces of bean pods as a substrate for his phytoalexin studies.

That the resistance mechanisms are mostly induced and that specificity lies much more in the induction process than in the mechanism proper is supported further by the fact that changes in the environment of the host, in its nutrient levels, or the employment of respiratory inhibitors will often bring about very marked shifts in the overall resistance of the host. In this direction seems to lie the road to fruitful research in the near future.

The widespread success, in human medicine, of the technique of vaccination as a means to disease prevention has led repeatedly to efforts in plant pathology based on the same general approach. For the most part these have not been markedly successful, probably as much as anything because plants do not have a comparable circulating system, but there have been a few promising indications. Several virus diseases show clear evidence of protection against a virulent strain when a healthy host plant is first inoculated with a mild strain; rather less evidence exists for fungus and bacterial pathogens.

Schnathorst and Mathre (1966) report convincing results with mild and severe strains of *Verticillium albo-atrum* on cotton with a variety of trials. They found, for example, that when conidia of the mild strain were sprayed on host roots a week prior to inoculation with the severe strain, up to two-thirds of the plants were protected (Fig. 7–3, *top*). Perhaps even more amenable to practical use is their finding that naturally infested soil could be rendered virtually hazard-free by adding rather large supplements of microsclerotia of the mild strain (Fig. 7–3, *bottom*). In their view, where the two strains occur together naturally, there may be significant retardation of the severe one, depending on proportions of inoculum in the soil.

Fig. 7–3. Cross-protection in *Verticillium* wilt of cotton. *Top:* Plants inoculated with mild strain of fungus only, plants inoculated with mild strain followed 1 week later with severe strain, plants inoculated with severe strain only (*left to right*). *Bottom:* Cotton growing in sterile field soil, cotton growing in nonsterile field soil, cotton growing in nonsterile field soil amended with inoculum of mild strain (*left to right*). (Schnathorst and Mathre, 1966)

A Note on Insects

Not all work on host-pathogen interaction has been done with fungi, although the preponderance surely has. In 1951 Painter, for example, considered at length the matter of resistance to insect attack, and set up an outline (Chapter 2, pp. 23–83) of mechanisms of resistance to insect attack based on what he called:

- Preference—the relation of mechanical, chemical, and visual stimuli to oviposition, food and shelter needs of insects
- Antibiosis—the impact of the host on the insect development and life history and on feeding mechanisms
- Tolerance—the ability, so to speak, of the host to repair, recover from, or withstand the effects of, insect attack

Of these three items the first two are rather clearly resistance of a predominantly "biochemical" nature.

8

Extrinsic Factors

This chapter does not concern itself with the direct effects of the environment on the host—a matter already dealt with in Chapter 3—or with its effects on pathogens. Conversely, matters pertaining to epidemic disease—disease in populations—are left to a subsequent section.

To a degree not encountered in human medicine, plant disease phenomena are at the mercy of the environment. Here the host has far less capacity to maintain stable conditions than does the warm-blooded mammal and is therefore subject to far greater diversity, both internally and externally. Thus the course and outcome of a given host-pathogen confrontation depends very much on the impact of environmental conditions, acting through separate but often simultaneous effects of those conditions on each of the two interactants.

Still further, two or more elements of the environment often interact with each other. Sometimes the interaction is direct and obvious, as when a rise in ambient temperature induces a corresponding drop in relative humidity, or when increased light intensity results in rising temperatures. At other times the phenomena are more obscure and will show up as alterations in the responses of pathogen or host. Optimum temperature for a given phenomenon at one moisture level may not, for example, be the same as that at another moisture level.

And finally not only are variations among individuals of a given species common, but responsiveness to environment tends to change during the life span of an individual plant. Values will usually therefore be expressed as a range between two extremes or, as the occasion demands, an average of divergent readings.

From the above it follows that each host-pathogen association must almost literally be approached as a separate and distinct entity—its environmental relationships cannot safely be deduced by extrapolation from some other situation. It follows, too, that the greatest caution must be exercised in translating experimental data from the laboratory into field situations—at best a move fraught with uncertainty. Part of the problem arises from the laboratory tradition of holding all but a given factor constant during an experiment, whereas inconstancy is the rule in nature. Traditionally, too, we deal with pure cultures of pathogens in experimental work, when the norm outside is a heterogeneous assemblage.

MOISTURE

Moisture relations of plants divide very naturally into the above-ground (atmospheric) and below-ground (soil) aspects. In both sites, but to varying degree, vapor and liquid water are importantly involved—the former more characteristic of the atmosphere, the latter of the soil milieu.

Although the powdery mildews are generally thought to be exceptions, the spores of fungi must be thoroughly wet if they are to germinate. Very often the needed amounts of water are provided by dew formed on the leaf and other exposed surfaces during the night hours. So critical is dew formation and its duration that it alone often determines whether a pathogen does or does not become established. As for diseases in populations of plants, the need for accurate data on timing and duration of dew is so important that recording devices of one kind or another have been developed to detect it. One of the simpler and more ingenious was that worked out by C. L. Taylor a number of years ago, employing a water-soluble colored pencil held against a moving paper disk. The design has since been elaborated into a 7-day recording device (Fig. 8–1).

Dew is related to humidity and temperature, of course, but one cannot assume from laboratory experiments precisely how pathogenic organisms will behave in nature. The former show, for example, that germination falls off very rapidly as humidity drops much below saturation, whereas field infection actually occurs at these levels. Almost certainly the nature of leaf surfaces and the transpirational water vapor immediately adjacent to this surface make spore germination and subsequent invasion possible at times when the general atmospheric condition would be judged unfavorable.

Flagellated cells, obviously, can function only in a liquid medium, whether on leaf surfaces or below ground. A familiar example is the process of infection of potato tubers by the pathogen of potato late blight. In this case spores formed on the foliage find their way to the soil surface and, if there is sufficient water, germinate to form zoospores that in turn swim about until some come in contact with a tuber surface, which they penetrate. The late-blight pathogen, however, is capable of adjusting to conditions of lesser moisture availability—the spores under drier conditions form hyphae, or germ tubes, rather than motile spores.

Fig. 8–1. Apparatus for recording 7-day occurrence of rain and dew. *Top:* Installation in banana plantation. *Bottom:* Main assembly, door opened to show hygrothermograph within shelter, with dew-recording apparatus (revolving disk and colored pencil) in place above the roof of shelter. (Theis and Calpouzos, 1957)

Bacteria, with the exception of those introduced into wounds, are entirely unable to penetrate host defenses unless a continuous liquid medium is available from surface through stoma or other natural openings into the interior. It has been known for a number of years that water-soaking, or perhaps better termed water congestion, is essential as a prerequisite to the establishment of many bacterial plant pathogens. The biology of the bacteria as plant pathogens is such as to make this an entirely understandable situation, both as to initial entry through stomata and subsequent multiplication, especially of course for those pathogens that are not vector borne. Williams and Keen (1967) find that either abundant water in the host or in the surrounding atmosphere (Fig. 8–2) is conducive to development of symptoms of cucumber angular leaf spot and that there is a definite loss of water from the cells into the intercellular spaces associated with the disease. This later event, in turn, hinges on changes in cell membrane permeability.

Water is demonstrably an almost universally necessary prerequisite to successful invasion by common pathogens. Once within the tissues of the host, at least the living tissues, a certain amount of moisture is always available. When conditions of the water economy of the host are such as to have resulted in water-soaking, then the fortunes of the pathogen are often signally enhanced —a situation true for fungi as well as for bacteria. Present evidence suggests a dual effect, one that is advantageous to the pathogen, per se, and debilitating to the host.

Both in host tissues and in soil one of the more immediate effects of high moisture is to inhibit the growth of conspicuously aerobic organisms by excluding, or at least diminishing, the air supply. Just as water-logged soil is harmful to the roots of many host species and works to the disadvantage of the desirable nitrifying bacteria, so it slows the activities of many fungus pathogens by establishing an oxygen-deficient medium. This situation is capitalized upon in several well-known control measures that involve flooding agricultural areas that are badly contaminated by recognized pathogens (the banana wilt is the classic example here) for a period long enough substantially to reduce the population of the unwanted organisms. Gäumann, in a less well-publicized situation, describes several instances of facultative wood-rot fungi that can survive in the bark, the sapwood, or the heartwood of living trees. For several pathogen-host associations, normal water content of sapwood is sufficiently higher than that which is optimum for the fungus that it protects healthy standing specimens from invasion.

High soil water content is not always detrimental to the development of disease. In cases where it proves to be relatively more favorable to host than to pathogen, disease is reduced. But if, as is the case with many bacteria, fac-

Fig. 8–2. Relation of relative humidity to development of angular leaf spot in cucumber, shown 3 days after inoculation with the bacteria. *Upper left:* 85%. *Upper right:* 90%. *Lower left:* 95%. *Lower right:* 100%. (Williams and Keen, 1967)

tors related to pathogen spread overshadow other considerations, then a high tissue water content or soil moisture level will favor the development of disease.

Although there is overwhelming evidence that the soil environment has a profound effect on the onset and course of root rots and related diseases, the interaction of factors is sufficiently tangled that the problem of sorting out the various elements in the picture is far from easy. From time to time instances of clearcut cause and effect emerge, as in the work reported by Ghaffar and Erwin (1969) on *Macrophomina phaseoli* on cotton. In this case two variables, soil temperature and moisture stress, were examined in greenhouse experiments. Of these, the latter was clearly the more critical in determining the eventual severity of disease (Fig. 8–3).

TEMPERATURE

Temperature fixes the geographic limits of hosts and pathogens, and hence of disease. It does not alone determine every facet of occurrence or nonoccurrence, but it does determine the major climatic zones of latitude and the diversity encountered with significant changes in attitude. With moisture—and the two are ecologically closely interrelated—temperature must be by far the most critically important extrinsic factor in the host-pathogen reaction.

Few experiments in plant pathology have been more frequently cited as evidence of environmental influence on disease than the classic work of J. G. Dickson in 1923, wherein he investigated the relation of temperature under carefully controlled conditions on three phenomena:

- The growth of the fungus *Gibberella saubinettii* in pure culture
- Seedling blight of corn caused by this pathogen
- Seedling blight of wheat

Three different maxima appear in the data. One, at relatively low temperatures, describes disease incidence in corn. Another, at relatively high temperatures, characterizes the disease in wheat. A third, intermediate between the two, represents optimum conditions for the fungus alone. Here, because other factors were controlled, Dickson could safely conclude that the temperature effect operates largely on the host in predisposing it to the disease. But this and countless other experiments have shown that each host-pathogen association must be examined individually.

Temperature does, within limits, bring about a significant acceleration in metabolic rate in living organisms as the environment becomes warmer. It should be noted that in the Temperate Zone much of the year is a period of

Fig. 8–3. Effect of water stress on severity of root rot by the fungus *Macrophomina phaseoli* on cotton. Plants 1 and 2 were watered regularly; plants 3 and 4 were subjected to stress. Plants 2 and 3 were, in addition, inoculated with a suspension of the mycelium. (Ghaffar and Erwin, 1969)

minimum activity on the part of both host and pathogen. When changes leading up to periods of minimum temperature are gradual—when there is a
"hardening-off" period—many species of cultivated plants will successfully
withstand extremely low temperatures without apparent injury. Sudden fluctuations, or below-freezing temperatures following immediately after extended periods of warmer weather, will cause damage. The point bears re-
peating that for host and pathogen alike it is the extremes of temperature,
high or low, that have the greatest impact.

In connection with the relationship between soil temperature and the severity of root rots, Ostazeski (1968) has reported that greenhouse tests on the
use of porous as against nonporous containers show a markedly higher temperature in the latter. This is apparently a combined effect of the heat-ab-
sorbing characteristics of the pots and the extent to which they are cooled by
evaporation. Tests of birdsfoot trefoil seedlings in soil contaminated with cultures of *Leptodiscus terrestris* showed marked differences in the length of
time required to produce permanent wilting; the porous pots, with a substantially lower soil temperature, required as much as twice the elapsed time. Not
only are we thereby shown the important role of soil temperature, but we are
reminded that experimental results may very well be misleading if so unlikely
an external factor as the nature of the pot itself is ignored.

Host

Because temperature strongly influences growth rate, it strongly affects the
course of disease in those instances where the host is susceptible to invasion
only during a given stage of development. In the case, for example, of a seedling blight it is clearly disadvantageous to the host if unfavorable temperatures prolong the period during which the plant is in this vulnerable condition. For many species abnormally cool temperatures bring about this very
situation. Obviously, inadequate moisture could also prolong the seedling
phase, but it would then be under conditions far more likely also to be unfavorable to the pathogen in question. In making this very point, Gäumann has
summarized observations on two diseases, the bunt of wheat and the onion
smut. In the first instance, the optimum temperature for disease development
is about 5°C. This is well below the optimum for both spore germination and
seedling development but is a temperature at which the seedling stage of the
host is so prolonged that it maximizes the chance for successful infection. In
onion smut temperatures below 10°C are most favorable for the disease, although it, too, is below that most favorable for either of the organisms sepa-

rately. At temperature readings above 25°C the host is so favored in relation to the pathogen that the disease rarely if ever becomes an important consideration.

A second temperature effect primarily centered on the host relates to wound healing and the formation of various tissue barriers. As a rule higher temperature tends to promote periderm formation and to lessen the incidence of invasion by pathogens. On the other hand, cell wall differentiation, with its consequent reduction in rate of pathogen spread, is often markedly less pronounced in plants that are developing at the accelerated rate characteristic of elevated temperatures. Not all host-pathogen interactions follow the same pattern, of course, but where the situation is governed primarily by the condition of the host, disease is aggravated as temperature rises, at least within the limits normally encountered under laboratory and field conditions.

There are temperature effects upon host-pathogen interactions the mechanisms for which are not wholly understood. For example, it has long been recognized that in using accepted tester varieties of wheat for the identification of rust races, it is of critical importance to maintain a temperature comparable to that established as standard for the technique. Identification of races depends upon a scoring and classification scheme that assigns the host reaction on each variety to one of several arbitrary categories—categories based primarily on the severity of the infection produced on the leaves of potted seedlings that have been dusted with uredospores of the unknown rust isolate. It soon became obvious that unless the temperature were standardized, very different reactions would result, with the result that at one temperature a given specimen would receive one race identification, while at another temperature the identical pathogen would key out to quite another race.

Pathogen

Temperature impinges very early upon the host-pathogen interaction, through effects on germination of fungal and bacterial spores. As with some seeds, temperature influences spores in several ways: in affecting dormancy, in its relation to the percentage of germination, on speed of germination, and in fewer instances, on the pattern of germination.

Dormancy in higher plants is characteristic of climates having either alternating cold and warm periods or, less commonly perhaps, wet and dry seasons. Many species of microorganisms display a quite similar tendency not to resume active growth until after an appreciable waiting period. Alternate freezing and thawing, for example, or heat shock treatments, are needed to

effect germination of some species of fungus spores. Close study of the life cycles of most of these organisms will show dormancy to have distinct survival
value and presumably to have evolved as a response to the pressures of the
environment.

Temperature also affects percent of germination, but not with anything
like the universality with which it influences speed. That is, some species
show clearcut correlations between temperature and percent germination,
but others are but slightly affected. In all cases, lower temperatures lead to
prolongation of the germination process.

In a few species, of which the late blight fungus is by far the best known,
temperature not only determines the speed of germination but actually the
form it takes. Within the lower ranges, spores germinate to form zoospores
typical of the taxonomic group of fungi to which it belongs; at higher temperatures a single hypha emerges from the spore.

Pathogens evidence a response to temperature by virtue of their being
characteristically either "high temperature" or "low temperature" organisms.
Not all of the effect can be attributed directly to the effect of temperature on
the microorganism. Cool temperatures may well be associated with higher
moisture levels, with reduced host resistance, with prolonged exposure. But
the fact remains that certain species of pathogen are clearly favored by low
temperatures, others by relatively high temperatures; still others are indif-
ferent to the range of temperature normally encountered during the growing
season.

A final point concerns the influence of temperature on what pathologists
usually refer to as the "generation time" of spore-forming fungus pathogens;
the concept is equally valid for generations of egg-laying nematodes and perhaps in rare cases for vascular parasites. The point is that most local lesion
type diseases of fungal origin show a characteristic pattern of inoculum – penetration – establishment – spread – sporulation – dissemination – inoculum –
penetration, and so on. The severity of disease is greatly influenced by how
long a period is required for a single cycle to be completed, because this directly determines the rate of multiplication—or at least the potential maximum rate of multiplication. Temperature, then, is one of the important environmental factors determining the duration of a given reproductive cycle.

Disease

There are several aspects of temperature effects that are more characteristic of the disease phenomenon per se than they are of either host or pathogen
(Fig. 8–4).

Fig. 8–4. Effect of temperature on the development of blue mold of tobacco seedling. *Top:* Seedlings held at 70° F at night, remaining healthy. *Bottom:* Seedlings not heated, showing severe damage. (Clayton and Gaines, 1945)

The first, incubation period, refers to the duration of the interval between the initial invasion of the host by the pathogen and the development of characteristic symptoms. This is related to, but not fully synonymous with, generation time in the sense that the incubation period is more directly a manifestation of host-pathogen interactions. It is also usually shorter, inasmuch as the production of the next increment of inoculum usually follows by an appreciable period the development of what might be called maximum symptom expression. And it would be entirely possible for a given host-pathogen association to develop characteristic symptoms without ever reaching the stage of producing new inoculum. Within these limits, temperature plays an appreciable role in determining the duration of the incubation period.

A second temperature-mediated disease phenomenon, the character and intensity of symptom expression, is well exemplified by virus maladies. It is widely recognized that in seasons when temperature is higher, the evidence of virus in plants is mostly, or even wholly, suppressed, whereas the very same host-virus association at a lower temperature will be conspicuous.

Finally, it appears that elevated temperatures may suffice to free a diseased host of an already established causal agent, a fact that becomes of special interest in terms of control measures.

It has been entirely obvious for a long time that environmental conditions affect the response of the host to invasion by pathogenic organisms. It is less easy to so sort out the various factors of the environment as to identify in reasonably precise fashion the impact of a single element on the disease picture. Brinkerhoff and Presley (1967) have succeeded in showing a striking effect of day and night temperatures on the bacterial blight of cotton as brought on by *Xanthomonas malvacearum*. In comparing immune, susceptible, and resistant strains of the host under conditions of relatively low night and relatively high day temperatures, relatively low night and moderate day temperatures, and relatively high night temperatures, they found consistent but strikingly different responses (Fig. 8–5). Still further, the susceptibility of different individual leaves of the susceptible varieties varied under the higher night temperature regime.

LIGHT

By contrast with temperature and moisture, there is not much to say about light in relation to plant disease in the context of this chapter. This situation comes about from the obvious fact that the basic nutrition of one partner to the disease association, the pathogen, is in no way light dependent. Light

Fig. 8–5. Relation of different temperature regimes to the reaction of cotton to bacterial blight. *Top row:* Resistant variety I. *Middle row:* Resistant variety II. *Bottom row:* Immune variety. Varieties shown in left column were grown at 19° C night and 36.5° C day temperatures; those in right column were grown at 19° C night and 25.5° C day temperatures. (Brinkerhoff and Presley, 1967)

plays an important role in the metabolism of the green plant host but is a rather insignificant factor in the biology of the pathogen.

There are, of course, some fairly common phenomena that are modified by light. Best known, probably, is the sporulation of fungi, which is in a number of species conspicuously accelerated by exposure to light. But it is not at all difficult to find species that seem to be wholly insensitive to this factor in the external environment. In the case of virus diseases, there seems to be a clear causal relationship between light and symptom expression, with the result that during the summer months many are difficult, if not actually impossible, to detect.

While individual instances of light effects are common, few meaningful generalizations are possible. Gäumann risks at least one when he argues that light is favorable to diseases caused by what he terms eusymbiotic pathogens (host-pathogen pairs showing a degree of tolerance to one another) and unfavorable to the parabiotic ones (an acute antagonistic interaction). To the extent that this view is valid, it appears to hold for both light duration and light intensity, although there are frequent exceptions to both.

The obvious dimensions of light, in the sense considered here, are intensity, duration or photoperiod, and quality or wavelength. Each aspect can be found to have an effect in this or that instance, in a frequency roughly equivalent to the sequence just noted—few data exist on the effects of light of different wavelengths, somewhat more on duration, and most on intensity. Light in one or more of its aspects can affect any phase of the host-pathogen relationship—inoculum survival, entrance, disease development, incubation, sporulation. But in the last analysis, it is certainly true that light has by far its most powerful influence upon the host and to predisposition of the host to disease.

By no means all information on the behavior of hosts and pathogenic organisms is derived from investigations planned in advance to elicit that information. Indeed, in an impressive number of cases, the initial observation is based on an apparently chance event and only then are the definitive experiments carried out. Just such an instance is illustrated by Duncan's (1967) article on the effect of light on rate of decay in pine sapwood. Here it was known for a considerable time that rates differed under experimental conditions that were presumed to be constant in all significant variables. When, however, comparisons of a number of tests in a single incubation room were made, it became clear that those farthest from the source of illumination were significantly less rotted than were those in higher-intensity light. More detailed comparisons of light intensity and wavelength suggested clearly that it was the lower spectral range that was most effective and that there was a positive correlation with increased intensities as measured in footcandles. Light is, of course, not essential for the action of the wood rot fungi, even though their activity is stimulated. Our tendency to associate wood rotting with darkness is more likely than not because in the main it is the unlighted parts of a wooden structure where moisture levels are most favorable to fungal growth.

OTHER ENVIRONMENTAL FACTORS

Most of the environmental factors other than temperature, moisture, and light do not greatly affect those pathogens and diseases that involve the above-ground parts of the plant host. This seems to be so because the very vastness of the atmosphere allows scant fluctuation or because the particular factor involved is but indirectly, or transiently, associated with the pathogen.

By way of illustration, consider the carbon dioxide–oxygen concentration in the atmosphere. While a few species of fungi have spores that will germinate in the total absence of oxygen, this property is hardly relevant to natural conditions, where the levels of these two gases do not vary sufficiently from one time to the next to make significant changes in the biology of disease.

The same is true of pH, another aspect of the environment that has perhaps some effect on spore germination of leaf and stem pathogens but is mostly rendered insignificant by the buffering effect of soluble materials in the droplets of fluid in which the spores are normally found.

As soon as one turns to the soil environment, however, carbon dioxide–oxygen levels and pH are discovered to be of considerable importance over and above their well-documented effects on the growth and development of the host plant itself. The same point can be made as regards nutrient materials, in both the macro and micro categories.

For many years it has been well established that certain soils-related diseases are closely tied to the acidity of the soil itself. Common scab of potatoes, for example, is cited in virtually every textbook of plant pathology as a classic case of a disease favored by alkaline soils. Its antithesis is cabbage clubroot, which develops well in wet, acid situations. Others among the many important diseases affecting primarily the root systems of plants can justifiably be placed in one or the other of these two categories.

As for oxygen–carbon dioxide, the situation varies much from one situation to the next. Generally, fungi are aerobes, but so long as the available oxygen does not drop too low it would appear that the predisposing, or at least damaging, impact of reduced oxygen on the host more than compensates for any inhibitory effect on the pathogen; in short, reduced oxygen tends in the main to favor disease.

In Chapter 3 some attention was given to nutrient deficiencies as they relate to the well-being of the host. A very considerable body of data has been accumulated on the question of nutrients in relation to diseases caused by pathogenic organisms, but like so much of the research on environment and the host-pathogen interaction, generalizations are most difficult to enunciate and to defend. Again and again observations pertinent to one disease do not seem to be applicable to the next.

What then can be said? Above all, it should be emphasized that most of the effects of nutrients are indirect. That is, the primary influence of the nutrient substance is upon the growth and development of the host plant, upon the pH of the soil, upon the availability of some other substance, or through some still different effect other than directly upon pathogen or disease. A few broad statements are worth risking. By and large, for example, excess nitrogen tends to increase disease incidence and severity, whereas relatively higher levels of potassium and phosphorus reduce damage. And, as might be expected, nutrient regimes favorable to the overall vigor of the host are at the same time inclined to aggravate the diseases caused by obligately parasitic fungi and viruses.

In Chapter 15 some of the practical means whereby nutrients can be manipulated in control of epidemic disease will be examined. It is by no means surprising, in view of what has been said already, that for every effective nutrient adjustment for which the mechanisms are reasonably well understood there are several that continue in use because they have been shown empirically effective, but that remain largely unexplained.

Although it is widely recognized that nutrition importantly affects the picture of disease and, further, that the presence of crop residues in the soil has an inhibitory action on root rots and related diseases, the details can be uncovered only by painstaking experimentation. Studies of *Fusarium* root rot of beans by Maier (1968) disclose that a high-nitrogen medium produces a more severe disease situation than if the fungus is grown in a medium of low nitrogen, or in one that contains none. Not only that, but it was significantly easier to recover the pathogen from high-nitrogen-content soils. From the standpoint of the host, those grown in a nitrogen-poor medium were more susceptible than those grown in one that had been enriched. Finally, the impact of barley straw residue on root rot was more pronounced if the infected plants were themselves vigorous than if they were unthrifty. At the same time, this suppression was counteracted most effectively by supplemental nitrogen if the infected plants had been grown on a high-nitrogen medium.

So many things influence the outcome of a given host-parasite interaction that one almost despairs of getting the entire picture clearly in hand, but progress is being made, bit by bit, in documenting the impact of this or that factor in the environment. Weinhold *et al.* (1969), for example, provide a clue as to the importance of the nutrition of the pathogen *Rhizoctonia solani* on its apparent virulence respecting cotton in laboratory and field conditions. When fungi taken from a medium containing 2 grams of asparagine per liter was compared with that from a medium containing only 0.5 grams, the former proved not only more virulent in terms of mycelial growth, but very much more effective so far as lesion development was concerned—that is, the nutrient requirement for maximum virulence is greater than that for vegetative growth.

IV

EPIDEMICS

The single diseased plant is in a way a contrived and artificial circumstance, although occasionally there is a proper and compelling interest in a particular individual. One thinks here of a cherished shade tree, a favorite shrub, or a long-tended ornamental. Upon these may be lavished a measure of concern out of all proportion to their intrinsic worth; they are the exceptions that prove the rule—the rule being that disease becomes of practical importance only when it involves a substantial number of individuals. Only in human medicine—and even here it is fully expressed only in more complex and technologically advanced societies—is the illness of a single individual considered worth the investment of substantial time and resources.

This is not to say that research on the biology of disease in small numbers of plants is ill-directed. By no means, for only by this approach can the detailed, critical data essential to an understanding of larger problems be accumulated. The point is, rather, that plant pathology contains a large element of practical concern for the impact of disease on populations and regions.

POPULATIONS AND ECOLOGY

As one moves from a consideration of individuals to a concern with populations, the multiplicity of factors that must be taken into account, often simultaneously, tends to discourage precision and to provide a false sense of safety in vagueness. Several points need constantly to be kept conspicuously in mind:

- The hard data for dealing with population biology must be derived from careful research on single-organism biology.
- Consideration of populations requires that the simultaneous impact of two or more elements in the system be taken into account, but must

211

recognize that the general phenomena of a community are in the main the net effect of a multitude of single, often unseen, events. In other words, population biology introduces vast complexities but it does not create phenomena that are wholly unique nor does it violate the basic laws governing single events within the system. To oversimplify, a people or nation stricken by an influenza epidemic is, in the final analysis, a multitude of individual cases of the flu. It is primarily the viewpoint, not the phenomena of disease, that changes.

• As the horizon widens to encompass large numbers of individuals, the attainable level of precision drops. This lesser degree of exactness must not be regarded as a fatal flaw. It is just that the stakes are higher. Where respiration rates in a mildew-infected leaf can be precisely measured, the onset of a regional late blight outbreak can at best be only approximated. Yet it can be cogently argued that an educated guess as to the probable severity of an epidemic is vastly more significant than carrying a carbon dioxide determination to the third decimal point.

PATHOLOGY AND ECONOMICS

Portions of Chapters 12 and 17 deal with economic aspects of plant pathology. Suffice it to point out here that the science of pathology, and even more particularly the art of pathology, is inextricably bound up with matters of practical value. The pathologist, rather more than those in the basic sciences that support his work, is ever concerned with the cost-benefit ratio of what he advocates. Plant pathology is not only a synthetic science, in the sense in which the word was used in an earlier chapter, it is inescapably an applied science. Many of the most exciting challenges are those that have economic implications.

Epidemics connote widespread and severe disease, which in turn means loss, hardship, danger, cost. As plant pathology operates in this sphere it can be likened to public health and is concerned with the same sorts of issues— detection of danger spots, prompt identification of outbreaks, predictions of potential spread and severity, instigation of countermeasures, assessment and alleviation of damage, and prevention of recurrences. Not all scientists are comfortable in the hurly-burly of this kind of campaigning—to others it offers a special challenge and a special appeal.

EPIDEMIOLOGY

The next three chapters deal with epidemics in plant populations. First consideration is accorded the devices by which pathogens move to new sites —the total assemblage of infective material summed up in the term inoculum.

On this point a distinction should be made that will exclude diseased plant material from the category of inocula. Inoculum should be thought of as the actual entity responsible for infection—diseased material is more appropriate to the problem of geographic spread—here included in the chapters on the dynamics of epidemic spread. The point is that while infective material can derive from a portion of a diseased plant, or indeed can multiply on or in such a fragment, the diseased tissue itself is not an infective entity.

Once one has the diversity of inocula and an awareness of how it accomplishes its journey to new sites in mind, the very complex question of the factors influencing rate of disease spread can be approached. Finally, the environment must be looked at from the viewpoint of climate and soil as they influence epidemics.

The viewpoint of Part IV is that of communities, of aggregates of factors, of net effects and multiple interactions.

9

Inoculum

INTRODUCTION

In their treatise on plant pathology Horsfall and Dimond bring out a variety of concepts that have developed about the term "inoculum potential." Most simply defined, it means the sheer mass, or perhaps better, density, of the infective material. If the concept is extended to include an assessment of the likelihood that disease will result from a given instance of association between pathogen and host, then virulence, susceptibility, and environmental influence enter the picture. Rough quantification of potential is based on estimates of infective units, separate lesions produced, or comparable data.

Identification of rust races is routinely carried out by assaying the particular pathogen in question against a selected and agreed upon set of indicator varieties of the host plant. The judgments themselves are made on the basis of the degree of infection achieved, ordinarily by putting the reaction on a given host indicator variety into one of several rather arbitrarily defined reaction types. That the reaction is subject to change with environmental conditions—and hence the need to maintain conditions that are constant—is well established. Davison and Vaughan (1964), working with bean rust, have shown that sheer inoculum density alone is enough to alter the reaction and hence affect the race identification. This seems to result from an effect on pustule size as a function of the closeness of one to another. They showed also that up to a certain point, in some experiments, the number of pustules increased only to drop down again at still higher concentrations, probably as the result of an inhibitory substance (Fig. 9–1). In other cases, the number of pustules rose steadily as the concentration of spores in the inoculum rose.

Whatever the particular point of view chosen, the central theme of inoculum potential lies in the notion that a target population lies under threat of attack by a pathogen population and that the crucial issue is what can be ex-

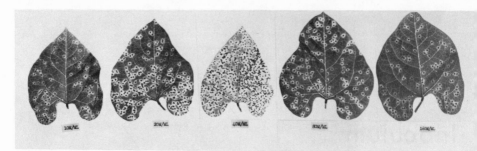

Fig. 9–1. Relation of inoculum concentration to number of pustules formed and to the size of pustules in bean rust. *Left to right:* Inoculum at 10,000, 20,000, 40,000, 80,000, and 160,000 spores per ml. (Davison and Vaughn, 1964)

pected to result from the interaction of the two. Environment plays its role in determining the outcome as it influences the chain of events from the initial production of infective material through its transport, invasion, and establishment.

What, then, is meant by inoculum? It is whatever can successfully reach and produce disease in a previously uninvolved host site. Its precise nature depends almost entirely on the taxonomic group involved. By way of illustration:

- *Viruses.* The only inoculum that need be considered in virus disease study is the virus itself; it would be virtually impossible to conceive of an entity so simple as a virus that possessed the ability to form anything analogous to the spores of fungi or the seeds of plants. Because plant viruses have little or no capacity to survive apart from living host cells one could even argue that the inoculum consists of the organism plus some at least of the host cell fluids, or virus plus insect saliva. Only in exceptional cases, e.g., tobacco mosaic, can virus remain viable outside the plant for long periods of time.
- *Bacteria.* As in the case of viruses, the entire bacterial organism is the inoculum. Bacterial plant pathogens are not spore-formers and act as individual vegetative cells to accomplish dissemination and invasion.
- *Fungi.* By all odds the most diverse and complex inocula are to be found in the fungi. Perhaps the only safe generalization is that fungi characteristically produce very large numbers of one-, or at best few-celled, infective units called spores that account for a major fraction of fungal inoculum. Even when spores in the strict sense of the word are not formed, fungi usually produce hyphal fragments that are more or

less comparable functionally. Only perhaps in the soil environment is the fungus, per se, likely to act as an inoculating agent.

- *Nematodes.* One could argue whether nematode larvae, or the eggs from which they hatch, are most properly to be thought of as inoculum. On balance, perhaps, the term should include both, for as larvae are primarily responsible for invasion of new host sites, so eggs are particularly effective in dissemination and survival.
- *Flowering plants.* Seeds provide, almost by definition, the means whereby dodder, mistletoe, and other vascular plants survive from one generation to the next and are dispersed to new hosts.

There is a general disparity between inoculum in the above-ground and the below-ground environment. In the former, air is the medium into which inoculum is discharged, through which it must move, and in which it must survive. Infective units are therefore most likely to be successful if they are of sufficiently low density to be readily carried by air currents, are resistant to injury by drying or radiation, and are of such nature as to adhere readily to surfaces upon initial impaction. Below ground, the premium is on self-movement, as by motile cells, on longevity or saprophytic growth as a compensation for generally slow dissemination, and on substantial freedom from the more acute rigors of desiccation or radiant energy.

A chronological description of inoculation phenomena seems entirely reasonable. The following account considers the sources of inoculum, its production, the means whereby it moves from point of origin to site of invasion, the problem of survival and the special implications of the soil environment. The focus of attention is thus first on above-ground phenomena, where movement is more spectacular, and emphasizes the diversity of fungus pathogens.

SOURCES OF INOCULUM

The sources of inoculum are the sites or substances from which the infective material comes, as distinct from the material itself. For example, a corn plant seriously damaged by smut is of itself no threat to surrounding healthy corn plants. The growth of mycelium through the corn tissues, with resulting hypertrophy and destruction of major portions of the host, is not pertinent to the question how the pathogen may get to and invade other individuals. Only when the active, vegetative, assimilatory phase of the host-pathogen relationship begins to taper off and to be replaced by the reproductive phase is it proper to speak of inoculum production. The fungus-invaded tissue is thus a source of inoculum but it is not itself inoculum. For that matter, the inoculum borne on a diseased host individual is seldom of much significance for that plant—spatially, the developing spores are identified with the diseased host, biologically they are important only to a potential, healthy target tissue.

Less frequently, the site of inoculum formation is not a diseased plant but some reservoir of the pathogen itself. It may take one of several forms, most usually a dormant or semi-dormant phase—such as the sclerotia of certain fungi, or a concentration of pathogen established on a nonhost substrate—such as a soil fungus subsisting on organic material in the soil. Here again, these sources are more potential than actual and become of significance to the eventual host only when infective material begins to form.

PRODUCTION OF INOCULUM

Except for the fungi, not much variation occurs in the basic patterns of pathogen multiplication: virus particles increase within the living cells of the host, bacteria multiply to produce enlarged populations of individuals, flowering plants develop large numbers of seeds, and nematodes form countless eggs by several patterns of reproduction. The total numbers of infective units in each of these groups is very large and the rate of increase often very rapid.

In sharp contrast to other organisms stand the pathogenic fungi. Here the diversity of detail is striking and the mechanisms of inoculum production and liberation highly effective, as Stakman and Harrar (1957) have amply documented in their summary of this topic (Chapter 11). Viewed from the standpoint of generalized environments, two broad categories appear—aboveground inocula and soil-related pathogens.

Above-Ground Inocula

Pathogenic organisms that attack the stems, foliage, and reproductive parts of the host plant produce inoculum above ground—i.e., in a gaseous environment. The infective unit is usually a spore—providing the essential qualities of abundance, transportability, and at least short-term survival. The spores of above-ground fungi are markedly successful in meeting the problem of pathogen dispersal and survival. Because transport is often passive and totally nondirectional, over considerable distances, fungi are successful only if the total number of spores produced is almost incredibly large. Because of the dual hazards of desiccation and radiation, spores moving in dry air must be resistant if they are to be viable upon arrival. Because the moving forces are usually weak it is advantageous to the species if spores are forcibly ejected from the site of formation and if they themselves are very minute. And so the typical inoculum of the above-ground pathogenic fungi is tiny spores, produced in prodigious quantity, often launched into the air by special mechanisms, and capable of surviving the common hazards of a journey through the atmosphere.

There are exceptions to these generalizations. The spores of the downy mildews, for example, are highly sensitive to dry air and are formed only in very humid, cool weather. Spores of insect-borne fungi are frequently sticky on the outside, the better to adhere to surfaces of vectors. And fungi spread mostly by splashing rain have spores with rather different attributes than those of strictly air-borne species.

Inocula of Soil Pathogens

The below-ground environment imposes on fungi conditions that are very different from those found in the atmosphere. There is much less premium on numbers of spores and on capacity for long-distance travel. Danger of injury by desiccation is appreciably less and from radiant energy virtually nil. On the other hand, means of transport are not so effective, with the result that self-motile inocula are probably more common. Indeed, the infective unit may not be a spore at all but may be the hyphal mass itself, growing outward through the soil from an already colonized food base.

Whatever may be the particular form and abundance of the fungus inoculum, as a general rule inoculum production occurs only after an appreciable period of association between host and pathogen. That is, following invasion, the pathogen ramifies through the host and derives nutrient materials from it during an intensive vegetative growth. Only after the phase of most pronounced damage to the host is well past does inoculum formation occur. By the time spores are produced, most of the damage at that particular lesion has already been done.

MOVEMENT OF INOCULUM

Inoculum must move from point of origin to point of new invasion. For the most part this means from diseased host tissue to healthy host tissue, whether separated by a few millimeters or by many miles. Varied indeed are the mechanisms and pathways by which this journey is accomplished.

Self-propelled Inoculum

There are at least two distinct aspects to self-propulsion: (1) autonomous movement that serves only to get the inoculum started on its way or to refine the discovery of a suitable site, and (2) movement that accounts in large measure for the total distance travelled. In most species the capacity to move falls into one or the other of these categories—intermediate situations are not common.

So far as is now known, viruses are totally incapable of movement; they rely wholly on extrinsic forces to move them about in the host or from one lesion to the next.

Bacteria—at least the bacilli—do move, by means of minute flagellae on the outer surface of the cell. Their activity is most pronounced, at least under laboratory conditions, when the cells are grown in a liquid medium and when the culture is a relatively new one. But because the cells are so very minute, total movement is for only very short absolute distances and can hardly accomplish much dissemination. Motility does, however, aid the pathogen appreciably in the last few fractions of a millimeter that spell the difference between successful invasion and failure.

Self-propulsion is very common in fungi and is accomplished in a variety of different mechanisms. The spores of many species are forcibly discharged from the hyphae on which they are formed and thus launched on their journey (Fig. 9–2). And while it may seem that the distances traversed are so tiny as to be of little consequence, it must be recognized that getting the spores into the airstream and getting them in at a propitious time often spells the difference between success and failure. After all, the statistical odds against a given spore arriving at a new site must be extremely high. Any advantage, however small, therefore becomes important.

Fungus spores are discharged in many different ways. For years it has been generally assumed that the spores of the Basidiomycetes are fired by a device that is signaled by the appearance of a drop of water at the point of attachment; Olive (1964), on the contrary, has published observations that he feels indicate that the "drop" is in fact a bubble of gas formed between inner and outer layers of the wall (Fig. 9–3). Other spores, particularly those of certain Phycomycetes and Ascomycetes are forcibly ejected as a result of sudden release of internal hydraulic pressures.

Fully as important as the fact of spore discharge is the adjustment of this event to take advantage of environmental conditions most favorable to further travel and so to maximize the likelihood of successful establishment. The

Fig. 9–2. Spore cloud from apothecia of *Sclerotinia libertiana,* photographed as the fruiting bodies, having been kept in a saturated atmosphere for 3 days, were left exposed to the atmosphere of the room for 1 minute. (Dickson and Fisher, 1923)

fruiting bodies of fungi commonly adjust themselves to gravitational stimuli, as in the case of gill and pore fungi, thus making it certain that spores will fall free after discharge. In other cases, the fruiting bodies and spore-bearing structures are positively phototropic, assuring the discharge of spores toward "open air." Directionally, by these and other devices, the inoculum of many species of fungi is given a favorable initial launch. But in timing, too, spore discharge is adaptively specialized. In some cases, spore discharge occurs in response to temperature and humidity conditions favoring dissemination, especially at times of low humidity. In other species, e.g., the ascospores of apple scab, discharge from old leaves on the orchard floor is so timed as to coincide with the appearance of the first new foliage on the trees.

So much for spore discharge, per se. For the most part, fungus species that discharge their spores forcibly are among those whose spores are themselves nonmotile—that is, they are inert ballistic objects at the mercy of external forces. Very obviously, the great preponderance of organisms of this kind are above-ground pathogens.

Somewhat less abundant, but still important, are the fungi whose spores are capable of intrinsic movement. Swimming spores, called zoospores, are not found in either the Ascomycetes or Basidiomycetes, but occur regularly in most of the Phycomycetes. In the important group of diseases called downy mildews—late blight, grape mildew, and so on—flagellated spores provide the same kind of advantages as does motility in pathogenic bacteria, by increasing the likelihood of successful stomatal penetration. Even in soil it is not easy to imagine zoospores as moving very far under their own power but it does seem clear that they can and do move for short distances that can be of

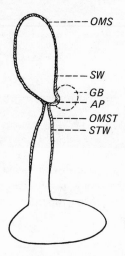

Fig. 9–3. Diagram of spore discharge mechanism in the basidiomycete *Sporobolomyces* (gaseous layer is cross-hatched): *OMS*—outer spore membrane; *SW*—inner wall of spore; *GB*—gas bubble; *AP*—apicular region; *OMST*—outer membrane of sterigma; *STW*—inner wall of sterigma. (Olive, 1964)

very great significance. For example, several recent investigations have clearly shown that the zoospores of pathogenic Phycomycetes move selectively to the roots of susceptible host species in response to concentration gradients of specific root exudates.

Nematodes, as larvae and adults, are capable of active movement by swimming in the films of water present in soil or on the surfaces of the root. In all probability, long-distance spread is passive, but local dissemination can be explained on the basis of self-generated movement.

Finally, a few of the pathogenic flowering plants, most notably the dwarf mistletoe, expel ripe seeds for considerable distances. This, plus the fact that the surfaces are sticky, is an important aspect of local dissemination.

Air Movement of Inoculum

It can be convincingly demonstrated, by using spore traps of one kind or another, that the atmosphere carries an impressive load of pathogen inoculum. Most research to date has been with fungus spores because they are easily recognized and conveniently handled. But it can be safely assumed that bacteria, seeds, even in some cases nematodes, are transported by air. There can be little question, too, that air movement accounts for most of the really spectacular geographic spread of pathogenic organisms (Fig. 9–4).

The forces acting on air-borne spores are three—gravitation, wind, and turbulence. The first is constant for a given particle under any particular set of conditions and tends to move the spore downward. Because the spores are so very small and of such low density, gravity alone cannot be counted upon to move them down from the air mass very rapidly. Several factors conspire to speed up or slow down the rate of fall—irrespective of the effect of vertical air currents. For one thing, the water content of the spores, as a reflection of

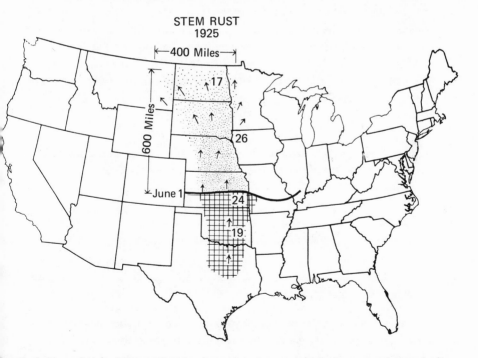

STEM RUST
1925

Fig. 9–4. Map of United States showing long-distance spread of wheat rust during the first week of June, 1925. Actual dissemination was even greater than that indicated, but infection in certain areas was prevented by dry weather. (Stakman, 1947)

atmospheric humidity, sharply alters their specific gravity. If they dry out they become less dense and hence fall less rapidly—conversely, moisture-laden spores drop more quickly. When rain is involved, quite different considerations come into play, of which the most critical is the size of the raindrop relative to the size of the spore and, obviously, the duration of rainfall.

Schrödter (1960) makes the highly important point that "the probable range of flight is directly proportional to the vertical mass exchange caused by turbulence and to horizontal wind velocity, and inversely proportional to the square of velocity of fall in calm air." By this set of criteria, a halving of the rate of fall would increase the distance traversed, other things being equal, four times.

The effect of wind on spore travel is direct and obvious. The matter of turbulence is far more complex. Schrödter, again, points out that the transition from laminar to turbulent states occurs suddenly at a critical value that in atmospheric currents is so routinely exceeded that for all practical purposes only turbulent air exists. The exception is at the immediate ground level, which underscores the very importance of spore ejection—serving as it does to move the inoculum out of the very thin layer of laminar air into the turbulence above it. When, because of this turbulence, particles move from one stratum to another, it becomes clear why spores can be found at considerable heights. Turbulence resulting from the contact of two air masses moving at different speeds and turbulence deriving from temperature gradients and consequent differences in air density combine to move spores vertically.

Table 9–1

Flight Range (X), with Different Values of Mass Exchange (A), Wind Velocity (U), and Velocity of Fall (c)

A (g/cm sec)	U (m/sec)	c (cm/sec)	X (km)
10	4	2	7.6
20	4	2	15.2
20	8	2	30.3
20	8	1	121.3

SOURCE: Schrödter, 1960.

The crux of the problem in plant pathology is the question how far, on the horizontal, a spore may go. In a series of three tables (Tables 9–1, 9–2, 9–3)° this has been brought out.

° From J. G. Horsfall and A. E. Dimond (eds.), *Plant Pathology: An Advanced Treatise* (New York: Academic Press, Inc.). Copyright © 1959–60, Academic Press, Inc.

Table 9–2

Probable Flight Range of Spores of Different Sizes with a Wind Velocity of 2 m/sec and a Mass Exchange of 10 g/cm sec

Spore Size (length/width) (µ)	Velocity of Fall (cm/sec)	Flight Range (km)
Small spores (5:3)	0.035	12,400
Medium spores (14:6)	0.138	800
Large spores (20:16)	0.975	16

SOURCE: Schrödter, 1960.

It can easily be shown empirically that the concentration of spores in an air mass falls off rapidly as distance from source increases. For example, extensive mapping of local wheat stem rust patterns as related to known infected barberry bushes, during the early years of the eradication program in the United States, showed very clearly that as one went downwind from the point of origin disease levels rapidly fell off. Behind this apparently simple relationship lies a complex of factors—spore size, height of release, vertical travel, wind velocity—to say nothing of complications introduced by irregularities in the ground surface, the filtering effect of other vegetation, and by the question whether conditions favor actual impaction on a host surface or deflection about it. This last, in turn, is determined by spore size and velocity and by the size and configuration of the host itself.

Only too rarely do investigators show the diligence and imagination to unravel the actual circumstances that surround a given observation of disease patterns. In the early days of the study of the relation between barberry and stem rust there were numerous case histories, as it were, developed that showed much of this meticulous attention to detail. Van Arsdel's careful study

Table 9–3

Probable Flight Range (X) of Spores of *Phytophthora infestans* Under Various Wind and Turbulence Conditions

A (gm/cm sec)	U (m/sec)	X (km)
0.1	2	0.09
1	4	1.8
10	6	27
20	8	72
50	10	225

SOURCE: Schrödter, 1960.

(1967) of white pine blister rust (see Fig. 9–5) in the Great Lakes region is a more recent instance. Here he showed that the time of spore release, at night, in relation to air flow patterns (which in turn were studied by observing the paths taken by smoke clouds) was the key to the situation.

Fig. 9–5. Smoke movements indicating air currents that match the observed spread of white pine blister rust from swamp currants to upland white pine. (Van Arsdel, 1967)

Water Movement of Inoculum

By comparison with air, the role of water as an agent for the dissemination of inoculum is equivocal. Almost certainly it is less effective than air in long-distance transfer of small particles but at the same time can carry larger bodies, especially those that float, for appreciable periods of time. Water can, also, move inoculum on the soil surface, through the soil, or from one point on the surface of the host to another.

Water is probably most important, however, as an adjunct to other factors. One can think of at least three ways, possibly more, by which this is exemplified. In the first place, spores of fungi that are not actively discharged from their point of initial attachment must be dislodged by external forces. Of these, water, particularly in the form of falling drops, is especially effective.

Water, as best seen in splashing raindrops, can account for very successful short-range dispersal—to other sites on the same host, to nearby plants, to protected areas that are but ill suited to deposition from moving air currents.

Walker and Patel (1964; see Fig. 9–6) have provided an experimental demonstration of the effectiveness of wind-blown splash dispersal of a bacterial
pathogen in two studies of the development of halo blight of beans from a
single infected plant centered in a rectangular plot as much as 160 feet long.

Finally, water augments the air transport of inoculum by providing especially favorable conditions for survival during and just after the journey.
Spores and bacterial cells of the kind characterized by appreciable amounts
of slime are more likely to be loosened and airborne under high moisture conditions. In a moisture-laden air they may well not move so great a distance as
in lower humidity, but the chances of survival during that movement will be
greatly enhanced and, upon landing, the chance of successful penetration will
be improved.

That the consequences of efforts to control plant disease may be other than
those intended is underscored by the observations (Dimock, 1951) that occasionally fungicides will augment rather than decrease the disease hazard. In
this instance, Dimock found that a copper quinolinate spray not only failed to
control snapdragon rust but indeed scattered the spores about and made matters worse. He reasons from this to the interesting possibility of raising a triv-
ial disease to a status of importance while trying, and even successfully, to
control another. It might well be, for example, that using the above-men-
tioned copper spray against *Alternaria* on carnations, for which it is very
effective, would at the same time materially worsen the inroads of carnation
rust (*Uromyces caryophyllinus*), which is generally of little importance.

Movement Resulting from Action of Insects

Viruses. By all odds the most intriguing interactions between pathogens
and their vectors are those involving insects; of these associations the most
complex and varied are certainly the insect-virus relationships (Fig. 9–7).
Many and diverse are the specific instances of such a pathogen-vector pairing.

Viruses by their very nature cannot move effectively from host to host, or
site to site, without an external agent. The vast majority of viruses cannot
even survive for any but very brief periods outside the living host. What better agent, then, can be imagined than the sucking insects, whose normal activities furnish an almost ideal, highly localized device for obtaining inoculum,
storing it in transit, and reestablishing it at precisely the proper point in a new
host location?

Most virus-transmitting insects have sucking mouthparts, especially the
aphids and leafhoppers, although white flies, thrips, some bugs, even grass-
hoppers, are known to be effective in a more limited sense. The degree of

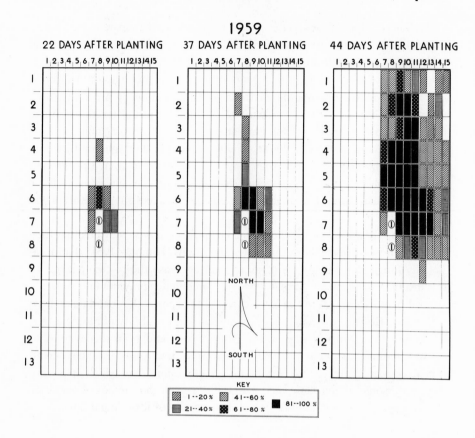

Fig. 9–6. Spread of halo blight from a centrally placed source of inoculum ⊕ in

specificity between virus and vector, indeed the whole biology of the virus in the insect, is highly variable, depending upon the particular association under study. Most workers, however, see two rather distinct classes, with less common intermediate forms. Very often these are termed "persistent" and "nonpersistent" forms, depending upon the relative length of time during which the insect remains capable of transmitting the virus.

The nonpersistent viruses—exemplified by the aphid-transmitted forms—are those where the mouthparts of the vector seem to become directly contaminated with virus and to transmit the material only so long as virus remains on their surfaces. In this sense the feeding operation is almost directly analogous to inoculation with a needle, except that it is a very delicately and precisely manipulated one.

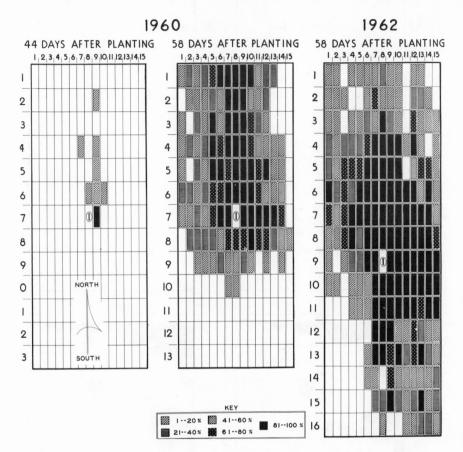

experiments carried out in 1959, 1960, and 1962. (Walker and Patel, 1964)

With persistent viruses—exemplified by the leaf-hopper forms—a number of new and complex factors come into play. Mostly, the specificity is more exact. Vectors display a noticeable difference in their ability to pick up virus depending upon whether or not they are starved prior to feeding on the host source. Differences occur between genetic variants of the vector. As a rule, the vector does not become infective for a substantial period after feeding but remains infective for a relatively long time.

All of these considerations very strongly suggest that in the persistent types, virus is taken up by the insect, moves to and through the gut, through the hemolymph, and comes to reside in due time in the salivary glands. Reinjection, along with saliva, accounts for reestablishment in a new site. Most workers have become convinced that actual multiplication of virus in the

Fig. 9–7. Diagrams showing successive spread of celery virus from adjoining weeds and then within the celery plots in a field near Sanford, Florida. (Wellman, 1935)

body of the vector takes place in a number of cases. For that matter, instances are of record where virus is transmitted to subsequent generations through the egg stage.

The feeding operations of insects are ideally suited to locate virus-bearing parenchyma or phloem, remove liquid cell contents and virus, store and move it to a new site, and reintroduce it into susceptible cells. The "journey" for viruses must be literally from cell to cell!

Swenson, in a review of aphids in relation to disease (1968), suggests that if the seasonal fluctuations in numbers of migrating aphids were better known, the information could be used to advantage in adjusting planting and harvesting dates and in applying insecticides. As effective as they are, however, the aphids do not measure up to what it would seem their potential must be because, overall, the transmission mechanism is relatively ineffective. There are many reasons for this, of course, but the more conspicuous include the brief time that the nonpersistent viruses remain in the vector and the high proportion of instances in which a particular insect fails either to pick up or to transmit the virus. Indeed, it is only when circumstances are more than usually favorable that serious losses occur—infected propagating stock, proximity to reservoir hosts, overwintering on alternate hosts, and so on.

While the transmission of a given virus may well be strictly limited to a particular pathway, the diversity of pathways that have been shown effective in at least one situation is very great indeed. The sour cherry yellows virus, for example, has been shown by several workers (Gilmer, 1965) to be transmitted by pollen from one tree to another and to be present in the seeds produced by the pollinated flowers as well as in the woody tissues on which the flowers were borne. Transmission by this means seems to take place, experimentally at least, in sweet cherry, in sour cherry, and to dwarf cherry from sweet cherry.

Bacteria and Fungi.   Rather less specificity characterizes pathogen-vector relationships involving fungi and bacteria than those discussed just above. Neither group of organisms ordinarily demands a living host cell for sheer survival, and there seems to be nothing quite comparable to the incubation period, even in those instances where the pathogen enters the body of the vector.

Insects disseminate the inocula of bacterial and fungus pathogens in a number of ways. They pick up the material either by contact as they move on the surface of diseased tissues or when inocula are, as in the case of Dutch elm disease, formed abundantly along the walls of insect burrows. In other instances the insect becomes contaminated in the process of feeding—some species of fungi and bacteria produce sweet or aromatic exudates—and may carry materials both inside and outside the body. If the spores or cells are adhesive, chances of transfer are substantially enhanced.

At the other end of the journey, new sites are inoculated by direct contact or by feeding and egg-laying. As a vector of fungi and bacteria, insects play a role analogous to the aphid vectors of viruses—the inoculum acting more or less as a contaminant and the insect as a self-mobile inoculating instrument. Not infrequently, the biological attributes of the two species have evolved into a rather intricate and complex association.

Active Movement.   By no means do all insect vectors fly, but the overwhelming majority do so in at least one of the life stages. Very local movement can result from mere crawling about; the more spectacular instances are attributable to insect flight, often augmented by air currents sufficiently strong to transport the individuals themselves. Weather, then, has an important role in disease spread by insects. When temperatures are low or rainfall heavy, most insects will move little if at all from one place to another. Rapid wind currents, low humidity, and warm temperatures will maximize the tendency to move about.

Movement Resulting from Action of Organisms Other than Insects

Other than man himself, there are a few animals whose role in the movement of inoculum, though relatively minor, deserves notice. After all, nearly any moving object can occasionally, entirely by accident even, become surface contaminated and serve as a vector. Birds are probably most widely held responsible for pathogen spread. Woodpeckers, for example, were considered to have been effective in carrying the chestnut blight organism at the peak of its destructiveness. And bird transfer can readily account for those infrequent instances of long-distance spread when the nature of inoculum or of inoculum formation seems to preclude direct air movement as an adequate explanation.

Other small animals—bats, nonflying rodents—may occasionally act in the capacity of vectors, although they do not seem to be generally important. The relationships between vector and pathogen in most of these instances is just too superficial to be convincing.

Last but not least, as noted in an earlier section, nematodes appear to serve as vectors of what have been called "soil-borne" viruses. Most of the importance of the nematodes to the pathogen lies in the latter's survival, but small increments of dissemination are attributable to vector movement.

EFFECTIVENESS OF INOCULUM

No word better expresses the general success with which a given inoculum brings about a new infection than "effectiveness." It is a multifaceted situation, involving the number of infective units in the inoculum under examination, the virulence of the pathogen, susceptibility of host, and the external environment. Effectiveness is the net effect of all these, many of them operating simultaneously. Yet if it were not for this constant threat of new disease we would be interested in inoculum only in the academic sense.

THE PROBLEM OF SURVIVAL

Along with all of the other variables, inoculum very often displays a highly seasonal variability. As might be anticipated, this variability is mostly related to production of the infective propagules. In spring, for example, the ascospores of the apple scab fungus are formed in the leaves lying on the orchard floor; in the height of the growing season asexual spores are formed on the surfaces of active lesions on foliage and fruit. The list of examples in this general category is endless.

But seasonal effects operate through another channel in that the amount of inoculum is conditioned by the success of the pathogen in surviving unfavorable environmental circumstances. One thinks immediately of winter, and this is probably the most frequently limiting, but not infrequently the high temperatures of the summer months, at least in the lower latitudes, are likewise limiting. Many microorganisms are aided in the matter of survival by having one or several resistant stages in the life cycle that enable them to withstand not only hot and cold extremes, but desiccation and physical forces as well.

Because phytopathogenic bacteria do not form spores, the tendency is to think of them as relatively short-lived contaminants of crops and soils, but studies of cotton angular leaf spot (Schnathorst, 1964) show that the organism can remain viable and pathogenic for as much as 7 years in dried leaves. This seems to explain why ginning machinery remains contaminated for very appreciable periods and why fields show disease even when all of the usual precautions—blight-free source of seed, soils not recently used for cotton culture, and so on—are observed.

Much of the difficulty experienced in control of soil-borne diseases results from the impressive ability of the pathogenic organisms to survive for very long periods. Hoppe (1966) has provided an instance of this in trials of air-dried muck soil kept at room temperature for 12 years. He found that *Pyth-*

ium, probably in the form of oospores, was not only able to remain viable for this length of time, but was effective in producing seed rot of corn when planted in the contaminated soils. Germination of corn was not inhibited by rot to the degree that it was in recently collected muck, but was even so reduced by as much as 60% when the dried samples were rewetted prior to the test.

As the search continues for ways in which to control plant disease by manipulating the natural populations of various competing species, the diversity of these manipulations increases. Klink and Barker (1968), among others, have conducted experiments on the relationships between a mycophagous nematode, *Aphelenchus avenae*, and several of the common root-rotting pathogenic fungi—*Rhizoctonia, Fusarium,* and *Sclerotium*. They found, in controlled conditions of sand culture, that the best control of root rot occurred when there were 4,000 to 6,000 nematodes per milliliter of fungal inoculum and that at this favorable rate, the inoculum was virtually destroyed (Fig. 9–8). Not only this, but the nematodes prevented the formation of sclerotia in the soil if they were added along with the fungus inoculum, presumably by destroying the mycelium of the sclerotia as rapidly as it grows out.

The hazards to survival that must be overcome are many, although not all types of inoculum meet these hazards in just the same way, nor with the same degree of success. Most conspicuous hazards are desiccation, temperature extremes, radiation and death from what might be called "old age." Clearly, it is the extremes of the environment that are important and one soon realizes that the ranges of values of environmental conditions and the possible combinations are simply enormous.

Not all inoculum is similarly equipped to face the hazards of environment. Some are extremely sensitive, others highly resistant, to each of the factors in turn. Where one organism emphasizes thickness of resting spore wall at the cost of loss in motility and minuteness, another sacrifices resistance to desiccation as the price of capacity for almost immediate germination and penetration of host tissues. In still others the body of a vector protects them from environmental extremes.

The crucial point is that if, on arrival, the inoculum is viable, we have a real interest in the fact that it has accomplished its journey. If not, the journey is of no significance.

THE SOIL ENVIRONMENT

S. D. Garrett, possibly more than any other one person, has clarified the special circumstances bearing on soil pathogens, particularly soil fungi, and

Fig. 9–8. Effect of the nematode *Aphelenchus avenae* on root rot induced by *Fusarium solani* f. sp. *pisi*. (A) On bean (*left to right*): control, fungus alone, fungus plus 475 nematodes per seed, fungus plus 950 nematodes, and fungus plus 3,000 nematodes. (B) On peas (*left to right*): control, fungus plus 13,000 nematodes per seed, fungus plus 6,500 nematodes, and fungus only. (Klink and Barker, 1968)

his writings are a must for the serious student who wishes to go more fully into the subject.

Viruses, bacteria, fungi, nematodes, and the seeds of vascular plants are all found at one time or another in soil—for many fungi and nematodes it is their most characteristic habitat. Soil-borne viruses were discussed in an earlier section. Bacteria may remain as inoculum in the soil as such, or may be carried by a subterranean insect vector. The fungi exist as spores and as masses of vegetative filaments of greater or lesser size and complexity.

Because movement over long distances in the soil is infrequent, unless the soil itself is transported, the more important question is that of survival during the interval from the demise of an infected host until another becomes available. Viruses persist in alternative host species, fungi or nematodes. Bacteria continue as vegetative cells or associated with such other organisms as insects. Fungi meet the situation in two ways:

- By forming a "resting stage"—a zygospore, chlamydospore, or sclerotium
- By persisting as a saprophyte on soil organic material during the absence of a susceptible host species.

Nematodes may persist as adult or larval forms or remain as eggs until conditions are favorable.

Movement through soil, though limited, does take place. Motile cells move through soil water, and the movement of soil water itself carries even inert cells along for considerable distances. To some extent, too, growth of a root system will bring tissue and pathogen together even though the inoculum itself is immobile. Conversely, in fungi with rhizomorphs the inoculum will reach new sites by virtue of its own growth in length.

While bacteria do not have the obvious characteristics of the fungi that facilitate their movement from host to host in the soil, they are not entirely unsuccessful in this regard. Kelman and Sequeira (1965) have studied the movement of the pathogen *Pseudomonas solanacearum* from an inoculated to an uninoculated plant growing a short distance away under experimental conditions. Using combinations of tomato, tobacco, and banana, they discovered that not only do uninoculated plants become diseased but they do so in the absence of direct wounding—observations suggest that the point of emergence of secondary roots is the site of entry. By whatever route, the evidence clearly shows that after symptoms develop, but before the plant actually dies, very large numbers of bacteria escape into the soil; presumably it is these cells that bring about the invasion of nearby healthy plants.

Lastly, the final entry of inoculum is much facilitated by the wounding of tissues by soil-inhabiting creatures of one kind or another. Much soil-borne inoculum owes its success to the activities of root-damaging species that serve to breach the early barriers of newly formed root tissues. Only in the case of root nematodes, which provide their own avenues of entry, can pathogenic organisms succeed without an external factor to assist in their entry and establishment.

10

Epidemic Development

The question of how disease becomes established in a population of host plants and how it then extends through that population has not been especially popular as a research topic in plant pathology. As evidence of this, when a committee of the American Phytopathological Society, about 1960, undertook to assemble a bibliography of "reviews" in plant pathology for the immediately preceding decade, all available summary articles and relevant doctoral theses were included. Under the heading "individual diseases" were about 260 titles, mostly representing monographic studies of a single-host-pathogen interrelationship. During the same span of time, the committee could find only 5 review papers on inoculum production, 18 on inoculum dispersal, and 10 on survival of inoculum. In the entire category of "Epidemic development" there were but 34, and of these a substantial number were the work of a very limited number of authors. A category entitled "Kinetics of epidemics" contains but seven entries. There must be significance to a situation that results in nearly 40 times as many analyses of individual diseases as of phenomena of disease dynamics, per se. One tends to reject the possibility that epidemics are intrinsically one-fortieth as important.

One finds in the literature of plant pathology very little, actually, that might fairly be called the "history" of plant diseases. Whether such a study would provide useful insights into the biology of disease is, of course, an unanswered question until the study is actually made. But it does seem likely that if careful records were compiled—assuming the data did not turn out to be simply too scanty to permit useful conclusions—it would be possible to chronicle the rise and fall of disease in a way that would be instructive. We have a few that are reasonably well known, such as the late blight of potato, but mostly it has not received anything like the attention given by medical historians to the story of human disease.

The problems of epidemics and their behavior are highly complex and introduce a number of variables. To attack the question has appeared so formidable a task that many have turned to simpler issues. The tools needed to do the job have seemed hardly adequate and the odds against success too great. The difficulty of getting precise data in an era that holds it dear has militated against work in this area.

But there are both theoretical and practical reasons why it is essential to understand why disease develops as it does and what are the underlying principles of its behavior. Not the least of these is the increasing pressure on growers and professional pathologists alike to find ways to reduce the use of chemicals in the control of disease and to lengthen the span of time through which a given genetically resistant variety maintains an effective degree of resistance. In short, there is great incentive to adopt cultural methods that will either substitute for, or enhance, the traditional means of disease control. Culture, as here used, means much more than mere cultivation practices. It means all those aspects of timing, spacing, sequential planting, and general programming that affect the target crops (see in this connection, Chapter 15). If this approach is to be successful, it will be necessary to know far more about the biology of disease and to understand far better than we now do the phenomena that underlie disease development and spread.

Of the relatively few persons who have attacked the question of epidemic spread head on, Dr. J. E. van der Plank, of the Department of Agriculture, Union of South Africa, stands out. The interested student is referred to his review paper in the anniversary volume of the American Phytopathological Society (1959), to his detailed chapter on analysis of epidemics in the Academic Press treatise on plant pathology (1960), and to his later book on the subject (1963). These are milestones in the literature of plant disease epidemiology that can be expected to have a lasting effect. The earlier classic work by Ernst Gäumann (1950) is a contribution of like stature.

The keys to van der Plank's approach seem to be, first, that he consistently subordinates factual data to a determined search for underlying principles; secondly, that he has the happy facility of discerning relationships even when they are so simple as to be easily overlooked; and thirdly, that he takes pains to carry his analyses to the point where their practical consequences can be demonstrated and thus wins credibility.

Van der Plank's material is sprinkled far more liberally with processes and events expressed as mathematical equations than is characteristic of most plant-pathological literature. To those of an analytical turn of mind, this mode of expression will be of appreciable benefit; to the mathematically less apt they will not detract noticeably from the force of the arguments. In the following pages, many of his insights are summarized as they apply to the epidemic as an abstract event, as it affects host, pathogen, and diseased individual, and as it applies to practical forecasting.

EPIDEMIC SPREAD—THE PHENOMENON

What Is an Epidemic?

The term disease epidemic usually brings to mind the sort of thing that has happened on several historic occasions—outbreaks of potato late blight, tobacco blue mold, or the widely publicized black stem rust of wheat. In these cases the growers have witnessed a dramatically rapid, widespread, and destructive attack of the pathogen over major acreages of the susceptible crop. Occasionally, if the damage is sufficiently conspicuous or destruction sufficiently great, epidemics of less rapidly developing diseases have been objects of general public concern. The chestnut blight, imported into North America from China about 1900, and the wasting disease of eelgrass on both the western and eastern coasts of the North Atlantic are two examples.

Van der Plank argues persuasively that epidemics should not be defined along traditional lines as suggested in the preceding paragraph, but that they should be recognized as a balance struck between those circumstances that produce new pathogen propagules and those that cause their destruction. In his terms, when "birth rate" exceeds "death rate," whether the processes in absolute terms are rapid or slow, there is an epidemic. He carries the point still further by characterizing high birth rate epidemics as local lesion diseases, to be controlled by fungicides or resistant varieties; conversely, low death rate epidemics are caused by systemic pathogens and are best controlled by cultural methods.

Whether one wholly accepts his view or not, it is interesting to speculate on why the more limited concept of epidemics has generally prevailed. Most likely it is the direct result of public familiarity with human disease, for in this connection epidemic means exclusively a rapidly developing outbreak. So pervasive is the emphasis on human disease that the habit of using "epidemic" in the more extreme, limited sense is firmly rooted.

How Does an Epidemic Behave?

At one extreme are the diseases that threaten every growing season and that, if conditions are right, have the capacity for explosive development. On several occasions the stem rust of wheat has devastated much of the great wheatlands of midcontinent North America, from Mexico into Canada, or the Soviet expanses of the Ukraine and adjacent provinces. Again and again the potato fields of northern Europe, of the British Isles, or of the United States have stood as grim reminders of how, almost literally overnight, a single pathogen can lay waste a major fraction of its host species.

The Dutch elm disease is very different. Introduced about 1930 into Baltimore, Maryland, on elm logs brought in for manufacture, the pathogen spread inexorably north and west until vast numbers of that most popular of all American lawn and street trees had been destroyed. But the time scale was years and decades, not days and weeks. Even today, nearly half a century later, there are cities still experiencing an active phase of the disease and still harboring large numbers of as yet unharmed trees. Generally speaking, the white pine blister rust and the chestnut blight have had patterns of development very like that for Dutch elm disease.

Whether rapid or slow-moving, an epidemic usually begins long before its presence is widely recognized. Studies such as those by K. S. Chester of the wheat leaf rust in Oklahoma years ago showed most graphically that the events of this very early period are critical in epidemics of the one-season type. That is, the generations of spore production necessary to bring the lesion count from one for every thousand leaves to one per leaf are critical in determining whether, in the remaining interval before maturity and harvest, there is time enough for a serious outbreak to occur. As we shall see, substantial reliance is placed on data from just this period in trying to forecast the eventual outcome of rust in a given year.

As available tissue is used up, so to speak, even the most virulent pathogen must show a measurable diminution in rate of increase. The general result, if the epidemic is assessed on the basis of lesion number or size, is a sort of "growth curve" pattern—slow start, period of maximum increase, then a tapering off. When attention shifts to the more slowly moving diseases, patterns are by no means so obvious but can be presumed to follow much the same route.

The ebb and flow of new—or newly noted—diseases tends to make us forget that a very substantial fraction of the total economic damage and of the time and attention of plant pathologists is directly related to a small number of very important diseases. How many make up this "small number" depends upon who is making the list and what criteria are used to determine the diseases that merit inclusion, but there would be little disagreement as to a dozen or two that should be voted into this kind of a hall of fame. And it is a valuable exercise to review the situation from time to time, lest the very familiarity we have with these old standbys lead us to underestimate their importance and the importance of continuing research upon them. Just such a summary statement has been provided by van der Zwet (1968) in a paper on the fire blight of pear, apple, and related hosts. As the maps show (Fig. 10–1)

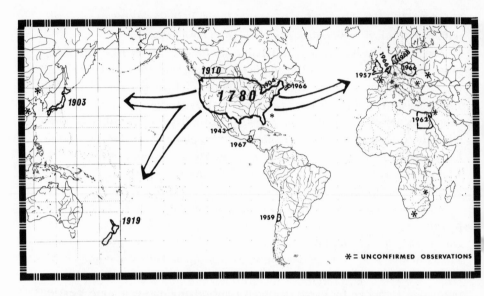

Fig. 10–1. World distribution of fire blight. *Top:* Map showing dates of earliest known observations of fire blight in 11 countries and locations of recorded blossom blights *Bottom:* Enlarged map of northern Europe, updated to 1970. (Van der Zwet, 1968)

the disease was first recognized in the orchards of North America in the late 1700's and spread in about a century from New York to California. It then moved to Canada, Japan, New Zealand, and Mexico and, since 1957, to England, Chile, Egypt, Poland, The Netherlands, and Guatemala—by "moved" in this case one can mean only that it was recognized in those countries for the first time in the period indicated.

As the author says, "Between 1901 and 1909, fire blight wrought such havoc in California as has seldom been known in a fruit-growing country. The State Board of Horticulture reported in 1902 that Fresno County has 125,000 pear trees and Kings County 43,700 trees. By 1904, fire blight had reduced these numbers to 1,500 and none, respectively . . . by 1908, two-thirds of the 'Bartlett' trees in the State had been destroyed by the blight."

Rate of Multiplication

Pathologists have recognized for a long time that the rate at which a given disease multiplies and spreads is the net result of a complex of interacting factors. Among the more obvious of these are host density and susceptibility, pathogen reproduction, inoculum dissemination. Each of these factors, in turn, comprises a subset of variables. Most are influenced by the atmospheric and soil environment. Indeed, a great deal of the aggregate effort of plant pathologists as a group is spent in trying to learn of and to understand the phenomena that, on balance, govern disease development.

Van der Plank adopts mathematical symbols and expressions to convey his philosophy of epidemics. In so doing he introduces the concept of "r"—specifically, "the rate of increase per cent per day (or other unit of time) up to the onset of the epidemic." Without, for the moment at least, concerning ourselves about the restriction of the use of r to the pre-epidemic phase, it is useful to point out that by letting r stand for the entire array of factors noted in the first paragraph of this section, van der Plank achieves a convenient shorthand expression that permits him to think about the consequences of differences in the value of r unhampered by need to spell out the detailed causes of these differences. Perhaps this device, while it makes no pretext of being wholly new, has permitted the author to pursue his thinking toward useful conclusions that would otherwise have been far less likely to emerge. For detailed treatment of the weather as an element in the process, the student is directed to Chapter 11.

Van der Plank calculates his r on the basis of the differences in the proportions of susceptible tissue that is infected at either end of a known time interval. If the latter is in days, then r becomes a value expressed as percent per day. By definition, he restricts the concept, which is basically a "compound interest" expression, to the period up to 5% total involvement, thus avoiding the complications arising from the progressive disappearance of available uninvaded tissue. Experience of a number of investigators clearly demonstrates that the early, even very early, dynamics of disease are fully indicative of the total pattern.

Epidemic Spread

In the last analysis growers of agricultural crops must face the fact that plant diseases can and often do spread with appreciable speed over wide areas. Just how fast and how far depends upon a complex of factors alluded to above—host susceptibility, abundance, and distribution; pathogen virulence, inoculum productivity and mobility; environmental conditions as related to host susceptibility, inoculum dispersal, and incubation period.

One may again look with profit to van der Plank for an analysis of epidemic pattern. He shows, for example, that if the characteristics of inoculum production, transport, and establishment are such that the number of new lesions varies inversely as the square, cube, or higher power of the distance from the source, epidemics will spread in a continuous fashion and may be easily traced. If, on the other hand, gradients are comparatively flat and vary inversely at values less than the square of distance, spread will be discontinuous and difficult to follow dependably. This particular relationship seems to hold pretty much irrespective of the actual distances involved—i.e., a given outbreak may move outward from an initial source at distinctly different speeds in two different directions—downwind vs. upwind, for example—without altering the basic pattern by which it moves.

And because distance affects rate of multiplication, local lesion diseases must inevitably have the highest potential for establishing new sites.

THE HOST AND EPIDEMICS

Are there aspects of the host plant that can be causally related to the behavior of epidemics? If this question can be answered in the affirmative it suggests a fruitful avenue of approach to aspects of disease control—control that, incidentally, may be less costly than any alternative means available.

In an earlier section we dwelt at some length on the changing patterns of agriculture and the strong tendency in modern practice to develop monocul-

tures. Where large plantings of genetically uniform crops are found, the supposition is that epidemic potential is sharply enhanced. So long as susceptible
host varieties and virulent pathogens do not coincide, the threat remains only
a threat. But so genetically variable are most pathogen species that it is hardly
likely that host populations will escape indefinitely. In plants and people
alike, the spectacular epidemics of history have usually moved through large
concentrations of host individuals.

Whether diseases become epidemic, in so far as the phenomenon is related
to host distribution, would seem to depend more than anything else on
whether inoculum is of the kind that moves only relatively short distances and
multiplies relatively slowly. These generalizations have implications for control by management of size and proximity of plantings of a given crop variety.
When, for example, the rate at which disease develops is at the upper end of
the spectrum, it makes comparatively little difference how concentrated and
how extensive is the host population—diseases will, within a growing season,
be established virtually throughout. When, on the other hand, disease is of the
kind that develops only slowly, isolated populations may either escape entirely or, perhaps more importantly, will receive inoculum so belatedly that
overall damage is minimal.

As van der Plank puts it, "The paradox is this. Bringing plants together
into fields increases the chance of epidemics; bringing them still further together, by increasing the area of the fields and correspondingly reducing their
number, may reduce the chance of a general epidemic."

PATHOGENS AND EPIDEMICS

Consider now primarily the pathogen. The dynamics of an epidemic is
very greatly influenced by aspects directly attributable to the pathogen as a
biological entity. If inoculum production is rapid and profuse, the potential
for invasion of new tissue and new hosts is greatly enhanced. If, in addition,
the pathogen moves rapidly and for substantial distances, the threat is compounded. This is not to overlook the importance of host resistance but rather
to point out that for any given level of host resistance, population density, and
so on, epidemics reflect the rate at which the pathogen reproduces and is disseminated.

HOST-PATHOGEN INTERACTION AND EPIDEMICS

From van der Plank comes a persuasive analysis of the patterns of epidemics of disease in plants. Where the time available is a single growing season—

i.e., in annual plants and in the new season's growth of perennials—disease in destructive proportions is possible only when percentage rate of increase (the value of "r" in his terminology) is high or the amount of inoculum available at the beginning of the growing season is large. Perhaps the only significant exception would be those cases where each lesion is so destructive that the first involvement of a given host plant is sufficient to cause its near destruction or death.

Where the host population survives for more than one year, a whole new set of considerations comes into focus. If the population is long-established and the pathogen indigenous to the area, stable levels of disease tend to prevail. It is only when either host or pathogen is introduced from a locality other than that under consideration that striking changes occur—where the term "epidemic" again becomes applicable. More on that point will be found in the discussion of quarantine (Chapter 16).

Where the host-pathogen relationship is systemic, severity of an epidemic tends to vary directly with the size of the host plant but inversely as the number of plants per unit area.

FORECASTING

Students of the philosophy of science point out that nothing so convincingly demonstrates the validity of a concept or set of postulates as does their successful use in forecasting an event stemming from those data and understandings. Plant pathology is no exception to this rule, even in dealing with the peculiarly difficult and complex phenomena of disease epidemics. Indeed, epidemics of a number of specific diseases are regularly predicted, to the considerable credit of those who accept this responsibility and to the economic advantage of the growers whose interests they serve. Much remains before the full potential of forecasting is realized, but it is even now an established aspect of the profession.

Useful Information

Each disease complex will have its own peculiar combination of factors that interact to determine how severe will be the damage in a single season at a given spot. There are, therefore, a number of *kinds* of information useful in developing a forecasting procedure that are more or less common to all situations. It is the details thereof and their importance relative to each other that must be carefully worked out case by case.

Inoculum. Especially where rate of multiplication is slow, the level of disease to be expected in an approaching season is greatly influenced by the amount of inoculum coming into contact with the target host population. In the temperate zone, initial inoculum is often whatever survives the winter season as dormant spores, mycelium, cysts, seeds, or other entity. Alternatively, pathogens may survive as established infections in overwintering portions of the host plant—as for example in reservoir species. Finally, inoculum may arrive on the scene from a point outside the immediate region for which forecasts are to be made.

Whatever the biological basis for inoculum levels at the outset, quantitative data on just what this level is are of very great utility as an indication of future disease severity.

Multiplication. For diseases characterized by a potential for rapid increase, it is less important to know how much inoculum is present at the beginning of the growing season than to know what factors of host and environment are present that will operate to accelerate or depress the rate of multiplication. Environmental conditions certainly head the list of items to be considered. Indeed, it appears that perhaps the majority of forecasting programs now in actual operation are primarily keyed to this aspect of the problem. Thus temperature and moisture are of the utmost importance.

Ancillary matters may need to be considered, not the least of which are levels of field resistance on the part of the host. Where generation times of pathogens are set by the period required before new lesions will produce inoculum suitable for dispersal, even partial resistance on the part of the host will have a significant impact on total disease intensity by reducing the number of generations that are possible in the interval prior to harvest.

Movement. A third category of data useful to the plant disease forecaster has to do with inoculum movement. Whether the disease be one depending largely on initial inoculum load or upon high multiplication rate, practical predictions for a given crop in a given region in a given year will be dependent in part on how far, in what direction, in what quantities, and at what speed the pathogen moves. In this context it makes little difference how the inoculum moves, although accurate information on this point will often contribute to the needed answers.

How far and in what direction are usually determined by the mode of transfer—airborne inoculum, for example, being dependent on such things as wind direction and velocity. Infective material may move from scattered individuals with the field, from reservoirs along the edge of agricultural plantings, from overwintering materials nearby, or from distant, often more advanced, plantings lying to the south.

Regional differences in the threat posed by a disease result from differences in land use patterns, in geography, in climatic and biological barriers, and so on. The point is that there can be no substitute for on-the-spot information about inoculum movement of specific relevance to the area for which forecasting is to be attempted.

Just as samples taken of pathogen levels on selected sites will help answer the question as to how much threat is posed by that aspect of the problem, so sampling of airstreams will often indicate what is taking place as regards inoculum movement. True, not all movement is through the air, but generally those diseases for which forecasting is in fact economically justifiable are caused by pathogens having airborne inoculum.

Vectors. Many pathogens, particularly viruses and bacteria, depend on insects and other vectors as a means of survival during crop-free periods, for overwintering, and for dispersal. Where the relationship is highly specific in the sense that one vector—or at best a limited number—is involved, it is often possible to base forecasting procedures on data concerning the vector itself. The bacterial wilt of sweet corn furnishes a classic example of this situation, wherein acceptably accurate predictions can be made on the basis of the beetle vector of the pathogen. The beetle population, in turn, depends upon how large a population survives the winter. True, the immediately observed phenomena are weather data, especially temperature, but the causal relationship depends upon vector survival.

Survival and the magnitude of pathogen-bearing spring populations are not the only contributions vectors make to epidemic development and thereby to forecasting, but thus far these two have proven by far the most useful.

Biology of Disease and Forecasting. Forecasting cannot succeed unless it is within the biological context of the host-pathogen association. We have noted already that where rate of increase is rapid, forecasting can be based on weather and carried out almost without concern for initial inoculum load. Where rates are low, it is imperative to include initial inoculum in a forecasting regime.

In his discussion of forecasting, Waggoner (1960) examines one by one the commonly recognized phenomena associated with disease—inoculum load, dispersal, infection, incubation, and so on—and shows in what ways these are useful in developing forecasting methods. After recognizing the complexity of the situation, he then points out that not infrequently one can, after sufficient study, identify one or more highly critical phases of the process upon which the outcome ultimately depends. Once the key events are identified, much of the remaining fabric of the host-pathogen association becomes more or less irrelevant, at least to this issue, and can be largely ignored. More often than not the crucial item turns out to be what the weather is like at a particular point in the sequence of events.

The Role of Weather

Chapter 11 will deal, among other things, with weather in relation to plant disease epidemics. All that need be said here is that, by and large, forecasting has been keyed to weather factors rather more than to anything else. Perhaps this results in part from the tendency to devote first attention to the spectacular, rapidly epidemic types of diseases—the cereal rusts and the downy mildews. To formulate dependable forecasting schemes, the usual approach has been to study correlations between known levels of disease and established weather records. Where the correlations are striking, it often becomes possible so to narrow the relationship that provisional forecasts can be made. Subsequent testings permit a more and more accurate approximation to actual events.

Utilization of Forecasts

Aside from the academic satisfaction of seeing how well an understanding of disease can be demonstrated by accurate forecasting, there are important economic benefits.

For example, if costly control measures are the accepted means of reducing losses, it is directly beneficial to know in advance what the risks are likely to be. This is especially true when the disease fluctuates greatly from one season to the next and where available control measures are rather transiently effective. Perhaps the classic example is potato late blight. Uncontrolled on susceptible varieties, if the weather is favorable, blight may give rise to losses that approach total destruction. The pathogen is highly sensitive to moisture and temperature, develops explosively when conditions are ideal, and remains static when the environment is unfavorable. Still further, chemicals applied as a control measure do not persist for long periods of time on the foliage and do not protect newly formed tissues. All of these factors combine to provide a situation where the individual grower, if he can but know in advance when disease threatens, profits immensely by increasing the precision of his control efforts. It is not necessary that a forecasting plan be faultless, only that it not fail to alert the grower to possible danger. That is, a system that warns of *all* serious outbreaks can be highly acceptable even if it also produces a few false alarms. What cannot be tolerated is failure, even occasionally, to forecast an outbreak of major proportions.

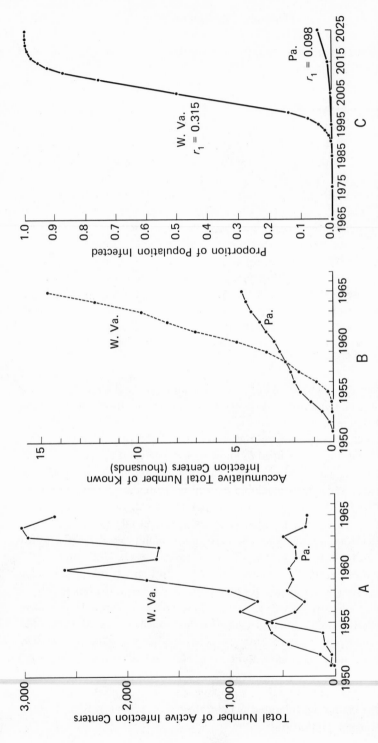

Fig. 10–2. Oak wilt in Pennsylvania and West Virginia. (A) Total number of active oak wilt infection centers, per year, in Pennsylvania and West Virginia. (B) Cumulative total number of known oak wilt infection centers in Pennsylvania and West Virginia. (C) Predicted course of oak wilt epidemics in Pennsylvania and West Virginia, based on calculated values for the period 1956–65. (Merrill, 1967)

250

Where control is not routinely feasible, as for cereal rusts, it is still economically important to know what damage is likely to occur in a given season. Occasionally substituted crops, rearranged harvesting and seeding schedules, or changes in storage and marketing plans may help to cushion the effect of high disease losses if they are known in advance.

Forecasting in plant pathology is a not uncommon event, but almost all of the effort has been devoted to the short term analyses that have been developed for potato late blight, the blue mold of tobacco, the cucurbit downy mildews. Here the concern is to assess the likelihood of epidemic development in a single growing season and to make estimates as to its probable timing and severity, with a view to effecting control measures. Merrill (1967) has turned to a very different disease situation, the oak wilt epidemics in Pennsylvania and West Virginia, and tried to invoke the van der Plank equations to predict what is likely to happen in these two states in the decades just ahead. Whether measured against the number of new oak wilt infection centers per year (Fig. 10–2A), the number of "break over" infections per year, or the accumulative total number of known infection centers (Fig. 10–2B), the story over the past 15 to 20 years shows a very similar picture—rapid increase in West Virginia, relatively slow increase in Pennsylvania. Merrill's specific prediction is that if present trends continue, 1 percent of the population in Pennsylvania will be infected in about 50 years, but that this same level will be reached in West Virginia by the end of 25 years, and that the latter state will have a 50 percent infection level within 40 years (Fig. 10–2C).

Although there have been extensive sanitation programs in both states since the early 1950's, it is not possible to tell what would have been the present situation without control effort. Neither are the conditions that influence the greater rate of increase in West Virginia known, although on a regional scale it does lie in the center of the area of oak wilt occurrence, whereas Pennsylvania lies on the northern border.

11

Environment

In the section dealing with the intricacies of the host-pathogen interaction, Chapter 8 examined how temperature, light, moisture, and certain other factors affect the processes that lead to the occurrence of disease in plants. It was a commentary, from a selected vantage point, upon the contents of the three immediately preceding chapters. In all of these it will be recalled the focus of attention was upon the individual host plant in interaction with, characteristically, a single pathogen. In much the same way Chapter 11 now takes a look at the role of the environment as it influences the course of disease in populations. Thus it too accepts the viewpoint of the chapters immediately preceding it. But it does not devote any space to noninfectious diseases as such; epidemics must by definition be of diseases caused by living organisms.

Epidemics are best considered in collective terms. We observe the net characteristics of a system made up of many individual plants, many separate but interacting processes, all modified by a complex of environmental factors. One cannot be unmindful of the bits and pieces that make up the final result but the epidemic, as the result itself, takes precedence—that plus the fact that under most circumstances it is simply not possible to know every last one of the individual interactions.

By way of emphasizing the multiplicity of factors involved, consider what are often called "phenological" observations, as related to the occurrence of disease in epidemic proportions. K. S. Chester, among others, has reminded us that outbreaks of certain economically important diseases in Western Europe have long been correlated with recognizable stages in the seasonal development of native flora. Obviously both are affected by a complex assemblage of interacting factors—temperature, moisture, light intensity, photoperiod—acting over an extended period. Sometimes the details are reasonably well known, sometimes very obscure. But the point is that the utility of the system does not depend upon one's knowing which of the components is critical and which are not. Attention centers on end results—understanding the intermediate steps, however desirable, is a sort of luxury.

By what device, then, is it best to approach the question of environment and epidemics? On balance, an anecdotal or historical examination of selected cases suggests itself. If attention is to remain centered on the *collective* effect of environmental factors on disease in populations, and if excessive detail is to be avoided, a study of concrete situations is called for.

On the matter of sensitivity, some disease epidemics are strikingly subject to modifications by extrinsic factors. These diseases are the ones first to mind when the term epidemic arises—those explosively spreading types epitomized by the downy mildews, cereal rusts, and other predominantly airborne pathogens. Other maladies are much less dramatically affected by changes in the conditions under which they exist—most of the systemic diseases, the vector-transmitted virus diseases, and soil-associated difficulties are examples. Part of the apparent difference is due to varying time scales—in the sense that the greater the tempo of disease development, the more vividly it reflects response to the environment. Most systemic viruses cannot possibly show the effect of environment so quickly as can airborne fungi. But part of the difference is real—diseases do vary significantly in the extent to which they reflect environmental impact upon their development course.

It should not be overlooked, either, that some of the differences in appearance are attributable to relative differences in what might be called sensitivity. That is, even in a given category of disease there are instances that are fundamentally less sensitive and that therefore reflect far less the vicissitudes of the environment.

CLIMATE AND GEOGRAPHIC LIMITS

Climate, which is weather over the long pull, sets not only the geographic limits of the host plant but also of disease. Neither host nor disease has in every instance occupied all of the total area available to it, of course. Other conditions—economic, historical, cultural—may have operated to limit distribution, but in a very real sense climate sets the potential limit beyond which disease epidemics may not go. Sometimes this is co-extensive with the range of the host species, sometimes far more restricted.

As one example, take the suggestion of G. H. Hepting (1963) in his review of climate in relation to forest diseases. (Forest species, tied as they are to a fixed locality over many years, afford an especially favorable object against which to measure long-term influences of climate.) In Hepting's view, there is a class of forest tree diseases that is relatively insensitive to the environment —he cites chestnut blight, Dutch elm disease, and mimosa wilt, all caused by well-known pathogens. This insensitivity results from the fact that the pathogens are so effective in producing inoculum, establishing themselves, and producing disease that they are successful over a very wide range of weather conditions. It is by no means that they are unaffected by weather. At the other extreme are to be found diseases so marginally successful that they rarely reach epidemic proportions. *Phytophthora* root rot of Douglas-fir in the Pacific Northwest, sapstreak of maple and yellow poplar in the Appalachians and pine pitch canker in the South are among those cited in this second category. Note that none could be considered well known and that each is geographically restricted—to the Pacific Northwest, in the Appalachians, in the South. It is precisely because the disease is seldom able to gain a foothold that more often than not we have scarcely even heard of them.

To the leaf diseases and the rusts Hepting ascribes the term "threshold," by which he means that they pose a potential, but ordinarily unrealized, threat. If one now postulates even very modest climatic changes, the possibility of very serious shifts in epidemic development becomes apparent. In evidence he offers the suggestion that observed increases in the incidence of pole blight of western white pine, yellow pine little leaf, and birch dieback are the result of climatic shifts in the corresponding geographic regions. He points out that an air temperature shift of but a very few degrees could be expected to bring on major changes in the forest disease situation.

Lest it appear that climatic change affects only forest diseases, recall the wasting disease of eelgrass. No more widespread and destructive pathogen has ever been recognized than the obscure *Labyrinthula* responsible for this epidemic. Yet, as a marine plant, the eelgrass host enjoyed what must be as stable and uniform an ecological niche as is readily imagined. Weather, in the short-term sense, could hardly have been responsible. While unanswered questions remain, the weight of circumstantial evidence points to a climatic shift affecting the entire North Atlantic as the probable basis for the epidemic.

WEATHER AND EPIDEMICS—SOME EXAMPLES

Late Blight of Potato and Tomato

Here is a disease almost tailor-made for introductory textbooks in plant pathology. It is widespread in the cooler climates and higher altitudes throughout the world, is responsible for serious losses to a food crop of very great importance, has been the cause of historic outbreaks in potato-growing regions for at least a century, has been the object of intensive study by pathologists in a wide variety of different research specialties, is dramatically responsive to the effect of weather, and is capable of explosive epidemic spread. Small wonder that late blight has attracted attention as a subject of disease-forecasting investigations.

The disease originates each year either from inoculum coming from more advanced regions to the south, or from diseased plants developing on local cull piles. Whatever the source responsible for the pathogen being present, what actually happens next depends upon the weather. On the east coast of the United States, for example, late blight reaches serious levels only if the weather is wet and relatively cool over a period long enough to permit massive spore production. Differences do appear from region to region, but it can safely be predicted that if "blight weather" persists for several consecutive days in potato-growing regions, blight itself is virtually certain to follow.

Apple Scab

A second standby of pathologists, at least in temperate climates, is the apple scab fungus. Here the weather relations are rather different than in the case of late blight. A major source of inoculum is the sexual stage of the pathogen overwintering within the tissues of fallen leaves on the orchard floor. Ascospores ejected from fruiting bodies are picked up in turbulent air and deposited on newly emerging foliage. Just when spores will mature, and more particularly the conditions under which they will be discharged, is determined by moisture and temperature. During critical periods it is customary for growers, or pathologists acting in their behalf, to make frequent microscopic observations of overwintered leaves and to use the data so obtained in deciding when initial fungicide applications will be most effectively applied.

Cereal Rusts

Like late blight and apple scab, cereal rusts are highly sensitive to weather conditions. But perhaps because of the classic work of Stakman and his associates, and a host of other workers since that time, there is a tendency to think of the cereal rusts in terms of the genetic variability of the pathogen. As a result, one gets the impression from the literature that the occurrence of epidemics depends very largely upon whether a race that is virulent on the commonly sown varieties is present.

In fact, a virulent race of pathogen is a necessary but not sufficient precondition of epidemic. Once this condition is met, the outcome in a given year depends on weather—wind to insure incoming inoculum, sufficient moisture in the form of precipitation or dew to permit of germination and penetration and, most important of all, sufficiently high temperature to account for minimum delay in each successive crop of uredospores. As is so often the case, epidemics depend upon how many generations of inoculum are possible before the crop is too far along to be vulnerable.

However meticulous the method, there is really no substitute for the susceptible host plant for determining the presence and the effectiveness of pathogenic organisms. Tu and Hendrix (1970) provide good evidence of this in a short paper on the biology of the stripe rust of wheat in southeastern Washington. From the benefit of many observations it appears that stripe rust disappears from the area in the hot part of the summer, only to reappear in the fall, even though there would seem to be a dearth of available host tissue once the crop has matured throughout the area. Spore counts were adequate to show that even when the disease itself seemed to be at a low ebb there was measurable inoculum in the air itself—whether viable or not was a different question.

To resolve the question, potted seedling produced in the greenhouse were placed in open fields nightly for about a month starting in early August and the test plants then removed to a growth chamber favorable to rust development. Results clearly showed that viable inoculum was present, that generally the longer the exposure the higher the incidence of rust development, and that given moisture and temperature conducive to rust, it will break out at any time. This seems to explain the reappearance under field conditions even though the climate and state of maturity of the host appear superficially unfavorable.

For each region there are special considerations of weather, topography, geography, and cropping patterns that affect the course of disease above and beyond the attributes imposed by the biology of the disease itself. Green et al. (1970) have given us a sample of this in relation to two cereal stem rusts—on wheat and oats—in Kenya for the year 1968. They point out that wheat is planted to take advantage of the long rains of March through August and of the drier conditions for harvest in December, January, and February. A simple chart (Fig. 11–1) reflects not only these relationships, but the periods of maximum occurrence of the two rusts themselves.

On balance, Kenya is an area where rust is a considerable threat—a growing season of 12 months, frequent dews and rainfall, temperatures favorable, and so on. High levels of resistance to all pathogen races is essential. Inoculum comes either from residual grains scattered here and there or from a number of native grass species that serve as reservoir hosts.

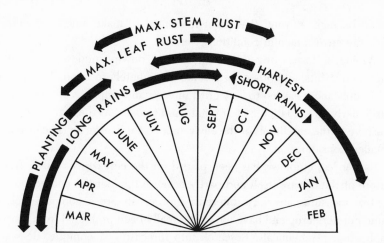

Fig. 11–1. Chart showing periods of planting and harvesting of wheat, periods of rainfall, and maximum occurrence of airborne uredospores of leaf and stem rusts in Kenya. (Green *et al.*, 1970)

WEATHER AND FORECASTING

Forecasting as "applied epidemiology," in the words of Paul Miller (1959), is introduced here to emphasize those aspects and disease situations where the outcome depends mostly on the weather and to show, by example, how this dependency comes about.

An early, very much weather-related, type of forecast has been noted by Miller in these words:

. . . occurrence and severity of bacterial wilt of sweet corn in the northeastern United States were associated with temperature of the preceding winters . . . using the sum of the mean temperatures of the three winter months, December, January, and February, as the basis for predicting occurrence during the following season at any given location. A "winter temperature index" of 90 or above indicated occurrence; 100 or more signified severe damage; below 90 indicated negligible occurrence or absence. The method is so accurate and so easy to use that it became a routine procedure in sweet corn growing. The correlation on which the method was based was later found to result from the effect of winter temperature on survival of the corn flea beetle, the insect vector in which the causal bacterium overwinters; . . .

K. S. Chester, in another classic example, although one that in retrospect seems oversimplified, found that wheat leaf rust epidemics in Oklahoma were keyed very closely not only to weather but to weather for a very limited period of time. He showed that if temperatures and moisture were favorable during winter and spring—about four months—the crucial early spore generations of the pathogen were made possible and subsequent disease levels would be high. Beyond that point it seemed to make much less difference what the environmental conditions were.

Whenever forecasting is considered, the downy mildews of potato, tobacco, cucurbits, and other hosts come immediately to mind. A combination of circumstances has led to very great interest and emphasis on these diseases, particularly on the late blight of potato and tomato. As these are diseases very sensitive to the conditions of the environment, they make a prime example for detailed consideration.

Rather less emphasis has been placed on the cereal rusts partly from the nature of the disease itself and partly because the logistics and economics of control measures are very different: the cereals are a comparatively low-value-per-acre crop and have not traditionally been protected from disease by application of chemicals. Research into forecasting techniques does go on, however, as evidenced by Burleigh *et al.* (1969), who have made comparative studies of the validity of forecasts in the United States midcontinent that are based on counts of uredia as against those based on urediospore numbers. In their view the mathematical formulations developed from spore counts—which are very much more economical to make—are fully as dependable as those based on uredia. They feel, too, that the forecasts are for all practicable purposes fully as valid for one host-pathogen pairing as for another, depending as it does more on weather and other environmental factors than on degree of resistance.

The United States has no monopoly on interest and accomplishment in plant disease forecasting. Miller and O'Brien (1952) in a detailed review of the situation, list no fewer than thirteen countries that have a specific program for potato and tomato late blight. The classic developments were those in Holland and England as early as the mid-1920's and 30's. In the first instance, Van Everdingen developed four so-called "rules," calling for blight to develop when there was a four-hour period of dew at night, a minimum temperature of 10°C, a "mean cloudiness" the following day of 0.8 or more, and at least 0.1 mm rainfall during the next 24 hours. To these, British workers found they should add a fifth requirement—a period of at least two days of relative humidity greater than 75%. With further study, it became possible to reduce British forecasting data to two criteria: minimum temperature of 50°F and relative humidity not under 75% for at least two days.

The United States Warning Service was organized in response to the situation reflected in a 1946 epidemic. Various regions with a history of damage were subjected to intensive analysis in an effort to discover useful correlations between known incidence of diseases and weather records.

One of the classic efforts to develop forecasting systems based on data from previous years was that in connection with late blight in the potato-growing region of Virginia. As shown in the accompanying figure (Fig. 11–2), temperature and rainfall lines for a 17-year period can be used, when they have been substantiated by actual comparison with disease occurrence, to establish conditions of high risk. Retrospectively, had forecasts been made during these years, control measures would have been recommended in only 4 of

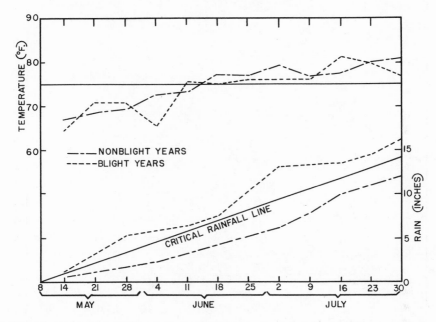

Fig. 11–2. Graph of data on temperature and rainfall for a 17-year period, indicating critical temperature and rainfall lines as related to forecasting the occurrence of potato late blight. (Cook, 1949)

the 17 years—it would actually have been needed in two of them. Perhaps more important, in none of the 13 "not recommended" years would it have been useful, indicating that forecasting would have been on the conservative side and that a very substantial savings in material and labor could have been effected. Actual rainfall records for four consecutive years are shown in Fig. 11–3; blight itself was serious in 1946 and 1948, but not in 1947 or 1949, although it threatened in the latter case early in the season.

Efforts to adapt the Norfolk study to the northeastern United States led Russell Hyre to refine the rainfall line so that each point stood for total precipitation for one week and so that each point on the temperature line repre-

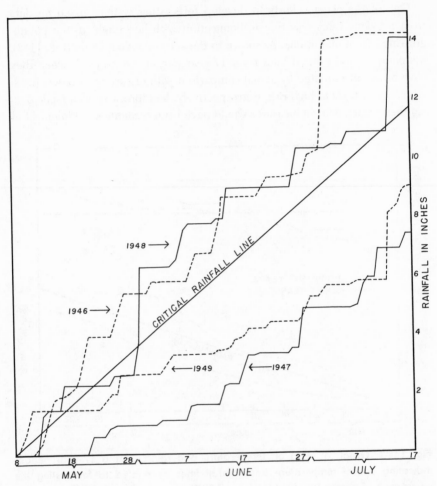

Fig. 11–3. Rainfall records for 4 consecutive years in Norfolk, Virginia, showing 2 blight years (1946, 1948) and 2 nonblight years (1947, 1949) in relation to the critical rainfall line. (Nugent, 1950)

sented average mean daily temperature for the same period. Even more precise forecasts were predicated on a ten-day system rather than one based on seven days, although development of disease after first appearance can be expected with substantially fewer days' favorable conditions.

Still further modifications proved necessary when attention turned to the Midwest, where humidity rather than rainfall seems to govern the appearance of the late blight disease. Without going into the details of this situation, it does indicate that the complexities of disease and environment are such as to require specific investigations at each spot under study—it is hardly ever safe to assume that what pertains one place can be transferred directly to another.

WEATHER AND INSECTS

In the monograph by Carter (1962) on insects and plant disease, easily two-thirds of the nearly 700 pages are devoted to insect-virus relationships. But relationships between weather and insects are much the same regardless of the pathogen they are transmitting. After all, the insect must get about if it is to serve as a successful vector—weather has demonstrable influences on where, when, and how far the insects move. Only rarely does the particular pathogen load being carried make a difference.

Carter finds that temperature, humidity, and wind velocity affect vector movement and can be expected to influence insect movement generally. He cites, for the peach aphid, conditions favorable to flight as being temperature over 70°F, relative humidity below 80%, wind velocity less than five miles per hour, and more than 12°F difference in maximum-minimum temperature during the day. Light, above perhaps 100 foot candles, seems not to make much difference; below that, flight activity is reduced.

To the extent that an insect, once launched, is a free-floating particle, to be buffeted about like any other tiny object, the generalizations applied in an earlier chapter to such inocula as fungus spores are germane here. Thus temperature, velocity, direction, etc., profoundly affect the aerial movement of a given individual. Trapping surveys repeatedly show not only that maximum numbers of insects in the air are near the earth surface but also that some can be recovered at great heights (several thousand feet) and at great distances from the initial source. Long-distance travel is a function of atmospheric conditions, not the result of autonomous flight.

Environment influences insect vectors in ways other than just movement. That it governs survival must be obvious, especially in the Temperate Zone, where populations reach high levels only if substantial numbers of individuals remain from the preceding season. In more tropical situations, fluctuations are far more likely to be in response to differences in rainfall—the latter is not wholly unimportant in temperate climates, of course. As a general rule, extremes of low temperature are responsible for insect mortality, but for some species in some areas general temperature levels are causally related to survival. It makes some difference, too, what stage in the life cycle of the insect is involved. Eggs, as a rule, are able to withstand climatic conditions that would be fatal to adults of the same species.

Climate, by setting the limits of survival, establishes the geographic range of a given species. When the insect in question is a sole vector of a particular pathogen, geographic limits to natural spread of the disease are thereby also set.

As in so many environment-organism interactions, it tends to be the extremes that account for the most conspicuous changes. Carter, for example, cites several instances where very high-velocity winds associated with hurricanes have drastically altered insect populations in the ensuing season. Yet it is the more routine influences of light, temperature, and moisture—on the level of insect activity, on the nature of that activity, and on the minutiae of insect-host-pathogen interactions—that in the long run constitute the crucial considerations.

THE MICROCLIMATE MODIFIER

One can think of microclimate as an added complex of factors that interpose themselves between the more general effects of weather and the observed phenomena of disease, just as weather could be considered a short-term modifier of the overall effects wrought by climate. Climate, as expressed in weather, is altered by immediate effect of microclimate. By microclimate in this context we are speaking of the above-ground part of the plant environment.

Yarwood (1959), among others, has analyzed several of the factors that determine conditions in the immediate vicinity of the plant surface where pathogen and host first come into contact and in so doing influence the course of disease outbreaks. Invasion and establishment are not the only aspects of plant disease subject to the "microclimate modifier," but these are surely the most critical phases.

The same factors that make up weather make up microclimate, but the emphasis is rather different. Attention centers not only on what microclimate factors do to the host, but the influence of the host population upon the environment. Generally, Yarwood notes, air movement velocity is reduced by plants, light intensity on soil surface and lower foliage is lessened, and atmospheric humidity is increased. In addition, temperature extremes at the soil are exaggerated over that prevailing in the atmosphere or over bare soil. In clear, still weather especially, temperature differences between day and night, and between individual low-level strata, are most pronounced. And the uniquely biological phenomenon of transpiration acts to increase atmospheric humidity and to reduce leaf temperature.

The chief basis for pathologists to be interested in microclimate is that from time to time the net effect is to alter the occurrence and course of disease. Very naturally, we are more inclined to take note of those situations where the effect is to worsen the disease picture—that is, to produce temperatures lower than that of the general atmosphere, increase the humidity, extend the period of surface wetness, or reduce air flow. But microclimate is also, perhaps less frequently, such as to decrease disease incidence and severity.

In describing microclimate, Waggoner (1965) approaches the problem from a sharply different angle and in so doing offers encouragement to those who might be disturbed by the apparent hopelessness of making accurate measurements of all the countless variations from one site to another, even within a modest-sized host population. His view seems to be the laudably pragmatic one that if a mathematical model can be erected and then shown to reflect adequately the observed phenomena of disease, then it matters not whether each instance is laboriously tabulated and taken into account. Historically, in his view, the important first impetus toward the formulation of workable predictive formulae was Gregory's work in demonstrating that the behavior of fungus inoculum followed the established rules of atmospheric diffusion. In support he recounts an interesting instance wherein an apparent inconsistency was actually nothing of the kind. In this case, it had been observed that the white pine blister rust appeared most abundantly near the tops of host trees a quarter mile or so from *Ribes*-infested swamp lands, although it would certainly have been expected to appear first in trees immediately adjacent to the alternate host and, probably, at regions not far above the ground surface. On the assumption that spores might behave like ordinary smoke, a simple experiment showed that at night, when spores would be most abundantly released from *Ribes*, a temperature inversion prevailed in the atmosphere such that the smoke drifted into the swamp—not out of it—then rose and flowed upland in a warmer layer above the vegetation (see Fig. 9–5). Thus, in fact, spores were most abundant in quite unexpected sites, with the clinical results noted above.

The crux of Waggoner's exposition lies in formulation of energy budgets in terms of radiation, convection, and transpiration, to be solved as statements of leaf and air temperature. More or less similar calculations lead to generalized values for the water relations of host plants. In Waggoner's own terms:

Measuring the temperature and humidity upon the diverse leaves that spores alight upon is a hopeless and entangling task. Fortunately, these factors that determine survival and prosperity of the pathogen can be predicted from a knowledge of environment and plant. First, the energy budget of a leaf is set forth. Then, the separate budgetary terms for radiation, convection and transpiration are expressed as functions of the difference between leaf and air temperature. The budget can then be solved for that temperature difference. Examples of importance to the spore have been constructed. Comparison of construction with observation verified the realism of the synthetic. The importance of this micrometeorological variety is exemplified by a well ventilated sunlit upper leaf—that would be only 0° to 3° warmer or cooler than the air—and a poorly ventilated sunlit lower leaf—that would be fully 15° warmer than the air if transpiration were nil.

The advantage is double if humidities upon the leaf surface where the spore may reside are synthesized. First, the variety of humidities would require countless observations. More important, however, their measurement is very difficult. The difficulty may be resolved, of course, for the same energy budget that yielded leaf temperatures also reveals water-vapor pressure or relative humidity at the leaf surface. Behavior of the relative humidity at the surface is illustrated by the same two leaves that were considered before. At the well-ventilated, sunlit upper leaf, the relative humidity would actually be lower than in air because moistening by transpiration is more than conteracted by warming of the leaf. At the dry, poorly ventilated sunlit lower leaf, relative humidity would be much lower than in air above, for the leaf would be very warm. On the other hand, transpiration would increase the relative humidity at this poorly ventilated surface markedly, showing the importance of transpiration in moistening the environment of a spore in a windless neighborhood.

The final synthesis attempted, and perhaps the most reckless and revealing of the state of our knowledge, is the attempt to integrate the effect of varying temperatures upon the course of disease. Essentially, the disease is presumed to increase at an exponential rate that depends upon temperature. The dependency was taken from experiments in temperature and the appearance of symptoms. Then, by means of climatological relations of temperature to time, season, or date, the increase of disease was expressed as a function of time alone. When this construction was completed for some well-known plant diseases, courses of disease increase with season in different climates were constructed that resemble the real state of affairs outdoors.[*]

The epidemiology of plant disease in arid areas is abruptly and markedly changed if, by any of several techniques, crops are brought under irrigation. Just what the changes are depends very much on the kind of crop, on whether the irrigation is by surface furrows, by flooding, or by overhead sprinkling, and on the pathogen that is involved in a particular disease situation. A number of these issues have been summarized in a review by Rotem and Palti (1969).

Generally, as would be expected, those soil-borne diseases that depend on pathogens favored by moist soils will be worse under irrigation. Generally, too, foliage diseases are more severe when overhead sprinkling results in conditions highly favorable for spore germination and initial penetration of the host. Finally, the overall effect of irrigation is greatly modified by the density of the host population and whether or not the weather conditions themselves are favorable.

[*] From P. E. Waggoner, Microclimate and plant disease, *Annual Review of Phytopathology*, vol. 3 (1965), pp. 123–24.

Any number of factors enter into the equations of disease severity: the inherent resistance of the host, the biology of the pathogen, the amount of water devoted to irrigation, the timing of application, the technique adopted, and so on and on. But the crux of the matter has to do with the general effect on microclimate much more than with any other single component; it is here the answers must be sought in trying to analyze a given instance of disease as related to irrigation.

SOILS AND EPIDEMICS

Striking differences prevail below ground compared to the atmospheric environment. These differences show up in the greater complexity of the ecological situation and, coincident with it, the far more difficult task of making observations. Thus the investigator has a tougher problem and the tools available to him are less effective.

The soil environment—the microclimate—governs the development of disease in almost every attribute. Take any aspect of disease—for example, inoculum survival or spread—and it will be obvious that within soil the rate and magnitude of that phenomenon are very much at the mercy of limits set by the surrounding medium. Sometimes the effect is to slow the process in question—inocula move poorly for the most part. At other times, soil is beneficial to the pathogen, as when it insulates against extremes of low temperature, excessive desiccation, or the hazards of radiant energy.

On the specific question of disease development, David Park in a recent review (1963) reminds us of a point that has often been noted but not always remembered. That is, when as a result of circumstances the soil environment is free of microorganisms other than the particular species in question, disease severity may in fact be exceptionally pronounced. Not only that, but on occasion organisms that are not usually considered to be pathogens will become so if they are not in competition with associated soil flora. He symbolizes the interrelationships in a diagram (Fig. 11–4) intended to show reciprocal effects of any two pairs of elements in the host-pathogen-microflora complex.

By then treating each of the postulated six pathways separately, Park documents his presentation with an array of specific examples. That is to say, there are identifiable consequences of the action of host on soil microflora, of microflora on host, of host on pathogen, and so on. Sometimes, of course, the consequences of this impact are beneficial, sometimes harmful. The course of plant disease is always affected, if only indirectly, although certain of the pathways more conspicuously govern the course of disease phenomena than do others.

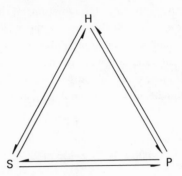

Fig. 11–4. Diagram showing interrelationships of host plant, soil microbial population, and pathogen. (Park, 1963)

The most important thing to be stressed here is that much interaction of possible importance in disease processes can take place without the direct involvement of the host, and even without its immediate presence. Of the six pathways chosen to represent the interaction, four do not at once involve the host. Moreover the soil microbia, "S", is not a single entity and, in fact, different sections of it may be doing different things at the same time. Also the S–S interactions that occur are able to alter in intensity or direction the effect of any overall S effect in the four pathways to which it contributes. Processes important to disease relationships, therefore, occur during rotation or fallow, and in the soil distant from the host plant.[*]

A convenient, detailed examination of soil as an environment in which pathogenic organisms—especially fungi—exist is to be found in the 1965 symposium volume entitled *Ecology of Soil-Borne Plant Pathogens.* The argument as to the importance of soil in disease development is here furnished as circumstantial evidence, for there is no more dramatic proof of how soil ecology governs disease than that "biological" control is more frequently employed against soil pathogens than against any others.

Under some circumstances, information can be gained by aerial surveys more easily and effectively than by any other device, although the techniques involved have been exploited far more in nonagricultural activities than they have in plant pathology. The possibilities are fairly obvious—to see more and to see it faster, to see patterns within large areas that cannot be detected from the ground, to see the same region repeatedly over a span of time, to compare levels of intensity within a pattern at a given instant in time. Obviously, one has to sacrifice the advantages of very close, detailed scrutiny of the kind possible only by ground observation, although the latter is a necessary adjunct to

[*] From D. Park, The ecology of soil-borne fungal disease, *Annual Review of Phytopathology,* vol. 1 (1963), p. 242.

Fig. 11–5. Two photographs of the same area taken at intervals of about 3 years. *Top:* Pattern of take-all and weeds in wheat in the summer of 1963. *Bottom:* Bare soil in the spring of 1966. Patterns in the latter proved to be due to a heavier texture and therefore higher soil-moisture content, which in wet seasons led to high incidence of disease. (Brenchley, 1968)

the former. One must also build up a fund of experience in interpretation as the measurable data on film are compared with traditional data in the field itself.

But within these limitations (Brenchley, 1968) plant pathologists are moving ahead in the detection and identification of disease, with the observations of patterns in disease distribution (Fig. 11–5) and epidemic development, and to a more limited extent, with the quantitative estimation of degree of damage. Techniques can be assumed to improve as time goes on and acceptance of the techniques of aerial photography to become more widespread; yet it augments, rather than rivals, more established methods.

V

DISEASE CONTROL

When disease control is considered, plant pathology takes on a brand new dimension. So long as attention centers on descriptive studies of the host, pathogen, or disease characteristic—or is concerned with unraveling the complexities of metabolic events—or is preoccupied with the interactions of environment and disease, pathology is much like other biological disciplines. It has problems and techniques unique to itself, true enough, but is still a branch of professional biology among many others.

The new dimension is, of course, the element of practical application. Plant diseases would be among the biological world's more fascinating problems even if we had not the slightest wish to control them. But we do so wish and it is essential that the rules of the game be clearly understood at the outset. In other words, what are the constraints imposed by the practicalities of control? And what are the special dividends afforded by this dimension of the problem? There are perhaps three factors to be examined: the public interface, the economic question, and the scientific component.

THE PUBLIC INTERFACE

When pathologists set out to control disease, they must forgo the sanctuary of laboratory and station field plot. Disease, in the sense that it is meaningful to control it, occurs in the marketplace. It appears to home owner, commercial gardener, florist, farmer, and forester as an immediate threat to his economic well-being. His relation to the practicing pathologist is often that of patient to physician—a person who wants results, not theory.

It is one of the rewards of plant pathology as a profession that it provides opportunity to deal directly with the public. To many, problems become more compelling and challenges more immediate when they take on the actuality of specific emergencies. There is for many persons no substitute for a situation where the welfare of real people is at stake and nothing quite matches the satisfaction of successfully resolving a genuine problem.

In a final chapter the related question of the interrelationships of the science of pathology with the public will be examined.

The parade of what seem to be "new" diseases goes on and on, although in fact they may be introduced from another area, explosions of hitherto obscure host-parasite associations, the result of more careful observation or of more critical diagnostic methods—or some combination of these. Whatever the basic situation, what one actually observes is the emergence of a disease outbreak that attracts attention because it becomes of economic importance to a number of growers. Very often, once the general pattern of symptoms has been recognized, the disease is found to occur in a relatively wide area and one tends to wonder just why it has not been recognized sooner—in some measure this seems simply to be a matter of focusing attention on the set of visible attributes that indicate an identifiable syndrome.

"Stem pitting" of peach is just such a "new" disease. The characteristics are described by Barrat et al. (1968) and by Mircetich et al. (1968, 1970) among others. Characteristically the lower trunk is enlarged at or below the ground level, the bark extremely thickened, and the wood pitted (Figs. V–1, V–2)—this associated with a general foliage symptom of girdling. The disease is widely encountered in the Middle Atlantic states and occurs on young orchard trees propagated in California, North Carolina, and Tennessee as well. Severity depends on the particular cultivated variety, whether of peach, apricot, or nectarine. As in so many cases of plant disease, the nature of the causal agent remains to be determined for an appreciable interval after the disease itself is recognized as important. It appears not to be an incompatibility phenomenon at the graft union, since it occurs also in unbudded seedlings.

By 1969 the stem pitting malady had become of sufficient importance in Pennsylvania that Stouffer and Lewis (1969) and Stouffer et al. (1969) could refer to it as the "single most important peach disease problem in Pennsylvania," in summaries of the symptoms and apparent spread of the disease. Not only this, but a very similar syndrome was to be found on other stone fruits, such as cherry and plum. Experiments at this stage were inconclusive, but indications of a virus as the cause of the difficulty were beginning to emerge.

THE ECONOMIC QUESTION

In many ways cost does not enter as a first-order consideration into the planning and execution of basic research. One is interested in answers to

Fig. V–1. Symptoms of stem pitting in peach (*left*) as compared to an apparently healthy trunk (*right*). (Barrat *et al.*, 1968)

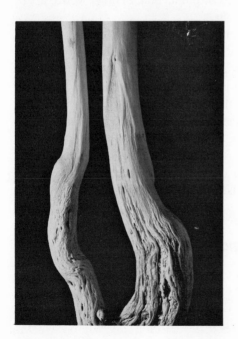

Fig. V–2. Symptoms of stem pitting on a nursery tree (*left*) and a 2-year old orchard tree (*right*). (Mircetich *et al.*, 1970)

questions, answers that need be arrived at only once, provided they are well and carefully worked out. In this context it is often justifiable to make substantial investments of time, equipment, and effort.

Control, on the other hand, except when it is itself a part of research, must pay its own way. The pathologist responsible for developing control measures cannot escape the obligation to consider the dollar cost of what he recommends as balanced against the good that it may be expected to accomplish. This is not to say that in the developmental stage only those controls that are clearly profitable should be pursued. It is rather to argue that development must not be considered complete until and unless it reaches a stage where it is economically beneficial to the user. The research dollar must be used responsibly, of course, but the practicing farmer's dollar must be treated with the utmost respect. In Chapter 12 this issue will be treated more fully.

We tend too often badly to underplay the importance of a single epidemic outbreak of disease. In 1916, for example, rust seems to have brought about the loss of 200 million bushels of wheat and 100 million in Canada, well over ten times the total productivity of the plowing-up campaign in Great Britain during World War I. We forget, too, that the loss need not nearly reach these proportions to take serious toll from an economic standpoint—after all, it is only the upper several percent of a crop that can fairly be thought of as profit; the remainder must go to pay the costs of production. In other words, a 10% loss in crop may be loss of *all* the profit.

The dramatic impact of a single climatic event, of the inroads of disease, and of the introduction of resistant varieties, is shown in the data on sugarcane production in Louisiana (Rands and Dopp, 1938; Fig. V–3).

It would be imprecise to say that every disease outbreak, even those that are on the face of it disastrous, is in the long run disadvantageous—although one must conclude that most are indeed in this category. Even so dramatic an outbreak as that of coffee rust, which appeared in 1869 on the island of Ceylon and in six years had completely ruined the 340,000 acres of plantations, had its beneficial side effects. In this case tea was introduced as a substitute crop and by 1930, total plantings had reached 500,000 acres, nearly 50% above that attained earlier by coffee.

THE SCIENTIFIC COMPONENT

Behind virtually every successful control measure must lie an assemblage of scientifically valid information. It has been argued that plant pathology is both an art and a science; nowhere is this view more appropriate than as it pertains to the disease control aspects of the discipline. The practical, eco-

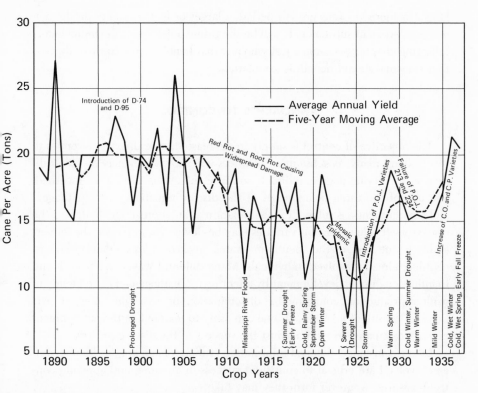

Fig. V–3. Graph showing 50 years of sugarcane production in Louisiana in terms of yield per acre in relation to root rot and other diseases, varietal introductions, and extreme weather conditions. (Rands and Dopp, 1938)

nomically profitable application of recognized techniques to field problems is an art. The laborious working out of measures that may be successfully put to practical use is a science. If the science component is inadequate or unsound, the application is endangered, although sheer luck may account for scattered successes. In Chapters 13 to 15 appreciable attention is given to the scientific base upon which effective control measures rest.

OBJECTIVES OF DISEASE CONTROL

Any measure invoked to reduce the amount of damage done by plant disease, whether infectious or noninfectious, is by definition a control measure. Under any but experimental conditions, the objective must be to benefit one or more groups of persons by assuring a larger number of desirable plants, a longer or more vigorous growth period, a larger or higher quality production of a wanted plant substance. It will be the prime objective of the immediately following chapter to examine just who it is that benefits from control efforts— that someone should benefit is axiomatic.

APPROACHES TO CONTROL

The objective of control is simply to decrease disease damage. Avenues to this goal are many, as subsequent chapters will show. They may be either direct or, to varying degree, indirect. So far as infectious disease is concerned, any one of the three components of the disease equation—host, pathogen, and environment—is subject to manipulation as an approach to control of the disease itself. Thus resistant varieties may be developed to reduce the vulnerability of the host, or therapeutic measures invoked to lessen damage to susceptible, already-involved individuals. Many different ways have been found to influence disease development by affecting the pathogen—i.e., reducing inoculum production, counteracting dissemination, or destroying infective particles at the site of invasion. Or one can essay to manipulate the environment in ways calculated to work against the success of the disease process.

In every instance, detailed information and understanding of the phenomena involved are crucial to consistent success in choosing and applying control measures, whatever form they may take.

12

Economic Considerations

In the real world of agriculture there is always an economic element involved, whenever actions are taken to alter the course of a disease outbreak. In the long run it can be assumed that someone, somewhere has made a choice between alternative actions—perhaps between action and inaction— and proceeded accordingly. It can also be assumed that this judgment was made on the basis of a sought-for economic gain. That is, decisions on what to do about disease are almost always taken with the profit motive very much in view. As, of course, they should be.

To say the above is not to level a charge of selfishness at those involved. Quite the contrary, it could be persuasively argued that the greater sin is to consider, much less put into practice, control operations that do not give promise of being economically advantageous. In this connection, the responsible plant pathologist will frequently find himself confronted by a peculiar compulsion on the part of growers—professional and amateur alike—to take action in the face of disease attack whether there is a recognized remedy at hand or not. It seems to be unacceptable to the sincere and diligent citizen to do nothing, even in those instances when a coldly objective assessment of the situation so dictates. All the more obligation upon the plant pathologist to keep his wits about him and recommend only those measures that are economically defensible.

In connection with the economic aspects of plant pathology, see the charmingly personal account of the profession by A. E. Muskett (1967) when he refers to his early initiation into the real world of practical agriculture in Northern Ireland upon becoming, as a young man, a lecturer in Queen's University, Belfast. He says:

My training in London had been biased towards fundamental science and, in what spare time I had, I commenced a fundamental nutritional study of one of the fungal parasites responsible for a disease of flax. I well remember explaining this to J. S. Gordon when he exclaimed "My goodness, and what good is that going to do the farmer!"

And I realized I had come to what was then a comparatively poor part of the United Kingdom where unlimited funds were not available for flights of fancy into fundamental issues. It was my job to go and find out what the farmers' problems were and to help them to try to solve them. Being the son of a farmer, and knowing something of the hardness and consistency of the work which often yielded but a poor return, I did not find it difficult to readjust myself accordingly. Within three years we had evolved a satisfactory spraying programme for the control of American gooseberry mildew. And since 1926 no bushes have been burned in Northern Ireland—the only method used until then for controlling the disease. By 1928 the thousands of acres of apple orchards in County Armagh were being systematically sprayed in accordance with a program evolved for the control of apple scab which had ravaged the main variety Bramley's Seedling. By controlling scab and incorporating insecticides for apple sucker, aphids, and caterpillars, the yields of the orchards were increased eightfold and the percentage of clean fruit raised from almost nil to ninety. By 1930, damping off diseases and weeds in the forest nurseries were being controlled by the use of dilute sulphuric acid watered into the beds at sowing time. Now I was happy—I was paying my way. County Armagh had become almost my home; it felt just like the accomplishment of a successful mission. I had been able to bring a greater measure of prosperity and peace to the garden county of Ireland.°

Decisions on control are and should be regularly predicated upon economic criteria, but they are not necessarily always valid. Mistaken estimates of costs and benefits can lead to quite unexpected outcomes. Viewpoints may be narrow, objectives selfish, interpretations faulty, data imprecise. But at the very least control measures are almost never taken unless they are presumed to be economically profitable, just as money is never invested in an enterprise that the investor feels will be a losing venture.

Time remains as a final dimension. While most control steps are initiated with the notion that benefits will accrue within a short time—usually the same crop year—there are situations where the gain is expected only after a longer period, or more indirectly. Removal of debris looks to the next growing season, elimination of natural reservoir hosts to a lessened disease incidence some time hence. Most quarantines are rationalized on their contribution to the welfare of a broad area in future years. Even when the relation is obscured by elapsed time, by space, or by some other factor, control and the economics of control are inseparable.

Nothing more underscores the economic imperatives of disease control than does the agriculture of the technically less advanced societies. Here the scale of economic strength is an entire order of magnitude below that of the industrialized nations and the margin available for maneuver almost nonexistent. Losses from disease are often enormous in the very spots where they can be least well withstood and where control measures can be least well

° From A. E. Muskett, Plant pathology and the plant pathologist, *Annual Review of Phytopathology*, vol. 5 (1967), pp. 13–14.

afforded. The considerations noted in earlier paragraphs are sharply high-lighted when production is at a subsistence level.

One clear reason for the greater economic vulnerability of the developing nations is the fact that for a large fraction of them a single crop represents a preponderance of total exports. Paddock (1967) provides the list in Table 12–1 in support of this situation, based on data from the U.S. Agency for International Development.

Table 12–1

Percentage of the Total Exports of Selected Developing Nations Represented by a Single Crop in 1957–1960

Country	Crop	Approximate Percentage of Exports
Nigeria	Peanuts	87
Senegal	Peanuts	85
Chad	Cotton	76
Colombia	Coffee	75
Burma	Rice	71
Guatemala	Coffee	69
El Salvador	Coffee	67
Panama	Bananas	66
Dahomey	Palm kernels	66
Yemen	Coffee	65
Haiti	Coffee	64
Ceylon	Tea	62
Ecuador	Bananas	60
South Vietnam	Rubber	60
Somalia	Bananas	60
Ghana	Cacao	59
Pakistan	Jute	58
Brazil	Coffee	56
Sudan	Cotton	56
Costa Rica	Coffee	56
Ethiopia	Coffee	54
Algeria	Wine	53
Ivory Coast	Coffee	52

SOURCE: W. C. Paddock, Phytopathology in a hungry world, *Annual Review of Phytopathology*, vol. 5 (1967), p. 382; based on data from the U. S. Agency for International Development.

An encouraging exception to the general paucity of material on the economics of plant disease control is the 1969 review by Ordish and Dufour. In this pleasantly breezy account they note some of the earlier studies in this general area and then relate the economics of disease loss to the standard supply and demand curves of everyday economic calculations.

To the three interested groups identified by the California team many years ago—consumers, individual producers, and groups of producers—they add the pesticide manufacturers and research workers. They then examine a number of facets of disease control and develop a provocative comparison of the behavior of three representative governments—capitalist, socialist and communist—when threatened by a hypothetical lasagna blight and spaghetti weevil. As they see it, pest control measures most favored in the capitalist economy tend to be chemical, because the economy is geared to the production of material goods and the sale of chemicals is more attractive than the imposition of biological controls. In socialist and communist countries, other things being equal, they would expect more emphasis on methods that cost less to the individual farmer and more emphasis on forward planning to bring supply and demand into balance. Indeed, they go so far as to make the generalization that technologists now set the pattern of the economy of the modern state, not the consumers, and that pest control is no exception to the rule that it produces the goods it suits large organizations to produce.

In the course of their analysis, which is well worth study in its entirety, they make a number of cogent points, a few of which can be paraphrased as follows:

- Plant pathologists are more interested in the interaction of host and pathogen than are entomologists in the interaction of plants and insects, the latter being rather more likely to concentrate on the insects themselves.
- That farmers are not in business to feed the hungry but to make money, as a result of which measurements of loss are meaningful to the majority of them only if they are expressed in monetary terms.
- One of the most important effects of disease control, from an economic standpoint, is to facilitate the fitting of supply to demand.
- Not only can developed nations cope more effectively with loss from plant disease, by using their economic reserves in a number of ways, but the underdeveloped countries are far more likely to depend upon a very small number of crops, sometimes a single crop—peanuts in Nigeria, coffee in Colombia, for example.

WHO IS HURT AND WHO SHOULD PAY?

There is no simple answer to the question who suffers from plant disease. Few have seriously tried to find the answer—possibly because it seemed at first glance that everyone already knew it.

History has numerous records of plant disease losses that have been so heavy and so widespread as conspicuously to affect the welfare of whole nations or societies. But the less dramatic losses of everyday agriculture are much more obscure and may not always be recognized even by those who suffer part or all of the consequences. It is usually the producers who first call for assistance in the face of a newly important disease outbreak and there is a tendency to measure benefits from control programs in terms of benefit to the producer. Yet the role of the producer is a variable one, not subject to routine prediction of relative gain or loss from crop fluctuations. To quote from the classic paper by Brooks (1935), "The fact seems to be overlooked that improving conditions . . . for one group of producers sometimes drives others to the wall and that the greatest importance of the accomplishment lies in the benefits given the consumers. That a small group of producers has found a more profitable market is actually a small item compared with the fact that many millions of people may have been supplied with a cheaper, better balanced or more healthful diet." It is the consumer who must, in the long run, pay for the loss that occurs along the way toward the produce that he buys in the eventual marketplace.

The individual producer, as distinct from producers as a group, is in many ways in the same category as the consumer—he will gain maximum income from maximum production with, of course, minimum expenditure of time and effort. "The real cost to society of plant pests and diseases is the amount of additional effort required to produce agricultural products on account of these pests and diseases . . . These costs to society cannot be measured in dollars and cents, and any statements attempting to show either losses or gains in money terms to society as a whole are meaningless. In the long run the consumers tend to pay all the costs and to receive all of the benefits except when some form of monopolistic control intervenes, and then consumers continue to pay all of the costs but do not receive all of the benefits . . . The consumer always benefits from an abundance of production." (Smith *et al.*, 1933)

The interests of groups of growers may be different from those of the individual. Sometimes, but not always, the cash price of a crop will be enough higher following disease outbreak that growers actually profit from the reduction in volume. The results are seldom predictable. Small changes in volume may have one tendency, large changes an opposite effect. More important, perhaps, is the fact that great disparities are likely to appear as between one group and the next.

In cases where disease affects the quality of a crop instead of or in addition to its quantity, economic relations are even more complex. It is now generally recognized that fruits and vegetables are sold largely on appearance and that in a highly competitive market the presence or absence of even superficial blemishes may make the difference between the possibility of marketing at a fair price and failure to sell at any price. However, it may well be that the enthusiasm of professional plant pathologists has carried them beyond the degree of plant disease control that is necessary for the best good of society as a whole.

It depends also on just what crop is affected and what role this crop plays in the economy of the society within which it is produced. If the item is readily transported from elsewhere, producers may lose sharply, whereas consumers are scarcely affected. If the item is pretty much within a self-contained economy, and if it is essential to the diet or industry of the society, slippages in supply will cause marked price rises. It has been pointed out, for example, that losses to the potato crop in England will cause such sharp rises in price that the producers' position is dramatically improved, to the mild disadvantage of the consumer. The situation within a given market area depends, also, upon whether reduction in one commodity can be easily made up by shifting to another different, but related, commodity. If so, price rises will be reflected in both, although disease losses are restricted to one.

Society as a whole is in the same position as the individual. Its interests are in the production of the largest crops practicable and in the highest degree of pest and disease control that is economically feasible. In the admittedly difficult decision as to when control measures are economic on the state or national level there will be room for much difference of opinion and need for real statesmanship.

The question who should pay for control measures entails not only simple profit and loss but the question of responsibility. When the disease is one that can be controlled locally within the confines of a single field and where the causal agent is sufficiently ubiquitous that what happens to it in one area will not significantly affect it in another, it is pretty clearly up to the individual grower to pay his own bills. He would presumably do this on the assumption that increased income from sales will more than repay the costs.

If, on the other hand, failure to institute control measures on one property will increase the hazard on adjoining fields, it can be argued that control steps should be taken even when the net cost-benefit result is not, on the face of it, advantageous to the individual owner. Only occasionally can voluntary cooperation or group persuasion effect the desired action in situations of this kind. Some measure of coercion, normally in the form of legal action, is almost always necessary.

Legal action can take at least two forms—it can require that the individual institute measures at his own expense or it can additionally bear the costs of the measures imposed. We are here concerned primarily with cost, but where actions are forced upon the citizen the question of financial responsibility is directly affected. There are several criteria to be applied in examining the thesis that governments should pay for control measures—assuming that any public program must meet the test of economic suitability:

- The extent the disease can spread from one decision unit to another, due to failure or inability to control it
- The extent to which action by more than one decision unit is required to effect control
- The extent to which danger from the disease or benefits from its control are realized by decision units removed from the affected area, but required to share the costs of a control program
- The extent to which all of the benefits of a public control program exceed the costs of such a program

In a related situation Smith *et al.* (1933) examined the question of responsibility as it pertains to plant quarantine legislation:

Since plant-quarantine regulations and the spread of plant pests and diseases do not affect all people alike, the question at once arises as to the number and kind of classes and groups of people who are to be considered in evaluating the economic effects. Obviously the advantages and disadvantages to different people must be compared in order to estimate the net benefit or loss to everybody or to society. But how many and which ones of the several groups of people shall be considered as constituting society? . . . the producers of a particular crop in California, all the producers of a particular crop irrespective of where they live, all the farmers in California, taxpayers in California, consumers in California, all the people in California, all the farmers in the United States, or all the people in the world?

Whatever may be a fair distribution of the costs of disease control, and regardless of how this is in turn reflected to the consumer, an important fraction of the total bill is not obvious at first glance. Take, for example, the matter of license fees for nurserymen—an item that is almost wholly attributable to pest and disease control. Or consider the very large amount of money spent by state and federal departments of agriculture on research and extension programs directly aimed at disease problems.

Bulletin 553 (Smith *et al.*, 1933) expresses the situation in these terms:

. . . In considering the costs of plant pest and disease control, it is essential to remember that in most cases the costs to one group or class become income to another. The growers' costs for hired labor equal the income to the farm laborers. The total cost to users of spray material . . . equals the total gross income from such products to manufacturers, wholesalers, and retailers. It is therefore practically impossible to make any estimate of the net cost of plant pests and diseases to all of the people of California. If there were no plant pests or diseases the entire social and economic organization of the state would be different.

WHAT, IN FACT, IS THE MATTER?

The detailed data needed for successful diagnosis are derived from careful study of the specific interactions discussed in earlier chapters. One must consider the myriad ways in which photosynthesis, respiration, water economy, growth, differentiation, reproduction, and so on are altered by the causal agent. For each disease, at a given level of severity, there will be a peculiar set of changes that, added together, spell out the nature of that disease. Knowledge of the possible alterations, of the variations inherent with each syndrome and—perhaps in the long run most critical of all—experience in the field, are the only dependable weapons in entering this arena. As in human medicine, there are those who seem especially gifted at the art of diagnosis.

One difficulty in reaching a diagnosis, except where the evidence of trouble is dramatic, is the general absence of anything that can safely be regarded as entirely healthy. This is particularly true in matters of yield levels, growth rates, or size comparisons, where absolute values are missing and where judgments must be made on the basis of statistical comparisons of two or more populations. It is certainly no accident that the true importance of virus diseases and diseases affecting the root systems of plants were recognized only belatedly. Here, with some exceptions, the observable effect of disease is most often a quantitative change, perceivable only by careful examination and comparative measurements. In the same way, many noninfectious diseases are substantially more difficult to diagnose than most infectious ones.

HOW SERIOUS IS THE SITUATION?

In the final analysis severity of disease is not the same as loss, and it is with the latter that mankind is really concerned. If diseased plants produced the same amount of food and fiber, of the same quality, as did healthy plants, we would be for the most part unconcerned about them. But measuring disease severity and translating it into measurements of loss is a rather complex question. For the outset they may be considered separately.

For many reasons, several of which have been suggested, it is difficult to arrive at realistic money estimates of the losses imposed by disease to crop plants. Perhaps this explains in part why the literature of plant pathology is so sparse when it comes to papers on disease damage and loss. But LeClerg (1964) has at least provided us with some useful figures from the decade of the

1960's, as shown in Table 12–2. His paper gives estimates for individual crops within each of the categories shown here. To the total might be added an estimated average annual loss from nematodes of about $375 million.

Table 12–2

Average Annual Loss in Value to Crop Groups Due to Diseases 1951–1960

Commodity Group	Average Annual Loss (000's omitted)
Field crops	$1,890,836
Forage crops and pastures and ranges	808,701
Fruit and nut crops	223,505
Ornamental plants and shade trees	14,099
Forage seed crops	23,584
Vegetable crops	290,389
Total	$3,251,114

SOURCE: LeClerg, 1964.

Disease Measurement

Ideally, disease should be measured in units that are generally accepted, by methods so standardized that they are dependable from one person to the next and from one place to the next. They should embrace all aspects of disease in so unequivocal a way that there can be no doubt as to their validity and usefulness. They should be sufficiently flexible to take into account local, seasonal, and varietal differences without losing their overall applicability. In short, they should be measured in the same straightforward way as one measures temperature, precipitation, or the passage of time. The truth of the matter is that virtually none of these conditions can now be met. We hardly know what measurements to make and in what units to make them. For the most part we do not measure at all, we estimate. And we do not always even know what estimates to make and how to make them.

The trouble lies mostly in the complexity and variability of disease phenomena. Take, for example, so well known a disease as apple scab. There are summer symptoms on leaf and fruit, overwintering mycelia on fallen leaves. Affected fruits are smaller than are healthy ones, deep cracks bring about dehydration, total photosynthetic tissue is lessened by scab lesions. How sick is the apple host, then? To find the answer what do we measure: Number of lesions, total lesion area, relative size of fruit, number of leaves lost prematurely, average reduction in fruit weight, retardation in photosynthesis? Or should we assess quality loss and reduced marketability? Actually, only detailed study of a given disease on a given host type can begin to provide an answer to questions of this kind. In a few fortunate cases, perhaps, a single, readily observable, easily measured manifestation of disease will give a direct, dependable index of disease severity. More commonly, the situation is far more complex, requiring selective measurement and a number of adjustments and correction factors.

Large (1966) gives a good account of the complexities of assessing disease by pointing out how much detailed study must precede even the most elementary effort to fix damage levels. As a general approach, he suggests that nothing less than a careful study of the morphology and development of the healthy host, and an equally meticulous examination of the course of the disease in question, suffices as a starting point. Given that, standard diagrams and field keys can be developed, to be validated by a series of field trials over a period of years. Finally, one is in a position to select an assessment scheme that best fits the disease in question and calibrate this in terms of yield reduction.

Above and beyond the question of finding dependable aspects of the disease complex to measure—getting a handhold on the situation, so to speak—there are many other difficulties in the way of a simple solution. K. S. Chester, one of the pioneers in this field, reminded us of a number of common defects as far back as 1950:

- Failure to allocate loss to its actual cause
- Failure to appreciate the destructiveness of factors that are relatively constant from year to year and not spectacular nor widely publicized
- Lack of a disease-free standard
- Lack of negative data to temper reports of epidemics
- Correlation of certain diseases with seasons of high potential yield, which obscures the actual losses sustained
- Correlation of certain diseases with freedom from other hazards
- Lack of correlation between field loss and lowered quality
- Subjective errors of judgment due to inadequate or biased training and experience
- Errors due to nonrepresentative sampling
- Errors due to an unsuitable method of appraisal
- Errors due to duplication and summation of loss estimates at different stages in the marketing of a crop
- Lack of an experimental basis for estimation
- Fear of prejudicial effect of loss reports on agricultural industry

When all is said and done, pathologists have no choice but to get on with the job as best they can with the tools available, staying alert for better tools. What, then, are the options available?

Numerical Measurement. A common device for assessing disease is simply to make counts or other direct measurements. For example, number of diseased plants per unit area, percent of diseased individuals, or percentage of diseased tissue within a single host, will at times provide a useful insight into the situation. Because these measurements are among the easier to make they tend to imply a maximum of objectivity and repeatability and are probably especially useful when used to compare the situation at one time with that at an earlier or later stage.

Scales, Indices, and Standards. There has been much attention over the years to the need for making disease severity evaluation as nearly uniform from person to person and place to place as possible. In moving toward this objective, pathologists have come up with an array of standardized devices to be employed in making estimates. Some are pictorial diagrams, as in the case of the well-known rust inventory scales. Others are verbal descriptions, each intended to correspond to an index number, in the hope that a quasi-quantitative value can be derived from what would otherwise be no more than descriptive prose. Perhaps the gravest danger in using these particular systems is the temptation, once having a numerical expression in hand, to manipulate it arithmetically as though it had the same hardness and objectivity as a physical value—that is, to forget how subjective were the initial observations from which the value first emerged.

Correlations. Correlations in disease management are analogous to marker genes in plant breeding. In both cases one seeks a readily visible, consistent characteristic that will reliably indicate a more obscure underlying situation. There need not even be, though there frequently is, any direct causal relationship. For example, red seed coats have been linked with host resistance to the southern anthracnose of red clover, although it is highly unlikely that the character itself is at all involved in the actual pattern of resistance— the practical value lies in the simple correspondence between coat color and resistance. It is an effective way of measuring by correlation a quality that would otherwise be very difficult.

Useful correlations in plant disease work are those wherein a more convenient index can be substituted for a less convenient: e.g., above-ground symptoms as related to root disease; leaf counts as related to individual lesion counts; relatively stable symptoms as related to transient ones; pathogen populations as related to disease damage; percentage of individuals affected as related to degree of injury to diseased host.

It is in the nature of correlations within the context of plant pathology that they can be uncovered only by diligent comparisons among phenomena and by painstaking, almost literally trial-and-error, examinations. This seems to be so because we understand so little of the underlying principles of disease, and because diseases are so many and varied that there are few if any really predictable relationships between the several phenomena. Useful correlations are not even necessarily between phenomena of equal significance. By and large it requires a thoroughly pragmatic approach to discover correlations most effectively.

Surveys. Of many and diverse kinds, surveys form a special category of disease measurement techniques. They are, for the most part, designed to develop estimates that are applicable to relatively extensive areas, as distinct from measurements of disease in single plants or in very limited populations. As in other field assays, whether for commercial or research use, a wide array of particular techniques and ways of assembling data have been used. But fundamental to all approaches is that a balance must be struck between sample sizes so small as to be unreliable and those so large as to be infeasible. Surveys are practical only when they fall between the two extremes.

Survey samples must also be maximally objective. To this end, trained statisticians have devised a number of techniques designed specifically to insure random samples. Which one, or ones, to employ depends greatly on the kind of crop, the kind of disease, under study.

One has many avenues for gathering survey data—questionnaire, interview, firsthand observation on foot, by automobile, by aircraft.

In the United States and elsewhere, surveys have been organized to monitor a number of the more important crop-disease complexes. Mostly they have been aimed at economically important problems, either as a guide to management and control practices, as a protective device in support of quarantine programs, or to provide data of economic importance in agricultural and forest planning.

Disease as Related to Loss

"Ground truth" is a term that comes from the jargon of remote sensing from satellites or aircraft and refers to the laborious verification, by detailed study of surface phenomena on identified test plots, of the images received by sensing instruments. After all, if aerial surveys of rusted wheat fields show clear variations in reflective spectra, the data are still of no value until a meticulously correlated relation to actual samplings from the areas scanned has been made. Until a dependable relationship is established between actual disease levels on the ground and recorded images in the sensing apparatus, nothing can be done with the survey tool.

In much the same way, measurements of disease intensity are of limited practical value unless they can be translated into loss. Loss, in the sense here used, refers to reduction in either quantity or quality of the marketable plant product being considered. Dollar loss may or may not reflect product loss accurately.

That disease intensity and product loss are by no means synonymous can be overlooked. But it is not difficult to think of situations where high disease intensity entails little or no loss, and of other circumstances that are very nearly the reverse. It all depends on what disease is involved, when that disease develops to a given level, and what plant commodity is involved. There are almost endless possibilities for variation—the important thing initially is to recognize that loss is different from disease and that each case is unique.

Why, then, if we are really interested in loss do we so often measure disease? The reasons are at least two:

- It is usually quicker and easier to assess disease than to measure loss.
- Once a correlation between disease and loss is established, it permits direct translation from the former to the latter.

Disease-loss correlations may be sought in a number of ways (see Chester, 1950), for the most part by comparisons between losses under conditions of differing disease intensity arrived at from every conceivable angle. Such devices as questionnaires, comparisons with weather records, crop prices, budget levels, and publication rates have been utilized, along with more conventional analyses of yield records over a span of time. As for experimental methods, they have included planned or intentional greenhouse or field infestations, use of resistant and susceptible varieties, comparison of untreated with pesticide-protected plots, and simulated damage produced by physical mutilation.

Despite the many difficulties and complications, useful correlations have been worked out, often in the form of graphs, formulae, or tables. Where the circumstances are such as to have predictive value, these correlations are useful in forecasting.

WHAT CAN BE DONE WITH THE INFORMATION?

There is an inherent satisfaction in the sheer ability of the scientist to appraise disease damage and to translate this appraisal into loss. Solutions, even partial solutions, to complex problems carry their own intellectual reward. But there are a number of immediately practical advantages to having data on disease levels and losses available. The advantages are almost exclusively economic, although not necessarily realized as direct increments of dollar income. By and large, benefits lie in increased income, in more economical use of manpower, in conserved labor and materials costs, or in more efficient use of available space and resources.

In the last analysis, disease loss information serves to ease the uncertainties of the decision-making process—decisions that range over a wealth of major and minor issues, decisions that confront the individual grower, the research administrator, the politician, the teacher.

Although it has been suggested that hazard ratings be attempted as a guide to new agricultural enterprises, in the sense that they might guide growers to avoid especially hazardous undertakings or discourage the introduction of especially vulnerable crops, there has been relatively little effort to put this into practice. Morris and Frazier (1966) provide one of the few examples of hazard ratings in their investigation of the factors that are responsible for the rate of spread of *Fomes annosus* root rot of thinned stands of pine. Of the many factors studied—host species, spacing, slope, whether planted or natural stands, age, amount of stump infection, time of thinning, competing stump and soil organisms, depth of litter, amount of organic matter in the soil, soil texture, depth of A horizon and height of the water table—the last three were assessed in terms of what they might contribute to establishing a hazard rating. Several generalizations were arrived at:

- As percentage of stump infection increased, damage to the residual stand increased, provided the soil was sandy loam, loamy sand, or sand.
- If there is a change in the horizon of the soil profile at 8 inches or less and if clay can be detected below that, hazard is reduced to moderate or low; if the sandy A horizon extends deeper than 12 inches before clay is encountered, hazard is high.
- If drainage is poor, regardless of soil texture or depth of the A horizon, hazard is sharply reduced.

From this work and subsequent field observations, formal guidelines were prepared and distributed to management foresters. They were as follows:

1. Examine all first generation pine plantations and all natural stands under age 30, prior to the first thinning, using the criteria of soil texture, depth of A horizon, and height of the water table to predict rate of spread should the stand become infected with *F. annosus*.
2. Hazard ratings based on soil texture as related to future stand management considerations indicate that:
   a. Clays and clay-loams can be considered *low* hazard soils.
   b. Loams and silt loams are *intermediate* hazard soils.

    c. Sandy loams, loamy sands and sands are *high* hazard soils if deeper than 10 inches. Deep sandy soils are the dangerous ones!

3. Exceptions to the above:

    a. If high hazard textural soils are underlain at 10 inches or less with a soil horizon in which clay can be detected in field examination, they become "intermediate" or "low" hazard as far as stand management is concerned.

    b. If the water table is high through 2 or more months of the year, as evidenced by surface water or soil mottling at 18 inches or less, these soils are "low hazard" soils, regardless of soil texture or depth of A horizon.

4. When a high or moderate hazard soil is encountered, give consideration to thinning only during the months of July and August when likelihood of stump infection will be lessened, to stump treatment to help prevent infection, or to delay of the first thinning until age 25.

MARKET PATHOLOGY, AGAIN A SPECIAL CASE

At the close of Chapter 3 the diseases that affect plant produce after it has been harvested were singled out as a special category of environmentally induced maladies, although it must be recognized at the outset that by no means all post-harvest problems are noninfectious. The rationale for commenting on market pathology at that point was that the issue of noninfectious disease was perhaps more conspicuously encountered there than elsewhere.

On much the same grounds, a case can be made for the special importance of market diseases in the economic sphere. For while economic factors are not necessarily any more fundamental than other considerations, they are appreciably more immediate and obvious, and in that sense the stakes are higher. There are several points here that merit a further look.

Economic Relationships Are Direct and Obvious

By the time agricultural crops or forested areas have been harvested, the point where goods are converted into money is usually very near at hand. Price, and total value, are closely related to the quality and quantity of the given commodity and will directly reflect any deterioration or loss. Thus the market middleman or retailer is keenly aware of the penalties imposed upon him in direct loss of income. He tends to make an immediate translation of specific disease loss to dollar loss.

By contrast, the grower of that same crop usually faces a substantially less obvious situation. Confronted by disease at, say, an early stage in crop development, he has to weigh the cost of control measures against an estimate of how much loss will take place if nothing is done. But making this last estimate is complicated by uncertainties as to how rapidly disease will develop and how much disease will mean how much loss. It cannot be fully known what other hazards will be faced later on, what unrelated diseases, mishaps, and environmental hazards will show up later.

The producer's situation is not unlike that of the golfer as he reacts to an unlucky or inexpert shot. If it comes early in the round it actually affects his total score precisely as if it comes on the final hole. Yet a poor showing on the first few holes is taken with philosophical calm—perhaps on the unspoken theory that it might have been a bad day anyhow. Let this same golfer play sixteen better-than-average holes and then do poorly on the last ones! He will be greatly upset at having thus missed the opportunity of posting a fine total score. He has, it might even be said, a "market pathology" point of view toward what happens at the windup of the game. Trouble at this stage seems ever so much worse than it would have earlier.

The Stakes Are Actually Higher

Not only does disease in market produce seem more severe than would the same damage earlier in the season, they often actually are worse. In the first place, it is no longer possible to invoke alternative procedures. The growing season is over and there is no way to recapture any of the time, labor, and money that has been expended—no way, at this point, to have done anything else with the resources used. Substitute crops, alterations in harvesting and management, are not possible. The die has been cast.

Secondly, unit value is at a maximum and loss of a unit is therefore maximally expensive. The economically most important part of the crop plant is the very part that is subject to attack in storage and shipment. It is often concentrated far more than at any point prior to that time. Actual cash has been invested and can be recovered with maximum profit only if nothing such as disease lowers the price and volume of sales.

Market Pathology as a Management Problem

Damage to harvested produce is the direct result of what might be called management in a broad sense. Mechanical injury, overripening, damage from imbalances in the gasses of the storage atmosphere, injury from toxic substances, and a number of pathogen-induced diseases show up when in one way or another the produce in question has not been stored, treated, or handled properly. To an extent seldom true in the field, modern facilities provide the means to avoid most post-harvest troubles, provided they are wisely used.

The tools and information are available to a substantial degree; there are far fewer uncontrolled, unpredictable variables to contend with than in the field. The crucial question is how these assets are managed, how well the threats that emerge are evaluated and met, how wisely are choices made among the alternative countermeasures available, and how astutely the financial issues are analyzed and resolved.

13

Chemical Control

INTRODUCTION

No approach to disease control is so familiar to the nonspecialist as is the application of a protective or therapeutic chemical. In the first place, man's common experience with disease prevention and cure involves the ingestion of medicines or the application of a medicinal compound of one sort or another. That public health measures rather than clinical practice are analogous to plant pathology usually escapes his attention.

Secondly, chemical control is by all odds the most obvious and direct means toward disease control. For the most part, chemicals are applied either at the very time of most obvious outbreak of disease or are used just before or just after disease appears. For this reason, it is associated closely with disease in the mind of the observer.

Thirdly, and perhaps in the long run most importantly, the effectiveness of chemicals in the control of disease is more readily apparent than is that of alternative methods. Most other approaches to disease control are either less direct or more protracted in time, or both. Resistant varieties, for example, require years to be developed and even then the relationship to disease incidence is often conspicuous only when experimental plantings of resistant and susceptible varieties lie side by side. Contrast this situation with the neat comparisons provided fortuitously by the juxtaposition, say, of sprayed and unsprayed plants or parts of plants. Small wonder that chemical methods get the bulk of the credit.

Finally, chemical control is by and large invoked by the individual grower. To a limited extent, of course, chemicals are used by outsiders—by crop-dusting contractors, soil fumigation organizations, and commercial seed firms. But for the most part chemicals are applied at the time of disease outbreak or threat by the person immediately responsible for and interested in the welfare of the crop. That the intensity of the effort varies from time to time and from one season to the next merely heightens interest in the program.

A distinction is often made between three general categories of fungicidal action—fungicidal here should be thought of in a nonspecific sense to refer to chemical action against pathogenic microorganisms, not fungi exclusively. In by far the preponderance of instances chemicals are applied to host plants or to soils in the immediate vicinity of host plants with a view to protecting the crop from a pathogen that presumably has not yet arrived—in short, to protect the plant. Much less frequently chemicals are used to eradicate a pathogen already established or to perform a curative role, alleviating the damage done by an established pathogen without in fact getting rid of it entirely.

History

Chemicals in disease control have been traced far back into history, although one cannot judge how effective the earliest efforts were. For the most part, disease control by chemical means has been seriously pursued for about a century and a half, commencing about 1824 with the use of sulfur as a means of controlling powdery mildews. Even so, it was not until a clear causal relationship between disease and microorganisms—especially fungi—was firmly established that much enthusiasm could be generated for chemicals as a means of control. By the late nineteenth century, De Bary had proven beyond all doubt that fungi cause disease, and Millardet had popularized that curious mixture of copper sulfate and lime that was famous for many decades as Bordeaux mixture. It is probably safe to say that no substance has been more widely used and aimed at a larger array of pathogens than has Bordeaux. One hundred years after its initial discovery, the familiar blue concoction is still used.

As time went on a new material, lime-sulfur, became very popular, especially for control of apple scab. It, with Bordeaux, rather dominated the field for years, only to be partly replaced by a whole array of materials in the early and mid-twentieth century. By the decade of the 1950's, an impressive list of materials was available. And along with increasing diversity came a far greater specificity for particular host crops and particular diseases.

For many years sulfur and copper, usually in analogous compounds with lime as lime-sulfur and Bordeaux mixture, were the mainstays of chemical control of plant disease. They had the advantage of being rather general in their protective action, economical, relatively stable, and generally effective. Only when the scientific and technical base of plant pathology had been substantially enlarged was it feasible to move toward the "tailor-made" fungicides characteristic of modern disease control.

Diversity

Over the years many compounds have been developed for disease control. The earliest materials were relatively simple, although to this day we do not know precisely the basis of their effectiveness. Sulfur, for example, has long been used in a number of forms and formulations, alone and in combination with other things, for control of several very important diseases. More recently, organic sulfur compounds, mostly carbamates, have been popular. In this guise the number of situations in which sulfur-containing fungicides are effective has been greatly enlarged to include many more above-ground diseases as well as soil-related problems and seed treatment. As a general rule, the more modern compounds are substantially more specific in their action than their more general-purpose predecessors. Generally, too, they are less phytotoxic.

Metals, particularly copper and mercury, are the active ingredients in a number of very widely used materials. Bordeaux mixture was long the old standby, but there is a whole family of copper salts useful in disease control. Mercury salts have come into use as disinfectants of seed and propagating stock and are therefore less widely used than copper. By contrast, the organic mercury compounds have proven more successful up to now than have the organic coppers.

As time went on, diversification became ever more pronounced, involving quinone-based substances, phenolics, heterocyclic nitrogen compounds, and a substantial number of volatile materials useful as fumigants. Not the least interesting is the appearance of oils as a spray in their own right, as distinct from their use as a carrier (see Calpouzos, 1966). At present, oil is especially well adapted to control of banana leaf spot, where the opportunity to use very low dosages per acre has solved what was with earlier fungicides a serious transportation burden. Apparently, it matters little whether the oil is a mineral oil, a plant glyceride, or a silicone—its low volatility and other physical properties are well suited to the task. Oddly enough, the effectiveness of oils was discovered almost by chance as an outgrowth of their use as a carrier for more orthodox fungicides. Just how the oils bring about their effect is still subject to speculation—it would appear to act through an effect on the host, as evidenced by reduced metabolic activity in the leaf tissue and an inhibition of stomatal penetration by the pathogen.

Oil sprays have been used very effectively in Israel (see Loebenstein et al. 1970) in the control of several virus diseases of bell peppers that are dependent on aphids for their transmission. Dilute sprays—1 to 2% of an 80% stock

Fig. 13–1. Effect of oil sprays in pepper plots showing the differences between (*left*) plants protected from the insect vectors of virus and (*right*) unprotected plants. (Loebenstein *et al.*, 1970)

preparation in water—applied with air-blast equipment to seedlings in nursery and field at intervals of a week or less—almost completely protected nursery seedlings and young field transplants, whereas unprotected beds developed as much as 60% infection within ten weeks or so of transplanting. The eventual difference in yield under these conditions was that between no harvestable crop in unprotected plantings compared to 5,000 to 6,000 kilograms per 1,000 square meters in sprayed areas. Oil sprays were less effective against virus in older plants (Fig. 13–1).

Not only are chemicals diverse; so are the sites and methods of their use. This is evident as one considers high volume and low volume sprays, dusting, slurries, fumigants, directed in turn toward fungi, bacteria, and nematodes. Chemicals may be used for temporary or extended protection, for therapy, as an antidote. They may affect host, or pathogen; they may be applied by hand sprayers or dusters, by machine, onto single plants or over broad areas by aircraft. They may be employed by the home gardener, the commercial grower, by the government. They may be used singly or in combination. They may be directed at one disease or several; they may be used as a specific treatment or as a generalized prophylactic.

A perhaps minor but none the less distinct barrier to communication in the general area of pesticides is the sheer length and complexity of the chemical name of many of the compounds involved. Yet because trademark names are usually, by custom, omitted from scientific writing—or may be confusing in the sense that substantially the same compound may appear from different companies under different trademarks—an effort has been made to coin common names that can be used whenever the details of chemical structure are not needed or when convenience dictates. W. D. McClellan (1966) has summarized the 78 common names given a measure of formal approval either by the Interdepartmental Committee on Pest Control of the United States government, which operated from 1947 through 1953, or by the American Standards Association, which took over the task. One has only to compare "endrin" with 1,2,3,4,10,10-hexachloro-6,7-epoxy-1,4,4a,5,6,7,8,8a-octahydro-1,4-*endo-endo*-5,8-dimethanonaphthalene to realize the advantages of the common name system.

There seems no substitute for the patient experimentation that leads to new techniques or new uses for established fungicides—no amount of theoretical knowledge can substitute entirely for laboratory and field trials. Littrell *et al.* (1969) have shown that by modifying the application method a material ordinarily used in one way can be highly effective in another. In this case chloroneb (1,4-dichloro-2,5-dimethoxybenzene), which is primarily a soil and seed treatment fungicide, was tried out as a foliar spray in protecting tomato, pepper, bean, and ryegrass from invasion by *Pythium aphanidermatum* inoculum applied by placing agar discs of the pathogen in contact with foliage. The results are clearly apparent in the accompanying figure (Fig. 13–2). These workers also discovered that the material protected foliage when applied as a drench, suggesting clearly that translocation within the host takes place from root to stem and leaf, although not in equal degree throughout the species tested.

Advantages and Limitations

The apparent simplicity and directness of chemicals in disease control carries with it great appeal. Results are frequently relatable to effort expended, are prompt and obvious. With care it is often possible to match expenditures reasonably well to estimated threat and to expand or reduce con-

Fig. 13-2. Control of *Pythium aphanidermatum* with chloroneb applied as a foliar spray 1 day prior to inoculation: top row sprayed, bottom row unsprayed. (Littrell *et al.*, 1969)

trol programs accordingly. But there are several inherent limitations that cannot be ignored and that represent, at best, constraints on use of chemicals in defending against the inroads of disease.

Toward the head of such a list must come the impermanent nature of chemical control. The main point here is that, with a few possible exceptions, the biological relationships of host and pathogen—as expressed by susceptibility, resistance, virulence, and so on—remain wholly unchanged by the chemical approach. In other words, every time pathogen and host come into contact in such a way as to invoke disease, control must be reinstituted. There is no hope of resolving the issue by chemicals once and for all.

Because chemicals must be used repeatedly, total cost tends to run high and control to be limited to those crops that have high per-acre value or that merit special consideration—fruits, vegetables, and ornamentals. Chemicals are economic only when value of the crop is high or when an especially inexpensive formulation and application technique is available. Sometimes, on a particularly valuable host, what might otherwise be an unacceptable cost is accepted. Conversely, new and more effective chemicals, or more efficient application methods—as for example low-volume spraying by aircraft—can bring wholly new crops into the roster of those to be protected or treated by chemicals.

It has been traditional to consider that except for very special instances, chemicals are too costly to be used in the control of diseases of cereals, with the result that emphasis has been almost exclusively on development of resistant varieties. While this is generally still the case, there is some activity directed toward chemical control, at least on an experimental basis. Rowell (1968) summarizes the situation in these terms:

One or two applications of existing fungicides result in only partial control of the cereal rusts. The short duration of activity of these systemic and protectant fungicides, compared to the length of the rust epidemic, limits their effectiveness. The need for fungicidal activity to persist through the last month of wheat development conflicts with the requirement for minimum residues in the harvested grain. Therefore, effective use of these materials requires reliable forecasts of the progress of rust epidemics to apply foliage sprays at the most favorable stage of development of the host and rust. Such limitations must be considered in the development of new fungicides and in the search for chemicals which control rust by increasing the resistance of the host or by altering the disease process. The delay of the early stages of rust epidemics by treatment at planting with the new oxathiin fungicides may overcome these limitations on the performance of subsequent foliar sprays for the control of cereal rusts.°

On the matter of toxicity to man and crops, controversy has raged back and forth for a long time. Disease control chemicals are poisons, designed to kill or at least seriously disadvantage pathogenic organisms. As such they are likely to be toxic to other organisms with which they come into contact. This effect is most frequently encountered as phytotoxicity when, by reason of unwise timing, incorrect preparation, or poor choice of materials, the host is directly injured by the chemical used. As will be noted later, much care is exerted in the commercial development of control chemicals to screen out those that regularly injure host plants. But there will still be occasional trouble, so thin is the dividing line between toxicity to pathogen, without which the substance is valueless, and toxicity to host.

Toxicity to man shows up in three ways. First are the routine hazards of inhalation, ingestion, or absorption through the skin during otherwise careful application. A second is the danger, as with any other toxic substance, of accidental poisoning through mistaking the stored pesticides for an innocuous substance. Most difficult to assess, and therefore most controversial, are the hazards represented by pesticide residues on plants and plant parts used for food or that accumulate in crops and livestock situated on land that has in it deposits of one or more recognized agricultural poisons. The legalities of the problem will be considered in a final chapter; suffice it here to point out not only that here is disagreement on effects as such, there is disagreement on

° From J. B. Rowell, Chemical control of the cereal rusts, *Annual Review of Phytopathology*, vol. 6 (1968), p. 258.

how much of what residues indeed exist. Changing analytical techniques, permitting detection of exceedingly minute amounts of material, have made it necessary to review the whole fabric of regulations bearing on the problem.

CHEMICALS IN DISEASE CONTROL

Foliage Diseases

The central objective in chemical control of above-ground diseases is to place the agent in question on the surface of the host—leaf, stem, flower, or fruit—in such a way and at such a time as to destroy or inactivate the pathogen. There are numerous modifications on this basic theme. At times the immediate objective is to destroy inoculum as it arrives at a healthy plant, before disease can be initiated. Mostly, too, chemicals applied to the foliage are designed to protect established crops.

Given, then, a population of plants subject to one or more pathogens, what are the options available to the concerned grower? The areas of choice primarily concern what to apply, how to apply it, and when to do so with the highest likelihood of success, at least cost in time and effort. All is on the assumption, of course, that an assessment of the hazard faced dictates that, of the options open, chemical control should be undertaken.

What to use? The choice lies among long-established, mostly general-purpose materials such as Bordeaux, lime-sulfur, or newer, more specific formulations such as the complex family of "organics." Knowledge of crop sensitivity and of the nature of the threat will help in reaching a sound decision here. The choice must needs also be made between liquid spray or dust—depending on equipment available, the size of the task, the dangers from drift, climate, and related factors. What to use in a particular situation will depend also on the future disposition of the crop under consideration: will it be used as food, as feed, or will it enter into commerce as a raw material?

Suppose then a choice as to the most suitable and promising pesticide has been made in the light of crop and pathogen and environment. How to apply the selected chemical depends on the complex of circumstances surrounding each situation. Very large or inaccessible areas may well be handled by aircraft, provided the nature of crop and chemical permit. Smaller plantings are best taken care of by mechanized surface equipment, either sprayers or dusters, that may carry large loads of the chosen material and move with facility through the crop. Individual home gardens, specialty crops, ornamental plantings, and so on are best treated with hand equipment or, in some cases, with small machines. How best to apply pesticide to plant is a rather different though related question. The key, of course, is coverage, particularly of those surfaces most likely to bear the brunt of the expected attack. Equipment design and the manner of its use seek to achieve maximum thoroughness of distribution over the host surface.

Finally, when pesticides should be applied hinges on the nature of protection sought. If, as is usually the case, the emphasis is on protection, chemicals must be in place when the inoculum arrives. If the latter can be dependably forecast, timing may be closely matched, but in most cases it is necessary to assume that the host crop is threatened and to act accordingly. A very great deal depends on whether the crop has stages of increased vulnerability, whether the disease is demonstrably seasonal, whether all or only a part of the plant is vulnerable, whether harvest time approaches, and so on. For some diseases it is necessary to provide continual, generalized control. For others, the timing can be precise. Most lie at a point in between.

The decision as to how often—that is, at what intervals—to apply pesticides can be wisely made only after weighing a number of factors. Several are obvious: tenacity of the material in the face of rains coming subsequent to application, resistance to degradation by light or other environmental element, retention of toxicity, rate of growth of new and hence unprotected host tissue, duration of pathogen threat and host vulnerability, cost of repeated applications versus risk of diminishing protection afforded by earlier application.

From this wealth of variables it must be evident that only a thorough knowledge of crop, pathogen, and environment can hope to provide satisfactory guidance. But here the grower is backed by an impressive array of expert advice. For most of the significant crops in a given region state and federal experiment station workers have developed large numbers of detailed recommendations on disease control, and incorporated this advice into readily available, inexpensive bulletins and pamphlets. There are but few crops for which up-to-date leaflets are not to be had for the asking. As new problems arise they become the subject of new publications, so that an intelligent, responsible grower can decide with substantial confidence what he had best do to insure a successful crop year. Failures there will be, for there are many answers as yet unfound, but on balance the record is good.

By far the most frequent employment of chemicals against above-ground disease is the use of sprays against fungus pathogens. In this category the most characteristic use is as a protectant against arriving inoculum. Several of the classic diseases—downy mildews, apple scab, brown rot of stone fruits, leaf diseases of ornamentals—are still controlled very largely by patient, faithful application of common fungicides at intervals during the growing season.

True, the campaign may be assisted by sanitation, by using resistant varieties, and by certain cultural practices, but in the long run the story is very simple —spray or fail.

In practice, spray formulations of one kind or another are used far more extensively than are dusts, but the latter are a not insignificant aspect of fungicidal application, taken overall. For the home gardener, in particular, but for certain commercial situations as well, dusts prove to be more convenient than liquid preparations.

The big difficulty, of course, lies in the matter of getting the particles of dust to travel from the application instrument to the surface of the host to be protected. In the first place, without the momentum of the fluid to assist, the distance to which material can be projected and the precision with which it can be aimed are substantially less in the case of dusts. Air currents, always a factor to be reckoned with, are far more troublesome to the operation when dusts are being dispersed than when a crop is being sprayed. Finally, it would appear that the very fact of passing dust particles through an orifice in the process of distributing it imparts an electostatic charge that may hinder deposition and retention even when that particle in fact comes into contact with the host surface. Assuming that the host itself is negatively charged, then positively charged particles of dust would seem most likely to remain fixed to the host surface. But the particle may be either negatively or positively charged depending on its size and upon its physical and chemical makeup—in fact a cloud must almost certainly contain a mixture of positive, negative, and neutral particles (see in this connection Whitman, 1926, Wilson et al., 1944, Gill, 1948, and Horsfall, 1956).

The Soil Environment

When the scene shifts to the soil environment, chemical control of plant diseases takes on a new measure of complexity. The dimensions of this complexity are, of course, three—organisms, soil, and chemical substances. As might be expected, the harmful organisms against which chemical weapons have been directed include insects, nematodes, and pathogenic bacteria and fungi. To an appreciable extent, the development of effective soil pesticides has grown out of efforts against one or more of these targets.

The soil itself has long been recognized as a highly complex physical entity, even so far as its inanimate components alone are concerned. The nature of the parent material, the texture and structure of the soil, the amount and type of organic matter, and the levels of water and gaseous substances therein, all influence in one way or another the behavior and effectiveness of a given soil pesticide. Finally, the soil pesticides are appreciably more diverse in their physical and chemical nature than is the family of "foliage pesticides."

Development of Materials.   If one considers soil chemicals in their broadest sense, attention seems first to have centered on fumigants in the control of harmful insects, especially the grape phylloxera. At least a century ago carbon disulfide was employed in this way, a practice that expanded with remarkable speed if we may accept Wilhelm's account (1966). He notes the tremendous increase in use of this compound from 1869, when "all the available carbon disulfide in Bordeaux amounted to only 38 kilograms," to treatment of 75,000 acres with 4400 tons of the chemical in 1884, 165,000 acres in 1887, and more than a million in 1900.

The parade continued, developing new materials and new usages as it went (Kreutzer, 1959). Sulfur was directed against onion smut before the close of the century, as was formaldehyde in 1900. Chemical seed treatment soon followed. Somewhat later, attention returned to volatile fumigants with the introduction of chloropicrin—first developed as a war gas—and methyl bromide, both directed far more at insects and nematodes than at fungi per se. This emphasis on insects held true also for the far less costly D-D (dichloropropene-dichloropropane) and ethylene dibromide, which came into favor in the mid-1940's.

More recently still an extensive list of materials has been brought out. Some are established fungicides from the arsenal of above-ground pesticides; more are formulations developed for the peculiar needs of the soil environment. It may therefore be instructive to take a quick look at the measure of diversity involved.

Diversity of Materials.   In Kreutzer's terms, "Soil biocides can be classified according to their chemistry, their biological properties, or their uses. A broad chemical classification of these materials would cover such groups as inorganic and organic heavy metal salts, the sulfur-containing dithiocarbamates and heterocyclics, aldehydes and unsaturated alcohols, halogenated nitrobenzenes, saturated and unsaturated aliphatic halides, organo-phosphorus compounds and antibiotics."

His most useful grouping, based on biological action, includes general biocides (volatile water-insoluble compounds, unstable chemicals, volatile water-soluble materials) and specific biocides (volatile eradicants, nonvolatile protectants).

It will be apparent that a wide range of chemicals, of varying degrees of specificity, having diverse modes of action, are employed in a number of different ways against a heterogeneous target. New facets are being added to the complex periodically.

Fig. 13–3. Hand application of chemical fumigants as used in the mid-1940's for control of root knot nematodes in shade-grown tobacco in Florida; see, for contrast, Fig. 16–3. (Taylor, 1946)

Application.   Not only are there many options available in terms of weapons and targets, but decisions must be made on how and when to bring the chosen weapon to bear. The actual technique, or technology, of application—whether by hand (Fig. 13–3) or machine (Fig. 16–3), whether as gas, liquid or solid, how positioned in the soil, and so on—is one thing. Quite another is the question how best to employ the chemical in relation to the phenomena of host-pathogen interaction. Kreutzer suggests four options on applications tactics so far as soil biocides go:

- General and continuous application of volatile and nonvolatile chemicals
- General and discrete application of volatile chemicals
- Local and continuous application of volatile and nonvolatile chemicals
- Local and discrete application of volatile and nonvolatile chemicals

To this list he adds the dimension of time—before, at, or after planting—which is determined mostly by the sensitivity of the host to the substance used. One must consider, all the while, the pathogen or pathogens involved, the cost/benefit balance sheet, and the foreseeable influence of the particular soil environment on the biocide selected—plus the kind of objective actually being sought, whether it be protection, eradication, control, or a combination of these.

Virtually everyone concedes that the soil environment is appreciably more complicated than the above-ground situation. Indeed, for many years the standard approach to soil-borne disease control was either to practice an ameliorative crop rotation or to move continually to previously uncropped land. The economics of land use and of the farm produce market often make this impracticable in the present day; a possible alternative is field-scale fumigation with wide-spectrum materials. Jones *et al.* (1966) have made comparative studies of a number of fumigants as used against an array of fungus and nematode pathogens and find that not only can the effectiveness be greatly enhanced by covering the soil with plastic film (Fig. 13–4) but that in a variety of ways the film alone is capable of reducing damage. Several possible explanations are offered, but it seems likely that retention of moisture, the possible effect of high-nitrogen fertilizers and, above all, prevention of reinoculation, account for the observed beneficial effects.

Time and again the complexities of the situation as encountered in the field bring about wholly unexpected complications. Whether or not the reasons behind these events can be discovered depends on the nature of the individual case and the ingenuity and diligence of the investigator. In the case of crown gall on Mazzard cherries, Deep and Young (1965) found that when nurserymen applied the fungicide dichlone to the soil in an effort to control several fungus root rots, the incidence of gall development increased. Careful experimentation seemed to indicate that the mechanism operative here was not a predisposition of the host, but a lessening of microbial competition with the pathogen, perhaps augmented by a tendency to increase the virulence of the crown gall organism.

Action in Soil. Goring (1967) provides a useful listing of selected pesticides, showing such values for each of them as vapor pressure, solubilities, and relative absorption by organic matter and water. If nothing else, the table clearly shows the enormous chemical and physical variety of the substances used. It might be noted that they have diverse uses as well—herbicides, nematocides, insecticides, fungicides. Finally, of course, soil is a complex mixture of mineral and organic matter, intermixed with air and water in various proportions and distribution.

What happens to biocides in relation to pathogens under these conditions is subject to few generalizations. For a given compound, used in a given way, effectiveness will be the net result of the separate influences of time of exposure, concentration, temperature, moisture levels, detoxification, absorption by soil constituents, decomposition of biocide, volatilization, and leaching. In more cases than not, increased temperature and moisture levels tend to enhance the effectiveness of soil pesticides. But where a given toxicant actually

Fig. 13–4. Use of plastic film in conjunction with fumigants. *Top:* Apparatus used to press beds before and after fumigation. *Bottom:* Fumigated field showing use of plastic film as a bed mulch. (Jones *et al.,* 1966)

goes within the soil environment, how fast it goes, and how long it stays there depends on how volatile it is, how soluble in water, how readily adsorbed, and how stable the molecule.

The interactions of clay and organic matter with toxicants are highly complex. A few generalizations emerge from Goring's discussion.

Clays thus exhibit: strong to weak sorption of organic cations with decreasing base strength of cation; moderate to weak sorption of organic anions with increasing acid strength of anion; increased sorption with decreasing pH for both anions and cations; strong sorption of non-ionic organics on dry clays; little or no sorption of non-ionic organics on wet clays.

Sorption by organic matter differs from sorption by clays in several important ways. Unlike clays, sorption by organic matter does not reach equilibrium rapidly. Initial sorption is rapid, but slow continued sorption follows. Presumably, sorption is a surface phenomenon with clay, whereas with organic matter surface sorption is followed by diffusion of the toxicant into the organic matter particles.

Even when reaction with organic matter does not occur, desorption is probably much more difficult for strongly sorbed chemicals like linear alkylate sulfonate than for weakly sorbed toxicants such as 4-amino-3,5,6-trichloropicolinic acid. Nevertheless, unreacted chemicals should eventually desorb completely, although months or years may be required under field conditions. When seasonal additions of a highly persistent toxicant are made to the soil, some constant amount will be carried over from year to year in the soil colution and soil organic matter in most instances.

Water solubility is an unsatisfactory parameter for judging sorption of toxicants by soils. The distribution ratio between organic matter and water should be measured, and is useful in accounting for the variation in the biological activity of toxicants in different types of soils. This parameter, together with data on the persistence of toxicants and their distribution ratios between water and air, can be used to predict doses of toxicants delivered to pest organisms.[*]

Specialty Situations

Seed Treatment. Although seed treatment seems a familiar and reasonably simple use of chemicals, Kreutzer suggests that it was not until 1913 that the efficacy of fungicidal substances for this purpose was established. At that time chlorophenol mercury was successfully used on wheat in control of bunt, or covered smut. Once the notion had been established, additional substances were tried, until the list presently available is lengthy: compounds of mercury, lead, and zinc; organic mercury compounds; several of the families of foliage pesticides, such as the carbamates, thiram, and dichlone.

There are a number of ways in which seed protectants are distinct, in degree if not in kind. Consider, for example, the matter of cost and convenience. So very small is the volume of the crop at this juncture that even the very heavy dosages customary in seed treatment incur only a minimal expenditure

[*] From C. A. I. Goring, Physical action of soil in relation to the action of soil fungicides, *Annual Review of Phytopathology*, vol. 5 (1967), pp. 297–99.

for the grower. Whether machine or hand sown, it is but little trouble to apply the pesticide, of minor significance in terms of labor time and cost.

Many of the problems that normally plague the practicing pathologist are avoided or minimized in seed treatment. Dosages are relatively huge, thus doing away with the question of coverage in the usual sense of the word and sharply reducing the requirement for adherence and persistence. Whereas foliage pesticides must be used so as to meet the need for thorough distribution and must be so constituted that they will remain active for a period of time despite the environment's impact, seed protectant chemicals are applied to a very small total surface. All that is really needed is a short-term protection— enough to get the seedling through a hazardous early period. Finally, because the seed itself is in a comparatively resistant state, phytotoxicity is very much less of a problem than would otherwise be the case.

Seed protectants are mostly applied as a dust or are first mixed with water into a slurry. They may be applied to small lots by hand but in larger operations are maneuvered by machines. More and more it is possible to buy seed that has already been chemically treated prior to distribution. A degree of care must be taken to see that the protectant used does not cause difficulties when the seed is planted by machines, such as clogging the channels by which seed move from the hopper to the soil.

To a limited degree seed protectants create a zone of safety about the seed, but there is a certain amount of movement into surrounding soil and interaction with soil. As Burchfield (1960) remarks, some of the organic fungicides that have proven of little value when used as general soil additives are useful on seed. Thiram, captan, and dichlone, for example, are effective seed protectants, where their tendency to react with soil does not seriously militate against their use.

Chemotherapy and Systemics. Opinions differ as to what should be included in chemotherapy, but as considered here it applies only to those materials that are purposely introduced into a plant for the express purpose of preventing, curing, or alleviating a pathogenic disease. Treatment of nutritional deficiencies is not considered chemotherapy in the true sense of the word. Neither is the use of curative chemicals as applied to the surface (foliage chemicals) even when the most conspicuous aspect of their use is to "cure" established lesions. But substances applied to foliage that enter the host, become systemic, and later exert a therapeutic effect, would be considered as chemotherapeutants.

Those who have worked most with chemotherapeutants seem agreed that three modes of action are involved—to kill the pathogen upon entry into the host, to alleviate a pathogenic condition already existing in the host, or so to affect the host that its *de facto* resistance is enhanced. In each case, if the chemotherapeutic agent is to be effective it must have certain special properties, because it comes to be much more closely incorporated in the host organism than do externally applied materials. Firstly, it must be fairly mobile, so that it is moved effectively about the host and thus brought to the site of actual or potential host-pathogen involvement. As an added dividend from this viewpoint, new tissues are protected as they are formed, quite unlike the situation with more orthodox pesticides. Secondly, toxicity must be clearly selective. That is, the chemotherapeutic agent cannot be significantly toxic to the host if it is to be acceptable, yet it must be effective against the target organism. In some instances, interaction between host and chemotherapeutant is such as even to enhance the biocidal potency of the latter.

Many and diverse chemicals have been employed as chemotherapeutic agents, probably commencing with organic phosphorus compounds as systemic insecticides and leading eventually to such materials as auxins and antibiotics, the last of special value in several bacterial diseases. There does not seem to be a clear pattern linking chemical structure with chemotherapeutic activity; the majority of the materials used have been developed in a largely cut-and-try manner—as indeed were many of the foliage and soil pesticides.

Chemotherapeutic agents can be got into plants in several ways, although convenience and economy suggest that for large-scale use they will probably have to be applied either as a foliage spray or soil drench. Experimentally, or where single perennials are being treated, liquids (even solids) can be introduced into holes in the trunks of trees and shrubs. But uptake is uncertain at best and distribution uneven. On the other hand, not all materials are able to penetrate the unbreached foliage and stems if applied as a spray and the uncertainty that soil drenches will be taken up unaltered is even greater. There is no question that the problem of devising a chemotherapeutic agent that will be selective and effective, and that can meet the rather demanding requirements for uptake by root or leaves, is so difficult as to have slowed substantially the advance of this approach to disease control.

There seems to be no escape from what is very nearly a trial-and-error approach to the discovery of new materials that are effective in the control of plant diseases. This is not a blind trial and error necessarily, but rather a search guided by close observation and close evaluation. Take, for example, the highly provocative report by Schroth and Hildebrand (1968) on chemotherapy of crown gall and olive knot, both of which are neoplastic diseases causing an appreciable amount of economic damage. Their starting point was the observation that the effectiveness of a cyclohexamide-kerosene mixture against rust galls in Monterey pine was in fact largely due to the carrier rather than the antibiotic itself. Reasoning, then, that certain of the very many hydrocarbons in kerosene might be effective, they tested a number of identified components of kerosene—paraffins, olefins, cycloparaffins, and aromatic compounds—for phytotoxicity and for action against the tumors themselves. From this work emerged a mixture of 1,2,3,4-tetrahydronaphthalene, diphenylmethane, dimethylnaphthalene, 2,4-xylenol, m-cresol—used in a variety of formulations—that has proven highly effective and economically feasible under actual field conditions in California. Indeed, a proprietary mixture under the trade name of Bacticin has been patented for commercial exploitation. This seems to be the first clear success of this approach to control of plant neoplasms.

The search and research continues, however, because of the special advantages of chemotherapy—the importance of systemic protectants, the curative action of at least a few compounds, and above all the capacity of chemotherapeutic agents to reach those very pathogens (vascular wilts and viruses) that are not easily controlled by conventional methods.

The search for chemotherapeutants that will effectively control such troublesome diseases as the white pine blister rust—where the economically important host is subject to a perennial canker that results in the eventual death of the tree—is tedious and thus far not very encouraging. Perhaps it is continued (see Phelps and Weber, 1969) largely because there is so little else that can be done, with present tools and understanding, against this very destructive parasite. Attention has centered on various growth-regulating substances, antibiotics, as well as conventional fungicides; perhaps most used in experiments thus far are cycloheximide and phytoactin.

Until recently the search for generally useful systemic fungicides made little progress and there were virtually no commercially available compounds that fell in this category. By 1970 there were nearly a dozen that showed real promise and were being adopted for practical use. The basic approach to their application was either as a soil drench or foliage spray, with the notion that they would then be moved throughout the plant host—in practice movement is only in the direction of the transpiration stream, and systemics have not proven overly successful in large woody plants.

In the late 1960's the literature on chemical control of plant diseases began to reflect very great interest in two systemic fungicides, benomyl (methyl 1-(butylcarbamoyl)-2-benzimidazolecarbamate) and thiabendazole (2-(4-thiazolyl)benzimidazole), that seemed to be effective in a number of situations (see Johnston, 1970; Coyeir, 1970; Daines, 1970; Smith et al., 1970; and Goldberg et al., 1970). These compounds, and most particularly the first named, benomyl, were reported in trials against a wide array of pathogenic organisms and against a diversity of disease types. In almost every case the results were highly favorable.

From time to time, and with a variety of fungicides and application techniques, pathologists have attempted to combat the apple scab fungus by preventing the formation of ascospores from the leaves in the early spring—it has long been known that one of the chief sources of inoculum in the orchard is the carpet of fallen leaves that harbor the parasite and in which the sexual stage of the fungus develops during the winter months. Initially, the favored approach was to apply chemicals to the fallen leaves in the spring, in the hope of killing or at least sharply suppressing spore production, but results were less than entirely satisfactory. More recently (see, for example, McIntosh, 1969) with the availability of the fungicide benomyl, experiments have been made with various dosages and application equipment that focus on spraying the leaves before they fall from the trees, but after the fruit have been harvested. Results of this technique are very promising indeed.

The term phytoalexin was coined to indicate any of a group of substances that are produced in plants when brought into contact with a pathogenic organism and act to protect the plant from the inroads of that pathogen. Explicit demonstrations of the presence and effectiveness of phytoalexins are rather difficult to develop, as much as anything because of technical complications and obstacles. Chamberlain and Paxton (1968) provide one clearcut example of this mechanism of defense in their work with susceptible and resistant varieties of soybeans in the presence of *Phytophthora megasperma* var. *sojae*. In this case, susceptible Harosoy plants were protected against infection by a phytoalexin produced in resistant Harosoy 63 plants and transported across via a string wick. Indeed, severed tips of the wicks themselves were sufficient to prevent infection. Several fractions of the phytoalexin, with differing properties, were isolated.

Whether phytoalexins turn out in the long run to be a major new field in fungicide research or remain a biological curiosity cannot be ascertained at the present time. They would seem to deserve intensive investigation.

In one sense, the application of chemical substances to woody plants to reduce the severity of invasion and rotting by fungi is a form of systemic fungicide, although it differs in several fundamental ways from the more orthodox compounds mentioned above. Very possibly the most widespread application of this technique has to do with the control of basidiomycetes in pine stands.

Because *Fomes annosus* is so very likely to cause trouble in pine stands, especially those grown in monoculture, various devices have been employed to reduce the degree of hazard. One such is to plant fewer trees per acre, thus delaying thinning and increasing the distance between stumps when thinning does have to be done—increasing also the distance between root systems. But in due time trees must be removed, *Fomes* can colonize the stumps and then, often through root grafts, the remaining trees. An accepted practice is, therefore, to coat the freshly cut stumps with substances that prevent the germination and invasion of the fungus spores. A number of different materials have been tried, of which, among others, creosote, urea, and liquid borate have proven effective in comparative tests (Weidensaul and Plaugher, 1966).

At the other end of the continent, *Fomes annosus* is also troublesome as an early colonizer of western hemlock, and under very much the same conditions as in the Virginia pinelands—that is, it invades stumps left in thinning operations undertaken prior to the age at which the timber is cut for lumber. Here again, various boron compounds have proven effective in reducing colonization: dry borax, solutions of borax in water, and solutions of borax, glycerine, and alcohol (Edmonds *et al.*, 1969).

In assessing the effectiveness of borax and urea in preventing stump invasion by *Fomes annosus*, Artman *et al.* (1969) have clearly demonstrated that it is not enough simply to make observations on the presence of fungus fruiting bodies. Indeed, careful culture work shows that a substantially higher proportion of untreated stumps contain the fungus as an invader than would be suggested by superficial indications. These investigators conclude that both borax and urea are effective, especially when used on the smaller stumps that are characteristic of first thinnings in young stands.

Postharvest Uses. Special problems and special opportunities arise when chemicals are applied under postharvest circumstances (see Eckert and Sommer, 1967), although management and handling of the produce has probably a more significant overall contribution to make. That is, chemical control of postharvest troubles is more typically an auxiliary than a principal approach, taking second place to temperature control, atmospheric monitoring, moisture control, and so on.

Even so, chemicals are a not unimportant means to the desired end, although there are a number of difficulties. For edible products the question of toxic residues becomes of immediate concern and rules out a substantial number of compounds that might otherwise be suitable. Time of application, whatever the substance chosen, must take into account the biology of host and pathogen: whether infection stems mostly from an earlier, preharvest condition, or whether it is directly related to the storage and handling phase. Some accommodations must be made for the span of time over which the produce in question is vulnerable to the pathogen or pathogens involved. And it is necessary to fit the control measures economically and logistically into the special characteristics of the produce involved, the customary handling methods, the storage facilities and duration of time in storage, and eventual sale and use of the commodity. Given these complexities, two major attributes stand out—the high value and the small volume, i.e., the "convenience," of the host material.

Over the years an array of compounds has been used. First were the chemical washes or dips—rather nonspecific antiseptics such as borax, hypochlorite, and sodium carbonate. Gradually more effective and more specific compounds were developed and brought into use—sodium O-phenylphenate, dithiocarbamates, and a number of "organics" (2,6-dichloro-4-nitroaniline, captan, thiabendazole, and others).

But market produce lends itself to other ways of chemical application. Because volume is small and surrounding atmosphere often reasonably well confined, volatile substances can be employed as fumigants, an approach that in many cases greatly simplifies the business of getting the active chemical to the site where it is most needed. Again, many substances have been used in this way, beginning a number of years ago with sulfur dioxide for those crops that can withstand its generally high phytotoxicity. Somewhat more recently, NCl_3 has come into common use for fumigation of citrus and other items. Ammonia and volatile aliphatic amines, too, are used in significant amounts as fumigants.

Fumigation, in a modified sense of the term, has been accomplished by putting solid materials into shipping or storage containers, whereupon it gradually volatilizes and forms a biocidal atmosphere. Of these compounds, diphenyl is among the more widely used, at least in the citrus trade, along with O-phenylphenol and some halogenated hydrocarbons. For the most part the technique of choice is to impregnate wrappers with the active substance or otherwise provide an evenly distributed source in close contact with the host itself.

Last but not least, one finds that antibiotics and growth regulators are useful in special circumstances—the first against bacterial diseases of market produce, the latter as a means to postpone senescence in fruits and vegetables when, if unchecked, it would lead to enchanced susceptibility and invasion by pathogens.

Virus Inactivation. As a general rule neither plant nor animal viruses have responded well to chemical treatment. In human medicine, drugs are administered to patients with virus diseases more as a way of preventing secondary infection than to ameliorate the primary attack. In most plant diseases, the systemic nature of viruses on the one hand and their intractability on the other have militated against chemical control. Yet virus, as such, is inactivated (see Matthews, 1960) by a large number of different compounds, at least some of which operate *in vivo*.

Stoddard (1947), for example, showed that the X-virus of peach was inactivated by soaking in zinc sulfate and by infusion with sulfanilamide. Other workers have been successful in related experiments that have included malachite green and other aniline dyes, thiamine, and several antimetabolites directed at the nucleic acid subunits. Generally, it would have to be recognized that chemical control of virus is primarily an experimental procedure, not an established technique, and that there is no clear evidence that it will soon become so.

Although chemicals have not been very effective against plant virus diseases, a few have been shown to have a limited usefulness. Hirai and Shimomura (1965), working with Blasticidin—an antibiotic derived from a species of *Streptomyces* and used against the rice blast disease caused by *Piricularia oryzae*—have found that it is highly inhibitory on tobacco mosaic virus at a low concentration, giving a 50% reduction in leaf discs at a concentration of only 0.05 ppm. The same concentration of the antibiotic almost completely inhibited local lesions on either *Nicotiana glutinosa* or pinto bean.

Bacterial Diseases.   In sharp contrast to the situation in human medicine, bacterial diseases of plants have been substantially more difficult to control effectively with the materials commonly used in chemical treatment than have fungus diseases. In part, the explanation may lie in the fact that much chemical control of fungus pathogens depends upon there being a deposit of material on the surface of the host prior to the arrival of the inoculum and the destruction of that inoculum before it can accomplish penetration. Bacteria, although subject to chemical action, are characteristically plant pathogens only if the host-pathogen interaction is such as to permit prompt entry and establishment. That is, the logistics of bacterial diseases seldom lends itself to routine control by chemicals. True enough, with the arrival of antibiotics as control substances, pathologists had a potent new weapon against the bacteria. But even in the impure form ordinarily used on crop plants, the antibiotics are rather too costly for routine use.

To a degree that is not always adequately recognized, a relatively few diseases not only occupy the attention of plant pathologists in their research, but stand out as especially intractable from a control standpoint. Among the latter would surely come the fire blight of pear and apple, which has been responsible for major losses in fruit-growing areas and has been under study by pathologists for many years. Even so, control is still far from satisfactory and one still finds research reports in the professional literature (see Zehr, 1968) that recount efforts to improve the situation. The antibiotic streptomycin remains the material of choice, although the comparative studies carried out by Zehr indicate the possibility of improving control in a few special situations—i.e., reducing progress of the infection from blossoms into blossom spurs—by mixing the streptomycin with dimethyl sulfoxide. Most of the fungicides and fungicide-antibiotic combinations tested were inferior to the antibiotic by itself.

One way of improving the effectiveness of antibiotics in the control of fire blight, a bacterial disease that has traditionally been very destructive to pear and apple orchards, is to apply the material at night when it can be anticipated that the spray will remain wet on the leaf surfaces for a maximum period of time (Powell, 1967), thus insuring maximum absorption of the active ingredient—in this case streptomycin. In this particular case, however, legal restrictions on the use of the spray severely limit its practical utilization.

MECHANISM OF ACTION

It is one thing to describe the way in which chemicals are actually used in combating plant disease; it is quite another to examine just how these substances bring about their effect, and thereby to achieve improvements either in the agents themselves or in their use. To do so requires a look at the chemical and physical properties of the materials in question and at the biological factors that further modify their performance.

Chemical and Physical Properties

The compounds used in control of plant disease may be grouped in various ways depending upon the focus of interest. In broad categories, they fall into organic and inorganic, with numerous subdivisions. In terms of general use, one thinks of such groupings as wood and fiber preservatives, bactericides, fungicides, nematocides. As for physical form and behavior, there are dusts, drenches, sprays, dormant sprays, fumigants, and so on. Control chemicals come as solids, liquids, or gases. They may be volatile or nonvolatile; water-soluble, oil-soluble, soluble in organic solvents. They may be stable, instable or intermediate, short or long lasting. They may be broad-spectrum materials or highly specific in their action.

The following list suggests at least a goodly number of the established materials (Woodcock, 1959; Rich, 1960):

- Metallic and nonmetallic inorganics
- Dithiocarbamates and other sulfur compounds
- Heterocyclic nitrogen compounds
- Quinones
- Phenolic compounds
- Halogenated and nitrated aromatic compounds
- Antibiotics
- Plant growth regulators

Most pesticidal chemicals have been discovered fortuitously and evaluated by pragmatic trial and error. Despite all the research that has gone on, precious little is really known about the mechanisms of toxic effect and how these relate to chemical structure and physical properties. We are a long way from being able to tailor molecules to predictable ends—and some of the best-known and most widely used fungicides act in ways that continue to baffle those who work with them.

With the exception of materials used on nonliving substrates, or used in areas apart from the host, or perhaps used on hosts in the dormant condition, biocides must act differently with respect to host and pathogen. They must be in that sense highly selective, while at the same time they must come into contact with the pathogen wherever it may be lodged in the host organism. This demand in turn raises the issues of solubility, stability, uptake, and distribution. Two difficult questions need to be faced.

First, what properties of the material influence the capacity to reach the pathogen? A surface-acting material need only be sufficiently soluble to be made into usable formulations and to enter into the pathogen cell. A number of highly effective compounds are not appreciably soluble in water but may have to be dissolved in another solvent first and then incorporated into the spray formulation. Indeed, too great solubility in water proves highly disadvantageous in terms of direct leaching and, in more subtle ways, in toxic action. So far as penetrating cells is concerned, a degree of lipid solubility appears to be essential. Within the host, the molecules must be at least stable enough to persist over a moderate time interval and to preclude premature interaction with the host itself. Obviously, if the substance is appreciably altered, it may lose all or most of its effectiveness. Finally, the substance in question must be, whatever else it is, inherently toxic through one or more of a number of possible mechanisms.

Secondly, what effect, or effects, does the control chemical have once it has arrived at the site of action? Toxic effects may come about in a variety of ways. Chemicals may directly interact with the pathogen and damage or destroy it. But at least in the case of materials used in or on a living host, the requirement of selectivity tends to rule out most of the very strong, direct-action biocides. For this reason, compounds that work in more subtle ways are generally more suitable. Most of these upset in one way or another the delicate chemical or physical organization of the pathogen. At times this is done through inhibition or overstimulation of a particular enzyme system, a molecular rearrangement that upsets the colloidal nature of the protoplasm or some fraction thereof, the chelation of a key metal ion, the hydrolysis of one or more proteins, the promotion of surface charges at a crucial time or place, or the dissolution, hydrolysis, or precipitation of essential cellular components.

For many commonly used fungicides, detailed studies have unravelled the complex mechanism of their toxic action on pathogens. It appears not infrequently to involve one or more chemical transformations in the pathway leading to the observed end result. At the same time, even for several well-known and long-established disease control chemicals, a convincing story of the mechanisms of toxic action still escapes the investigator.

Biological Aspects

Biology and chemistry have much in common but the focus of interest here lies in the relation of the toxic compound under consideration to the pathogen cell rather than in the mechanism of action, per se. We are concerned with how the material gets into the pathogen, the site of action, and the development of tolerance.

Penetration. If any of the mechanisms cited above are to operate, toxicant and cell must come into intimate contact. As Sisler and Cox (1960) point out, this means getting a mostly insoluble substance from outside the cell to the inside—that is, the material must be mobilized and it must penetrate. As for the former, data on hand seem to show that metabolites formed by pathogen or host often accelerate appreciably the movement of toxicants into the surrounding medium and in so doing promote its entry into the pathogen. Actual uptake, by spores or other parts of the pathogen, of the now mobilized toxicants quite regularly exceeds by far the concentration of those compounds in the medium itself. This phenomenon can easily account for the surprising effectiveness of some inherently rather mildly toxic substances. At the same time, many fungicides do not seem to produce desired results unless they accumulate to comparatively very high levels in the pathogen cell.

Site and Mode of Action. Where the biocide effects its change depends on circumstances. The first barrier is the cell wall, the second the cell membrane; either may be the site of deepest penetration, either may be the site of toxic action. The cell wall itself can hardly slow the intake of low-molecular-weight compounds except in those instances where adsorption operates to inhibit movement through the wall. Very large molecules, on the other hand, are significantly less able to get through the cell wall proper. As for toxic effect on the cell wall, evidence at present is rather scanty save for a few instances where inhibition of cell wall formation is indicated.

Not so the cell membrane. This lipoprotein barrier is subject to disruption by a number of toxicants and may itself greatly affect the movement of toxicants into cells. All the considerable body of information on membrane structure that has been developed over the years is pertinent to the question of toxicant action. It suggests strongly that lipid solubility greatly enhances entry of molecules and that the size, nature, and polarity of the molecules must also be taken into account. Where metabolically active sites occur at the cell surface or where the selective permeability of the membrane is destroyed, toxic effects can eventuate even without further penetration.

The most effective materials penetrate both cell wall and membrane, thus subjecting the interior to the toxic action of the pesticide. Once in the cytoplasm, a given compound may exert its effect by one or more of numerous mechanisms. Generally, acting as an antimetabolite or reacting at one point or another with a metabolic process—with enzyme, coenzyme, metal ion—the net effect is to disrupt the orderly chain of events within the cell and bring about its death or at least sharply reduce its activity and prevent its successfully establishing and maintaining itself.

The detailed chemistry of fungicidal action is a special consideration in itself and has been the subject of specialized papers and monographs. It might well be recognized, however, that we know a very great deal more about the empirical facts of fungicidal action—what amounts of what compound will have what effect in disease control—than we do about the mechanisms by which that action is brought on. This is not nearly so much an indictment of the research workers who are involved in this investigation as it is a mark of the complexity of the situation they are trying to understand. As one small step toward that understanding, Lukens and Horsfall (1968) have examined the role of several compounds related to glycolic acid as to their capacity to inhibit glycolate oxidase, which in turn seems clearly related to sporulation in the test organism, *Alternaria solani*. They suggest that the effectiveness of the compounds tested depends on the hydrophobic binding property and on their ability, in this particular fungus at least, to migrate from the culture medium to the basal cells of the conidophore and the terminal cell.

Tolerance of Host and Pathogen.   At times, through a developed tolerance, the expected impact of a biocide fails to materialize. By tolerance is meant here any mechanism by which the toxic effect of a given compound is blunted. Although a substantial portion of the work on fungi has been done experimentally in the laboratory, instances of tolerance in significant amounts under field conditions are not uncommon.

One can make several dependable generalizations. In the first place, fungi are in practice conspicuously less apt to develop resistance than are bacteria, probably because most fungicides are rather nonspecific and depend for their effect on comparatively high concentrations per unit volume of pathogen cell. Secondly, resistance to metallic compounds used as fungicides is more widely encountered than is resistance to organic compounds. Lastly, the mechanisms of resistance mirror the mechanisms of toxicity—that is, when resistance appears it must do so by blocking, counteracting, or swamping whichever of the many avenues of toxicity is operative in the particular case.

For some time there has been uncertainty as to the basis for developing resistance in microorganisms, particularly perhaps in the familiar cases of heavy metal tolerance of fungi. The evidence now seems to favor a genetic basis for the phenomenon, although extra-genetic phenomena cannot be ruled out entirely.

LOGISTICS OF DEVELOPMENT AND USE

Commercial Development and Evaluation

In 1958, as part of its fiftieth anniversary meeting, the American Phytopathological Society convened a symposium on fungicides that included discussions of the commerical development and evaluation of fungicides. The student whose special interest lies in this area is well advised to turn to the report of that symposium for a particularly worthwhile summary (Wellman, 1959).

To find, evaluate, and market a new fungicide is a time-consuming and expensive task. Estimates vary, but $2,000,000 has long been cited as the approximate cost over a period of several years—a government commission looking into the general question of pesticides in 1969 came up with a price tag as high as $5,000,000! The pattern of development is pretty much uniform, although details vary from instance to instance. First, by routine laboratory screening of large numbers of newly synthesized compounds, a toxic compound is singled out. The tests are run against standardized biological materials and serve to eliminate those substances that have no promise. At this stage each test is relatively inexpensive of either time or money.

As a second general step, for those compounds surviving the early screening, more diverse and elaborate criteria are established. customarily involving greenhouse experiments, followed by field tests. These last are so inconvenient and expensive that they are justified only for the very most promising materials—and are absolutely indispensable for them. The point is that conditions of actual use cannot be simulated in laboratory or greenhouse, yet a pesticide must measure up to the many stresses of the outdoors environment if it is to have any likelihood whatever of competing successfully with those already well established.

A third and final step for those very few compounds that withstand the rigors of weather, resist chemical decomposition, and prove nontoxic to the host plant, is a complex of development and marketing activities. By present-day standards the candidate pesticide must not only be shown to be effective, but exhaustive data on toxicity are required—a requirement made much more controversial, in a legal sense, by the marked improvement of residue-measurement techniques and instruments. Once efficacy and safety are established, most of the remaining activities are closely controlled by economics— market demand, costs of manufacturing and distribution, diversity of use, value of crops involved, competition from other compounds, patentability, advertising and promotion, shifting disease patterns and severities, and so on. In the last analysis a pesticide will succeed only if it makes money for the manufacturer. And even here it cannot with impunity stir up too much concern on the part of nonusers who, rightly or wrongly, fear its impact on general environmental quality.

Application

Control chemicals must be got to the actual site where they will interact with the pathogen or, in fewer instances, with the host itself. For the most part, this means application to the above-ground host, or to soil, and by machines, either hand- or power-operated. Success depends on when, where, and in what physical form the substance arrives at its destination.

An as yet almost wholly unsolved question, except in a very general and crude sense, is how to get even a major fraction of the pesticide into direct contact with the host and assure that it remains there. Despite every care and precaution, it must be admitted that most of the spray or dust released from the application instrument goes other than on the host—much less to that portion of the host where it would be directly effective. It may, in fact, be impossible to improve substantially, but clearly it would make possible very large reductions in total amounts used and cut sharply into the residues that accumulate in soils and waters.

Machinery.   (See Allen, 1960; Fulton, 1965.) Chemicals are delivered in many ways, from the simplest hand sprayer or duster to large mechanized vehicles and aircraft. The choice of application device depends on how much of what kind of substance is to be delivered where. "How much" takes into account the range from single plants in the house or home garden to large acreages of orchard, forest, or cropland, and whether application rate is to be high or low. "What kind" dictates the choice between duster or sprayer, and the design of the storage tank, nozzle, and pumps. And "where" will determine whether application is by air (Fig. 13–5), surface vehicle, or subsurface injection. As a practical matter the individual must select his equipment on the basis of investment (i.e., cost) in relation to the kind and extent of use. The diversity of the equipment must match, at least reasonably well, the diversity of uses to which it will be put—and this in turn the diversity of crops to be handled.

In the never-ending search for more effective chemical control of plant disease, the gadgetry as well as the formulations are open to new developments and new modifications. Witness the experiments by Stretch and Springer (1966) on the possible use of what they refer to as a "ground-effect" machine in applying pesticides to cranberries—a crop that is not particularly amenable to spraying with wheeled vehicles, since the vines intertwine to cover the entire ground surface. The machine itself is of a type developed by several aircraft companies as a transportation device and rides on a cushion of air expelled below the machine (Fig. 13–6). Initial tests suggest that the apparatus has potential for a number of crops that are planted in rather large acreages and that tend to cover the entire surface—potatoes, tomatoes, alfalfa, turf, and so on. The particular machine used in the New Jersey tests is shown in the accompanying figure.

Practices.   Given a certain disease situation, control chemical and application equipment, the grower still has substantial responsibility for accomplishing successful control. He must consider timing, so as to put the materials on the host at an optimum point in the chronology of events. This may be before planting, during the dormant season, early during growth, or toward the end of the season—or it may be necessary to make repeated applications at intervals. He must consider dosage, so as to achieve adequate material at the site of activity, yet at minimum cost and at levels below that likely to damage the host. He must be concerned with coverage, both in the selection of a proper formulation and in the actual manipulation of the apparatus. In short, it is of little avail to choose an effective compound and then to use it unskillfully—success depends critically on putting the right amount on the right place in the right way.

Fig. 13–5. Helicopter adapted for application of granular pesticides to cranberry bogs, a crop that would be damaged by wheeled vehicles. *Top:* Helicopter moving up to lift off container of pesticide. *Bottom:* Airborne machine distributing pesticide over the crop. (Courtesy of P. R. Morse)

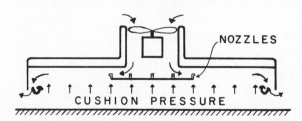

NOZZLES

CUSHION PRESSURE

Fig. 13–6. Changes in the technology of fungicide application. *Top:* Horse-drawn sprayer in use in Arkansas strawberry fields about 1920. *Middle:* "Ground-effect" machine as used in experimental application of materials to cranberry. *Bottom:* Diagram of the working principle of the latter. (Diagram and photo of machine from Stretch and Springer, 1966)

For special circumstances there must often be special techniques, a truism borne out by a suggestion of Anzalone (1970) based on experimental work with incorporation of fungicides under an increased atmospheric pressure. In this case, the problem lay primarily in the fact that sugarcane planting practices in Louisiana are such that seed pieces put in during September and October remain mostly inactive for several months. Under these conditions, the red rot fungus, *Colletotrichum falcatum*, tends to invade the stem sections and damage the buds. A partial solution of the difficulty is to immerse the seed pieces in fungicide at 10-psi pressure, as a result of which control is measurably improved.

In a second example, one of the handicaps that has plagued efforts to control the feeding of the beetle vectors of the Dutch elm disease is the simple fact that during the dormant season, in many regions at least, the air temperatures are too low for the standard spray equipment and spray formulations to be used without great likelihood of freezing. Epstein (1969) reports experiments in which both methoxychlor emulsions and DDT emulsions were made usable under feeezing conditions by adding 10 to 50% technical grade methyl alcohol. Depression of freezing point was roughly proportional to the amount of alcohol—30% alcohol reduced the freezing point to about minus 10°C. An added advantage of the alcohol was to insure deposition of the active ingredients of the spray formulations to an extent comparable with that of application under above-freezing temperatures.

Fulton (1965) in a general discussion of the evolution of fungicide application techniques toward reliance on low-volume methods, makes the interesting point that in high-volume methods employing hydraulic apparatus the final deposit density of the fungicide is proportional to the original concentration, but independent of volume applied. On the other hand, with low-volume machines, relying on air-blast for carrying the active material, the final density is more nearly proportional to the concentration and to the volume applied. The point is, of course, that in the former instance, all of the material falling on the host, beyond that retained by the surface initially, simply runs off and is lost. Fulton's paper underscores the importance of such factors as droplet size, number, configuration of the host, velocity of the airstream, nature of the target host surface, weather, and so on, and recognizes that with the advent of low-volume spraying it becomes necessary for research and field work to become far more exacting and precise in its use of terms, its analysis of the events that are taking place, and its implementation of the results of those tests.

Deposit. Except for fumigants, chemical materials that do not become affixed to the surface of the host cannot influence the course of disease. Much attention in research and testing programs, therefore, goes into questions of droplet or particle size, the wettability of the compound in question, and to the role of so-called stickers and spreaders. On one point, the matter of electric charge effects, data seem not only scanty but inconclusive. Plant surfaces are said to be electrically negative. Dust and spray, especially when released at high velocities from nozzle aperture, pick up charges of their own. When this charge is opposite to that of the host surface, it is assumed that the deposit is enhanced. But too few precise data are available. Add the aerodynamics of air moving past plant structures of different sizes and shapes and the picture becomes ever more uncertain.

Subsequent Fate

On Plant Host.   Although every effort is made to get dusts and sprays evenly and thoroughly distributed on the host, and in minimum particle size, the fact is that, with the exception of Bordeaux mixture, chemical sprays do not adhere particularly well to plant surfaces. Weathering—rain and wind primarily—causes these substances to be rather quickly lost, so that it is commonly necessary to apply new materials at frequent intervals. Among the factors contributing to loss are dissolution by water, a small reduction by direct volatilization, and degradation of the substance by photolysis, oxidation, or other physical-chemical event. Up to the present time, counter-measures such as the use of stickers have not been overly successful, partly because additives are inclined to reduce the effectiveness of the chemicals. In the case of those compounds that actually enter the plant, there is considerable evidence that they are to a greater or lesser extent metabolized in the plant tissues and thereby undesirably altered.

In Soil.   In soil, wind has little if any effect. Neither, of course, is the question of adherence to plant surfaces crucial to the same degree as above ground. On the other hand, so far as fumigants are concerned, volatilization becomes much more important and leaching no less so for the mostly nonvolatile compounds. New hazards are encountered here also—particularly chemical reaction with soil organic matter and biological degradation. On balance, then, the status of soil biocides is probably no less uncertain than that of above-ground materials, despite the superficially greater protection from the weather they seem to enjoy.

14

Disease-Resistant Crops

Two approaches to disease control, chemicals and resistant varieties, far outweigh all others in importance. Whereas chemicals are applied preferably in direct relation to a specific presumed risk, resistant varieties are employed more as a general insurance measure even though they are used against a highly specific threat. Paradoxically, chemicals may be much more broadly effective even though they are invoked for a specific risk.

In the case of chemicals, investment by individual growers is immediate and substantial; it is minimal and indirect when it comes to resistant varieties. Although he is but dimly aware of the investment that has gone into the research and development leading to the appearance on the market of a given pesticidal chemical, the producer is keenly aware of the cost in money, labor, and time that goes into the chemical control of a particular disease. His investment in control by resistant varieties is minimal and indirect.

Producers are acutely aware—often to their considerable self-satisfaction —of personal involvement in using chemicals to combat disease. They have the gratification that comes with having actively participated in the battle with the enemy. By contrast, disease-resistant varieties are almost exclusively the product of professional research establishments, although not necessarily governmental ones. Their adoption and use by the growers reflects an acceptance, mostly on faith at first, of the claims laid down by the research scientist. They are used as an insurance against disease rather than as a cure in the way that pesticides are. In a very real way, costs are concentrated in the research and development sector.

PROS AND CONS OF RESISTANT VARIETIES

Unquestionably, disease-resistant varieties represent one of the more important and effective measures available in the control of plant disease. Their use affords several clear advantages:

- Costs are comparatively low.
- Protection in many instances is highly successful and therefore economically very advantageous.
- There are no hazards to man or livestock from toxic residues, which prove so troublesome an aspect of pesticides.
- Control is for the most part independent of the age and vigor of the host, unaffected by vicissitudes of the climate, and steadfastly present throughout the life of the plant.
- They offer an approach to disease control that can be invoked for crops and under circumstances where application of chemicals would be impossibly difficult or time consuming.
- Resistance through genetic characteristics has been developed for diseases, notably the viruses, for which chemicals are as yet ineffective.

In all of plant pathology there is scarcely a more clearcut example of success in developing resistant varieties than in the case of asparagus rust control. The crop itself has been cultivated in Europe for over 2,000 years and was brought to New England prior to 1672. The rust fungus was described in Europe as early as 1805, although there seems to have been only one really severe epidemic in the United States, that in the decade or so following 1896, when it was first noted on the Atlantic seaboard. By 1900 the rust had reached the Dakotas and Texas; by 1904 it was reported from northern California (Fig. 14–1). Losses ran very high in these years and before long the variety preponderantly grown throughout the country at that time was virtually eliminated. As a result of this epidemic, an intensive breeding program was initiated by J. B. Norton that met with marked success; in 1913 the varieties Martha Washington and Mary Washington were introduced, and since about 1919 these two have practically replaced all other varieties in the United States. As anecdotal evidence of the success of the breeding program, one can note that the 1926 edition of Heald's text on plant pathology contained 7 pages devoted to the disease—the 1933 edition just one and one-half lines!

But there are inherent disadvantages. Perhaps the most conspicuous drawback is the fact that genetic variations in the pathogens all too frequently permit it to outflank the host, so to speak, and thus render a promising variety worthless (Fig. 14–2). In short, to achieve a disease-resistant variety is almost certainly a but temporary victory—the search must go on and on as the genetic array of the pathogen shifts. A second problem arises from the fact that most resistant varieties are successful against only one pathogen—that is, of course, unless the breeding program has been extended to include a second or third objective. And in those cases where a single variety has been produced that is resistant to several pathogens, the investment of time and money is

Fig. 14–1. Map of United States showing approximate dates of first appearance of asparagus rust as reported in the literature.

commensurate with the added attributes. That is, it takes roughly five times as long and costs five times as much to produce a variety resistant to five organisms as to produce the initial variety resistant to one. Finally, resistant varieties are hardly usable as an emergency measure. Should a new disease problem arise, something must usually be done to stave off disaster for the considerable length of time necessary to carry out a breeding program.

If one leafs through an elementary textbook prepared in the late 1940's (Chester, 1947), he comes upon sentences like the following: "The uniformity of hybrid corn, while an advantage agronomically, is a potential hazard pathologically . . . When, as in the hybrid corn program, we plant vast populations of very similar plants, we are creating the possibility for totally effective epiphytotics should there appear virulent pathogens to which the hybrids are not resistant."

It took a quarter of a century to prove the truth of this statement, which had of course been recognized by a number of persons, when the United States corn crop was seriously damaged by a mutant form of *Helminthosporium maydis,* the pathogen responsible for Southern corn blight. In this case the great preponderance of the corn carried a so-called "Texas" male-sterile cytoplasm that makes possible production of seed corn without the laborious manual detasseling of the female parent inbred. Yet because susceptibility to the mutant pathogen is apparently closely linked to the male-sterile cytoplasm, most of the acreage was affected and in some parts of the United States losses were very high indeed (Fig. 14–3).

Fig. 14–2. Susceptibility of oat variety Victoria, and Victoria derivatives, to the fungus *Helminthosporium victoriae,* a pathogen not even recognized until a few years after the introduction of this then-promising variety. *Left:* Victoria. *Center:* Vicland. *Right:* Resistant Bond variety. All three have been inoculated with a suspension of spores. (Litzenberger and Murphy, 1947)

The 1970 outbreak of Southern leaf blight (*Helminthosporium maydis*) on corn in the United States appears to be an almost classic example of the risks that are accepted when, in order to achieve the production advantages of hybrid vigor, an ordinarily cross-pollinated crop such as corn is converted into a highly homogeneous one (see Scheifele *et al.*, 1970; Hooker *et al.*, 1970). To a nation whose agriculture is so heavily linked with the success of this one crop, the impact of a disaster of this kind is very great indeed.

Fig. 14–3. Illinois cornfield virtually destroyed by the epidemic of Southern leaf blight in the summer of 1970. (Photograph by Curt Beamer, courtesy of the *Champaign-Urbana Courier*)

GENETICS AND PLANT BREEDING

Much fascinating work has been done in the genetics of microorganisms and many highly significant findings have been achieved. But it is not the nature and mechanics of the genetics of the host-pathogen relationship that is directly relevant to the *control* of disease. It is the practical utilization of these data and insights that is important, even though it must be confessed that the basis of success in a given resistant variety is more often than not unknown. Common practice is to establish resistance by wholly empirical means of testing. Success is measured by the extent to which disease damage does not occur under challenge by the pathogen.

There are several points that must be kept in mind if the special promises and difficulties attendant to utilization of disease-resistant varieties are to be adequately understood:

- The genetics of plant breeding so far as the host plant is concerned is the same as that of any other problem in the genetics of higher plants.
- The genetics of the pathogen—viruses, bacteria, and fungi, at least—

presents some special additional complications beyond the orthodox genetics of higher organisms. Many are haploid in the stage at which they interact with the host, which means that recessive genes are fully expressed in the phenotype. As nutritionally dependent organisms, physiological characteristics are far more significant—or at least more conspicuous—than in higher plants. But surely the most widely recognized attribute of microbial pathogens is their extreme genetic plasticity (Fig. 14–4)—in case after case, these organisms display many different races, varieties or physiological strains, whatever the term of choice. By no means all of this variability is in terms of virulence or pathogenicity, of course.

• Certain special genetic mechanisms have been elucidated in viruses, bacteria, and fungi—parasitic flowering plants and nematodes are genetically like the host plant—that have not as yet been shown in higher plants and animals. This may be only because the vast numbers of individuals that can be conveniently examined and the sophisticated means of detection make it possible to detect rare or obscure events. Even so, the fact remains that direct transfer of genetic materials from one organism to another, mitotic segregation and recombination, and related phenomena, are known for a number of microorganisms and can fairly be presumed to occur in others.

• Because the filamentous fungi are morphologically so adapted—having aseptate filaments or perforated septa, for example—and because they form anastamoses readily, multinucleate, genetically heterogeneous complexes are very common. When this situation is coupled with the fact that the nuclei are usually haploid, it is not difficult to see that the genetic result is at best uncertain.

• The genetics of *both* host and pathogen is involved—the genetics of resistance to cold, drought, or other noninfectious disease is a single-organism system. There is now evidence, particularly in the work by H. H. Flor (1959), that the relationships between the two is more than a simple random addition of the genetics of host and pathogen. In now classic work on flax rust, Flor finds a gene-for-gene relationship between pathogenicity in pathogen and resistance in host; as more host-pathogen interactions are investigated other instances may well appear.

One of the earlier conclusive demonstrations that both host and pathogen were involved in the development of new races of microorganisms—or perhaps more precisely stated, in the development and relative prevalence of races of microorganisms—was the discovery that there were substantially more races of the black stem rust of cereals in areas where the alternate host, barberry, was present and infected. In this case, of course, the sexual phase of

Fig. 14–4. Origin and inheritance of mutant characters in corn smut fungus. The white culture (center top) is a mutant of the brown culture to its left. The three vertical rows of four cultures are colonies from each of the four haploid sporidia (basidiospores) from three different chlamydospores (diploid) from a cross of the white mutant at the top with the brown line designated $10I_1$. Several of the white lines are again sectoring. (Stakman *et al.*, 1943)

the pathogen occurs on barberry, leading to new genetic combinations. The accompanying map (Fig. 14–5) gives some indication of the diversity of rust races isolated from naturally infected barberry.

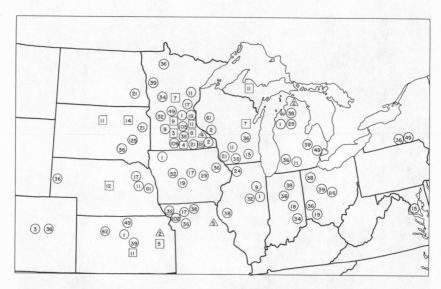

Fig. 14–5. Relation of barberry to the development and survival of races of black stem rust. Geographic distribution of physiologic forms isolated from naturally infected barberry is shown by number designation. *Circles*—var. *tritici. Squares*—var. *secalis. Triangles*—var. *avenae.* (Stakman *et al.,* 1934)

Again, the complexity of factors that determine virulence in sugarbeet curly top virus is shown in the relation between strains brought in from surrounding breeding grounds and those coming from the beet fields themselves (Bennett, 1967). Apparently, the more virulent strains of the virus kill the plant hosts in the desert breeding grounds of the leafhopper and tend to be self-eliminating. In beets themselves, on the other hand, the stunted plants characteristic of virulent strains of virus are also ideal for leafhopper increase, by contrast with the larger plants that are less severely affected. As the season goes along, then, the populations of vectors carrying virulent strains tend to outnumber those carrying less virulent strains. By the end of the season, most of the plants will be infected with the more virulent viruses.

Selection in the desert breeding grounds tends to work against virulent strains; selection in the beet fields tends to work in their favor. When management practices, such as irrigation, shift the balance toward a preponderance of vectors from the immediate vicinity of beet fields, the severity of the disease can be expected to increase, even to the point of damaging varieties of host usually considered resistant.

For many years the matter of bringing order into the taxonomic treatment of physiologic races of important plant-pathogenic microorganisms has been handled by international studies or agreements that establish a set of selected host varieties as a uniforming screening mechanism. Just such an arrangement was published in 1967 (see Atkins *et al.*) as the result of a cooperative study by United States and Japanese scientists in relation to races of the rice blast fungus, *Piricularia oryzae.* In this case it was possible to use as few as 8 varieties of the host to identify 32 races of the pathogen. The definitive paper provides not only a table to be used in identification, but a superb color photograph that distinguishes resistant, moderate, and susceptible host reactions. It can be taken for granted that additional races are likely to turn up and that in time it may even be necessary to modify the indicator variety lists, but the basic approach has been well established through usage with other pathogenic organisms in a wide variety of host-pathogen interactions.

THE STARTING POINT

The starting point for developing a plant variety that is resistant to a given pathogen—or environmental hazard for that matter—must be the existence, somewhere, of resistant genetic materials. The breeder may expect to look in a wide diversity of places. He may even perform certain operations so as, seemingly, to create resistance. But he must find it somewhere. Plant breeding is in essence the manipulation of existing materials into desired combinations.

What then is the desired end product? Primarily the breeder seeks to combine a high level of disease resistance with an established, recognized, and cherished variety, sacrificing as little as possible of the desired horticultural and agronomic qualities. In a significant number of cases the latter can even be improved upon.

Given a choice, plant breeders will use a source that requires minimum time and trouble, provided the nature of the genetic material being dealt with is equally desirable. On the other hand, a whole battery of breeding techniques is available for accomplishing quite remarkable transfers and manipulations.

The starting point, then, for a given program in plant breeding is an other-

wise desirable crop plant that is subject to a disease not effectively or economically controlled by other methods, plus a source of genetic resistance
that can, through available techniques, be incorporated into the host plant in
question.

SOURCES OF MATERIAL

Individuals of the Same Variety

Where the host is a seed-propagated plant, especially an open-pollinated
one, there will be substantial genetic variation within the population of a
given variety. Other things being equal, it is a substantial gain to find the
sought-after disease resistance within the variety, for it is usually easier to utilize it than if found elsewhere. Even in vegetatively propagated varieties, resistant individuals are possible but the chances of their occurring in company
with otherwise desirable characteristics is at best remote.

Related Varieties of the Same Species

When a search within the same variety proves unavailing, the next most
convenient territory is probably among other varieties of the same species.
Not only does this greatly enlarge the range of genetic material under scrutiny, but it permits the breeder to work with less concern for undesirable horticultural characteristics than will often be the case if he must go to other species. That is, the desired resistant genes are less likely to be linked to
unwanted genes for other characteristics.

Related Species

Often, desired resistance cannot be found either within the host variety or
within related varieties in the same species. When this is the case a search
must be made more widely. The search becomes most dramatic when plant
explorations range to foreign countries and involve the accumulation of a
wide array of native species belonging, ordinarily, to the same genus as does

the host plant under study (Fig. 14–6). Research strongly suggests that the most profitable approach is to explore those regions of the world where the genus can be presumed to have come first into cultivation. A half-dozen or so such centers of origin of cultivated plants have been suggested by students of the problem—especially the Russian N. I. Vavilov—that involve both eastern and western hemispheres, and it is to these centers that much attention has been directed. As a result there exist for many of our important crops a large collection of related species kept solely as sources of genetic material—not only for resistance to disease but for a number of other wanted characteristics. Even when these plants are themselves worthless—often strikingly so— and would not seem at first glance to provide a very likely source of material with which the plant breeder can work, experience shows that an impressive number of successful breeding achievements have started at this point.

UTILIZATION OF MATERIAL

If the breeder cannot find a source of resistance in any of the several reservoirs known to him, the matter is closed. But if he can there is no automatic guarantee that it can be utilized successfully; he must resort to one or more of several strategies.

Hybridization

Except in those cases where resistance is discovered within the initial host variety and can be successfully obtained through selection from a mixed population, or where resistant individuals can be propagated vegetatively, an essential first step is to cross-breed susceptible host varieties with resistant plants. For obvious reasons, this is usually far easier to accomplish when the two are closely related than when they are taxonomically more distant. At times the gap is so great that it simply cannot be bridged.

There is a distinction to be made between self-pollinated and "open"-pollinated plants. The former are highly homozygous, through generations of inbreeding, and are therefore genetically uniform. The latter are conspicuously heterozygous and, furthermore, are subject to accidental, or random, pollinations, with the complications this entails. Controlled inbreeding of open-pollinated crop varieties tends to produce homozygous lines, which are then used in hybridization. But whatever the nature of the pollination system, carefully

Fig. 14–6. Use of interspecific crosses as sources of genes for disease resistance. (*Top*) Reaction of species of *Nicotiana* to blue mold. *From left to right:* first and third are varieties of *N. tabacum;* fourth is *N. sylvestris;* second is *N. debneyi.* (*Bottom*) *From left to right:* N. *debneyi;* hybrid of *N. debneyi* and *N. tabacum;* susceptible *N. tabacum.* (Clayton, 1945)

controlled cross-breeding is a necessary first step in getting resistant genes from where they are to where they are wanted. The trick is to accomplish this move without also carrying numbers of unwanted genes for other characters.

Testing

Assuming the two plants in question can be successfully crossed, there will be a first-generation hybrid having a mixture of the characters of the initial parents. Almost certainly it will not at this stage be satisfactory as a commercial variety. On the contrary, it will be necessary to continue the work until a commercially valuable, disease-resistant variety is obtained in genetically stable form.

How, then, is one to know, in each generation, which individuals to save and which to discard? Only by testing, by challenging the plants with the pathogenic organism in question to see what happens (Fig. 14–7). If inoculation is easily accomplished, if unmistakable symptoms appear promptly, and if they can be induced early in the life of the host plant, testing is relatively simple. But if the converse is true, testing can become a very slow, troublesome, and expensive part of the program.

F_1 plants, presumably, will be alike. One need only show that resistance has been carried to them from the parent. If so, it remains to retain that character while moving on toward an acceptable variety. Should the desired end product be a variety very like the initial susceptible parent—except for the vulnerability to disease, of course—then the breeder resorts to "back-crossing," i.e. crossing the F_1 with its cultivated, susceptible parent type. The offspring of such a backcross will be genetically heterogeneous and only those individuals that retain the characteristic of disease resistance will be of value for future use. At each successive backcross resistant plants are identified and further selected for resemblance to the original variety in size, quality, and so on. Step by step the process goes on until after a number of generations a marketable new variety is achieved.

It is not always wise or necessary to try to approach the susceptible parent in all characters other than disease resistance. Many, perhaps most, breeding programs have multiple objectives, with the result that the additional crosses are made with varieties other than the initial susceptible parent and that selection for several characteristics is made simultaneously. There is probably no procedure that could be called standard for all situations.

In practical plant breeding complications arise. And among the more vexing is the phenomenon of genetic linkage. Simply stated, this means that genes for resistance are on the same chromosomes as one or more unwanted characters, with the result that, in a sense, one cannot have resistance unless

Fig. 14–7. Testing of varieties for resistance to sugar beet curly top virus. *Top:* Breeding plot in Twin Falls, Idaho, showing center rows of the susceptible European variety, flanked by resistant varieties on either side. *Bottom:* Tests in State College, New Mexico, under conditions of severe exposure, of a number of new varieties of sugar beets. (Coons, 1949)

he accepts the package of genes that are tied to it. If some are undesirable, the situation is unfavorable to say the least.

Because chromosomes do occasionally break, the linkage they impose on groups of genetic characters also breaks—and in so doing permits the breeder to surmount the obstacles facing him. Without going into the details of chromosome morphology and behavior, one can think of the likelihood of two genes on the same chromosome—that is, two linked genes—becoming separated as being proportional to the distance between them. This is not literally the case, but from a practical standpoint it is the closely linked genes that give trouble for the simple reason that they are the least likely to be separated by chance crossing-over. In any case, separation is a random event and the separation of an unwanted gene from a gene for resistance can be detected and taken advantage of only through patient search among the progeny of a given cross.

What then are the chances of success and how long will the process take? Both answers depend upon how readily the two initial parents hybridize, how great is the overall difference between them, or between the resistant hybrid and the desired end product, and how troublesome is the linkage problem (how many undesirable genes are how closely linked). To these variables must be added a number of others not thus far emphasized in this discussion. The generation time (seed to flower) of the plant, for example, sets the lower limit on how many crosses may be accomplished in a year—for woody perennials, the generation time is much longer. The nature of the disease in question, how time-consuming is the testing of progeny, and especially how early (or late) in the life history of the plant can disease resistance be determined, all have a great deal to do with how long the total process of bringing out a new variety takes. Finally, because the job must be done "gene by gene" a great deal hinges on how many steps must be taken (more on this point later).

Commercial Release

So far as the grower is concerned, a new variety is unavailable until it is released from the experiment station, or by the commercial seed company in whose laboratories and field plots it was developed. Total requirements of seed stocks for any of the major crops is very substantial and supplies must be available for sale through established outlets. By and large, the research and development phase of the work ends at about this point—too often the important role of the seed-producing and -distributing apparatus is overlooked.

In practice, varieties are usually given an identifying name by the time they are released into commerce. By this time, too, it is possible to detail fairly completely the prominent characteristics of the plant, not only its disease resistance, but other useful data on growing season, yield, and cultural requirements. It will, after all, be competing with other varieties already on the market and will succeed or fail on the strength of its acceptability to the majority of growers of that crop. Hence it must be advertised, in the better sense of that word, and its strong points brought to the attention of potential customers.

Whether, in the long run, a new variety succeeds depends upon its performance under the multiplicity of conditions and varied handling of a host of individual farmers. Even the most exhaustive field testing cannot possibly achieve the wealth of diversity of actual use, nor can it fully simulate the harsh economic measures by which, in the long run, a variety will be judged. In a very real sense, a "successful" variety is simply one that succeeds in actual use.

Multiply-Resistant Crops

Crop plants are subject to a number of pathogens. It is thus seldom adequate simply to produce a variety resistant to but a single disease, although the pressures for relief may be so great, or the trouble caused so conspicuous, that varieties are released when they represent no more of an improvement than the addition of a single kind of resistance. It is far preferable, however, to incorporate an array of resistances, one that will protect against all, or at least most, of the troublesome pests and diseases then widely encountered. The difficulty in this, of course, is that resistance is to be found, as a rule, only in widely different sources. One is obliged, then, to go through the whole laborious process of identifying a source, hybridization, further crossing, testing progeny, and so on, each time a new character is added to the host—all necessarily done without losing the characters established in earlier programs. It can and has been done, with signal success, but it is a difficult, time-consuming process.

SPECIAL PROBLEMS AND ISSUES

Field Resistance

Where resistance is clearly correlated with specific genes, the patterns of inheritance and often the mechanisms of resistance itself are comparatively

clear. Dominance and recessiveness, segregation of characters amongst progeny, and all of the other trappings of orthodox genetics are part of the picture.
It is with this kind of situation that most of the classical successes of plant
breeding are associated. But for many years it has been recognized that certain varieties of plants, in actual practice, suffered less in the field than would
have been predicted on the basis of known genetic characteristics and plot
trials. That is, they worked out rather better than it seemed on the face of it
they should.

This kind of highly pragmatic resistance has picked up the name "field" or
"horizontal" resistance, and is mostly considered—in contrast to "vertical"
resistance—to derive from the net effect of a number of genetic characteristics that in one way or another act to lessen disease damage. Often the actual
number and mode of action of the characters are not even known. One simply
finds that the incidence of disease is less and takes advantage of the discovery.

Field, or polygenic, resistance is not conveniently manipulated by the
plant breeder; there are too many unknowns. But in terms of benefit to the
producers its value cannot easily be overestimated. At the very least, field-re-
sistant varieties can be used to buy time while the more precise and manageable monogenic types are being sought and developed. In other cases, field resistance is to be preferred.

Impermanence

The point has been made repeatedly that success in developing a resistant
variety can never be more than a temporary victory over the pathogen in
question. As living organisms, the viruses, bacteria, or fungi concerned are
themselves mutable and are thereby producing new genetic combinations,
some of which can be expected to show pathogenic attributes against established host varieties that are not expressly protected against them. When this
is the case there is no recourse but to begin the whole breeding program all
over again.

From a practical standpoint, the problem is met by maintaining stocks of
genetic materials—seed stocks, plantings of native species, international collections, and so on, in full realization that new items will be constantly
needed. Along with this, especially in dealing with pathogens of marked genetic plasticity, there must be a scheme for rapidly recognizing and typing
any suspected new strain that appears, an approach that is probably best seen
in cereal breeding programs. What is as yet less well established is a system
for detecting what are in fact likely to be the new pathogens and pathogenic
races just around the corner, although some research on this problem is going

on. True, it might be impracticable to predict that a particular mutation was going to show up in a given place at a given time. Yet exploratory studies do seem to show that by making plantings of important crops in selected foreign countries it would be possible to discover just what pathogens in those areas are most to be feared.

Testing

With but few exceptions new hybrids and later progeny must be tested for resistance to the pathogens against whose inroads a solution is sought. Wholly aside from the time and labor required, testing of this kind is a substantial problem for, in the long run, it just is not easy to produce disease in an experimental population at will. If susceptible control plants in a given trial do not show symptoms, then the whole trial must be discarded. Indeed, when for any host-pathogen association a dependable routine for inoculation, holding and incubation, and disease severity measurement can be developed it represents a major contribution to the success of plant breeding efforts.

Van der Plank has been highly critical of commonly practiced field testing for resistance (1963). Generally, he feels that by demanding very high levels of resistance breeders have set up unnatural conditions and thus overlooked what are in reality very promising new host varieties. His arguments are closely reasoned and buttressed by specific examples, but they add up to the basic contention that field tests, designed to be statistically sound and otherwise scientifically unimpeachable, commit the serious practical error of putting fully susceptible crops (the traditional "controls") in close proximity to those being tested. In so doing, conditions are established that are favorable to a rapid buildup of inoculum and an exaggerated pathogen challenge to the variety being tested. Van der Plank is saying that "field resistance" is not only a wholly respectable kind of resistance but that it is likely to be overlooked in currently accepted variety-testing procedures—the system is weighted in favor of orthodox, single-gene resistance.

Tricks of the Trade

Plant breeders are not without recourse even when initial attempts to find and exploit a source of desired resistance meet with failure.

Induced Mutations. At the outset the point was made that resistance cannot be created, that it must be found. There are, however, techniques for increasing the likelihood that such a search will be successful, for while genetic mutations can be neither predicted nor directed, the rate at which they occur can be accelerated. A whole battery of possibilities lie at hand—mutagenic chemicals, heat treatment, irradiation. Of these, possibly the use of radiant energy of one wavelength or another has been most publicized and generally most successful. In practice, large numbers of seeds or pollen or plant embryonic tissues are subjected to sublethal doses of the chosen radiation band and the resulting individuals screened for desirable mutant forms.

As for chemical mutagens, the tremendous increase in knowledge of the chemistry of the genetic apparatus of the cell and of the mutagens themselves has made it possible to ascertain what kind of chemical changes are brought about when the two are brought into interaction with each other. While there remains a large component of the cut-and-try approach to induced mutation, the trials may be associated with certain known mutant types and the choice of mutagen made in relation to the kind of change sought.

Induced Polyploidy. When two taxonomically distant parent plants fail to produce viable, fertile offspring, a common explanation is that they either possess unequal numbers of chromosomes or possess chromosomes so genetically different that they do not proceed through a normal meiotic division. If, for example, one parent provides pollen with five chromosomes and the other has egg nuclei with seven, the resulting hybrid even if it survives will produce bizarre gametes when it matures, for the simple reason that pairing and redistribution of chromosomes will be irregular.

There are ways of surmounting this difficulty. The most popular involves treating young tissues of both parents—or the hybrid offspring—with an alkaloid called colchicine. This curious drug, derived from a species of autumn crocus, has the interesting quality of suppressing the action of the mitotic spindles and thus causing the nuclei to re-form with a double set of chromosomes. When this occurs, pollen and egg carry two sets apiece and it makes little difference if they are unlike as between pollen and egg—when meiosis occurs each chromosome can readily pair with its homologue and fertile offspring are produced.

Embryo Culture. At times failure of seeds to produce viable seedlings can be traced to incompatibility of embryo and the tissues in which it lies embedded. When this is the case, the breeder can often solve the problem by dissecting out the very young embryo, discarding the remainder of the seed, and growing the embryo itself in sterile tissue culture. Care, a certain minimum of facilities, and some investment of time are essential for success, but it is a well-established technique.

Genetic Mechanisms.   Gene linkage is troublesome to the plant breeder when undesirable characters are closely tied to the cherished resistance factors and there is difficulty in getting the two separated. But linkage can also be very convenient. Suppose, for example, the disease in question is of such nature that resistance to it is hard to detect, or must be delayed until late in the life of the host, or requires elaborate and expensive screening programs. It would be of great practical advantage in cases of this sort to have a gene, closely linked to that for resistance, that manifests itself as a conspicuous, readily recognized character appearing early in the life of the plant, even in the seed itself. When this is the case, one does not screen directly for resistance, but for the conspicuous, linked gene—a "genetic marker." True, crossing-over will result in a small percentage of mistakes in identifying resistant individuals, but the error will be far more than compensated for by savings in time and trouble.

Asexual Propagation.   When resistance is discovered in plants that can be vegetatively propagated, the breeder's task is immeasurably easier. This is true even when resistance must be established first in the new variety by conventional means. Thus strawberries or potatoes must be handled like seed-propagated crops during the process of developing new varieties. Once achieved, however, vegetative propagation assures a stable progeny without need for a lengthy period of stabilizing the seed.

In quite another sense asexual propagation, especially grafting, permits genetic resistance to be utilized in interesting ways. Rootstocks resistant to soil pathogens are regularly grafted to desirable fruit and nut varieties. Combinations of root, trunk, and top have helped solve several of the diseases affecting rubber culture in South America.

Variety Management

Given a well-integrated and enlightened agriculture, it should be possible to accomplish worthwhile objectives through planned use of existing varieties as well as by continual development of new ones. It has been suggested (Stevens, 1949) that for certain crops it would be worth trying a rotational system involving sequential use of several varieties that are genetically resistant to different groups of pathogen strains. This approach would be analogous to crop rotation, in which different crops are used in such a way that soil pathogens can build up only so far before they are presented with a crop that is highly resistant. Another suggestion is that selected varieties be used so that in any given year the target presented to the pathogen has a wide range of susceptibilities and no one variety predominates. One might, for instance, use a combination of five varieties so selected that a single prevalent pathogen strain could, even if totally effective against a susceptible variety, destroy only about one-fifth of the crop.

Van der Plank has advanced a number of primarily "management" proposals, based on his views of resistance and its role in epidemic development. He would urge, among other things, that moderately resistant varieties not be exposed to heavy attack by virtue of having susceptible plantings nearby in which the pathogen inoculum level can quickly skyrocket.

And finally, in the general category of management, the combined use of chemical control and resistant varieties must not be overlooked. The two have very different primary objectives and avenues of approach. Where compatible, on the other hand, they can nicely complement each other to the substantial benefit of disease control efforts.

The constant seesaw shifting of host and pathogen dominance in the cereal rusts—and many another host-pathogen association for that matter—is thoroughly established. The question is whether a change in strategy might not be effective in breaking the cycle and moving the disease-control effort a full step forward. Browning and Frey (1969) feel that if only enough attention were devoted to this end and if plant breeders would forego their preoccupation with pure line cultivars, success would be achieved. They recommend a "continental" control program that combines the use of fungicides in special circumstances with tolerant varieties, pureline strains that have polygenic resistance—"horizontal resistance," in van der Plank's terms—and multiline cultivars. It is with the last that they are most concerned; the remaining are well-established disease-control techniques.

Multiline cultivars may be devised by physically mixing in equal proportions, and with a view to the pathogen strains most likely to be encountered, ten or more agronomically similar resistant varieties. This is the approach taken by workers in the Rockefeller programs in Central and South American grain improvement programs. A modified system has been developed in Iowa. Experimental work clearly indicates that in the face of disease inroads, the losses in multiline populations are less than in uniform populations, as would have been predicted. Their success is even more marked when the length of the growing season is sufficiently short to take full advantage of the tendency for disease to develop at a slower pace in multiline populations.

Browning and Frey spell out several advantages of this approach: it provides a mechanism for quickly synthesizing well-buffered, horizontally resistant populations; it makes possible utilizing several resistance genes at the same locus and resistance genes that are linked; it extends indefinitely the life of a given resistance gene; it permits the farmer to optimize production of a given multiline cultivar by removing the rust hazard; and it permits the distribution of host varieties to distant points without the risk of worsening the threat of a given pathogen strain.

15

Cultural Control

By the end of the 1960's, environmental quality had become an overwhelming concern of a substantial segment of the technologically advanced societies of both hemispheres. When one makes the necessary allowances for the distortions arising from special interest groups, political opportunists, and just plain ignorance, the fact still remains that people generally had begun to think seriously about the need for careful attention to how abuses to the environment might be minimized and how most effectively to utilize the limited resources available to mankind's ever increasing numbers. For plant pathology these new emphases and enthusiasms have special significance as they relate to cultural practices in disease control and raise the status of cultural control measures as compared to more conventional methods.

Cultural control is an assemblage of diverse techniques by which the producer of agricultural crops aspires to improve his husbandry and maximize his efforts by the way in which he manages the operation. It includes agricultural cropping practices, harvesting and storage methods, crop rotation, tillage, variety selection, land-use planning, timing of schedules, and many related aspects. By contrast, the traditional approach to disease control has been by the application of agricultural chemicals or the adoption of resistant crop varieties. The former, especially, comes under hostile scrutiny by those who are greatly concerned about the dangers of harmful residue accumulations.

It is hardly surprising that chemical control and resistant varieties have won wide acceptance in practical agriculture. The former, which is aimed primarily at the pathogen, has the obvious appeal of a direct attack on a visible or imminent enemy. It bears a simple, one-to-one relation to the situation at hand. The latter, centering on the host, has the advantage of economy and ease of implementation.

Viewed against this backdrop, cultural control must often seem both complex and uncertain. It is concerned with the environment as it affects crop and pathogen, the interaction of crop and pathogen, and with these interactions as they operate through time. In a very real sense one has to know a great deal more about the biology of the situation to institute cultural control measures than to invoke either chemicals or resistant varieties. At the same time, where sufficient knowledge is available to assure sound premises, cultural control offers many exciting possibilities and at the same time makes possible economies in effort and materials while it avoids some of the common hazards of more traditional methods.

We are concerned in this chapter almost exclusively with control of infectious diseases by cultural methods, because it is in this area that the more intriguing problems lie. At the same time, it would be an oversight not to recognize that a substantial fraction of noninfectious diseases are most directly alleviated by what amounts to cultural methods. Deficiencies or excesses of soluble materials, irregularities and extremes in such factors as temperature, moisture, and light, and toxic gases in soil and atmosphere damage appreciably the well-being of crops and forests. The importance of cultural control tends to be overlooked because it is so very obvious. After all, once the cause of a noninfectious malady is identified the steps that need to be taken are often obvious, even in those cases where considerations of cost or practicability preclude their being put into operation. If nutrients are insufficient, they should be added; if frost kills the fruit buds, the crop must be moved to another area, protected by smudge pots, or planted later in the season. If water is deficient, irrigation is called for.

GENERAL CONSIDERATIONS

Basis of Cultural Control

Full realization of the importance of the environment awaited the discoveries that clearly established the infectious nature of many plant diseases, although at first the role of the pathogen itself was much overemphasized. By the end of the mid-1930's the pendulum began to return and interest now continues unabated. To recognize that environment is a powerful factor in determining the cause and severity of infectious disease is to suggest that to alter the environment should constitute a potent weapon in disease control. The real challenge is to sort out those aspects of the environmental fabric that can, by manipulation, be turned to the advantage of man in his efforts to produce healthy crops.

Not all of the measures properly classified as cultural are as direct as those employed against noninfectious diseases. Some are, particularly when they are centered primarily on either the diseased host alone—rogueing, sanitation, eradication, storage mechanisms, heat therapy, variety selection—or on the pathogen alone—pathogen-free seed, certified propagation material, soil sterilization, flooding, disinfection. Others are more indirect—vector control, soil amendments, dispersal or isolation of fields, crop rotation, elimination of alternate and reservoir hosts, establishment of trap and buffer crops.

In the more indirect approach the grower seeks by manipulation of one or more components in a chain of events to interrupt the development of disease and lessen its impact. By destroying the vector of bacterium, virus, or fungus, he seeks to intercept the movement of inoculum. By soil amendment he seeks sometimes to abet host resistance, sometimes to inhibit pathogen growth. By dispersal, isolation, or barrier plantations he seeks to avoid the juxtaposition in time and space of susceptible crop and virulent pathogen.

Disease control by cultural methods is not only often indirect, even obscure, but it is very likely also to involve more than one operation, to require the joint application of two or more practices. Thus attention not to seeding rates alone, but to seeding rates, timing, and depth of sowing are required for results to be satisfactory. Care in storage avails but little unless preceded by care in harvest. Vector control must often be supplemented by destruction of weed hosts and by sanitation within the crop.

In summary, the essence of cultural control is to invoke every aspect of cropping practice that will promote crop growth; inhibit or otherwise obstruct the pathogen; avoid, delay, or lessen the impact of disease, should it ensue—and rigorously to discover and eliminate any and all practices that operate in a contrary direction. No association is more intertwined than that between cultural measures and what is often dubbed biological control, especially since it is by no means certain whether the ultimate effectiveness of a given practice is attributable to the one or the other; available evidence suggests that the immediate result is so to alter the environment that growth of nonpathogenic organisms is accelerated at the expense of pathogenic forms.

We perhaps too often forget the extent to which agricultural practices that seem to have been perpetuated from generation to generation from sheer adherence to tradition are, in fact, grounded in sound disease control. A letter from John S. Niederhauser, written from Mexico in 1951, contains this example:

In the area bordering the Gulf of Mexico . . . when the grower considers that the corn is nearly mature, the stalk is broken over about one internode below the ear attachment. This is done by hand. It has apparently been practiced there for as long as anyone can remember. The people who practice this stalk-breaking do so for several reasons. First, since the corns in this area are quite tall, there is considerable danger late in the season that the corn will be blown down, and the prostrate corn is much less likely to give a good ear. Second, drying of the corn in the mature ear is an important problem in the moist tropics. Since there is hardly ever a satisfactory storage for harvested corn, the ears are left to dry on the stalks, and dry much more effectively if they hang down. Likewise, during this drying period, they are less likely to blow down. And third, as the ear matures and the husks begin to spread, rain finds its way into the upright ear much more readily, and more rot occurs, especially at the base of the ear, if it is left upright. Breaking over the stalk actually results in less rot in the field.

When asked why they do it, most of the growers who practice stalk-breaking will give one or more of the reasons I have given. A certain number, of course, just say that they do it that way because that's the way to grow corn!

Economic Aspects

In no aspect of disease control are economic considerations more directly relevant than in the application of cultural measures. As N. E. Stevens pointed out (1938b), except for ornamentals, control should cost demonstrably less than the losses that would be sustained in the absence of control can fairly be expected to. In their zeal for demonstrating their ability to solve difficult problems of disease control, plant pathologists seem a little like the old-time volunteer firemen who were more interested in beating the other outfit to the fire and putting on a good show there than in saving the building. Pathologists seem sometimes to forget that the real purpose of agriculture is not to control plant diseases but to grow profitable crops. For growing profitable crops, disease prevention is often better than disease treatment.

One suspects that rather more demanding criteria of economic feasibility are often applied to cultural practices than to chemical control or the use of resistant varieties. It is not uncommon to find sprays and dusts recommended, and applied, in situations where the economic soundness of the program is not clearly demonstrated—if, indeed, considered at all. But only rarely do we see cultural procedures undertaken until there has first been serious thought given to whether it will "pay off" in increased crop value.

Naturally, those cultural measures that are synonymous with, or only a slight modification of, practices and programs already being carried out in the routine planting, tillage, and management of crops will cost little if anything and can be instituted without undue concern for their economic outcome. In a word, there are instances when, as the saying goes, "it doesn't cost anything to try." The main point, however, is that when it does cost something to try, the probable gain must be rather clearly shown before the grower can be persuaded to take the suggested steps.

The higher the cash value of the crop, the greater is the expenditure of time, effort, and money that is justified in its defense. Other things being equal, one can wisely expend more upon a perennial than upon an annual crop, more upon ornamentals than other commercial crops, more upon horticultural than agronomic varieties. Forest stands are traditionally not subjected to measures having a high per acre cost. When they have been converted into processed materials, they attain minimum volume and maximum value, and can be protected by the more expensive measures characteristic of storage and market pathology.

The producer must nearly always make the effort and pay the cost of cultural control, although he will in the long run pass these costs along to the consumer. Even more importantly, perhaps, he is acutely aware of having to assume the costs; chemical control and resistant varieties do not always appear so directly chargeable to the individual producer, because the costs of development are hidden in the budgets of government experiment stations or industrial laboratories. Thus while the total real cost of cultural methods may be the lowest of all alternatives, the apparent cost is sometimes highest—the result is that too little serious attention is given to this avenue of disease prevention and control.

Growers must not only pay the cost of cultural control, they often bear the responsibility for invoking it. Where the immediate cropped area is the only one affected the owner can decide what to do entirely on the basis of selfish interests. But if adjacent areas are implicated—most vector control falls in this category—grower responsibility includes his obligations to his neighbors. Smith et al. (1933) point out the important difference between requiring a grower to control a pest or disease that otherwise continually threatens his neighbor and requiring him to eradicate it. They argue that if a reasonably effective control is available at moderate cost, it can be assumed to be to the mutual advantage of all to adopt these measures and that the individual can be held liable if incidence on his property reaches a state that menaces others. He is not, however, fairly held responsible for the occurrence of disease or pest organisms on his property above and beyond ordinary methods of control, and ought to be compensated for any considerable cost in excess of this or for any destruction of property involved in eradication. In their opinion, compulsory control is a proper function of the police power, but compulsory eradication, since it deprives the grower of valuable property for the benefit of society, is an altogether different matter and should be fairly compensated.

Successful application of cultural methods often requires cooperative action. The grower who chooses to apply chemicals to his crops, seed, or soil may do so with impunity and on his own initiative, secure in the conviction that some direct benefits will accrue whether his neighbor on either side chooses to act accordingly or not. He may plant seed of resistant varieties or employ disease-resistant propagating materials and expect improvement in his situation whether or not his colleagues follow suit. But the success of an unorthodox measure often rests on its simultaneous, conscientious application by a group of individuals—a cooperation that frequently has to be initiated by law and supported by public opinion.

The greater complexity of cultural control situations stands as a hindrance to their adoption because there is the risk of making matters worse. In this they tend to differ from spraying and dusting. In the latter instances even if ineffective the maximum loss is that of money and labor. In the same sense, use of resistant varieties is a thoroughly safe approach for the most part. But in the web of interacting variables within which cultural control operates, a given practice has the potential for harmful rather than helpful effect. Adjusting the environment is, at best, a risky business.

Elements of Cultural Control

Disease control by cultural methods is complex and faces a general reluctance of those involved to think and act decisively. Over against these disadvantages is a sharpening interest in nonchemical approaches to agriculture generally and a partial disenchantment with many traditional plant breeding techniques. But far and away the most crucial single factor in the situation is the amount and accuracy of the biological data available in a given instance.

Graham (1951) has provided an especially convincing piece of evidence of the absolute necessity for sound biological data as a prelude to cultural control. He points out that the white pine weevil was for many years studied only where it was abundant, until it eventually dawned on someone to examine those areas where it was normally scarce. This approach soon showed that where the trees grew from infancy in dense stands a good crop was invariably produced, whereas scattered plantings were always severely damaged, and that pines growing intermixed with hardwoods were practically never attacked. Obviously, forest management could be designed to take this knowledge into account.

He showed too that the spruce budworm—an insect estimated to have destroyed in one decade enough timber, piled as cordwood, to encircle the earth 10 times—was seldom destructive in stands of spruce-fir that had in the upper crown less than 50% balsam. Here the balsam serves as an ideal site for survival of the hibernating insects. In a related form attacking pine, outbreaks can be controlled by cutting out scattered, large-crowned trees; these bore an excessive number of staminate cones, which correlates closely with insect damage.

Satisfactory progress in the identification, development, and application of cultural control measures will be achieved only through correspondingly meticulous and persistent researches on the biology of disease in plants, coupled with close observations of the effects of empirical field tests and a genuine willingness to evaluate objectively the long-established, tradition-based practices of the commercial producer.

Where large geographic areas are involved, cultural control is best carried out as a venture that involves a community or group of individuals, particularly if the areas involved are scattered. Valleau (1953) made this point in a discussion of tobacco blue mold in the southeastern United States. As he says, any informed tobacco grower can with comparatively little labor be certain that his farm does not originate an epidemic. Hence the joint efforts of a majority of tobacco growers in the region could reduce losses to the vanishing point. By eliminating the pathogen from Georgia, where it survives the winter on living plants and as oospores, the spore showers to which tobacco in the Carolinas and Virginia is subject could be prevented. Very likely the disease could be for all practical purposes eliminated from those more northerly regions.

The Diseased Plant. The diseased plant itself—as distinct from the diseased population—is a prime element in cultural control because infectious disease is clearly the sum of innumerable specific interactions between individuals of the pathogen population and individuals of the host population. Control is the net effect of the particular measures invoked upon these specific interactions.

We have noted in earlier chapters that the individual host plant has one or more of a number of defensive mechanisms—disease escape, histological resistance, hypersensitivity, tolerance to the pathogen, and so on. When cultural control comes into play it operates through these mechanisms and takes advantage of growth habit, rate of maturation, morphologic changes, or any of the many related attributes of the plant. In short, the host population is manipulated so as to maximize the net effect of all available individual resistances.

Host plants not only display a number of resistance mechanisms, they are subject to environmental forces—nutrition, temperature, moisture, light, soil conditions—that act to predispose them to pathogen attack. Viewed from the standpoint of cultural control, the way in which a crop is handled may well influence how effective are these predisposing factors. In this case, of course, the objective will naturally be to keep predisposition to a minimum.

The Pathogen. If the individual host plant is one element of cultural control, and the diseased population another, then the pathogen is clearly the third element needed to complete the picture. In this case, the grower searches for vulnerable spots in the life histories of the pathogenic organism—in, for example, its reproduction, pathogenicity, or dispersal mechanisms—and tries to exploit those weaknesses by adroit management.

Some foliage diseases, for example, that are serious when hosts are crowded and when humidity in the immediate vicinity of the leaf surfaces is high can be favorably altered by reducing the seeding rate. Others, such as the aphid-transmitted peanut rosette virus, are made worse by dry weather and can be partially controlled by sowing more thickly. In any event, plants requiring much moisture, if it be supplied by irrigation, do not normally suffer from pathogens requiring high humidity.

Spore germination, viability, survival and longevity, resistance or sensitivity to extremes of light, temperature, drought—all these elements of the pathogen are in the last analysis influenced by the environment and hence are affected by cultural practices.

Reproduction is a part of the biology of individual pathogens; inoculum production is the cumulative result of the process as carried out by a given population of pathogens. But all along the line the environment has its effect and can be manipulated to decrease or to accelerate the processes involved. When the result is a consciously produced decrease in reproduction rate or inoculum productivity, we call it cultural control.

CONTROL BY DIRECT EFFECTS ON THE HOST

So many miscellaneous items are fairly considered as cultural control techniques that a rough classification becomes convenient. First in such a grouping comes those maneuvers that directly affect the host plant, even though what is done may have additional objectives that are not immediately pertinent to disease.

Manipulation of the Host Plant

The often routine practices of the grower—management, tillage, handling, and so on—are frequently influential in setting the level of disease damage. Growth habit, for example, which can be set to some extent by selection of crop varieties or by pruning, affects the disease propensities of the host largely because the microclimate they engender is different.

As for mechanical damage, there are endless instances of injury to orchard, shade, and ornamental trees, to perishable fruits and vegetables, and to other agricultural crops that result from careless or unskilled handling. There are no magical or obscure measures needed to rectify this difficulty, just the obvious need. for meticulous attention to the situation as day-to-day operations are carried out. Avoidance of poor techniques is, of itself, a positive measure in disease control by cultural methods.

Choice of soil type, where alternatives are available, and tillage practices, in addition to a number of obvious direct effects on crop welfare, are related to disease incidence. Gäumann (1950) has cited the influence of heavy- and light-textured soils on tuber infection with late blight, and comments on the widely recognized importance of soil reaction and humus content.

Soil, soil management, and cropping practices are clearly influential in determining the severity of a number of root rot diseases, which have long been recognized as the cause of substantial losses. "Take-all" of cereals, particularly of wheat, is made worse by continuous cropping, by weeds in competition with the crop, and by low soil-moisture levels, apparently because under these conditions diseased roots are not replaced rapidly. According to Simmonds (1953), dry topsoil is especially unfavorable.

On occasion burning has proven effective as a means of reducing disease damage, the best-known instance probably being the preparation of tobacco seedbeds. As long ago as 1938, Stevens (1938a) pointed out that destruction of diseased plant parts by burning in order to reduce inoculum was very often recommended in the literature. He cited a 5-year study of the brown spot needle blight of longleaf pine seedlings that showed a single fire greatly reduced the disease for a season or two, and that once seedlings were established, controlled winter burnings every three years served to keep the disease under control. Ten years later Hardison (1948) noted control of blind-seed disease of perennial rye grass in Oregon for at least a year by burning straw and stubble. As might be expected, other measures are needed to reinforce the control—inspection of seed samples, ageing of seed for two years, and planting to a depth of at least one-half inch to prevent emergence of apothecia.

Removal of Host. Roguing is the systematic removal of diseased individuals from a host population. It is characteristically a hand operation that requires undeniably high labor costs and probably seldom achieves fully satisfactory control by itself. This is in part because by the time disease symptoms are sufficiently conspicuous to indicate that plants should be removed, inoculum is likely to have spread to nearby healthy individuals. The most appropriate use of roguing is in support of other control practices, as in the production of virus-free propagation stock, as a preliminary step to chemical disease control in small plantings, and in combating diseases of forest and shade trees.

Removal of volunteer plants, usually holdovers from the crop of the preceding season that serve as a source of inoculum or as a way whereby the pathogen overwinters, is akin to roguing. These plants may also act as a bridge for nutritionally fastidious organisms between successive cropping periods or as a site for buildup of viruliferous vector populations. Whatever their role, it is wise to be rid of them.

Alteration of Host.   Girdling, poisoning, root severing, desiccation, and defoliation are some of the ways in which disease can be lessened by physical alteration of the host plant.

From the literature on root rots of woody species (Berkeley, 1944) come several instructive examples. He notes that the *Armillaria* root rot of tea in Nyasaland is reduced by ring-barking trees before they are felled when land is being cleared. The practice prevents passage of carbohydrate from leaves to roots and is most effective when carried out just before trees break into leaf, thus accelerating the rate at which roots die. Trees that die slowly should be felled one year after ringing. In a comparable situation, tea in Ceylon is protected against *Poria* when planted in jungle clearings, as is tung in Nyasaland. When the stumps are injected with sodium arsenite, the effectiveness of the method is still further enhanced because decay is hastened and saprophytic fungi invade at the expense of the pathogenic species.

Wagener and Davidson (1954) argue that methods of control useful in forest stands must be applied to populations of trees, because forests are not sufficiently valuable to justify the care given other woody perennials. Selective thinning and similar silivicultural measures are often well worthwhile, and rot can be much reduced by thinning hardwood sprouts before a bridge of heartwood forms at the base. Low-origin sprouts and those coming from small stumps should be retained rather than those of high origin and from large stumps. Decay in young conifer stands can be reduced by pruning of crop trees while the branches are still small, a practice that tends to prevent entry by such fungi as *Polyporus anceps*.

Oak wilt, a disease that has for a number of years been observed to progress slowly through local groves of oaks, is another disease to which control measures involving physical alteration of the host have proven applicable. Tree-to-tree spread is accomplished in large measure by vascular transfer of inoculum across root grafts, which can be controlled experimentally by poisoning a circular strip of trees immediately surrounding the infected individuals or by passing a large subsoil knife, drawn by tractor, between diseased and adjoining healthy trees, thus severing the root connections (Kuntz and Riker, 1950). Formation of fungus mats beneath the bark—which contributes to overland spread—is substantially reduced by early felling of wilted trees, by deep girdling in the early part of the growing season, or by application of sodium arsenite to a band of exposed heartwood.

With the advent of highly effective chemicals and of means for their economical application, destruction, defoliation, and desiccation of plants as adjuncts to disease control have become rather commonplace. In the case of potato late blight, tuber infection occurs at the time the potatoes are dug if the tops of the plant are still green at that point. To guard against this it is common practice to kill the above-ground stems and foliage and allow them to dry thoroughly before the crop is harvested—the potato-growing sections of Long Island, New York, or Aroostock County, Maine, present a dramatic spectacle of this each year as the time for harvest draws near.

Defoliation is of demonstrated value in reducing disease and pest damage. In cotton culture, defoliation seems to induce lodged plants to return to an erect position and to reduce boll rot and the injuries caused by leaf-feeding insects. When the leaves of nursery stock being dug preparatory to storage or shipment are removed, diseases ordinarily associated with foliage are reduced. Several means are available: hand beating; application of ethylene gas to stored stock, either from tanks or by including a bushel of apples for every 400–500 cubic feet of the storage chamber; or, as in the case of California roses, simply by allowing sheep to graze prior to lifting the stock (Addicott and Lynch, 1957).

Field defoliation has been advocated as an aid in bacterial canker of stone fruits, which invades the host through freshly exposed, incompletely healed leaf scars. The procedure of choice is to defoliate the trees in mid-autumn and then to protect them with a single spray application until leaf scars are fully healed.

As the cost of hand labor increases, and perhaps also as its general quality goes down, there is an understandable urge to find other means. In the case of the hop downy mildew (Romanko, 1964) it was common practice for many years to remove infected leaves and systemically infected shoots manually and similarly to remove surplus basal shoots and all leaves and branches to a height of 4–6 feet. Understandably, this is a costly and at times ineffective means of control. Some success has been obtained in eradicating the causal organism (*Pseudoperonospora humuli*) with streptomycin sulfate, but an apparently more promising approach is to selectively eradicate diseased plant parts, or to destroy diseased plant parts by nonselective methods. In Romanko's experiments, either 0.75% sulfuric acid used generally late in the season, or 3% acid used early in the season, was effective. Similarly, applications of DNOSBP (55% dinitro-O-sec-butylphenol) in early midseason brought about rapid and near total eradication of infections and susceptible sites at the base of the hop plants without reducing growth of productive bines.

Sanitation and Eradication.   Sanitation as a direct means of disease control and as an adjunct to use of chemicals can be summarized in the following terms (Stevens and Stevens, 1952):

One of the simplest of all these means is, of course, removal and destruction of diseased plants or plant parts. In the home garden, especially the ornamental garden, and in the greenhouse, this is of far greater utility than is generally realized. In fact the very obviousness of the method is one of its greatest weaknesses—it is not exciting; it is not expensive; and makes no appeal to the imagination. Sanitation is also of utility in the orchard, primarily for such diseases as black rot of apple, and some stone fruit viruses.

The effectiveness of this type of sanitation in the home garden is due to the fact that infection is almost always heaviest in the immediate vicinity of a source of infection. Falling off in concentration of spores or other inoculum is at first very rapid. At greater distances the rate of falling off is much slower, but the concentrations are so much lower that this is of less practical importance. As sanitation is the simplest of all methods of attempting disease control it may well have been one of the first attempted.

Sanitation takes many forms—the removal of infected plant parts, the removal of the body or reproductive portions of the pathogen (cedar apple rust galls, wood rot fungus conks, leafy mistletoe, corn smut galls). It may be cleanliness in the literal sense of avoiding dissemination of tobacco mosaic virus on the hands. It may be housekeeping, the removal of surface litter, the burning of stubble in fields troubled with flag smut, excision of infected buds in controlling anther smut of carnations, or the mechanical removal of bunt spores from seed grain. It may be an adjunct to other control measures. It may take bizarre forms; witness the practice in some areas of the southwest United States of leaving obviously diseased lettuce heads in the fields at harvest, to be consumed by sheep moved onto the area later.

Eradication differs from sanitation only in the matter of degree; it aims at the complete removal of diseased plants or infective material and is probably most commonly encountered in relation to initial invasions by exotic pathogens. Hence it becomes an issue primarily within the general context of plant quarantine.

Syracuse, New York, furnishes a case history of value in trying to assess the efficacy of sanitation methods in the control of Dutch elm disease that can be compared with the studies in Illinois (see Miller et al., 1969). The graph of percent loss for the years 1951–1967 (Fig. 15–1) is convincing evidence that under these conditions, losses can be cut sharply by sanitation even though

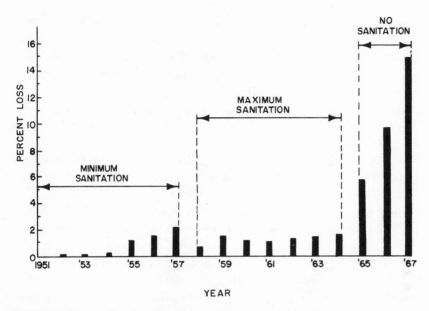

Fig. 15–1. Graph showing relation of level of sanitation effort to yearly losses from Dutch elm disease in Syracuse, New York, 1951–67. (Miller *et al.*, 1969)

financial stringencies and failure fully to appreciate the value of carrying out other control and preventive measures, such as dormant spraying with DDT, left the total effort far less than ideal.

When the disease was discovered in 1951, the city had nearly 54,000 trees; by 1968 it still had of the order of 30,000, although many of these could well have had inconspicuous symptoms. From 1951–57 sanitation was incomplete because many privately owned trees were not removed, and disease incidence increased rapidly. From 1958 to 1964, sanitation was enforced for all properties, public and private, and disease incidence remained at a low level of increase or, in some years, declined. As for 1965–67, when sanitation was abandoned, incidence of disease soared. On the basis of this, and in the face of rising opposition to dormant spraying with persistent compounds such as DDT, the authors come to the general conclusion that consistent, thorough, continued sanitation, augmented by measures that will prevent transmission by root grafts, can enable a community to keep its Dutch elm disease incidence to an acceptably low level.

So preoccupied are plant pathologists with their work on the biology of disease, the control of present-day diseases, and the examination of apparently new maladies that they all too infrequently take the trouble to reexamine events of the past and make the information readily available to modern

students. A pleasant exception is Sinclair's (1968) updating of the story of citrus canker and its eradication from the southeastern states in the early 1900's.
This program, which has been cited endless times as the first successful large-
scale effort and the first instance of federal funds being specifically appropri-
ated for this purpose, was aimed at a bacterial pathogen almost certainly imported from Japan with a shipment of infected trees into Texas. Whatever the
details, the situation by 1914 was clearly of crisis proportions and the eradication undertaken.

Sinclair's account deals with the situation in Louisiana, where a number of
abandoned groves of Satsuma oranges on trifoliate rootstocks gave rise to
large numbers of seedlings. A number of other factors contributed to the
difficulty in Louisiana and well illustrate how complex are the factors that impinge on plant disease phenomena: there were many abandoned groves; trifoliate orange was used as an ornamental; wild seedlings abounded; much of
the state was swampland; and, not unimportant in this context, the citrus industry itself was relatively minor. In the last instance, it meant that federal interest in Louisiana was secondary to that of the major citrus-producing states.
In any event, Louisiana as a state took action before the federal authorities
and cooperated with them through the whole campaign, which lasted for several decades before complete success was assured.

An accident of history may have been a key to the success in that the stun-
ning economic depression of the 1930's and with it the work programs of the
national recovery effort made available an abundance of manpower that
would in all likelihood not have been possible in more prosperous times. Meticulous search for individual seedlings was possible under these unique circumstances (Fig. 15–2)—one is reminded of nothing so much as a military
base in peacetime, when surplus manpower makes possible a measure of
cleanliness and order that would be wholly out of the question in a civilian establishment where each man-hour must be justified on economic grounds. Be
that as it may, no trace of the disease has been found in Louisiana since 1941,
after a total of nearly a quarter million trees had had to be destroyed.

Harvest and Postharvest Operations. Handling practices and the care
with which they are executed have much to do with the ultimate welfare of
agricultural commodities particularly as they relate to highly perishable fruits
and vegetables. "This is one of the simplest methods to explain and to understand. It is also one of the most difficult of all to maintain at a really effective
level. So in everyday plant disease control it is easier to sell patented processes, machinery and appliances than to convince each of ten thousand (or
even ten) strawberry pickers that he should keep his fingernails trimmed"
(Stevens and Stevens, 1952). Repeatedly, studies have clearly demonstrated

Fig. 15–2. Hand eradication of citrus seedlings during early successful attempt to eliminate citrus canker from the southeastern states, about 1935. (Sinclair, 1968)

that decay can be very substantially reduced by exercising care during harvesting. Some well-organized industries seem better aware of this situation than others, taking every precaution to insure minimum injury and introducing special methods for the express purpose of cutting down on loss of produce during shipping and storage.

There is an extensive literature on how the conditions of harvest and prestorage handling affect the quality of lumber and forest products. In general, heart rots are reduced by preliminary light sanitation cuts, which permit prompt removal of defective trees, for the danger from sporophores formed on felled trees is less than that if the trees remain standing. Adjustment of cutting age, special salvage cuts in fire- or storm-damaged stands, protection against fire and wounding, clear cutting where practicable, and where decay is related to age, harvesting before heavy losses occur—each of these practices enhances the quality and the quantity of the final product. As for preventing decay losses in lumber, chemical treatments can wisely be augmented by handling methods—storage of logs in water, quick utilization of logs, minimum delay prior to application of chemicals, reduction of time in bulk piles, and maintenance of good air-drying conditions.

Modified atmospheres of several types are utilized to control market and storage diseases—sulfur dioxide, nitrogen chloride, ozone, ethylene oxide, and methyl bromide. Nonvolatile materials, oiled wraps, copper-impregnated materials have been proven useful. But by all odds the most widely adopted of all preventive measures is temperature control, from precooling to transit refrigeration and cold storage—although the optimum temperature for different kinds of produce varies. As for stored grains, damage is least when they are protected by fungicides, stored in an atmosphere of toxic or inert gases (CO_2) and, above all, dried to the point were they will not support the active growth of fungi (Christensen, 1957).

Physiological Effects

Host plants can also be rendered less vulnerable to disease by cultural means that do not so much affect their structure as they do their physiology. The medium of this action is often not known but it usually involves an alteration in the environment that increases disease resistance, reduces the host's vulnerability to disease establishment, or gets rid of associated pathogens.

We know all too little about the effect of routine farm practices on the welfare of crop plants and to the diseases of those plants. When, for example, red clover is cut from one to eight times per season and the plants themselves then dug and compared for root vigor (Siddiqui et al., 1968), there is clear indication of the progressive effect of this treatment (Fig. 15–3). Not only is the severity of root rot increased, but so is the frequency of isolating species of Fusarium, which seems to be the organism most frequently associated with the observed difficulty. The whole picture also reflects a decrease in the number of nonparasitic organisms isolated as the total number of cuts per season increases.

The most obvious category of measures that affect the physiology of the host is the alteration of the nutritional situation. The circumstances of control by this approach are complex and have been dealt with in detail in a number of research reports; the point to be made here is that from a disease control standpoint, manipulation of the nutrients available to the host is without question an important component of the total fabric of cultural methods. The grower may not himself see clearly all of the interconnections, but how he manages the nutrient supply impinges directly and significantly on the disease relations of his crop.

Heat therapy is an important, though not widely applicable, device for reducing disease without imposing a physical change in the host. In this case

Fig. 15–3. Effect of frequency of clipping of red clover plants in relation to the incidence of root rot. *Top:* Cut once per season. *Upper middle:* Cut twice. *Lower middle:* Four times. *Bottom:* Eight times. (Siddiqui *et al.,* 1968)

heat—usually as hot water or steam—is employed to rid seeds and other plant parts of fungi, nematodes, or viruses.

Nyland and Goheen (1969) have summarized the pertinent information about heat therapy of perennials affected with viruses and provided an extensive table of published results in which they group the data into several distinct categories: yellows-type viruses (possibly mycoplasmas) (Fig. 15–4), those that are hot water labile, those that are hot air labile (inactivation in 28 days or less and therefore considered easily inactivated), and those that required comparatively very long periods in the heat chamber to achieve results. A final listing includes perhaps two dozen viruses that have thus far resisted all atempts to inactivate them by heat therapy.

Fig. 15–4. Heat inactivation of peach yellows: lateral branch, the lower portion produced prior to, the upper portion after, being held in a hot air chamber. (Kunkel, 1936)

Heat inactivation of viruses within host tissue, without permanent damage to the host itself, has been accomplished in a number of disease associations, utilizing both hot water and hot air techniques. There is at least one published record (Frazier *et al.*, 1965) of virus inactivation by growing the plants in a natural high-temperature environment. In this case, strawberries carrying one of five viruses were grown in the Imperial Valley of California during the 1959 and 1961 growing seasons. Of the five, strawberry crinkle virus was inactivated very noticeably, strawberry mottle virus to a slight extent, and mild yellow edge, necrotic shock, and veinbanding not at all. Maximum temperatures during these years reached about 40°C in July and August.

Where vegetative propagation is the routine means of multiplying a host variety, the likelihood of spreading virus with each new generation of plants is very good indeed. Crops such as potato have been badly plagued with a number of viruses for many years and the effort to reduce the difficulty is great. Tuber indexing, selection of virus-free individuals, control of insect vectors, heat therapy, chemotherapy, meristem culture, have all been used to various degrees in the campaign against potato viruses. Stace-Smith and Mellor (1968) bring to us a promising technique that combines several of the traditional methods and thereby achieves a measure of control higher than any one of the components by itself. They point out that such viruses as potato virus X and potato virus S are so ubiquitous that the commoner varieties are for all practical purposes universally infected with both. Yet it proves possible to get virus-free individuals by growing the plants for a number of weeks in air temperatures varying diurnally from 33 to 37°C and soil temperatures about 30 to 32°C. At intervals axillary buds were excised and grown in liquid sterile medium (Fig. 15–5). By the end of 8 weeks, X virus-free plants had increased to 50% of the total and by 18 weeks virtually to 100%; only about 20% of the X virus-free plants were also free of the S virus, even at the longer exposure times. Indexing for X-virus was against a local lesion host (*Gomphrena globosa*); S-virus was sought by electron microscopy of plant material.

An ingenious modification of heat therapy has been developed in India, where seed grain is exposed to the sun as a way of elevating the temperature. A similar approach has been used in Nigeria to free cotton seed from the bacterial wilt organism. Hot water has been used successfully against strawberry nematodes, and against nematodes infesting chrysanthemums, violets, and begonias, and against the fungus mycelium of mint rust and tomato brown rot.

Heat is more regularly employed against viruses than against other kinds of pathogens. Under these conditions, heat is consistently effective in freeing valuable clonal material from viruses or preparing planting stock of such crops as sugar cane—in Queensland, Australia, steam therapy is carried out on a very large scale indeed.

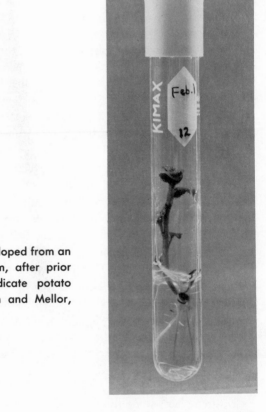

Fig. 15–5. Potato explant developed from an axillary bud on liquid medium, after prior treatment with heat to eradicate potato viruses S and X. (Stace-Smith and Mellor, 1968)

Finally, there are a host of miscellaneous techniques that have been employed from time to time and that operate through the host by affecting its physiology. The following list is indicative only, not inclusive.

- Use of various chemicals to improve rooting of cuttings, thin blossom from fruit trees, control preharvest fruit drop, regulate time of flowering and ripening, control weeds, or break or prolong dormancy—each of which may well, in turn, affect disease situations.
- Fermentation of tomato fruit pulp to free the seed from the bacterial canker pathogen.
- Prevention of cranberry leaf drop by withdrawing the water from beneath the ice during the winter.

INDIRECT EFFECTS ON THE HOST

Practices Involving Number

One way of compensating for disease damage, and one that is indeed often called into play, is simply to plant more of a given crop than would be needed if it were to remain healthy. Not surprisingly, this is rather more successful when damage occurs in the seedling stage—overplanting, minus killed seedlings, results in a normal stand. In a different sense, perhaps, overplanting can be thought of as coming into play when additional areas are sown to a crop because disease is expected to reduce the per-acre yield.

Numbers of plants, in terms of density per unit area, affects disease severity in the case of several cereal diseases—an obvious approach to control is to adjust the rate accordingly. Root rot in wheat seems to increase with increased rates of seeding, as does bunt. On the other hand, either very sparse or very dense planting, particularly the former, aggravates the harm done by cereal leaf rusts. To some extent, high rates of seedlings correlate with a later dense stand and a highly humid microclimate; under these conditions disease damage is inclined to be greater than in less dense stands.

Practices Involving Position

Placement.   Important effects upon disease may result from the proximity of host plants to each other. The microclimate—conditions of moisture, temperature, and air movement in the immediate vicinity of the host—rather than overall meteorological conditions most influences the rapidity with which many diseased conditions worsen. Close spacing tends to raise the humidity, encourage sporulation of the pathogenic fungi, and reduce air circulation. Growth habit of the host, whether dense or sparse, contributes to or reduces the effect of spacing on microclimate.

Placement also implies selection of planting site. This may involve not only the nature of the soil, slope, elevation, exposure, and so on of the immediate site, but its relation to other plantings. In an even more specialized sense, placement may call for no more than a modest change in farming practice—i.e., planting in ridged as against nonridged fields.

Dispersal.   As man developed agriculture and as his agriculture became more and more intensive, there has been increasing tendency to concentrate vast numbers of host individuals in contiguous plantings. Disease hazard is thereby increased. Stakman and Harrar (1957) put it this way:

The greatest need for plant disease control is in connection with those crops that are artificially cultivated. . . . one acre of wheat may contain approximately a million individual plants, all more nearly identical than individuals in any group of human beings; and the plant pathologist is concerned with the fact that the crowding together offers optimum conditions for the development of epidemic diseases. This crowding is a deliberate modern agronomic technique designed to promote maximum agricultural production through the use of improved varieties and soil management, but it provides highly favorable conditions for the devastating attacks of plant pathogens.... Every successful effort to improve yield by adding to the carrying capacity of the soil intensifies disease problems which must be met if agriculture is to progress.°

Despite this, one finds very little in the literature regarding dispersal as a means of disease control. Within the severe practical and economic limitation imposed, it is an obviously desirable tactic, to be taken advantage of whenever possible. In this sense it is a partial return to primitive agriculture.

Barriers.   Barriers act primarily to interrupt the movement of inoculum. They may be topographic (mountains, bodies of water, deserts), biological (absence of host plants or vectors, territory preempted by competing species), or climatic. Absolute barriers can be traversed only through the intervention of man.

On a very much smaller scale, barriers in the form of trenching have occasionally been used to stop the advance of soil-inhabiting fungi. It is apparently the only known method for controlling the fairy ring caused by *Psilocybe* in cranberry bogs and has been recommended for halting the spread of *Armillaria* and *Rosellinia*. The cotton root rot fungus has been confined by trenching and also by artificial barriers consisting of galvanized iron sheets and by soil barriers formed by mixing in oil, sulfur, acids, or copper sulfate.

Geographic Location.   Commonly, cultivated plants have a more extensive geographic range than do their pathogens, although this is not always the case. When this does occur, disease may be avoided by the obvious expedient of growing the crop in an area where the pathogen has not yet become established. The classic examples of this device are cultivation of rubber in Southeast Asia, where it is free of South American leaf blight, and the coffee industry of the Western Hemisphere—in the latter case, after decades of freedom from coffee rust the pathogen finally arrived in the late 1960's. Another, possibly analogous, approach is to dodge disease hazard by planting the crop out of season—i.e., in the dry season under irrigation rather than during the normal humid months.

Temperature is often the limiting factor in seasonal and regional incidence of disease, as determined by both latitude and elevation. This means that for

° From E. C. Stakman and J. G. Harrar, *Principles of Plant Pathology* (New York: The Ronald Press Co.). Copyright © 1957, The Ronald Press Co.

all practical purposes disease shifts about from one season to the next, a fact that has important implications for both the timing and location of particular plantings of susceptible crops. Moisture too, particularly the distribution of rainfall throughout the year and the frequency and intensity of fogs and dews, influences the seasonal and the geographic distribution of disease. It, too, must enter into the equation that tells the producer what risks he will encounter in moving along a particular cropping pattern.

As an explicit effort to capitalize on available information, it has been suggested that "disease hazard" maps might be prepared for the guidance of growers thinking of introducing new crops into a given area. Time and again new ventures have failed because of the inroads of disease; predictions as to what might have occurred, based on knowledge of climate and the limits of disease tolerance, might have prevented some of these mistakes.

Geographic location, in a more limited sense than that noted just above, is brought into play whenever plantings are isolated for the express purpose of disease control. This approach is most promising for those pathogens that do not produce aerial spores and is most often resorted to in connection with seedbeds and seed-increase plots. Because the total area that must be isolated is relatively modest, fungicides can be economically employed on crops that would be impracticable to protect under ordinary field conditions. For example, small quantities of seed of either wheat or barley affected with loose smut are first freed of possible pathogens by hot water or comparable treatment, and this nucleus of pathogen-free seed then increased in isolated plots a few hundred yards from the nearest commercial grain fields, often under the care of an informed grower.

The widespread practice of isolating tobacco seedbeds as a way of minimizing blue-mold damage is well known. Less so is the practice in the Pacific northwest of isolating cabbage plant beds from cultivated crucifers that harbor the aphid vector of several virus diseases.

Practices Involving Timing

Noncoincidence of Host and Inoculum. The precision with which host and pathogen must synchronize and the span of time over which successful infection and establishment are possible vary greatly from one disease to another. Inoculum is usually effective for only a relatively short time; if the host is vulnerable only during a particular phase of its development or if only transient organs or parts are susceptible, the overall likelihood of disease getting a foothold is greatly reduced. Disease control consists of capitalizing on the situation by upsetting the timing of host and pathogen association such as to produce a crop in spite of general presence of the inoculum and of a susceptible host variety.

Early-maturing varieties often complete their growth before the threat from disease materializes. Varieties of cowpeas are available that mature before the season for wilt and root-knot arrives; some kinds of potatoes commonly mature before the appearance of late blight, although they succumb readily enough if planted later in the season. Much the same end result can be achieved by planting a given variety rather earlier than usual, provided other factors make this option possible. Fischer and Holton (1957) recommend that winter wheat be seeded early, when temperature and moisture are unfavorable for germination of bunt spores and infection of the seedlings—with the result that the seedlings get beyond the susceptible stage before the pathogen is active. Other diseases for which early seeding is worth considering are flag smut of wheat, pupation disease of oats, and flax rust.

Sometimes, there are contradictory responses to seeding time selection. Bunt of wheat is favored by slow growth of the seedlings, scab (*Gibberella*) by rapid growth. In this case laboratory research showed that a rather similar situation regarding *Gibberella* on wheat and corn could be explained in convincing terms; here wheat is attacked at high temperatures, corn at low temperatures. When soil is cold, rapid hydrolysis of wheat starch results in seedlings that are rich in sugar, that have thick cell walls, and reduced susceptibility— protein formation and tissue growth are accelerated at higher temperatures, with consequent increase in susceptibility. In corn, on the other hand, low temperatures stimulate formation of cell walls of unmodified pectic materials, whereas at higher temperatures more resistant suberized cell walls develop.

Possibly the most extreme instance of noncoincidence of crop and pathogen is the imposition of a crop-free period by legislation or by common consent. In the early 1940's, for example, California celery growers agreed to break the continuity of Western celery mosaic virus propagation by a complete stoppage of celery culture for a limited period; the state legislature formalized the move shortly thereafter. With a relatively brief campaign along these lines, yields were brought back to levels commonly reached before the virus had become serious.

Noncoincidence is a factor in still another way as it relates to depth of sowing, in the sense that deeply sown seed requires a longer period for emergence of the seedling, other things being equal, and thereby increases the likelihood of invasion by soil-inhabiting pathogens.

Age and Life Span.   Cultural practices based on timing include those situations wherein the grower takes advantage of the age or life span of the host in avoiding disease. To every generalization there are exceptions, but seed-lings are often more susceptible than mature plants; mature or moribund leaves are more likely to be invaded than those less aged. Stage of develop-ment of the host is significant when the pathogen produces inoculum only after a given time or for only a limited duration, when the host itself is suscep-tible for only a limited part of its growth, or when both these conditions pre-vail.

Life span denotes the length of time needed for a crop plant—usually as applied to an annual or biennial—to develop from seed to harvest. Both it and age are really special aspects of noncoincidence. Attention to life span tends to lead to the selection of early-maturing varieties that can avoid the severest inoculum threat; if the inoculum can coincidentally be slowed down, as by deep plowing of infected stubble, so much the better. At times the indiscrimi-nate use of varieties developed for the climate and photoperiod of one region in another region with differing environment will lead to unfavorable matur-ing dates.

Early harvesting, instituted as soon as a marketable crop is available even though it may not be optimum, has the same end effect as would the use of early-maturing varieties. In special cases, as for example in trying to produce potato tubers free of virus, early harvesting is regularly practiced. In this case the virus is introduced by vectors into the foliage during the growing season but does not, hopefully, have time to migrate into the tubers before they are severed from the stems.

Longevity of Inoculum. The focus at this point is on special situations that permit the host material to be freed from associated pathogens simply by al-lowing sufficient time to elapse.

When seed of crop plants is held beyond the customary interval so that in-oculum borne therein may be eliminated or reduced, the grower is taking ad-vantage of the greater longevity of the host as against the pathogen. For ex-ample (Arndt, 1946), cotton seed can be freed of much of its load of the anthracnose organism (*Colletotrichum gossypii*) if stored for substantial peri-ods of time, particularly if the moisture content of the seed is up to 16% or better.

Practices Involving Sequence

Specific Sequences. Crop rotation generally is widely practiced. In a por-tion of the instances there is a specific relationship between the two crops

Fig. 15–6. Effect of a given cover crop on the vigor of crop plants that follow. In this case the tobacco to the left is following lambsquarters, that on the right is following horseweed. (Lunn *et al.*, 1939)

that come in juxtaposition to each other (Fig. 15–6), although the mechanism of this interaction may be direct toxicity, a biological relationship, or indeed unknown.

There are many examples from which to choose. Damping-off of sugarbeets is increased when the crop follows a legume, decreased when it follows corn, soybeans, or small grains, apparently as a result of the higher nitrogen levels reached in the first instance. Tip rot of the sugarbeet, which is widely distributed in Iowa and which reaches damaging proportions if beets are cropped successively, can be substantially reduced by a prior planting of alfalfa. Scab, wilt, and *Rhizoctonia*, which become troublesome in virgin soils and in some rotations, can be brought to a minimum when alfalfa immediately precedes the principal crops. Finally, the brown root rot of tobacco—due primarily to invasion by the meadow nematodes—seems generally to be favored by preceding crops of timothy or corn.

The directly toxic effects of plant residues are on occasion responsible for the damage one sees in following crops. It may be further aggravated by secondary rootrot organisms.

Not only field crops but also woody perennials can be affected by the particular species that occupied the land immediately beforehand. This occurs, for example, when ornamentals are set on stumpy land, only to be damaged by fungi presumably remaining in the roots of the felled trees. Similarly, replanting of peach is generally less successful than when peach follows other fruits, presumably because of accumulated breakdown products of amygdalin.

Crop to crop interactions do not necessarily follow in a time sequence, although this is probably the commoner circumstance. Coincident plantings are sometimes beneficial: there is little trouble from take-all of barley when the latter is undersown with trefoil. They are sometimes harmful; *Verticillium* damage to stone fruits is enhanced when a susceptible species is used as an intercrop, as is true also for nematode injury to peach orchards if a susceptible cover crop is sown at the same time. Admixtures of rye and wheat suffer increased damage from bunt in rough proportion to the amount of rye in the mixture.

The roster of crop-to-crop relationships is much longer than that suggested in the foregoing paragraphs. It is not, even from a more complete list, possible to derive useful generalizations—within present understanding of the situation each instance has to be treated in isolation and the rational explanation of the effect uncovered by careful investigation of the immediate case in point. Often, too, the effect itself is a chance discovery based on general observation of the result of a wide assortment of crop sequences.

While plant pathologists frequently encounter instances of this or that practice being recommended on the basis of tradition and hearsay, it is all too infrequent that controlled testings of these suggestions are actually carried out. Just such a situation is reflected in the widespread notion that plantings of marigolds are effective deterrents to damage by harmful insects and other organisms. In this case, at least as regards control of nematodes, Miller and Ahrens (1969) have made comparisons of this plant with rye, buckwheat, pigweed, and crabgrass as cover crops—and compared these in turn with ethylene dibromide fumigation. Generally, their results showed that following a crop of marigolds, several economically important crop plants were as favorably affected as following standard fumigation; in several cases the suppressing effect of the marigold planting on the two species of nematodes studied was even greater than that of the fumigant (6 gal. per acre). Not only this, but the cost of seeding with marigolds and treating the seeded fields with a preemergence herbicide was economically competitive with the chemical treatment. An admitted disadvantage, in many situations, was the fact that the marigolds to be effective had to remain through an entire year.

Crop Rotation. Diseases caused by soil-borne pathogens are the most likely targets on which crop rotation is brought to bear. The efficacy of rotation as a disease control measure lies in the fact that, in the absence of susceptible crops (i.e., in the presence of nonsusceptible crops), the population of a given pathogen materially decreases. Other pathogens, those to which the alternate crop or crops are susceptible, must as surely increase; but by rotating crops subject to widely different pathogens, effective control is often achieved.

Crop rotation is a very old and widely adopted cultural measure. As far back as 1938 Leighty listed 24 diseases of 17 crops controlled solely or mostly by this approach, and the list could be made much longer. Throughout the literature on crop rotation it is clear that the major obstacles to success are either pronounced longevity of the inoculum or a pathogen that has a wide host range. The former may result from the resistance of the pathogen to unfavorable environments or a capacity to survive as a saprophyte, or both, but if it takes a decade or so for the inoculum to disappear from the soil then crop rotation becomes impracticable. If a large number of possible alternative crops are susceptible it becomes economically infeasible to find a suitable rotation scheme. There is no escape, in the last analysis, from the obligation to employ in a rotation scheme a sufficient number of monetarily valuable crops to make the whole operation profitable to the grower.

A possible device for extending the principle of crop rotation to a sequence of selected varieties was suggested in 1949 (R. B. Stevens, 1949), in these terms:

Why not practice a rotation of host varieties, rather than of distinct, often widely divergent, crops species? While focusing our attention on the striking and often disturbingly rapid increase in "new" races or species of pathogens in the presence of newly emphasized host varieites, we should not forget that some, at least, of the "old" races are correspondingly decreasing. There is likely as significant a decrease in the inoculum of hitherto prevalent pathogens as there is increase in hitherto rare ones! This, coupled with the very possible fact that the old host varieties well may be resistant to the new pathogen, leads to our main thesis: that varietal rotation should be studied as a means of disease control.

The simple fact that a pathogen is new stands as direct evidence that the older varieties were highly resistant to it, and that it was therefore formerly rare. After five or ten years of widespread plantings of a new host type, it may well be that formerly well-known species or races of pathogens will have become scarce, and that older host varieties can be replanted with profit. By selecting for a given crop, such as wheat or oats, several commercially desirable varieties of widely differing susceptibility, it should be possible to work out a type of rotation which would hold disease losses at a low level.[*]

[*] From R. B. Stevens, Replanting discarded varieties as a means of disease control, *Science*, vol. 110, 1949, p. 49.

PRACTICES AFFECTING ELEMENTS OTHER THAN THE HOST

Inoculum

Disease-Free Seed and Stock. Seeds and propagating material may be disease-free either because it has been produced without coming into contact with the pathogen—i.e., raised in pathogen-free areas, in protected seed blocks, or has been selected from a larger population by one of several techniques—or because it has been freed of pathogen inoculum in some manner.

Seeds of several legumes, for example, are regularly produced in the semi-arid areas of the western United States, a device that is effective against such pathogens as those of anthracnose, bacterial blight, and *Ascochyta*, which cannot readily be destroyed by available seed treatments. Because spread during the growing season is dependent on atmospheric moisture, the disease does not develop in a dry climate even when the seed used initially is contaminated. Seed produced under these special conditions can safely be made available for planting in commercial production in any part of the country.

Heat therapy has already been mentioned briefly in an earlier section; it is one of the commoner means of ridding seeds and propagating stock of pathogens, perhaps especially in the case of the blossom-infection smuts of wheat and barley. An alternative—sometimes complementary—technique is to soak contaminated items in a solution that will differentially affect the pathogen more severely than the host.

The concept of pathogen-free seed and stock leads directly to the notion of its being so certified to the buyer; this in turn almost inevitably introduces the question of legal regulation. Of these there have been a substantial number, usually at the state and local level, but augmented by federal action. In its simplest form it may consist only of inspection by a governmental official—as of nursery stock prior to certification for sale.

As might be expected, certification programs have emphasized perennials and vegetatively propagated plants, because these are the very ones where difficulty, particularly with virus diseases, is most likely to arise. One finds fruit trees, bramble fruits, currants, strawberries, and potatoes (Fig. 15-7) high on the list of crops subject to regulation in this regard.

Strawberry certification in California, by the mid-1950's, covered yellows, crinkle, nematodes, and red stele, having been first officially sanctioned in 1941 and then much on the initiative of the growers. Fees to make the program self-supporting were set and a system devised that featured low tolerances on pests and diseases, intensive pest control, roguing, isolation, and

Fig. 15–7. Tuber-indexing in the production of virus-free seed potatoes. *Top:* Each pot contains a plant grown from a single eye; if the plant shows virus symptoms the tuber from which it was grown is destroyed; if no disease symptoms appear the remainder of the tuber is planted in an isolated plot. *Bottom:* Two index plants, the one on the right showing leaf roll symptoms. (Dykstra, 1946)

plant indexing. Four field inspections were carried out the first year before plants were set in increase fields, and three in the second. A registry of foundation stock indexed and found to be virus-free was provided for.

Indexing, incidentally, is often used in programs to develop certified stock when the pathogen in question is a virus. It consists of grafting material from the plant to be tested onto a selected host that is known to produce consistent and recognizable symptoms and makes possible confirmation of the presence or absence of virus even if systemic symptoms on the original host are masked or uncertain. As a general rule each distinct virus must be separately indexed although occasionally more than one can be checked in a single operation. Not infrequently, the indicator host is one that produces local lesions.

Very specialized techniques are needed when the biology of the host-pathogen relationship suggests a vulnerable spot. Vaughan (1956) has taken advantage of this kind of exact information in his method for eliminating the red stele fungus from valuable strawberry stock. Knowing that the fungus does not invade the crowns and stolons, even in susceptible varieties, that it grows poorly at temperatures above 65° C, and that it does not thrive in adequately drained soil, he prepared sterilized flats with wire bottoms and set the whole apparatus at a level above the potted plants being treated. New runners were kept free from the soil in the pots, glass wool used to prevent splashing, and the runners pegged down to the surface of the clean soil in the flats. As soon as possible after rooting, the new plant was cut free and later checked to make certain that the fungus had been left behind; this check was made by growing the plants under conditions favorable to red stele.

Eradication of pathogens from host tissue by immersion in chemicals has proven effective in only a relatively small number of instances. One such successful venture is reported by Beute and Milholland (1970) in their work with the stem canker disease of highbush blueberries. This disease, caused by *Botryosphaeria corticis*, is regarded by them as the most important limiting factor in production of blueberries in the southern blueberry region, North Carolina, Georgia, Florida, Alabama, and Mississippi. Because the crop is vegetatively propagated by stem cuttings, there is very considerable dissemination of the disease into new plantings.

Both hot water and chemicals were used to treat cuttings, but it proved infeasible to hold cuttings in water at temperatures sufficiently high (53° C) to kill the pathogen because the host itself was too badly damaged. One chemical, BSM-11 (50% potassium 2,4,6-trichlorophenate plus 10% phenylmercuric acetate), used in concentrations of 2500 ppm for four hours was highly effective at eliminating the fungus without materially reducing the viability of the cuttings.

The control of viruses through propagation of virus-free material has been summarized by Hollings (1965), who points out that there are four related aspects:

- Recognition and characterization of the virus diseases in each crop
- Development of reliable indexing methods to detect healthy stock, to sort treated plants, and to detect symptomless carriers
- Techniques to rid selected plants of virus and establish foundation stocks
- Machinery for maintaining and distributing the foundation stock

In the main, these are established aspects of the situation, but on each there have been some new developments as time goes on and research continues. For example, new techniques of inoculation, and particularly, much improved serological methods have made indexing of certain viruses simpler and quicker, although infectivity tests by traditional graft inoculation is still the accepted norm for most viruses. By the same token, hot air treatment continues to dominate the mechanisms for eliminating virus from infected plants, although it may be augmented by culturing excised meristem tissue. The latter is often effective by itself, of course.

Soil Treatment.   Application of chemicals to soils as a way of controlling plant pathogens is hardly a cultural control measure, but there are several other approaches to the problem available to the grower under suitable conditions. Of these probably the most commonly employed is heat, for achieving partial or complete sterilization of the soil, which can be sought by using steam, hot water, or dry heat.

There are a number of ancillary effects that must be taken into account. Beneficial microorganisms, such as nitrifying bacteria, are likely to be killed, while undesirable spore-forming species survive. Soluble salts are frequently liberated by heat, or colloids destroyed, the latter leading to deterioration in soil structure and loss in capillarity and water-holding capacity.

Steam heat—used more than anything else against nematodes—has the advantage of being simple and effective. It dissipates almost immediately after application ceases, leaving no undesirable residues, although reinvasion by fungi is likely to take place rather quickly. Commonly used apparatus includes inverted pans, buried perforated pipe or tile, steam harrow or rake. Less widely applicable techniques utilize hot water, which is less effective than steam, firing—as in the preparation of plots for seedbeds or the deliberate firing of existing vegetation—and occasionally electrical sterilization based on the resistance of the soil itself or some form of heating coils containing resistance units. Rarely, outside soil temperatures reach lethal levels, and it is not difficult to raise greenhouse temperatures to very high levels simply by closing the ventilation system and turning on the heat during a midsummer day.

Over the past century, perhaps longer, flooding has been used as a way of reducing the amount of inoculum in soils—against the *Phylloxera* in French vineyards, wireworms in California, root knot nematode, garden centipede, and so on through a long list. Easily the best-known examples of flooding on a major scale are the efforts to control the Panama wilt of cultivated bananas in Central America and to reduce inoculum of *Sclerotinia sclerotiorum* in Florida truck crop plantings. The *Fusarium* responsible for banana wilt can be materially reduced by several months' inundation of the soil, after which it will not again reach troublesome levels for perhaps a half-dozen years or so. Much of the time this treatment is augmented by plowing under the top several inches and by chemical treatment. As for *Sclerotinia*, three to six weeks' flooding suffices; if, in addition, summer plantings of lowland rice are incorporated into a crop rotation, the time can be shortened to as little as 20 days. In a quite different sense, flooding is used as a means of disease control in cranberry bogs, a crop that grows normally in very moist situations.

A miscellany of soil management and treatment practices completes the roster of control measures directly related to soil. In some cases tillage—usually the plowing under of surface inoculum—is recommended as a means of reducing disease hazards. The more commonly used approach is the addition of organic residues of one kind or another (Fig. 15–8), or adjustment of the soil pH toward a value unfavorable to the particular pathogen in question, provided its tolerance is known and the soil is not thereby rendered unfit for the following crop.

Because the mechanisms are often so obscure as to make it rather a hit-or-miss proposition in the experimental phase, all too little attention is given to cultural and managerial practices that have the effect of reducing hazards from pests and diseases. One such instance is the use of sawdust or straw mulches on such crops as tomato or cucumber as a means to reduce the populations of white flies and thereby the threat from the viruses that these insects carry (Nitzany *et al.*, 1964). In this case the mechanism seems to be that in the early stages of plant growth the air temperature above the mulches is substantially higher—5 to 6°C—than that above unmulched soil. This, in turn, exceeds the lethal point for the vector and markedly reduces the population, thereby eliminating for a time at least the need to control the insect chemically.

In an era when chemical control of plant disease is suspect in many quarters, there is an added incentive to find what might be thought of as managerial techniques that can substitute for application of agricultural chemicals.

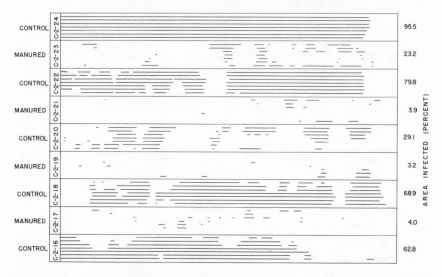

Fig. 15–8. Aerial photograph (*top*), with corresponding chart (*bottom*), showing the effect of adding organic material to plots of Acala cotton. The four darker plots have been manured, and most plants are alive and green; the light areas represent dead plants. In the chart, black lines indicate dead plants. (King *et al.*, 1934)

Just such a suggestion emerges from experiments by Papavizas (1966) on the effect of adding relatively small amounts of residues from crucifers to soils as a way of combatting the common *Aphanomyces* root rot of peas (Fig. 15–9). In this work it seems clear that several crucifers, particularly perhaps cabbage, are effective in reducing damage from the root rot, and that the inhibitory effect lasts up to 15 weeks or more from time of initial supplementation. The author suggests that the information might be put to practical use if a rotation of cabbage and peas were established and the debris from the former incorporated into the field following harvest; under the slower decomposition likely to occur in natural conditions, it seems entirely possible that a measurable effect would persist until planting time the following year.

Trial and error have produced a number of instances wherein addition of organic matter to soils has affected the incidence of root-infecting microorganisms and the degree of disease damage. In large measure because there are so many variables, the predictability of the outcome of a given amendment on a given crop is highly uncertain. When partial answers are to be had it is only at the cost of considerable effort and usually only after the situations are examined one by one. Gilpatrick (1969) has looked into the relation between soil amendments and the root rot of avocado caused by *Phytophthora cinnamomi*. Among other things, he discovered that some of the degradation products of the organic materials used not only directly affect the welfare of the pathogen, as by preventing zoospore formation or by toxic action on the mycelium, but also show substantial phytotoxic effect on the roots of the host. It would seem that the latter phenomenon works both to harm the host directly, and to render it less vulnerable to the parasite, thus making it necessary to give concern to timing, duration of effect, relative levels of amendment, and so on. He points out that performance under actual field conditions is far less uniform than in the laboratory and that one of the difficulties in trying to control this disease is that, since the host is a perennial, there is no opportunity to let amendment and pathogen interact prior to introducing the host into the system, as can readily be done with annual crops. Among the materials used as amendments, in addition to alfalfa meal, which was the one most under study, were: wheat straw, soya bean straw, soya bean meal, bean straw, cotton waste, redwood and pine sawdust, and sphagnum. Ammonia seemed in this study to be the degradation product of alfalfa meal that had the most conspicuous effect.

It has frequently been noted that when crop residues of one kind or another are added to soils the net effect is the reduction of pathogenic organisms. One of the common explanations—and doubtless there are many differences from one instance to the next—is that the additional organic matter

Fig. 15–9. Effect of Dexon, β-methylaspartic acid, and cabbage amendment on *Aphanomyces* root rot of peas. *Top* (*left to right*): Control, Dexon, MAA, and cabbage (0.6%). *Bottom* (*left*): Control; (*right*) 0.5% cabbage leaves and stems. (Papavizas, 1966)

promotes the development of an increased population of competitive, but nonpathogenic species. An additional possibility has been outlined by Patrick et al. (1965) in reporting experiments with the effect of decomposing rye on two plant-parasitic nematodes, Meloidogyne and Pratylenchus. In this case the purified extract of the rye was directly toxic to these organisms, and far more so than to several saprophagous species also used in the experiments— 50% of the parasitic forms were immobilized at concentrations of 380–440 ppm, whereas it took roughly ten times that amount to immobilize 50% of the saprophagous ones.

Although soil treatment with either heat or chemicals is commonly employed in combatting microorganisms harmful to plants, there have been comparatively few instances of success with radiation as such. An exception is reported by Eglitis and Johnson (1970) in tests with radio frequencies of about 27 MHz. on samples of greenhouse soil contaminated with Fusarium, Pythium, Rhizoctonia, and other common pathogens. In this case as little as five minutes' treatment was sufficient to increase markedly the germination rates of crimson clover (Fig. 15–10). To a certain extent this could be attributed to an overall rise in soil temperature, but probably also involved direct electrical effects on the cells of the fungi. This latter point is supported by the fact that fungi were eliminated more successfully than were bacteria, whereas in ordinary steam sterilization the two show no such differences.

Use of Chemicals. Chemical control, in the usual sense of the term, refers to the application of materials to the surface—sometimes to the interior—of the host plant as a prophylactic or therapeutic measure. But in special cases it can be worthwhile to direct chemicals against the inoculum as such. Eradicant sprays, for example, have been used to reduce the amount of viable overwintering ascospores of the apple scab fungus. In cases such as this the crux of the matter lies in whether the pathogen has a rapid rate of multiplication on the host; if so, it is not very significant whether the initial amount is large or small.

Chemicals are also useful as disinfectants for containers, equipment, and vehicles when there is danger of spread to new areas, as a drench or wash in handling specialized produce, and for the control of inoculum in special instances such as virus contamination of field workers' hands.

Vector Control. Vector control illustrates very well the diversity of cultural control; virtually every aspect of the biology of transmission by insects suggests a possible device through which to hamper the success of that series of events. The same might be said of transmission by birds or any other of the several classes of vectors.

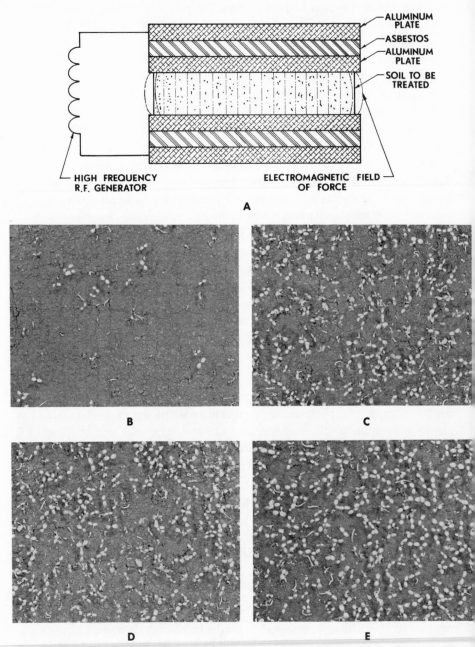

Fig. 15–10. Effect of radio-frequency energy on control of seedling damping-off. (A) Sketch of electrodes for treating soil in greenhouse flats. (B) Crimson clover seedlings in control flat. (C) Treated 5 minutes. (D) Treated 10 minutes. (E) Treated 15 minutes. (Eglitis and Johnson, 1970)

Provided the ecology of the situation is adequately known and the biology of the vector role understood, one can expect worthwhile results. Sometimes diseased plants can be removed before there is time for the pathogen to be carried to new hosts or where the diseased host serves as a site for increase in vector populations. Erection of physical barriers or removal of native reservoir hosts can contribute to the desired end. Occasionally, readjustments in crop rotation or rescheduling of sowing dates can be instituted to upset the pattern of reproduction, hibernation, and dispersal of the vector. Or it may be opportune to invoke a biological control of the vector species.

When insecticides are used against vectors, it is often wiser to direct them against the populations on the source plants—to reduce the number available for transmission—or to rely on persistent chemicals put in place prior to arrival than to attempt killing the vectors after they have arrived. The point here is that the percentage kill must be very nearly 100 if disease is to be avoided for an extended period.

Secondary Hosts

Alternate and Reservoir Hosts. Removal of the economically less important host species has been vigorously attempted in North America in three instances: barberry (Fig. 15–11), currant and gooseberry, and cedar. The corresponding diseases, of course, are the stem rust of wheat, the white pine blister rust, and the apple rust. Each campaign reflected the importance of the biology of the organism and its host relations, the economics of crop production and eradication costs, the strategies of mobilizing public opinion, and the traditions and technicalities of legal codes. Where the pathogen must go from one host to the other each season, as it must go from cedar to apple every spring, eradication of the wild species is highly effective. Similarly, new infections of white pine must come from currant or gooseberry, but in this case the lesions occur in perennial tissues—not the leaves and fruit—and a tree once infected will be progressively damaged even if the alternate host is later entirely removed. If, on the other hand, there are spore forms that can spread the pathogen within species—the uredospores of wheat stem rust can reinfect wheat—eradication is much less dependable. In this case, the campaign tended to shift from an effort to control rust to an exercise in reducing the number of new physiological races of the pathogen, this because the sexual phase of the fungus occurs on barberry.

By the term "reservoir hosts" is meant those species that provide an additional site of persistence or of multiplication for a pathogen, but without the precise biological relationship characteristic of alternate hosts. It would include species that are sanctuaries for the survival and multiplication of vec-

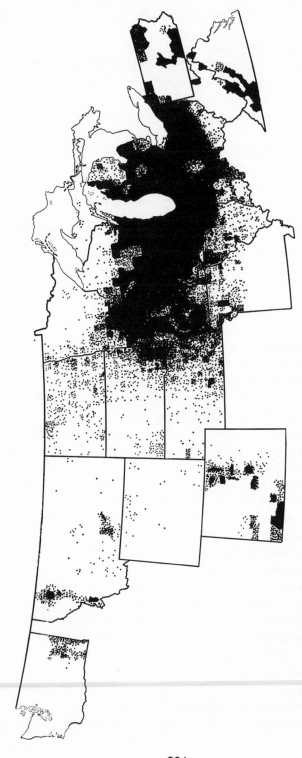

Fig. 15–11. Map of barberry eradication program in the United States, 1918–49, in those states cooperating in the wheat stem rust control program. Each dot represents one rural property cleared, a total of 141,377 properties, involving more than 373 million bushes and seedlings. (Courtesy of R. O. Bulger, USDA)

Fig. 15–12. Spread of yellows into a bed of endive from nearby weeds that serve as reservoir hosts. (Frampton *et al.*, 1942)

tors (Fig. 15–12), or where new pathogenic races might arise, or where the pathogen can persist in the absence of the cultivated host on which it is more commonly encountered. Finally, the term includes what might be called carrier species—species of crop plants in which viruses that cause trouble in other species or varieties seem to persist without causing visible symptoms.

The unwanted plants can be eliminated by mechanical, biological, or chemical methods, or by a combination of these. General emphasis has tended to shift from mechanical to chemical methods with the rapid development of herbicides, which have greatly favored the economic aspects by reducing the cost of labor to a fraction of its former level. There has been doubt expressed here and there about the safety of using herbicides in such very

large amounts in some instances and about the ecological wisdom of generalized brush control by chemical application, but the efficiency of the method is
inarguable.

Piemeisel (1954) describes a form of weed control he terms replacement
control: "changes in vegetation in relation to control of pests and diseases."
This is, really, a special instance of applied ecology or of range management
whereby pest populations and pathogen load are reduced through changes in
the population away from weeds and other ephemerals toward grasses and
native perennials. He points out that the further the vegetation has been altered from its original state, the more difficult it is to deal with and the longer
it takes. He cites as a good example of replacement control the success of reducing curly top of sugar beet by returning all lands not being continuously
farmed to good desert range, thus reducing the annual population of the vector leafhopper.

Biological control has so many connotations that it is a term of very limited
usefulness. To many it means pitting one organism against another, as when a
parasitic wasp is intentionally used to reduce the populations of an unwanted
insect species. To others it means nothing more specific than so managing the
environment that the population dynamics of the several species are shifted in
a direction favored by the producer. In trying to define the situation more
precisely, Piemeisel and Carsner (1951) suggest the term "replacement control" for a particular technique. In their words: "in replacement control,
though the immediate objective may . . . be the elimination of a particular
kind of plant species, the process involves the control of other plants of similar habits of growth . . . its objective may be multiple in effect, as: control of
a plant pest, plus control of an insect that is the vector of a disease, and, con-
sequently, control of the disease, plus improved forage, plus improved plant
cover as a protection for the soil." They stress the use of natural secondary
plant successions, with special reference to uncultivated lands as used for
grazing. They cite several examples of actual replacement control, particularly the establishment of stable communities of native perennials in an effort
to reduce the populations of leaf hoppers in the vicinity of sugar beet fields.

Trap and Buffer Crops.   When plantings are used as buffers they are, in reality, only a special instance of physical barriers. In a way, isolated plots can
be thought of as extreme cases of barriers, wherein the intervening land acts
as the barrier and in area greatly exceeds that of the crop. But a more useful
concept confines the term to situations where the principal crop occupies
most of the area and the buffer is marginal.

Forest windbreaks seem to reduce appreciably the overland movement of
air-borne inoculum, although they may at the same time alter the microcli-

mate on the downwind side and thus favor disease development in the crop in question. There is evidence that when legumes are sown with commercial rubber plantings they form root barriers that retard the growth of the mycelium of the root rot fungus—comparable relations could hold for citrus, grapes, orchard fruits, and other valuable perennials. Sideris (1955) recounts that the leaf tip necrosis of pineapple growing within one and a half miles of the seashore can be partly avoided by establishing multiple rows of *Casuarina* on the seaward side in order to trap sea water being blown inland.

Trap or catch crops are used in a way as bait to divert, as it were, the pathogen from a highly susceptible primary crop, with the notion of destroying the former, both host and pathogen, at a subsequent time. Trials in Hawaii have shown that tomato can be used in this way along with pineapples to reduce the damage due to the pineapple root knot nematode, provided the tomato is destroyed before eggs are produced by the pathogen. Reduction of the levels of infestation, not eradication, is the prime objective. In a different sense, catch crops can be used to establish the presence and extent of a threat from soil pathogens by planting one or more quick-growing, susceptible species in an area planned for subsequent culture of an expensive perennial; the methods have been used for example in Ceylon prior to setting a new rubber plantation.

Biological Control

In the sense used here, biological control refers to the reduction of disease incidence or damage as a result generally of the antagonistic interactions of two living organisms. Usually one of these is a recognized pathogen, the other a competitive, nonpathogenic species. It would not be at all difficult to find the term used in quite distinctly different ways.

Sometimes the antagonistic effect can be readily demonstrated in the laboratory, as indicated in the accompanying figure (Fig. 15–13), although this does not necessarily mean that it will operate in precisely the same way in nature nor, indeed, that it will be effective under field conditions. More frequently, perhaps, biological control is first recognized as a chance phenomenon in natural conditions and then investigated more carefully later.

A measure of the complexity of immune-like responses in plants to invasion by pathogenic organisms is provided by Goodman (1967) in his studies of protection of apple stem tissue from the fireblight organism, *Erwinia amylovora.* Besides showing that avirulent isolates of the species protect against a subsequent inoculation by a virulent form, he was able to demonstrate protection by several other bacterial plant pathogens that do not normally invade apple

Fig. 15–13. Antagonistic effects of fungi, showing antibiosis of *Trichoderma* metabolite on the pathogen *Rhizoctonia*. *Left to right: Rhizoctonia* inoculated into filtrate from *Trichoderma; Trichoderma* inoculated into filtrate from *Trichoderma; Rhizoctonia* inoculated into filtrate from *Rhizoctonia; Trichoderma* inoculated into filtrate from *Rhizoctonia*. (Allen and Haenseler, 1935)

at all. Not all species are effective, however. In this case the duration of protection seems to depend on the population of nonvirulent organisms present at the time of inoculation, and this in turn presumably upon the capacity and rate of multiplication in apple host.

Although the work was confined to controlled laboratory conditions, Cooke and Pramer (1968) have provided an intriguing look at the possibility of using nematode-trapping fungi in control of plant-parasitic nematodes, a suggestion that has surfaced from time to time. In their experiments, however, they were interested in the basic relationships between the two organisms under reasonably isolated and standardized conditions. To effect this, they grew the organisms in agar culture, and chose as the nematode a species that feeds on fungus mycelium, *Aphelenchoides avenae*. As a fungus component they used five species of nematode-trapping organisms. Under the conditions of this particular trial, there was a brief period of trapping after the mycelium had covered the surface of the culture, but eventually the nematodes increased to the point where the fungi were killed off. This suggests that, since the populations of the nematodes were not greatly affected, the latter may under natural conditions have a marked effect on the survival of the nematode-trapping fungi. This, in turn, bodes ill for the possibility of controll-ing parasitic nematode species by introducing trapping fungi.

Two questions that come to mind in thinking of manipulating populations are these: (1) Are there species of nematodes that can be used in the control of plant-pathogenic fungi? (2) Can the nematode-trapping fungi be used as a biological means for effectively controlling the nematode species that infest plants? It is to the second of these two questions that Cooke (1968) addresses a summary paper. He points out that contrary to previous general assumption, the nematode-trapping fungi do not seem to have a unique nutritional pattern nor do they behave differently than other soil fungi to a significant degree. More importantly, it seems rather clear that arbitrary addition of either fun-gus inoculum or organic amendments to soils is hardly likely to succeed and that until very much more is known of the biology of the interaction, practical measures of biological control of plant-parasitic nematodes with predaceous fungi are not available.

Except by a very few specialists, mycorrhizal fungi have been traditionally regarded rather as a curiosity by plant pathologists. To some they have seemed more in the province of plant physiologists, to others they are thought of as belonging to the mycologist. As their ubiquity is increasingly recognized and as the phenomenon of competition between species becomes of in-creasing interest in terms of disease control, the question naturally arises whether the mycorrhizal fungi play a significant role in relation to root patho-genic fungi and bacteria. Marx (1969) has reported preliminary observations on the antagonism of a number of pairs of fungi in culture, where one of the pair was an ectotrophic mycorrhizal fungus from pine roots and the other a commonly recognized root parasite. Of a total of nearly 50 pathogenic organ-isms, nearly half were inhibited by pine mycorrhiza—*Leucopaxillus cerealis* var. *piceina* was especially effective, inhibiting 92% of the test pathogens. The mechanism of inhibition seems to be the production of an antibiotic substance by the mycorrhizal fungus.

On the matter of biological control of plant pathogens one can hardly quarrel with the remarks by Wicker (1967) in his note on the control of dwarf mistletoe by a *Colletotrichum* blight. He reminds us that despite the successes here and there that have been chalked up by the entomologists, particularly against introduced species, plant pathologists in general have not really warmed to this method of disease control. Whether the great emphasis on risks of pesticides that emerged during the 1960's will swing the pattern to-ward biological control is an unanswered question. In the case here cited, Wicker has compared the four known fungal parasites of the dwarf mistletoe

(*Arceuthobium*) and concludes that the effect of *C. gloeosporioides* is appreciably more drastic than that of any of the remaining three. Killing of the host shoots is rapid, the pathogen has an ecological amplitude so as not seriously to endanger its usefulness, and it affects about a quarter of the shoots available —which latter can fairly be considered a significant measure of control.

Biological control of *Fomes annosus* on pine stumps during a first thinning cut by applying an inoculum of the fungus *Peniophora gigantea* has been reported (see Artman *et al.*, 1969; Artman and Stambaugh, 1970) as effective and in ways preferable to chemical control by either borax or urea. But in either case, the private landowners must go to the trouble and expense of a special application to the cut stumps. To remedy this, Artman and Stambaugh conceived of the possibility that spores of *Peniophora* might be added to the lubricating oil and the oil in turn employed in the chainsaws used in thinning. As it turned out, the spores survived well in the oil and were almost entirely effective as an inoculum when directly applied to stumps, but for one reason or another did not suffice as an inoculum when application depended only on the material that remained on the stump after the chainsaw had been used to cut the tree in question.

Occasionally, biological antagonisms can be put to use in rather unexpected ways, as when French and Schroeder (1969) carried out experiments on the utility of the oak wilt fungus to kill unwanted oaks, rather than working on means to reduce the effect of the disease on valuable trees, as plant pathologists would normally be expected to do. In this case, in a period from 1953 to 1967, inoculation with the fungus resulted in 92 to 99% mortality at a cost per tree of about 2 cents or less. By contrast, application of chemical silvicides was less effective and more expensive. Lest this seem a foolhardy venture, the fungus spread under the conditions of this test to only three uninoculated trees outside the 6–7-acre trial region, in central Minnesota.

16

Redistribution and Quarantine

Those means of disease control treated in Chapters 12 through 15 are a matter of direct concern to only a relatively small number of persons, those immediately involved with the disease in question. The producer of the crop, the extension specialist, the research pathologist, the representative of industry—all have first-hand knowledge of the situation and possess a measure of specialized knowledge that relates to it. These individuals stand to gain or lose, as individuals, depending upon the outcome of the attempted control program—if not monetarily, then in less immediately tangible ways.

In the case of quarantines and related measures the point of action is often far removed from the grower, and a very significant number of persons or groups of persons are involved who do not commonly come into direct contact with plant diseases. These include the general public (as distinct from the consumer as such), the legal and other related elements of government, and the transport and shipping industry.

In order to set plant disease in a proper context, envision a hypothetical world—at least the terrestrial part of it—in which all biological communities have reached comparative stability and in which wind, water, man, and animals do not move about appreciably. Under these clearly unrealistic circumstances the host-pathogen associations of any given area would be essentially stable and there would be no point in invoking quarantines as a disease control measure. If one now recognizes that wind, water, men, and animals *do* move, it becomes obvious that from time to time a new host-pathogen association will come into being. And it has long been recognized that when a species is introduced into a community in which it had not previously occurred, it may initially develop at a rate far in excess of what would be its long-term norm. When the introduced species is an insect, vertebrate, or vascular plant, the observable result is an invasion of pest or weed. When it is a plant-pathogenic virus, bacterium, or fungus the observable result is an outbreak of a "new" disease.

Thus the biological event against which quarantine as a disease control measure must be weighed is the pronounced tendency of a species when brought into a new geographic area to multiply at an abnormally rapid rate and to produce a very high population density. This capacity to multiply is characteristic of all biological organisms and would not of itself account for the explosive nature of the initial period of occupancy. The phenomenon must be ascribed to the absence of countervailing factors—factors such as host resistance—that would have evolved in the host species inhabiting the site from which the migrant pathogen came but which, in the absence of the new pathogen, could not have evolved in the hosts inhabiting the new area.

It would be quite wrong, of course, to conclude that every time a pathogen species moves or is moved to a new area it elicits epidemic disease there. As we shall see later, all kinds of factors may militate against this outcome. But the point is that the circumstance of introduction into a new area can, and not infrequently does, operate to permit disease development of a severity far beyond that previously encountered. It is the word "can" rather than "will" that provides the arguments for, and introduces the uncertainties about, quarantine as a disease control measure.

DISEASE INTRODUCTIONS—FAILURES AND SUCCESSES

Much of the evidence for and against quarantine as a disease control measure must be *ex post facto*. As a consequence, the most telling arguments for imposition of quarantines are drawn from the instances wherein they have failed or were not instituted. This is not quite the paradox it seems; it means simply that quarantine is the only disease control measure not subject to direct experiment. One cannot, obviously, try a "little" quarantine to see whether a full-scale one would be worthwhile, nor can quarantine be postponed for a period of years to see whether the inroads of a new pathogen are indeed as great as the more pessimistic estimates suggest. Nor, finally, can a quarantine be tried one place to see whether it would be worthwhile in another. The decision to invoke or to forgo plant quarantine must be applied uniquely to each situation and must be based on a reasoned assessment as to the probable cost of not invoking it. Inevitably, the official charged with this responsibility will be influenced appreciably by the record of major outbreaks of the past—by the failures of quarantine in some instances—because in a way it is the only hard evidence available to him.

A comprehensive list of the more notable events in the history of plant disease migrations would be very long indeed. If such a list were made, it would have near the top the introduction of grape powdery mildew and potato late blight into Europe from the New World, the movement of citrus canker, chestnut blight, Dutch elm disease, and golden nematode into the United States, and the two-way movement of white pine blister rust between North America and northern Europe.

Potato Late Blight

Phytophthora infestans is generally thought to be native to Mexico, where it occurs on native species in the wild. In any event, there is likely no better known instance of epidemic development than the mid-nineteenth century invasion of the British Isles and northern Europe. First observed in 1845, two or three years after it was known to be established in the potato-growing regions of the United States, by 1850 it had reduced the population of Ireland by over one million persons and caused enormous hardship and suffering. The disease is now found in almost every area to which the host plant itself has been distributed.

Grape Downy Mildew

Another "contribution" by America to the European scene was the fungus, *Uncinula necator*, showing up at almost the same time as the potato late blight and sweeping in about five years through much of the French vineyard region, whence it moved eastward and south along the borders of the Mediterranean. Some measure of its effect can be seen in the tabulation of wine production given in Table 16–1.

Table 16–1

Impact of Downy Mildew on French Wine Production

Year	Production in million hektoliters	Production per Hectare in hektoliters
1850	45.3	20.7
1851	39.4	18.1
1852	28.6	13.2
1853	22.7	10.4
1854	10.8	4.9

In short, production was cut to less than 25% over a period of only half a decade.

Citrus Canker

The United States is recipient as well as donor of destructive pathogens. Of these, citrus canker (*Xanthomonas citri*) has been much cited as one of the few examples of a successful eradication campaign. The pathogen appears to have been brought from Asia in the early 1900's and was found in Florida in 1912—the year of the first major federal quarantine act—and required heroic measures before it could be eliminated. It has not, apparently, successfully re-established itself in important citrus regions of the United States since that time.

Dutch Elm Disease

In the case of Dutch elm disease we know not only the site from which the pathogen came, and when it came, but we know almost certainly how it got here—on logs shipped from Holland to the East Coast for furniture manufacture and other uses and then redistributed about the eastern half of the continent. In the period between 1933 and 1942 vigorous efforts were made to wipe out the invader, to no avail, and at the present time the public has largely resigned itself to the loss of a major portion of the street trees in many American cities and towns.

Despite all efforts, although certainly not unaffected by those efforts, the Dutch elm disease continues to spread further and further from its point of initial invasion on the Atlantic Coast. Davis (1970) provides a map (Fig. 16–1) showing that the disease was detected in Georgia in 1965, in Idaho in 1967, and in Alabama, Mississippi, and South Dakota in 1968. In 1969 North Dakota was added to the list, and finally Texas in 1970.

A 1970 note in *Nature*, the British journal of science, brings out the fact that after years of relatively low-level damage, the Dutch elm pathogen is finally making significant inroads against the English elm and bids fair to destroy the beauty of many a village in just the way it ruined the appearance of the old towns and communities in the northeastern United States (Anon., 1970a).

In the years since the Dutch elm disease was introduced into the United States there has been a continuing difference of opinion as to whether municipal control efforts are sufficiently effective to merit their continuation. All are agreed, of course, that eradication is totally impossible at this stage. The issue seems actually to depend on circumstances in the community in question, if

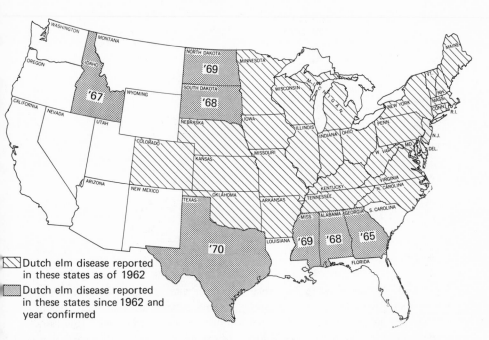

Fig. 16–1. Distribution of Dutch elm disease in the United States as of 1962 and 1970. (Davis, 1970)

we can judge from the experience in Illinois (Neely, 1967). In that state the situation seems to be rather as follows.

The disease was discovered in 1950 and by 1959 was known in every county of the state. In the south, where the very destructive virus of elm phloem necrosis acted as a complicating factor, control proved virtually impossible and the net result was the death of nearly all elms in southern and central Illinois. To the north, on the other hand, municipal efforts have been able, where vigorously and consistently pushed, to keep annual losses in the neighborhood of 2%, with total losses in the period 1957–1966 of 5 to 15%, as against 80 to 95% in cities that do not have control programs. The possibility that one city might exert control and a neighboring one forgo the effort without seriously affecting the first lies in the fact that in a prairie environment there is a substantial measure of isolation from one municipality's elms to another.

In this case, a "complete" control program includes compulsory destruction of elms that serve as a site for vector buildup, spraying of healthy elms with a dormant insecticide, and use of a soil sterilant to kill elm roots and prevent transmission through root grafts.

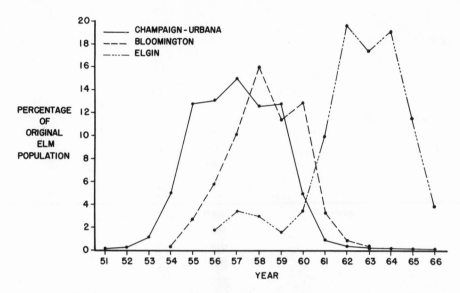

Fig. 16–2. Graph showing incidence of Dutch elm in each of three Illinois communities, all curves having roughly the same pattern. In Champaign-Urbana and Bloomington, the virus disease phloem necrosis complicated the picture and made control efforts ineffective; in Elgin, where necrosis was not present, there was no municipal control program. (Neely, 1967)

The accompanying figure (Fig. 16–2) shows how closely the pattern of destruction in a northern city (Elgin) without control program follows that of the central cities where phloem necrosis and Dutch elm together wiped out the entire host population.

Golden Nematode

By contrast with many invaders, the golden nematode (*Heterodera rostochiensis*), although highly destructive and hence much to be feared, has moved rather slowly in the United States and has been relatively unsuccessful. Partly, of course, this is due to the soil-borne nature of the pest, but also to strenuous application of rigid quarantine measures. Whatever the explanation, it apparently took 60 years for the pathogen to move from Germany through West Europe and the British Isles to Long Island, where it has been since held pretty much in check.

First discovered in the United States in the potato fields of Long Island in 1941, strictly enforced regulations halted the spread until such time as soil fumigation methods (Fig. 16–3)—now augmented by breeding programs seeking resistant varieties—could be developed and the industry rescued from economic distress (see Spears, 1968). Yet vigilance cannot ever be relaxed, for the pest has been found in 1967 in Steuben County, New York and even more recently (Spears, 1969) on a potato farm in Delaware near the Maryland border.

Chestnut Blight

Few if any diseases have, in terms of effect upon the native host, been as destructive as the fungus *Endothia parasitica*, which appears to have been introduced from the Orient about 1904. Within fifty years the native American chestnut, a conspicuous species in the hardwood forests of the eastern United States, had been virtually eliminated (Figs. 16–4, 16–5). True, the wood was so resistant to rot that many dead trees still stood, but it was impossible to find healthy trees and any sprouts that came from old stumps were, within a few years, themselves diseased. By 1948 the pathogen was established in Italy and a bit later in Switzerland. In these two countries there was the additional hardship caused by the fact that chestnuts formed a part of the national food supply.

Here we have an instance not only of the "importation" of a pathogen into the United States, from China, but subsequent "export" to Europe, in each case at vast cost to the recipient region.

Fig. 16–3. Large-scale application of nematocides to infested potato fields in Long Island as a measure to control the disease and prevent its dissemination to other areas. (Spears, 1968)

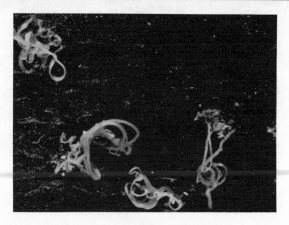

400

White Pine Blister Rust

In the case of white pine blister rust there has been a curious combination of circumstances leading to tragic destruction of 5-needle pines in the United States and an extremely troublesome and expensive control and eradication program (Fig. 16–5). Generally, the stage seems to have been set by there being a generally unimpressive pathogen, *Cronartium ribicola*, in Central Europe about the mid-1800's, which had perhaps in turn been introduced from Asia. To this scene, a few years later, quantities of white pine from North America were brought but, as all now know, proved highly vulnerable. It took only reimportation of European-propagated seedlings to transport the disease to North America, where it wrought havoc in the vast areas of this forest species spread all across the northern part of the continental United States.

During World War II, there was substantial concern that the agent of coffee rust might be intentionally introduced into South America; it seemed almost ideally suited as a candidate for this kind of biological warfare, in view of the hemisphere's dependence on coffee and the presumed total absence of immunity in the common varieties throughout the area. So far as anyone knows, such an attempt was never made, certainly not successfully made. But the pathogen, which has destroyed the coffee industry in Ceylon, south India, Sumatra, Java, the Philippines, south Africa, east Africa, Indochina, Malaya, and other parts of the tropics (Wellman, 1970a), has at last arrived in South America and is performing just as the most pessimistic had predicted (Fig. 16–6). In January of 1970 it was reported in Bahia, Brazil, and is moving rapidly and inexorably through the area. How it got there—by air currents, through international commerce, or some other means—is unknown. As Wellman notes, control work is being started, resistant cuttings and seedlings are being planted as a source of seed, but, in Brazil alone, there are billions of trees that will have to be replaced and it will be 3 to 4 years before the first resistant seeds will be harvested.

Wellman has spoken of it as "the most serious thing that has occurred in this part of the world in plant pathology in the last hundred years." Evidence from various sources suggests that it may have been present for as much as

Fig. 16–4. Blight of the American chestnut. *Top:* Dense stand of the native tree before the arrival of the blight from the Orient. *Middle:* Dead trees along the Blue Ridge skyline in Virginia left standing many years after the disease had swept through the area. *Bottom:* Spores oozing from the bark of a diseased tree, then to be disseminated by wind, rain, insects, and birds. (Courtesy of G. F. Gravatt, USDA)

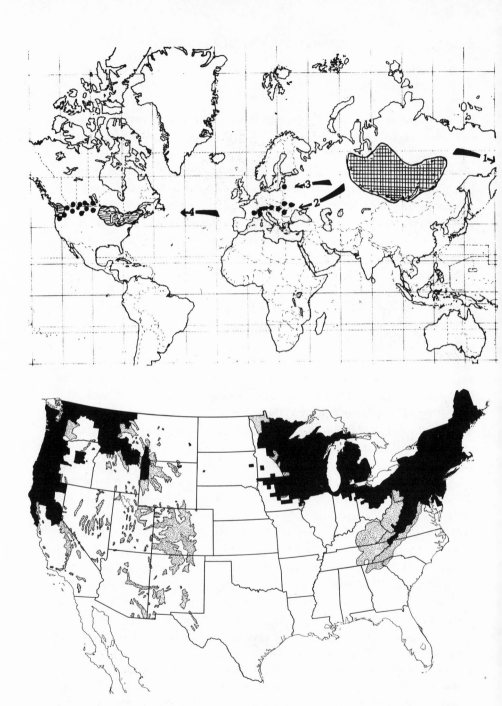

Fig. 16–5. White pine blister rust. *Top:* Original distribution of the disease in Central Siberia and direction of movement to Kamchatka, Carpathian Mountains, Alps, West Europe, and North America (Leppik, 1970). *Bottom:* Distribution of 5-needle pines (*stippling*) and of rust (*black*) in the United States as of 1948. (Courtesy of J. F. Martin, USDA)

five years. By July of 1970 it was possible to confirm the fact that the disease was present. The overall region of known infection measured roughly 300 by 700 miles. Thus a little over a century after the economy of Ceylon was destroyed, that of Brazil, to which the industry was driven, is in very real jeopardy (Wellman, 1970b).

The world's No. 1 grower and exporter of coffee is seeing whole plantations destroyed and an industry that provides more than 12 million jobs and nets almost $860 million in foreign exchange threatened. As might be expected, efforts are being made, at great expense, to isolate the disease in the areas now occupied. The 70,000-square-mile northern area is being isolated from the even more important plantations to the south by preparing a "sanitary corridor" 35 miles wide and 250 long, running from Rio de Janeiro to Belo Horizonte. Five to six million coffee trees are being uprooted in the process and a strict ban placed on moving any trees whatsoever across the barrier. Whether the ploy will be successful is by no means certain.

RATIONALE

Plant disease control by quarantine is much debated.

The evaluation of plant quarantine is, however, more than a biological problem. To be sound, not only must its objectives be reasonably probable of attainment from a biological standpoint, but it must be economically justifiable; it must have proper legal sanction; and it must not unnecessarily restrict the rights and the liberties of the people. Thus the problem will be seen to be an exceedingly complex one.°

What this means is that to an extent not ordinarily true of other control measures, plant quarantine is required to defend itself in each particular case, possibly because in most instances the explicit enactment of regulations is involved. One need not persuade others of the rightness of control by chemicals before applying a spray to threatened crops nor defend beforehand the introduction of a new host variety. But, as Smith and his colleagues say, invocation of plant quarantine must be contingent upon a prior consideration of both biological and economic factors. Once the decision is made, it still remains to develop an administratively feasible approach.

In an assessment of the feasibility of quarantine, one must always reckon with the possibility that even the most effective surveillance of certain avenues of entry may be entirely—or partially—circumvented by other means of spread. In the absurd situation where a political unit might, for example, establish rigid control over the movement of plant materials carrying infestations of a pathogen that was readily wind or vector borne, the expenditure of energy would be pointless. In retrospect, for example, it is perfectly safe to as-

---

° Only too rarely one comes upon an analysis so perceptive as to merit the term "classic." Such is the 1933 Bulletin of the California Agricultural Experiment Station (Smith et al., 1933).

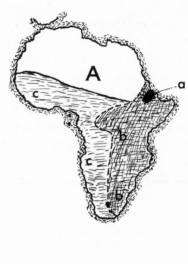

sert that no state in the Middle Atlantic region could have had the slightest success in stopping the inroads of the chestnut blight fungus once it had been initially brought to the United States from China. The crux of the matter, presumably, is the relation of the biology of dissemination to the facts of a given quarantine situation. If the Pacific Ocean is such a formidable barrier to chestnut blight spores that they cannot cross it unaided, then a quarantine between China and the United States, had the threat been recognized in advance, would have been a rational and possibly effective venture. Where chestnuts lay in an unbroken belt over much of eastern United States, state or regional quarantines against this virulent and mobile pathogen would have been meaningless.

Carl Hartley, one of the U.S. Department of Agriculture's more distinguished forest pathologists for many years, long ago recognized that by the time a pathogen has reached this country it is rather too late to do much about it. He recommended not only observing foreign plantings of American species, but going one step further and making plantings for this purpose alone—what he termed "trap plantings." For as he noted, in the case of cultivated plants resistant varieties can be found that will grow well, but that in forest species a resistant variety would have to be one that would reproduce and maintain itself in free competition. In his view, the chances of meeting a disease introduction by this device is relatively poor in the case of forest trees. He also reminds us that the hazard from Asian introductions is especially great because of the parallelism between United States and Asian tree flora; while Europe has a relatively poor flora and the Southern Hemisphere has mostly very different genera, Asia is full of relatives of our best timber species. Asia has nearly all of the world's pines, 70 oaks and 90 species of *Fraxinus* in the temperate part of the continent, and *Pseudotsuga, Liriodendron, Picea, Populus, Salix,* and *Liquidambar* are represented, to say nothing of *Ulmus* and *Castanea,* where the damage has already been done.

Fig. 16–6. Coffee rust in South America. (*Top of facing page*) Outline map of Africa and South America: (*a*) site of first observation in 1861; (*b*) extent of spread by 1942 in east Africa; (*c*) further spread to west Africa by 1963; and (*d*) first arrival in South America in 1970. (*Bottom left*) Map of eastern Brazil, showing the areas of coffee plantations and of the rust invasion, and the ineffective 40-mile-wide barrier zone. (*Bottom right*) Photograph of almost totally defoliated coffee tree, taken in Simonesia, Brazil, in April, 1970. (Top map and photo, courtesy of F. L. Wellman. Bottom map from Goodsell, 1971; reprinted by permission from *The Christian Science Monitor* © 1971 The Christian Science Publishing Company; all rights reserved)

Biological Factors

Whether a quarantine should be imposed and, once imposed, whether it will be effective depends to a substantial degree upon whether the disease in question would have "succeeded." Each disease situation is unique, a complex of factors that in the long run establishes the odds on whether the apparent threat is real and whether the proposed measures will be effective.

In essence, the earth's surface can be thought of as a complex of biological communities, each with its largely stable assemblage of populations of species. To the extent this stability is not disrupted by man, disease outbreaks of the kind to which quarantines are applied would not take place. But even if man made no attempt whatever to avoid or prevent the introduction of pathogens into new areas—ignored the whole matter, so to speak—it is by no means certain that every disease would become distributed throughout its entire theoretically potential range. There are three considerations that bear on this issue: the probability of introduction, the probability of establishment, and the actual importance if introduced and established.

Probability of Introduction.   A pathogen will be introduced into a given area only if all of a number of circumstances prevail. It will depend for example on the nature of the pathogen itself and therefore on the form in which it moves or is moved about. It will depend upon the resistance of the inoculum to environmental hazards likely to be encountered and upon the number and availability of host plants in the recipient area. It will depend upon the climatic requirements of the pathogen in relation to the topography and geography of the areas intervening between points of origin and of deposition. And it will depend very much upon whether the different seasons of the year vary as to their suitability for survival of the pathogen.

Because so substantial a portion of the actual movement of pathogens by man is a consequence of shipments in commercial trade, it makes a lot of difference just how the host and pathogen are related to the specific item being shipped. How frequently is it shipped? How far? In what quantity and how regularly throughout the year? What part of the host is moved from place to place, and what stage and what portions of the pathogen are associated with it? Under what conditions does the material exist in transit and how does this relate to the biology of the pathogen? These questions, and others, point up two issues:

- It cannot be taken for granted that a pathogen will inevitably be introduced into a given area.
- The probability of its being so introduced hinges upon so many interacting considerations that any conclusion can be at best an informed guess.

Probability of Establishment.   Assuming a pathogen surmounts the complex of obstacles facing it and is introduced into a given area, it still may not become established there. Whether it will or not depends upon a number of considerations, each of which must be met affirmatively. There is the question whether the amount of arriving viable inoculum is sufficient and whether it comes into contact with a susceptible host. If the pathogen requires an alternate host, both host species must be present in the local flora. And the pathogen must not only contact a susceptible host, it must do so through a vulnerable tissue at a season of the year when establishment and reproduction are possible. What is true of introduced pathogens is generally also true of introduced hosts (Fig. 16-7).

That establishment is uncertain is no way better demonstrated than by the number of times intentional introduction of exotic species has failed. There are no authenticated cases of intentional establishment as an act of biological warfare, but time and again insects have been introduced as a means of biological control of an unwanted host species. More often than not, even when much effort was expended to assure establishment, the introduction has failed.

Of course, the more frequently a pathogen is introduced, the more likely it is to become established. To some extent, plant quarantine is predicated on recognition of this fact and tries to reduce the frequency of introduction—on the assumption that establishment can eventuate from any one introduction, provided the biological demands are adequately met.

Importance.   In the final analysis, society as a whole is concerned only with those diseases that, if introduced and if established, will develop to the point where they are more than a pathological curiosity. This means that the climate must be favorable, that host-pathogen interactions must be such as severely to damage the former, and that needed vectors or alternate hosts are present. Here again, the answer must be that plant quarantine as a philosophy assumes there is at least a potential for significant damage in the situation to which it addresses itself, and seeks to lessen the odds of such an outcome by reducing the number of introductions as the first step in the sequence of events.

Economic Aspects

The economics of quarantines is determined primarily by the economics of plant disease itself. If disease were not costly, quarantines would be irrelevant, but there are certain economic considerations that apply with special force to quarantine issues. Whereas, ideally perhaps, there might be ways of excluding plant pathogens without costs and without interruption of trade,

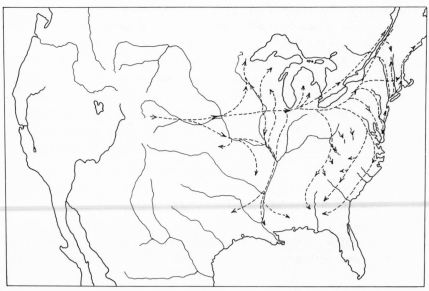

the fact is that costs are incurred and that "the economic consequences resulting from the spread of pests and diseases or from the regulations preventing the spread of pests and diseases are not uniformly distributed among all people. Until adjustments are made some individuals benefit directly, others only indirectly, or not at all" (Smith *et al.*, 1933). It is with these "adjustments"—in production, prices, land values, wages, taxes, consumption patterns, etc.—that the responsible official must reckon in assessing the wisdom of imposing quarantine restrictions.

Points of view, and therefore opinions, differ depending upon the relation of the individual to the crop, disease, or quarantine. To the nonagricultural citizen, almost totally ignorant of the facts and factors involved, the cost of disease is obscure and the existence of a quarantine an annoyance. To the tradesman it may well be one more expense in the array of costs that press in upon him. But to the grower, with predictable exceptions, quarantines appear as a needed barrier to the possible arrival of another biological threat to his crops. Growers can be depended upon to support most quarantines.

The California bulletin examines in great detail the central question of economics as related to society, first asking: "How big is the concept of 'society' to be: the producers of a particular crop in California, all the producers of a particular crop irrespective of where they live, all the farmers in California, taxpayers in California, consumers in California, all the people in California, all the farmers in the United States, or all the people in the world?" After thorough analysis, three generalizations emerge:

- "The real cost to society of plant pests and diseases is the amount of additional effort required to produce agricultural products on account of these pests and diseases.
- "Society considered as a large group of producers and consumers has interests almost identical with those of individual producers.
- "The consumer always benefits from an abundance of production."

While it must be accepted that the establishment of a new disease always results in a net social loss, this loss may be shared by growers and consumers in varying proportions depending upon the circumstances of each particular instance. Against this general truth must be balanced the cost of exclusion versus the threat of disease damage, and of disease damage after attempted

---

Fig. 16–7. Advance of the Colorado potato beetle in the United States, 1859–1904, as a result of introducing a new host into an area already occupied by the insect. *Top:* Prevailing wind directions during the summer are shown by arrows (dotted lines indicating advance as of year noted). *Bottom:* Chief trends of migration of beetle, showing natural highways of dispersal along river valley developments and coastal plain. (Tower, 1906)

control by available means, or of altering cropping patterns in the event tolerable levels of control cannot be achieved.

Finally, because of the very close and direct association between quarantines and trade, the economics of the excluded commodity, as distinct from the economics of the protected crop, enters the picture. The California bulletin examines this issue at some length, pointing out that, properly used, a quarantine is not a protective tariff and is not readily useful as a tool in price manipulation. The argument is based mostly on the assertions that "tariffs, to be effective in raising prices by practically the amount of the tariff, must apply first to all of the product, and secondly to all forms of the product," and that "the other aspect of tariffs on which there usually is agreement is that an import tariff on a commodity produced in such volume that some or a large part of the supply is exported has no effect on prices unless there is some form of monopoly control behind the tariff wall." While organized, monopolistic groups of growers admittedly could manipulate prices behind a quarantine just as they can behind a tariff, they could not succeed against organized buyers, who would insist the quarantine be removed. Or consumers, particularly in adjoining political units, could substitute "counter-quarantines."

A point raised by Horsfall and Dimond (1960) on the rationale of quarantine deserves attention. They advance the thesis, based on van der Plank's symbolic analysis of plant disease epidemics, that quarantine is suitable for a disease with a low "birth rate" if the diseased material can be surely and readily detected, and for diseases of high birth rate if the value of "r" (rate of increase) is low. They point out that quarantine affects only the quantity of inoculum and invokes the question how long an epidemic can be delayed, especially in view of the inherently low level of r in new areas.

MEANS

Assuming that the decision is reached to invoke quarantine measures, what are the means available to do so? Various authors organize their response to this question differently, but in the long run there are but two elements—where an action is taken and what that action is.

Quarantine has as its central goal to disrupt the flow of a pathogen—usually a commodity of one sort or another bearing a pathogen—from one place to another. *What* can be done, ignoring for the time being the question of feasibility, falls somewhere in the spectrum from completely prohibiting any movement whatever between the two points in question to permitting wholly unfettered exchange. Total embargo is invoked under certain circumstances, as when the economic penalties thereof are not especially great or when the risks of any importation at all are judged to be excessive. Mostly, however, quarantines rely on a measure of control of movement, or movement subject to certain qualifications and restrictions.

Inspection and Enforcement

For there to be qualified movement, there must be an effective means to determine whether the material in question measures up to the qualification —i.e., inspection and enforcement. As a matter of convenience, these tests are focussed on the point of origin, during shipment, or at point of entry.

- *Point of Origin.* Inspections at point of origin may take the form of field inspections of nurseries, seed production centers, or other commercial enterprises, or it may be instituted at the time of packing and shipping for export. In the latter case, the measures taken will greatly resemble import quarantine, but will differ as to time and place.
- *During Shipment.* Most inspections cannot readily be made while produce is actually in transit, but in some circumstances it has been found possible to regulate the conditions of shipment in such a way that goods will be freed of pathogens before they arrive at their destination. By the same token, poor conditions during shipment very often cause pathogens to emerge and the produce to deteriorate greatly before arrival at port of entry.
- *Port of Entry.* The key role in quarantine inspection rests with the importing country at time of arrival. Maximum interest in, and therefore responsibility for, plant quarantines lies with the receiving political unit. It is hardly surprising that they are most diligent in establishing and enforcing inspection procedures. For a number of trade items there are additional post-arrival measures that can be helpful—such things as fumigation, isolation during a holding period, and post-entry quarantine.

Biology of the Pathogen

It makes a substantial difference just what kind of a pathogen is involved in the disease situation against which quarantine is being contemplated. In some cases the evidence of there being a disease is so conspicuous that inspection quickly and surely reveals it. In many others the odds are discouragingly against its being discovered—inconspicuous or invisible pathogens, obscure symptoms, or latent infections greatly increase the difficulty. It is important, too, whether or not the material being shipped can be conveniently examined. Complex assemblages of plant material, soil, packing materials, and like substances are virtually impossible to inspect fully. Similarly, it is very difficult to screen out those organisms that travel as resistant propagules apart from the host plant—e.g., sclerotia lying free in otherwise healthy produce—or to apprehend an organism that enters as a relatively innocuous associate of the plant species being shipped—e.g., the chestnut blight organism.

Magnitude of the Task

Even if the many handicaps could be overcome, the sheer bulk of the inspection effort constitutes a serious problem. Trained manpower is required and is in short supply, as are the funds to pay for it. For many kinds of perishable produce, only a limited amount of time is available, lest the delay be harmful and expensive. For large shipments, or if the material is elaborately packaged, inspection of anything more than a sample is out of the question. The result of having a small team facing a huge task is that the very best that can be done is only partial—much must be left to chance, on the hope that inspection will reveal most of the quarantine violators, and that experienced personnel will continue to capitalize upon their skill in determining just which shipments most merit close examination.

To a considerable extent the difficulties inherent in inspections can be offset by counterbalancing moves. For example, if all material is to be treated, e.g., by heat or fumigation, it makes relatively little difference if a contaminated item has got by the initial scrutiny. Or if all plant material of a given type is held in isolation for a specified period under conditions favorable to the development of disease, a number of dormant or incipient infections will show up and be detected.

There is an inherent conflict between the necessity of keeping virus-infested plant materials from reaching the United States and the need to bring new materials in for plant propagation. Even when symptomless introductions are brought in by experienced collectors, the materials are held under quarantine for specified periods of time and then indexed for latent viruses against established indicator species. The results of such indexing are dramatic (see Kahn *et al.*, 1967). Whereas the percentage of introductions showing symptoms in the decade between 1957 and 1967 was about 20% for *Solanum* and less than 10% for *Citrus*, and *Prunus*, and about 15% for *Vitis*, these values rose sharply when indexing for latent viruses was taken into account. Percentages were 67, 56, 75, and 62 respectively for *Citrus*, *Prunus*, *Vitis* and *Solanum*—an overall count of 62% for a total of 1277 introductions.

Kahn suggests that much time and money might be saved by international co-operation under which introduced plant materials might, as much as possible, be chosen from institutions where virus-free stocks had been developed and maintained. While this would not relieve the recipient country from further indexing, it should sharply increase the number of virus-free introductions and therefore the per-unit cost—after all, introductions that do not pass the indexing test are destroyed and the cost and labor of obtaining them, to say nothing of holding and testing them, are lost.

One need only follow the pages of the *Plant Disease Reporter* to become aware of the shifting fortunes of this disease or that in the United States. In the latter half of the 1960's, for example, there were flurries of articles on dwarf mosaic and stunt of maize, on Southern leaf blight, and several others. Of the "new" diseases that appear in a given region within a given time span, a not inconsiderable number are, of course, introduced from some other area. Usually these are entirely unpredicted in the sense that they are already present for several years before being detected and in the sense that while the total array of possible threats is reasonably well known, it is virtually impossible to guess which will in fact be successfully introduced. With this in mind, and citing a number of examples to support his argument, Paul Miller (1966) restates the case for an isolation laboratory for plant diseases comparable to the Plum Island Animal Disease Laboratory of the U.S. Department of Agriculture. In such a laboratory it would be possible to make preliminary examinations of the more threatening foreign pathogenic microorganisms and, at least in some cases, be in a better position to deal with them when and if they arrive.

Experimentation in the absence of very careful safeguards is particularly dramatically brought out—in the field of entomology rather than plant pathology, to be sure—by the escape of the African honey bee into Brazil and surrounding countries in 1954. In sixteen years it has rather completely replaced the resident bee colonies as a result of far greater aggressiveness and swarming vigor. The point, however, is that the bee was intentionally introduced from Africa for breeding purposes and escaped through the carelessness of one of the geneticist technicians. In 14 years it colonized an area equal to that of the 48 continental United States and bid fair to extend its range still further.

Diversity and Speed of Transport

Whenever chance is involved—and chance cannot be eliminated from the picture—an increase in totals inevitably increases risk. That is, an introduction that is very unlikely to occur under conditions of limited trade becomes almost a certainty if trade movement becomes massive. In the same way, hazards are increased as the interval between departure and arrival is reduced. This is particularly true of delicate or short-lived pathogens, and those that can survive only on vigorous, living host tissue.

In the light of the unprecedented development of rapid, long-distance transport vehicles and the equally unprecedented increase in total passenger and commodity movement, it is small wonder that from a plant-disease standpoint the hazards have never been so great.

Air travel has unquestionably made the task of the quarantine inspector and the whole matter of quarantine enforcement very much more difficult. In no place is this more dramatically shown than in the frequency and speed with which movement now takes place between the United States and Europe, South America, and Asia. As for California, a state that traditionally for many years stopped all automobiles at the border for careful examination, it is now possible to fly into any of a number of airfields without any check whatsoever. It would appear almost as though authorities in that state had despaired of enforcing an effective quarantine against domestic importation of plant and animal material.

Countervailing Pressures

Not all of the obstacles to effective plant disease inspection and quarantine derive from the objective facts involved. Some are man-made.

Most citizens are well intentioned and law abiding, but there are always those who resent any intrusion upon their comfort, convenience, or economic well-being. There are others who derive a certain odd satisfaction from what they regard as outwitting the established codes and restrictions. As a result, of course, quarantines are either ignored or circumvented by a few persons regardless of how biologically sound they might be. Nothing much can be done to win the cooperation of these people; the only countermeasure is to recognize that they exist and to plan the inspection and enforcement procedures accordingly.

LEGAL IMPLICATIONS

Ernst Gram, in his review of quarantines (1960), provides a rather detailed discussion of the legal and international aspects of the issue. In so doing, he provides a limited amount of historical data and a few examples of various kinds of regulations and ordinances that have been formulated.

While the majority of formal measures to control pathogen spread are based on regulatory control by one or more governmental agencies, a few are voluntary in the sense that there is no established legal instrument upon which they are based. Mostly they are agreements of one kind or another between closely allied members of a group of growers who have come to recognize that in the long run their interests are best served by this kind of cooperation. For that matter, a good bit of the success for orthodox quarantine depends upon the voluntary compliance of those who might be in a position successfully to circumvent it.

Quarantines Are Laws

Quarantines invoke the police power, with all of the advantages and penalties implicit therein. Most growers, shippers, distributors, and the general public cannot be expected to observe the provisions of an inconvenient and expensive requirement unless they are forced to do so—forced in the sense that there are penalties for failure to comply. This means that the decision to impose a quarantine rests with governmental authorities and not with the people directly. Like any other governmental power, it is subject to abuse.

A common charge leveled at quarantines is that they are used as a means to control trade—a disguised economic tariff. Indeed, this has doubtless been true in certain circumstances and will occur occasionally despite all precautions. But if citizens are alert to the danger, aware of the criteria for justifiable quarantine measures and, perhaps above all, insistent that outmoded quarantines be promptly rescinded, the danger will be minimized.

Quarantine Statutes Are Complex

Because quarantines depend upon governmental action and impose penalties, they involve many technicalities and legalisms. Great care must be taken to see that the provisions of the quarantine regulations are explicit, precise, and realistic. All individuals must know just what is expected of them, how they will be affected, what is and is not permitted, and what the penalties are.

To be both equitable and effective, quarantines must be administered by trained and dedicated personnel. Most quarantines involve inspections of one kind or another, and it is a continuing responsibility of government to see that there is an adequate number of trained inspectors to handle the work to be done. Too often this is not wholly possible, with the result that delays, or inept examination of goods, diminish public regard for the quarantine procedure as such.

Quarantines Involve Political Units

Except for rare instances of "volunteer" quarantines by private groups, quarantines are established by political bodies representing a given constituency. They must, almost by definition, be directed against one or more other political areas—states, nations, regions. For this reason, quarantines very often have an international focus, since the most-feared organisms are likely to be from areas a considerable distance away. To some extent, at least, international treaties and conventions have served to regularize and implement the complex provisions of quarantine measures and to bring about a wider acceptance on the part of those affected by them.

VI

CONTEXT

17

Pathology and the Public

Plant pathology has always been closely associated with the human society within which it is carried out. Those who practice the art and science of plant pathology do so with a keen awareness of the applied aspects of their work if they wish that work to be effective.

Because pathology maintains this contact with the "real world," it is buffeted by the changes that take place in that world, and must remain aware of those changes. No one can say with certainty just what changes will take place in the future nor how much those changes will alter plant pathology. But at the same time the decade of the 1960's was one of more than average unrest at the interface between science and society. Its impact on plant pathology is important in itself and may, in many ways, serve as a partial guide to the trends that are to follow.

CHANGES IN THE WORLD PICTURE

Food

In several ways the food situation worldwide, sharply influenced by population pressures, changed in the decade before 1970. Add to this the simple fact that greatly increased speed of communication has brought the matter quickly and forcefully to our attention. Whatever may be the individual's reaction to the scenes before him, the great majority of citizens now clearly recognize how large a fraction of the human race is inadequately fed.

Not all changes have been for the worse, even though rapidly mounting demands have cancelled out, all too often, many of the gains in productivity that result from improved technologies. But dramatic improvements in the varieties of basic food crops—especially new varieties of rice and wheat—

have made possible what has been dubbed the "Green Revolution." Very possibly the greatest danger is that responsible officials will be so impressed by the magnitude of the problem on the one hand, or by the successes achieved on the other, that they will take an extreme position on one side or the other. If they do, the result will be the same—inaction.

A second dimension lies in the area of nutritional quality. More and more it is being recognized that while calories may be the most basic food insufficiency, protein malnutrition is a sinister threat, particularly to the normal development of the young child. Much effort therefore goes into programs that will provide an improved nutrient level and balance, as well as increased total food intake.

Population

From a subject once virtually barred from polite conversation and shunned by governments in their formal pronouncements, population limitation became in the 1960's a matter for open and serious consideration. If one were to judge by the amount of comment in the public press and mass media, he might be misled into feeling that matters were on the verge of straightening themselves out. Regrettably, this is by no means the case. For though it is clearly a step forward to make discussion of population respectable, little has actually been done in concrete terms to solve the problem. Ignorance, social custom, economic weaknesses, and a host of other barriers lie between mankind and the successful management of his population.

The Food-People Balance

Much is being written and said today about food, people, the environment, the impact of technology, energy resources, and the future of man. Much is profound, much is nonsense—the task is to distinguish between the two. There are no firm rules to this end, but it is probably safe to say that most of the extreme statements are without factual basis and can be discounted. So too can those that insist there is nothing at all to worry over.

A brief, but seemingly balanced presentation is available in the proceedings of a 1970 symposium under the chairmanship of R. D. DeLauer (1970). In this thin volume are to be found summary papers on population increase, world nutritional resources, interactions with nutritional resources. They cannot be adequately summarized here, but of all the lessons inherent in the message they convey none is more obvious than that food and fiber lost to pests and disease is an unacceptable waste of an all too scarce resource. Plant pathology cannot in a sense solve the food-people balance problem, but it is hard to see how solutions can be found unless loss from disease is taken into account and minimized. At the very least, as the 1970 report of the Food and Agriculture Organization of the United Nations shows (Anon., 1970b), the past quarter century has been a period when it has been possible to maintain an unprecedented population increase in the world without losing ground disastrously so far as food supplies go.

Most would agree that there must be strenuous effort to reduce the rate of population increase or, perhaps better, bring it to a complete halt. Most would also agree that for the foreseeable future the bulk of the effort in food and fiber production must be through traditional modes of agriculture. Yet thought is, and should be, given to a number of speculative techniques that may, should they prove economically feasible, furnish significant amounts of needed materials. Again, there is hardly space to go at length into the question of single-cell proteins, algal culture, synthetic foodstuffs, marine protein harvesting, and so on. As just one sample of the kind of effort being envisioned, Hodges (1969) speaks of "food factories in the desert." He cites the work going on at Sonora, Mexico, along the Gulf of California, where the peculiar extremes of that desert seacoast are utilized to provide, on a pilot basis, substantial amounts of fresh produce (Fig. 17–1). Another is being planned in the Sheikdom of Abu Dhabi, on the Arabian Peninsula.

Transport

No aspect of the current scene spells out the disparity between nations and groups of men more starkly than does the mode by which they travel. Most of the world's inhabitants still walk or go by the traditional means known to their forebears. But the affluent citizens of technologically advanced countries move at high speeds for great distances; many of them travel vast distances in relatively short spans of time. In this direct, physical way the world has indeed become "one world" to at least a minority of its citizens.

Aspirations

Although the worldwide trend in human society is to ever sharper contrasts between the "haves" and the "have nots," there is a critically significant

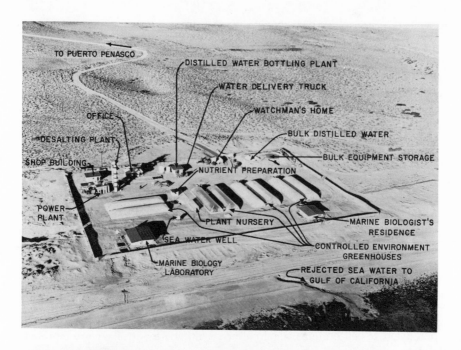

Fig. 17–1. Experimental "food factory." *Top:* Layout of power-water-food experimental facility at Puerto Penasco, on the coast of the Gulf of California. *Bottom:* Cucumbers grown in the greenhouse at the pilot plant shown above. (Hodges, 1969)

factor moving into the picture. It is simply this, that whereas the less fortunate peoples of an earlier age lived in general unawareness of the disparity between their lot and that of their richer neighbors—or at least accepted as immutable the condition in which they found themselves—today they are unwilling to remain docile in the face of what they see. Mass media have awakened in individuals, in groups, and in nations an aspiration for change—an aspiration that may be unrealistic as to degree and pace but that has the profoundest implications for the future of all mankind. If accommodation can be reached between disparate societies the lot of all will be improved. If not, there is grave danger that the technological culture of the advanced nations will suffer from the stresses of the conflict, but without achieving anything useful to the less favored groups in the process.

International Cooperation

There has always been a measure of cooperation between nations, but as communications become ever more rapid the ties between different societies become firmer and firmer. These ties are not so much at the political level as they are at the scientific and technical. In the latter sense, the United States government has for many years devoted substantial funds and attention to the assistance of developing nations and to international cooperation in science with the industrialized countries. Along with these efforts have gone very large investments by private foundations in the interests of peoples overseas. Foremost, surely, are the programs of the Rockefeller and Ford Foundations in Mexico, Colombia, many African and Asiatic countries, and cooperative ventures such as the International Rice Research Institute in the Philippines.

The traditional programs have been, on the whole, extremely effective and deserve much credit for their success. In the long run, however, it is just possible that the International Biological Program (IBP) will come to be regarded as the starting point of a new look at the relation of man to his environment and a new milepost in international cooperation. It was no doubt launched, in the early 1960's, on the strength of the highly successful International Geophysical Year, which had been organized to make possible coordinated measurements of a number of physical phenomena about the earth's surface. But the emphasis of the IBP lay in two areas that became incorporated in the central theme—the biological basis of productivity and human adaptability. Research, targeted for an initial five-year period, centered in the United States on such topics as analysis of ecosystems, aerobiology, phenology, marine upwelling, high altitude adaptations, and migrant populations.

The most nearly unique aspect of the entire IBP is that for the first time the new tools of ecological research are being used in a coordinated fashion by a substantial number of biologists and supporting physical scientists and mathematicians to the end that the intricate workings of several biomes—grassland, deciduous forest, desert, and so on—can be elucidated. Without the momentum of large-scale financing and the existence of the IBP as a formal mechanism for "big biology" it is highly unlikely that this kind of research effort could have been mounted successfully.

Plant disease is an important factor in biological productivity and is formally included in the IBP, especially those aspects that have a peculiarly international flavor such as the air transport of infectious particles. The main point, however, is not so much whether plant pathologists became involved in the IBP—some did—but to underscore the fact that those who "do" plant pathology in the latter third of the twentieth century will be doing it in a world where thoughtful people are newly alert to the place of mankind in the complex physical and biological environment. The plant pathologist deals with a different public than ever before, one that is perhaps often poorly informed but is at least no longer disinterested.

CHANGES IN THE UNITED STATES

Population Shifts

It is so obvious as to require no statistics to establish the truth of the statement that the United States is becoming a nation of city dwellers—urban and suburban, to be more precise. Data quoted in any one year are outmoded in the next. This is a trend of the utmost importance for plant pathology, signaling as it does the dwindling of small farms, of single-family ownership and operation. And it means a general public almost totally unaware, first hand, of agricultural matters. Farming takes on more and more of the attributes and complexities of large business enterprises, where costs and income are carefully monitored and where management is by a team of specialists. Money stakes are large, and advances in technology eagerly sought and quickly adopted. While productivity is at an all-time high, that sector of the population directly engaged in production of agricultural goods has shrunk to just a few percent of the total. It is this special situation in which the plant pathologist must work, depending for general public support on persons most of whom can comprehend only dimly what he is about. Some of the tensions that inevitably result will be examined later.

Food Handling and Technology

Changes in production agriculture have been accompanied by changes in food handling and technology. Indeed, as the total number of individuals on farms has dropped, the numbers who devote their time to seeing that farm products reach the consumer has correspondingly increased. A number of factors contribute to this trend.

In the first place, most products that go into human food or trade goods must be moved, physically, from site of production to site of use. No longer do most Americans live on the farms where materials are produced. To some extent this is also true of animal feeds. Thus collection, storage, shipment, marketing, distribution, and so on are a vastly more important part of modern agriculture than was true a generation or so ago.

Secondly, regional and seasonal differences are rapidly being submerged to the demand for continuous access to all kinds of products, in every part of the country, and throughout the year. When this is coupled with a demand for greater diversity, the result is a greatly increased complexity in the products-handling system.

Thirdly, and a matter of special significance to plant pathologists, United States consumers have been conditioned to demand a degree of freedom from blemishes in fresh produce that may well be unrealistic. Substantial additional effort is regularly invested in disease and insect control solely to achieve the last few percent of improvement in the quality of the final product as delivered to the consumer.

Finally, modern trends in food purchasing and use call for a very significant component of what has been summed up in the term "convenience." What this means is that what was a generation ago put on the grocer's shelves just about as it came from the fields is now machine-picked, washed, sorted, cut, packaged, frozen, dried, freeze-dried, and otherwise manipulated prior to sale.

As a result of all this, pathologists find themselves dealing in a different context than formerly, with highly specialized, complex, interlocking production, processing, and management systems. They must tie their activities into this fabric of people and functions.

Research Approach

With the explosive development of new knowledge and new techniques, and with the enormously more involved and diverse research problems that are being carried on, major changes have taken place in the way research is actually done. It now very much tends to be left to specialists working in teams rather than to the lone investigators. Plant pathologists find themselves assisted by teams, or as members of teams, organized to attack major research objectives. Even the traditional generalism of the extension worker is giving way to a measure of specialization as the customer, too, becomes more specialized, the operations more complex, and the monetary stakes higher.

DEVELOPING TENSIONS

Sheer numbers of people, accelerated tempo of activities, and general affluence are adding to the complexity of modern technological society. This complexity has led to a number of tensions within that society, some of which impinge directly on plant pathology and on pathologists.

Support of Science

Science, in the end, is paid for by the general public. Support for science has its ups and downs as the public enthusiasm for what science does—or at least what the general public thinks science does—swells and recedes. From the end of World War II to the mid-1960's, science rode on the crest of a wave of unquestioning loyalty and support, although it can hardly be claimed that nonscientists have a clear understanding of what it is they support.

As the decade drew to a close there developed a distinct public disaffection with science, in part attributable to a still broader anti-intellectualism. But in part it stemmed from a simplistic tendency to blame all science for what its critics regarded as the improper use of some of the knowledge derived from science. And in part it was surely due to a general resistance to the amounting dollar costs of doing science and to a mounting conviction that scientific results were worthy of support only if they were immediately and conspicuously applied to the benefit of man.

Plant pathology, with its long history of direct contact with the everyday problems of society probably enjoyed some freedom from the inroads of the financial stresses of this period—an advantage partly offset by the fact that the agricultural component of the population had shrunk to a few percent only of the total.

Environmental Quality

Public interest tends to run from one enthusiasm to another. By 1970, the center of the stage was unquestionably held by the issue of environmental quality; indeed, one would need to seek far in recent history to find a more emotional issue—except probably that of military conflict. But in fact matters were becoming worse, and comparatively rapidly so and thus caught the fancy of the popular press and the mass media.

The issue of environmental quality has profound implications for pathology and pathologists, because so much of the work is directly in support of agriculture and because agriculture, in turn, is the target of so much criticism.

Consumer Safety

In the past, at a time when infectious disease terminated the lives of a large portion of the populace before the normal lifespan was reached, attention tended to center on measures to combat the agents of those diseases. To an impressive extent the battle against infectious maladies has now been won. In a sense, people now live long enough to die of metabolic diseases, of coronary troubles, of cancer, or of the complications associated with biological senescence. Under these circumstances, professionals and laymen alike are becoming alert to the possibility of damage from chronic contact with one or more of the many substances in the environment that may be toxic. This new awareness is occurring at the very time when the diversity of these substances—pesticides, food additives, detergents, agricultural chemicals of all sorts—is large and getting ever larger.

Concern for environmental quality and for consumer safety—two facets of the same issue—confront plant pathologists with grave questions, more especially so in the context of developing pressures for increased overall production of agricultural materials. It means that the public is demanding on the one hand better disease and insect control and on the other that some of the more widely useful agricultural chemicals be eliminated from the arsenal of weapons or their use at least sharply reduced. Very possibly this can in fact be done, in the long run, given enough time and research support to develop adequately effective alternative measures. But until that time, intemperate statements on either side of the debate are of no help, and the decisions taken must balance risks and gains if the final position is to be both useful and wise.

LEGAL AND GOVERNMENTAL INVOLVEMENT

For many scientists there is only a remote connection between their research work and the everyday operations of laws and governmental regulations. For plant pathology—at least for practicing plant pathologists—the impact is direct and pervasive.

In the early years of the *Botanical Review*, Dr. Edmund H. Fulling began a series of articles with the appealing title "Plant Life and the Law of Man"

(Fulling, 1943) that was, regrettably, never carried fully to completion. In the first two of these articles he examined in detail such classic instances as barberry eradication legislation, the laws affecting cedar and apple culture, and similar materials. These, and the even better-known rules, regulations, and conventions bearing on quarantine, are long-standing examples of the constraints under which the pathologist must work.

Of more immediate concern is the situation that develops directly and predictably from the situation described just above, that is, the misgivings amounting to outright distrust on the part of the general public. It is difficult indeed to see how plant pathology can fail to be affected by a substantial fraction of the laws that are enacted in response to the public clamor over the environment, particularly those designed to restrict the use of agricultural chemicals, including those employed for disease control.

Restriction of chemicals is not necessarily bad, provided the regulations are based on carefully weighed data and wisely enforced. What is troublesome is the thought of laws established for primarily political reasons, or formulated in haste and anger, or administered without due regard for the interplay of advantages and disadvantages to each interested party. Pathologists cannot directly control this situation but they had best be alert and ready to work within the constraints they face. And they owe it to themselves and to society to provide guidance to those who must handle the regulatory responsibility.

A second possibility is that governments will find it necessary to formulate and implement overall agricultural management schemes, fitting land use to a plan that seeks to minimize disease loss. If trends go in this direction, plant pathologists will certainly be called upon to help devise the schemes and to implement them.

IMPLICATIONS FOR PLANT PATHOLOGY

Complexity

The production, handling, and marketing of agricultural and forest products is now so complex a procedure, and the interlocking relationships of private industries, individuals, and various levels of government are so many and so diverse, that it is in vain to wish for a return to the simpler times of the past. Plant pathologists must for better or worse resign themselves to working within the framework of modern technological societies.

Stability

Despite the major changes that are taking place in the way science is done, the complexities into which each specialty is developing, and the increasing tendency of one specialty to interlock with another, the basic approach of science remains unchanged. It is still a matter of objectively testing alternatives, narrowing down the areas of ignorance and reducing the diversity of possible explanations, holding to a given hypothesis only until such time as new data or new insights require that it be changed.

In plant pathology there is no escape from the requirement that the biology of the host—and in infectious disease the biology of the attacking organism as well—be recognized as the key element without which none of the related information is meaningful. These imperatives do not change as time goes on.

Responsibility

Three groups of persons are directly involved in the phenomena of plant disease: the producer of the crop, the consumer or user of the product, and the pathologist himself. All in one way or another play a responsible role in the total picture.

The Grower. The grower has a selfish responsibility to maximize his production at minimum cost by being alert to the appearance of disease, aware of what measures are available to combat it, and willing to seek the advice of experts when his own experience is inadequate. He has the additional community responsibility to cooperate in regional disease control programs, to invest reasonable amounts of his resources in control measures that will protect his neighbors, and to support worthwhile effort in plant pathology even when directed to crops that he himself is not at the moment growing.

The Consumer. The consumer, especially in our urbanized times, seems often to be distantly removed from any immediate concern with plant disease. Yet consumers in the aggregate must furnish the bulk of the economic resources that support plant pathology. To do so in a timely fashion, in adequate amounts, and in the right way, they must be at least minimally informed. Just how this can be facilitated at a time when first-hand acquaintance with agriculture and forestry is less and less available to the average citizen is a very troublesome question.

The consumer has an additional obligation to avoid levying unrealistic demands upon the system—whether in terms of produce quality, regulatory controls, or other facets of the system. He must by all means cooperate in quarantine enforcement, disease control ordinances, and related efforts designed to prevent needless worsening of the impact of disease on society.

The Pathologist.   The professional plant pathologist has his own responsibilities and obligations, above and beyond the obvious need to be as fully prepared and diligent as circumstances allow. For example, he is enjoined to provide advice that is in the best interests of *both* the producer and consumer, to avoid measures that are economically unsound, even if scientifically intriguing, and generally to recognize that an applied science must operate within the constraints of what is often called the marketplace.

Economy

The factors that influence the economy of disease are now the same as they were in the past in a general sense; the relationship of consumers and producers, singly and as groups, remains essentially unchanged. What does seem to be happening is an increased emphasis on certain aspects of the complex of interactions.

For example, as consumers get increasingly removed from the site of production and as fewer and fewer have a rural background, the criterion of sale price as an indicator of disease control activity becomes ever more remote. That is to say, as the number of persons who handle agricultural produce, from the time it leaves the grower until it is purchased by the consumer, increases, the producer and consumer have less and less awareness of each other. Modern-day buyers, as individuals, have little to say on what shall be the farm produce available for purchase. The middleman is the purchaser of produce and it is he to whom the grower must direct his attention. Decisions as to the economic wisdom of instituting a particular control measure will be based in good measure on whether it is likely to influence the prospective middleman.

While the old relationships between cost and benefits persist, the stakes tend to be higher. Production is concentrated on fewer, larger units. Costs of materials and labor are moving up. Skilled competition has pushed the margin between cost and sales price ever smaller. Total capital investment is usually very large. As never before it is important for the practicing plant pathologist to make very careful assessments of the situation before making recommendations to the client.

One more element moves into the economic picture more strongly as time goes on: the regulatory arm of government. To a long-standing interest and involvement with plant quarantine measures must now be added an augmented concern for food safety, especially as regards pesticide residues, and with nutritional quality. All in all, it seems inevitable that the plant pathologist of the future will need to reckon carefully with the legal aspects of each disease situation as he moves toward a final decision on an economically sound course of action.

Society

Pathology in many of its activities is an applied profession. Because of this it suffers rather less from lack of public awareness and support than do some of the more esoteric sciences. Yet even here so large a majority of the citizens of a modern technological society know virtually nothing of agriculture and the biological environment in general that public support of plant pathology is at best vague and uncertain. With the single exception of the health-related fields, science generally has not been especially successful in making its case with the public. The constituency of pathology must remain, for the foreseeable future at least, the informed producers, a few legislators, fellow scientists in related disciplines, and the consumers as represented by the middlemen who buy and process the output of the nation's farms and forests.

Education

Except at the technician level, the day of apprenticeship in science is virtually at an end. For some years now it has been possible to enter plant pathology almost solely through formal professional education. While there are exceptions, the usual path to professional work in plant pathology is through a graduate degree involving demonstrated research achievement.

Education programs in schools of agriculture, where plant pathology is often lodged, are changing, even though agriculture has long been a conservative part of the university scene. One can see a gradual movement away from rigid departmental lines within schools of agriculture, a weakening of barriers between agricultural schools and the liberal arts colleges, an infusion of more basic science instruction into agricultural school curricula, and a tendency to substitute general introductory courses for the battery of traditional crop-oriented classes.

Plant pathology itself has moved noticeably in the direction of the basic sciences and is demanding of its students a sharply increased amount of mathematics, physical sciences, and biology. Most training of professional plant pathologists emphasizes the science over the art—it is geared much more to the production of research pathologists than of practitioners. In all fairness, this same trend is conspicuous in the medical profession. Indeed, the time may be at hand to reexamine priorities and to consider seriously whether the balance should not be redressed, whether a sector of the students should not be consciously provided with more training in public relations, communications, economics, and commercial law in preparation for careers as practitioners.

Manpower

Populations, worldwide, have increased to the point where most thoughtful persons are deeply concerned with the implications for the welfare of man generally. At the same time, increased knowledge and ever more complex technologies put a heavy premium on skilled and educated manpower. The net effect of these trends is to create what amounts to rising unemployment—often masked by offsetting social welfare measures—in the less well-educated and less able segment of the manpower pool and a sharpening competition for workers in the skilled professional ranks.

In the competition just noted, sciences usually thought of as "agricultural" tend to come off second best. The truly superior students in schools of agriculture are every bit as good as the best in biology generally, or in the physical sciences. But there is no gainsaying the fact that, on the average, plant pathology and its sister sciences in agriculture do not compete successfully on an even basis with nonagricultural sciences, and particularly with the most popular of the physical sciences. No simple means to rectify the situation is apparent.

As for quantity, plant pathology suffers no serious manpower shortages. The supply emerging from graduate schools is such as to fill most of the vacancies that exist and conversely, most graduates experience no special difficulty in getting suitable posts. What troubles do exist are sporadic and subject to readjustments as occasion demands.

In one employment area, that of the skilled technician, sciences in the United States are weak. Not having the traditions of northern Europe, which imparts status to the position, very few persons seem willing to devote a lifetime to the supporting role in science. Plant pathology is no exception, with the result that most technicians are graduate students in need of financial support for a few years, unsuccessful aspirants for a professional career, educationally underprivileged individuals, student wives, and a miscellany of others. The effect of this situation is to impose on most professionals a burdensome and recurrent training obligation, an inadequate supply of supporting staff with but uncertain permanence and, too often, the obligation of doing their own technical work. In times of dollar shortage in support generally, the extravagance of working with inadequate technical support is even less tolerable. Means must somehow be found to provide the technician role with adequate status and to achieve the stability and competence that stems from the existence of a bona fide technician class. One encouraging development is an awakened realization that by no means all young people are best advised to attend regular colleges and the establishment of new technician-training programs for their special benefit.

Information

By no means least in the roster of changes that plant pathology encounters as it faces the future is the question of information handling. By all odds the most critical factor is the sheer mass of information to be coped with. Estimates vary, but no one argues that the problem of data accumulation is of less than near-crisis proportions, partly because it is more diverse and complex than it used to be, but primarily because so many more persons are working at science in this than in any previous generation.

What to do? What are the resources that can protect science from a total strangulation in its own information?

Virtually everyone who tackles the information explosion places his faith in automatic data processing—with emphasis on computer technology—as the only tool with the potential of making the situation manageable. There can be no question but that the advent of high-speed computers opens up two very important avenues of exploitation: they make it feasible to record and process data in a quantity and wealth of detail hitherto impossible, and they make handling of a given volume of data enormously faster and easier than in the past. Less spectacular technologies include IBM punch cards, xerographic reproduction, microfilm, and so on.

There are hazards in relying too much on automatic data processing to solve information problems. No machine can do more than speed up operations that are inherently possible by older methods. No machine can invent new relationships nor think for itself. They can only perform those operations programmed into them by the man who controls their patterns and sequences. It is highly misleading to speak of "mechanical brains," when in truth the technologies perform only the task—crucial though it is—of removing the tedium from data manipulation.

Three major tasks lie before the scientific investigator if the information dilemma is to be solved, even with the help of modern systems and techniques:

- Data must be accumulated selectively, as opposed to haphazard storage of whatever comes to hand.
- The fragmentation and confusion brought on by the existence of a profusion of subdivisions and specialties within biology—i.e., its tremendous diversity—must at the very least be met by assuring interconvertibility of terms.
- Systems of data and information handling must take into account the existing regional and local systems—which in turn must be modified where essential so that they are all compatible with the national network.

CAREER OPPORTUNITIES

Education

The student who aspires to a career in plant pathology is under heavy pressure to pursue his formal education through the Ph.D. degree. It would be incorrect to say that persons with lesser academic degrees have no place in the profession, but equally incorrect not to recognize that failure to hold the doctorate degree is a serious handicap.

It makes but little difference what research specialty is chosen. At one time virology or nematology will seem to be getting the lion's share of attention, at another the physiology of disease, at still another epidemiology. Plant pathology, like virtually all other human activities, is subject to fads and fashions, just as a department in one university is unlike that in another. So diverse is the field and so varied the schools and curricula that an individual is often wise to select his career specialty largely on the grounds of its appeal to him as an individual, then to seek training in an institution where that specialty is strong.

Practical experience in the field, either as part of a structured curriculum or as summer employment, is a highly beneficial aspect of education whenever it can be arranged for.

Overseas Activity

The long-standing practice of bringing foreign agriculturists to the United States for advanced training and education has much to be said for it, but there are drawbacks as well. It becomes fairly evident that conditions in many countries, especially tropical ones, are so very different from those in the temperate zones that direct transfer of knowledge and skills ranges from difficult to impossible. Research facilities in the home country too seldom measure up to those in the more affluent nations, and the returnee may well be relatively ineffective upon his return to his homeland.

If the situation is to be improved, it will require at least two significant and demanding changes. First, it will be necessary to learn a great deal more than we now know about the agriculture in general—and the pathology in particular—of less developed parts of the world. And second, scientists in the more favored lands must be willing to go overseas and remain there long enough to make the work effective. Of the two, it may prove to be the latter that is the more difficult. Traditions, the inconveniences of extended overseas sojourns, the pressures of family obligations, the possibility of delays in career advancement, all conspire against the easy establishment of a cadre of pathologists who meet the overseas obligations of the profession.

Personal Relations

The science community, by comparison with a generation or so ago, has changed by the very fact that it has increased sharply in total numbers. As a direct result, members of a given disciplinary group can no longer know each other personally as they once did—at least the individual scientist's circle of acquaintances is a far smaller fraction of the total than it once was. Several additional circumstances derive from this general expansion and depersonalization of the science community:

- The old-fashioned devices by which persons have traditionally been recruited and appointed to positions on university faculties or experiment station staffs—sometimes characterized as the "old boy" technique that depends on word-of-mouth inquiries and recommendations—is less and less suitable for the current scene. Job opportunities are less widely publicized and candidates less exhaustively and objectively sought than would be desirable. The continuing prejudices against open advertising of vacancies and open application for consideration for employment need badly to be overcome.
- Scientific meetings tend to become ever larger and more diverse, and the informal interaction of the attendees ever more cumbersome and difficult. Countermeasures lead to more and more fragmentation of professional meetings into specialty groups, with consequent loss of contact outside these specialties.

- Improved communications technologies, and vastly more rapid means of transportation, have made the professional societies relatively insignificant as an avenue of contact among scientists. Except as a medium for the organization of meetings and for the publication of research, the bulk of professional societies and similar organizations are not very effective.

Publication

Traditionally, the results of research investigations have been made available to others through being published in scientific journals, monographs, and occasionally books. These have been augmented from time to time by photographs, demonstrations of material, specimens, and other visible and tangible aids. Over the years great significance has been attached to priority of publication; in very large measure the reputation and professional advancement of the research pathologist have rested on the amount and quality of his formal publications. To some this situation has meant that they are tempted to bring out published reports of scarcely proven hypotheses, or to emphasize the number of individual research papers over the quality of their content. On the other hand, evaluation of published research is a reasonably satisfactory measuring stick and has been seized upon in most quarters as a way of arriving at estimates of personal worth and ability.

There is but little indication, even if one argues that there should be, of an easy alternative. At the same time, the greater speed with which results can be reported by techniques other than the printed page and the mounting diversity of the research community suggest that it may be time seriously to consider phasing out the traditional scientific journal by which complete copies of all papers are provided to all subscribers. Alternative possibilities are many:

- Publication of abstracts only, the full paper to be distributed individually upon request
- The pooling of data within computers, to be sought only upon posing specific questions or sets of questions
- Microfilm reproduction

The list could be expanded greatly, but the central point is relatively simple—the printed page no longer stands as preeminent as it once did as a device for recording and disseminating the results of scientific discovery.

Fig. 17–2. Potato late blight—a century of progress. *Top:* Diseased potato plant typical of the disease in its severest form. *Bottom:* Luxuriant field of healthy potatoes in County Cork, Ireland, from which the inhabitants fled by thousands a century ago. (Courtesy of W. J. Zaumeyer)

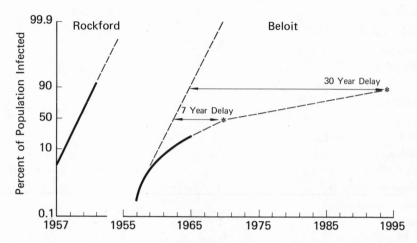

Fig. 17–3. Disease and public policy—Dutch elm in the upper Midwest: graph of disease development in Rockford, Illinois, and Beloit, Wisconsin. Extensive control measures in the latter have delayed losses as shown. (Merrill, 1971)

PROGRESS

It has been more than a century since the dramatic outbreak of the potato late blight devastated much of the food supply of Ireland and forced a major migration of that nation's people to other lands. Compare, then, the condition of what must have been typical of most of the potato fields in that unhappy time (Fig. 17–2, *top*) with the waist-high luxuriance of that same crop today in County Cork, not far from the port of Cobh, from which so many thousands fled to America (Fig. 17–2, *bottom*). Plant pathologists do not claim unvarying success, nor sole credit for such successes as are achieved. But the specter of plant disease is held back, at least in part, by the patient efforts of those who account themselves as plant pathologists. Examples could be cited by the score—in field and forest, orchard and garden, park or plantation.

Yet it is perhaps more typical of the relationship—an increasingly effective relationship—between pathology and the public to consider a much less publicized interaction. One could choose from a thousand instances, but any will serve the purpose. Consider, then, the simple question whether it is wise or unwise for a community threatened by a major disease to institute control measures. Merrill (1971) succinctly treats just such a question in comparing two upper midwestern towns in reacting to the Dutch elm disease (Fig. 17–3). In Rockford, Illinois, where no control was instituted, virtually all of the elms were gone at the end of a decade. In Beloit every reasonable effective measure—removal, pruning, soil injection, and spraying—were vigorously pursued, and the 50% level of loss postponed for seven years. Projections to the future convincingly show that near-total loss would be postponed only about 30 years, despite a very costly control program. The crucial point here is to understand what is plant pathology and what is public policy. It is up to the pathologist to tell the citizens what can be done to control a given disease. It is up to him, further, to provide estimates as to cost and effectiveness of available measures. Finally, where possible, it is up to the pathologist to forecast the probable outcome of alternative courses of action—just as Merrill has done in this case. But to the questions "Is the control program worthwhile?" and "Should it be instituted?", only the citizens themselves can provide the answer.

Literature Cited

ADDICOTT, F. T., and R. S. LYNCH. 1957. Defoliation and desiccation: harvest-aid practices. Adv. in Agron. 9:67–93.

ALBERSHEIM, P., T. M. JONES, and PATRICIA ENGLISH. 1969. Biochemistry of the cell wall in relation to infective processes. Ann. Rev. Phytopath. 7:171–194.

ALEXOPOULOS, C. J. 1962. Introductory Mycology. 2nd Ed. John Wiley, New York.

ALLEN, M. C., and C. M. HAENSELER. 1935. Antagonistic action of *Trichoderma* on *Rhizoctonia* and other soil fungi. Phytopathology 25:244–252.

ALLEN, M. W. 1960. Nematocides. In Horsfall and Dimond, 1959–60, vol. II, pp. 603–638.

ALLEN, P. J. 1959. Metabolic considerations of obligate parasitism. In Holton, 1959, pp. 119–129.

ALLINGTON, W. B. 1938. The separation of plant viruses by chemical means. Phytopathology 28:902–918.

ANONYMOUS. 1965a. America-Canada-Russia. Christian Science Monitor, March 10, 1965.

ANONYMOUS. 1965b. Stopping the spread of witchweed. Agri. Res. 13:6–7.

ANONYMOUS. 1970a. [Note on Dutch Elm] Nature 228:304–305.

ANONYMOUS. 1970b. Food for the future. Nature 228:1021–1022.

ANZALONE, L., Jr. 1970. Air pressure incorporation of fungicides into short stalk sections of sugarcane for the control of red rot. Phytopathology 60:741–742.

ARNDT, C. H. 1946. Effect of storage conditions on survival of *Colletotrichum gossypii*. Phytopathology 36:24–29.

ARTMAN, J. D., D. H. FRAZIER, and C. L. MORRIS. 1969. *Fomes annosus* and chemical stump treatment in Virginia—a three-year study. Plant Dis. Rept. 53:108–109.

ARTMAN, J. D., and W. J. STAMBAUGH. 1970. A practical approach to the application of *Peniophora gigantea* for control of *Fomes annosus*. Plant Dis. Rept. 54:799–802.

ATKINS, J. G., ALICE L. ROBERT, C. R. ADAIR, K. GOTO, T. KOZAKA, R. YANAGIDA, M. YAMADA, and S. MATSUMOTO. 1967. An international set of rice varieties for differentiating races of *Piricularia oryzae*. Phytopathology 57:297–301.

BARNES, E. H. 1964. Changing plant disease losses in a changing agriculture. Phytopathology 54:1314–1319.

BARRAT, J. G., S. M. MIRCETICH, and H. W. FOGLE. 1968. Stem pitting of peach. Plant Dis. Rept. 52:91–94.

BAWDEN, F. C. 1964. Plant Viruses and Virus Diseases, 4th ed. Ronald Press, N. Y.

BECKMAN, C. H. 1966. Cell irritability and localization of vascular infections in plants. Phytopathology 56:821–824.

BELL, A. A. 1969. Phytoalexin production and *Verticillium* wilt resistance in cotton. Phytopathology 59:1119–1127.

BENNETT, C. W. 1967. Epidemiology of leafhopper-transmitted viruses. Ann. Rev. Phytopath. 5:87–108.

BERGMAN, H. F. 1959. Oxygen deficiency as a cause of disease in plants. Botan. Rev. 25:418–485.

BERKELEY, G. H. 1944. Root-rots of certain non-cereal crops. Botan. Rev. 10:67–123.

BEUTE, M. K., and R. D. MILHOLLAND. 1970. Eradication of *Botryosphaeria corticis* from blueberry propagation wood. Plant Dis. Rept. 54:122–125.

BISHOP, C. E. 1969. Effects of changes in economic structure upon the quality of rural living. In Proceedings, 18th Annual Meeting of the Agricultural Research Institute (pp.17–30). National Academy of Sciences–National Research Council. Washington, D.C.

BITANCOURT, A. A. 1945. Plant pathology in Brazil. In Verdoorn, F., ed. Plants and Plant Science in Latin America. Ronald Press, New York. Pp. 302–304.

BONNER, J. 1962. The upper limits of crop yield. Science 137:11–15.

BONNER, J., and A. W. GALSTON. 1957. Principles of Plant Physiology. W. H. Freeman, San Francisco.

BRACKER, C. E. 1968. Ultrastructure of the haustorial apparatus of *Erysiphe graminis* and its relationship to the epidermal cell of barley. Phytopathology 58:12–30.

BRATLEY, C. O., and J. S. WIANT. 1950. Diseases of fruits and vegetables found on the market, and means of controlling them. Econ. Bot. 4:177–191.

BRAUN, A. C. 1959. Growth is affected. In Horsfall and Dimond, 1959–60, Vol. I, pp. 189–248.

BRAUN, A. C., and R. B. PRINGLE. 1959. Pathogen factors in the physiology of disease—toxins and other metabolites. In Holton, 1959, pp. 88–99.

BRENCHLEY, G. H. 1968. Aerial photography for the study of plant diseases. Ann. Rev. Phytopath. 6:1–22.

BRINKERHOFF, L.A., and J. T. PRESLEY. 1967. Effect of four day and night temperature regimes on bacterial blight reactions of immune, resistant, and susceptible strains of upland cotton. Phytopathology 57:47–51.

BROMFIELD, K. R. 1967. Some uredospore characteristics of importance in experimental epidemiology. Plant Dis. Rept. 51:248–252.

BROOKS, C. 1935. Some botanical aspects of perishable food products. Sci. Monthly 40:122–137.

BROWN, W. 1965. Toxins and cell-wall dissolving enzymes in relation to plant disease. Ann. Rev. Phytopath. 3:1–18.

BROWNING, J. A., and K. J. FREY. 1969. Multiline cultivars as a means of disease control. Ann. Rev. Phytopath. 7:355–382.

BURCHFIELD, H. P. 1960. Performance of fungicides on plants and soil—physical, chemical and biological considerations. In Horsfall and Dimond, 1959–60, Vol. III, pp. 477–520.

BURLEIGH, J. R., R. W. ROMIG, and A. P. ROELFS. 1969. Characterization of wheat rust epidemics by numbers of uredia and numbers of urediospores. Phytopathology 59:1229–1237.

CADMAN, C. H. 1963. Biology of soil-borne viruses. Ann. Rev. Phytopath. 1:143–172.

CALPOUZOS, L. 1966. Action of oil in the control of plant disease. Ann. Rev. Phytopath. 4:369–390.

CAMPBELL, R. N., and R. G. GROGAN. 1964. Aquisition and transmission of lettuce big-vein virus by *Olpidium brassicae*. Phytopathology 54:681–690.

CARLEY, H. E., and R. D. WATSON. 1967. Plant phytotoxins as possible predisposing agents to root rots. Phytopathology 57:401–404.

CARTER, W. 1962. Insects in Relation to Plant Disease. Interscience Publishers, New York.

CASPER, R., D. LESEMANN, and R. BARTELS. 1970. Mycoplasma-like bodies and viruses in *Opuntia tuna* with witches'-broom disease. Plant Dis. Rept. 54:851–853.

CHAMBERLAIN, D. W., and J. W. GERDEMANN. 1966. Heat-induced susceptibility of soybeans to *Phytophthora megasperma* var. *sojae*, *Phytophthora cactorum*, and *Helminthosporium sativum*. Phytopathology 56:70–73.

CHAMBERLAIN, D. W., and J. D. PAXTON. 1968. Protection of soybean plants by phytoalexin. Phytopathology 58:1349–1350.

CHESTER, K. S. 1947. Nature and Prevention of Plant Diseases. Blakiston, Philadelphia.

CHESTER, K. S. 1950. Plant disease losses: their appraisal and interpretation. Plant Dis. Rept. Suppl. 193:190–362.

CHI, C. C., and E. W. HANSON. 1964. Mechanism of wilting incited by *Fusarium* in redclover. Phytopathology 54:646–653.

CHIARAPPA, L. 1970. Phytopathological organizations of the world. Ann. Rev. Phytopath. 8:419–440.

CHRISTENSEN, C. M. 1957. Deterioration of stored grains by fungi. Botan. Rev. 23:108–134.

CHUPP, C., and A. F. SHERF. 1960. Vegetable Diseases and Their Control. Ronald Press, New York.

CLAYTON, E. E. 1945. Resistance of tobacco to blue mold. Jour. Agr. Res. 70:79–87.

CLAYTON, E. E., and J. G. GAINES. 1945. Temperature in relation to development and control of blue mold. Jour. Agr. Res. 71:171–182.

CLOUD, P. E., Jr. 1969. Resources and Man. W. H. Freeman, San Francisco.

COOK, H. T. 1949. Forecasting late blight epiphytotics of potatoes and tomatoes. Jour. Agr. Res. 78:545–563.

COOKE, R. 1968. Relationships between nematode-trapping fungi and soil-borne phytonematodes. Phytopathology 58:909–913.

COOKE, R. C., and D. PRAMER. 1968. Interactions of *Aphelenchus avenae* and some nematode-trapping fungi in dual culture. Phytopathology 58:659–661.

COONS, G. H. 1949. The sugar beet: product of science. Sci. Monthly 68:149–164.

COUEY, H. M., and M. N. FOLLSTAD. 1966. Heat pasteurization for control of postharvest decay of fresh strawberries. Phytopathology 56:1345–1347.

COYEIR, D. L. 1970. Control of storage decay in 'D'Anjou' pear fruit by preharvest applications of benomyl. Plant Dis. Rept. 54:647–650.

DAINES, R. H. 1970. Effects of fungicide dip treatments and dip temperatures on postharvest decay of peaches. Plant Dis. Rept. 54:764–767.

DARLEY, E. F., org. 1968. Symposium on trends in air pollution damage to plants. Phytopathology 58:1075–1113.

DARLEY, E. F., and J. T. MIDDLETON. 1966. Problems of air pollution in plant pathology. Ann. Rev. Phytopath. 4:103–118.

DAVIS, D. D. 1970. Distribution of Dutch elm disease in the United States. Plant Dis. Rept. 54:929–930.

DAVISON, A. D., and E. K. VAUGHN. 1964. Effect of uredospore concentration on determination of races of *Uromyces phaseoli* var. *phaseoli*. Phytopathology 54:336–338.

DEEP, I. W., and R. A. YOUNG. 1965. The role of preplanting treatments with chemicals in increasing the incidence of crown gall. Phytopathology 55:212–216.

DEILER, F. G. 1970. The pollution spectrum, with some recent technological contributions to air and water conservation. Chemurgic Digest 28:18–37.

DELAUER, R. D. 1970. The Food-People Balance. National Academy of Engineering, Washington, D.C.

DICKSON, F., and W. R. FISHER. 1923. A method of photographing spore discharge from apothecia. Phytopathology 13:30–32.

DIENER, T. O. 1971. Potato spindle tuber "virus" IV. A replicating, low molecular weight RNA. Virology 45:411–428.

DIMOCK, A. W. 1951. The dispersal of viable spores of phytopathogenic fungi by fungicidal sprays. Phytopathology 41:157–163.

DROPKIN, V. H. 1969. Cellular responses of plants to nematode infections. Ann. Rev. Phytopath. 7:101–122.

DUBEY, H. D. 1970. A nitrogen deficiency disease of sugarcane probably caused by repeated pesticide applications. Phytopathology 60:485–487.

DUNCAN, CATHERINE. 1967. Effect of light on the rate of decay of three wood-destroying fungi. Phytopathology 57:1121–1125.

DUNLAP, A. A. 1948. 2,4-D injury to cotton from airplane dusting of rice. Phytopathology 38:638–644.

DYKSTRA, T. P. 1948. Production of disease-free seed potatoes. USDA Circular 764.

ECKERT, J. W., and N. F. SOMMER. 1967. Control of diseases of fruits and vegetables by postharvest treatment. Ann. Rev. Phytopath. 5:391–432.

EDMONDS, R. L., C. H. DRIVER, and K. W. RUSSELL. 1969. Borax and control of stump infection by *Fomes annosus* in Western hemlock. Plant Dis. Rept. 53:216–219.

EGLITIS, M., and F. JOHNSON. 1970. Control of seedling damping-off in greenhouse soils by radio frequency energy. Plant Dis. Rept. 54:268–271.

EPSTEIN, A. H. 1969. Low temperature sprays for Dutch Elm disease control. Plant Dis. Rept. 53:304–306.

ESAU, KATHERINE. 1967. Anatomy of plant virus infections. Ann. Rev. Phytopath. 5:45–76.

FISCHER, G. W., and C. S. HOLTON. 1957. Biology and Control of the Smut Fungi. Ronald Press, New York.

FLENTJE, N. T. 1959. The physiology of penetration and infection. In Holton, 1959, pp. 76–87.

FLOR, H. H. 1959. Genetic controls of host-parasite interactions in rust diseases. In Holton, 1959, pp. 137–144.

FRAMPTON, V. L., M. B. LINN, and E. D. HANSING. 1942. The spread of virus diseases of the yellows type under field conditions. Phytopathology 32:799–808.

FRAZIER, N. W., V. VOTH, and R. S. BRINGHURST. 1965. Inactivation of two strawberry viruses in plants grown in a natural high-temperature environment. Phytopathology 55:1203–1205.

FRENCH, D. W., and D. B. SCHROEDER. 1969. Oak wilt fungus, *Ceratocystis fagacearum*, as a selective silvicide. Forest Sci. 15:198–203.

FREY, H. T., O. E. KRAUSE, and C. DICKASON. 1968. Major uses of land and water in the United States—summary for 1964. USDA Econ. Research Service, Agric. Economic Rept. 149.

FULLING, E. H. 1943. Plant life and the law of man. IV. Barberry, currant and gooseberry, and cedar control. Botan. Review 9:485–592.

FULTON, J. P. 1967. Dual transmission of tobacco ringspot virus and tomato ringspot virus by *Xiphinema americanum*. Phytopathology 57:535–537.

FULTON, R. H. 1965. Low-volume spraying. Ann. Rev. Phytopath. 3:175–196.

GARRETT, S. D. 1959. Biology and ecology of root-disease fungi. In Holton, 1959, pp. 309–316.

GÄUMANN, E. 1950. Principles of Plant Infection. Hafner, New York.

GERBER, J. F. 1970. Crop protection by heating, wind machines, and overhead irrigation. Hort. Sci. 5:428–431.

GHAFFAR, A., and D. C. ERWIN. 1969. Effect of soil water stress on root rot of cotton caused by *Macrophomina phaseoli*. Phytopathology 59:795–797.

GILL, E. W. B. 1948. Frictional electrification of sand. Nature 162:568–569.

GILLASPIE, A. G., JR. 1970. Evidence that ratoon stunting disease of sugarcane is caused by virus and not mycoplasma. Phytopathology 60:1448–1450.

GILMER, R. M. 1965. Additional evidence of tree-to-tree transmission of sour cherry yellows virus by pollen. Phytopathology 55:482–483.

GILPATRICK, J. D. 1969. Effect of soil amendments upon inoculum survival and function in *Phytophthora* root rot of avocado. Phytopathology 59:979–985.

GOLDBERG, C. W., H. COLE, and J. DUICH. 1970. Comparison of systemic activity of thiabendazole and benomyl soil amendments against *Sclerotinia homeocarpa* and *Rhizoctonia solani* in the greenhouse. Plant Dis. Rept. 54:981–985.

GOODMAN, R. N. 1967. Protection of apple stem tissue against *Erwinia amylovora* infection by avirulent strains and three other bacterial species. Phytopathology 57:22–24.

GOODSELL, J. N. 1971. Brazilian coffee besieged by rust. Christian Science Monitor, June 26, 1971.

GORING, C. A. I. 1967. Physical aspects of soil in relation to the action of soil fungicides. Ann. Rev. Phytopath. 5:285–318.

GRAHAM, S. A. 1951. Developing forests resistant to insect injury. Sci. Monthly 73:235–244.

GRAM, E. 1960. Quarantines. In Horsfall and Dimond, 1959–60, vol. III, pp.313–356.

GREEN, G. J., J. W. MARTENS, and O. RIBEIRO. 1970. Epidemiology and specialization of wheat and oat stem rusts in Kenya in 1968. Phytopathology 60:309–314.

GROVES, A. B. 1946. Weather injuries to fruits and fruit trees. Va. Agr. Expt. Sta. Bull 390.

GUTTER, Y. 1967. A new method of applying biphenyl for the control of citrus fruit rots. Plant Dis. Rept. 51:58–61.

HARDISON, J. R. 1948. Field control of blind seed disease of perennial ryegrass in Oregon. Phytopathology 38:404–419.

HART, J. H., W. E. WALLNER, M. R. CARIS, and G. K. DENNIS. 1967. Increase in Dutch elm disease associated with summer trimming. Plant Dis. Rept. 51:476–479.

HATFIELD, W. C., J. C. WALKER, and J. H. OWEN. 1948. Antibiotic substances in onion in relation to disease resistance. Jour. Agr. Res. 77:115–135.

HAWKER, LILIAN E. 1957. The Physiology of Reproduction in Fungi. Cambridge University Press.

HAWKSWORTH, F. G., and D. WIENS. 1970. Biology and taxonomy of the dwarf mistletoes. Ann. Rev. Phytopath. 8:187–208.

HEPTING, G. H. 1963. Climate and forest diseases. Ann. Rev. Phytopath. 1:31–50.

HIBINO, H., and H. SCHNEIDER. 1970. Mycoplasmalike bodies in sieve tubes of pear trees affected with pear decline. Phytopathology 60:499–501.

HILDEBRANDT, A. C., A. J. RIKER, and B. M. DUGGAR. 1945. Growth in vitro of excised tobacco and sunflower tissue with different temperatures, hydrogen-ion concentrations and amounts of sugar. Amer. Jour. Bot. 32:357–361.

HINDAWI, I. J. 1970. Air pollution injury to vegetation. Natl. Air Pollution Control Admn, Env. Health Serv., Raleigh, N. C.

HINDS, T. E., F. G. HAWKSWORTH, AND W. J. McGINNIS. 1963. Seed discharge in Arceuthobium; a photographic study. Science 140:1236–1238.

HIRAI, T., and T. SHIMOMURA. 1965. Blasticidin S, an effective antibiotic against plant virus multiplication. Phytopathology 55:291–295.

HODGES, C. N. 1969. Food factories in the desert: accomplishments. In Proceedings, 18th Annual Meeting of the Agricultural Research Institute, pp. 113–123. Natl. Acad. Sci., Washington, D.C.

HOLLINGS, M. 1965. Disease control through virus-free stock. Ann. Rev. Phytopath. 3:367–396.

HOLMES, F. O. 1946. A comparison of the experimental host ranges of tobacco-etch and tobacco-mosaic viruses. Phytopathology 36:643–659.

HOLMES, F. O. 1968. Trends in the development of plant virology. Ann. Rev. Phytopath. 6:41–62.

HOLTON, C. S., ed. 1959. Plant Pathology—Problems and Progress, 1908–1958. Univ. Wisconsin Press, Madison.

HOOKER, A. L., D. R. SMITH, S. M. LIM, and J. B. BECKETT. 1970. Reaction of corn seedlings with male-sterile cytoplasm to Helminthosporium maydis. Plant Dis. Rept. 54:708–712.

HOPPE, E. 1966. Pythium species still viable after 12 years in air-dried muck. Phytopathology 56:1411.

HORSFALL, J. G. 1956. Principles of Fungicidal Action. Ronald Press, New York.

HORSFALL, J. G., and A. E. DIMOND, eds. 1959–60. Plant Pathology: An Advanced Treatise, 3 vols. Academic Press, New York.

HUNTER, L. 1965. A doctor for the apple. The Analyzer 6:7–9.

JOHNSON, F. 1941. Transmission of plant viruses by dodder. Phytopathology 31:649–656.

JOHNSTON, C. O., and E. C. MILLER. 1934. Relation of leaf rust infection to yield, growth, and water economy of varieties of wheat. Jour. Agr. Res. 49:955–981.

JOHNSTON, H. W. 1970. Control of powdery mildew of wheat by soil-applied benomyl. Plant Dis. Rept. 54:91–93.

JONES, J. P., A. J. OVERMAN, and C. M. GERALDSON. 1966. Effect of fumigants and plastic film on the control of several soil-borne pathogens of tomato. Phytopathology 56:929–932.

KAHN, R. P., R. L. MONROE, W. B. HEWITT, A. C. GOHEEN, J. M. WALLACE, C. N. ROISTACHER, E. M. NAUER, W. L. ACKERMAN, H. F. WINTERS, G. A. SEATON, and W. A. PIFER. 1967. Incidence of virus detection in vegetatively propagated plant introductions under quarantine in the United States, 1957–1967. Plant Dis. Rept. 51:714–719.

KAMEI, T., Y. HONDA, and C. MATSUI. 1969. Intracellular appearance of turnip mosaic and bean yellow mosaic virus particles. Phytopathology 59:139–144.

KELLOGG, C. E. 1957. Home gardens and lawns. In 1957 Yearbook of Agriculture, pp. 665–688.

KELMAN, A., and L. SEQUEIRA. 1965. Root-to-root spread of Pseudomonas solanacearum. Phytopathology 55:304–309.

KING, C. J., C. HOPE, and E. D. EATON. 1934. Some microbiological activities affected in manurial control of cotton root rot. Jour. Agr. Res. 49:1093–1107.

KLINK, J. W., and K. R. BAKER. 1968. Effect of Aphelenchus avenae on the survival and pathogenic activity of root-rotting fungi. Phytopathology 58:228–232.

KLINKOWSKI, M. 1970. Catastrophic plant diseases. Ann. Rev. Phytopath. 8:37–60.

KLISIEWICZ, J. M., and L. B. JOHNSON. 1968. Host-parasite relationships in safflower resistant and susceptible to Phytophthora root rot. Phytopathology 58:1022–1025.

KRAFT, J. M., R. M. ENDO, and D. C. ERWIN. 1967. Infection of primary roots of bentgrass by zoospores of Pythium aphanidermatum. Phytopathology 57:86–90.

KREUTZER, W. A. 1960. Soil treatment. In Horsfall and Dimond, 1959–60, vol. 3, pp. 431–476.

KUIJT, J. 1955. Dwarf mistletoes. Botan. Rev. 21:569–627.

KUNKEL, L. O. 1946. Heat treatments for the cure of yellows and other virus diseases of peach. Phytopathology 26:809–830.

KUNTZ, J. E., and A. J. RIKER. 1950. Oak wilt in Wisconsin. Wisc. Agri. Expt. Sta. Stencil Bull. 9.

LACASSE, N. L., and A. E. RICH. 1964. Maple decline in New Hampshire. Phytopathology 54:1071–1075.

LARGE, E. C. 1966. Measuring plant disease. Ann. Rev. Phytopath. 4:9–28.

LeCLERG, E. L. 1964. Crop losses due to plant diseases in the United States. Phytopathology 54:1309–1313.

LEPPIK, E. E. 1969. The life and work of N. I. Vavilov. Econ. Botany 23:128–132.

LEPPIK, E. E. 1970. Gene centers of plants as sources of disease resistance. Ann. Rev. Phytopath. 8:323–344.

LEWIS, SALLY, and R. N. GOODMAN. 1965. Mode of penetration and movement of fire blight bacteria in apple leaf and stem tissue. Phytopathology 55:719–723.

LIBMAN, G., J. G. LEACH, and R. E. ADAMS. 1964. Role of certain plant-parasitic nematodes in infection of tomatoes by Psudomonas solanacearum. Phytopathology 54:151–153.

LIN, S., C. LEE, and R. CHIU. 1970. Isolation and cultivation of, and inoculation with, a mycoplasma causing white leaf disease of sugarcane. Phytopathology 60:795–797.

LINDBERG, G. D. 1969. Separation of a mildly diseased from a severely diseased isolate of Helminthosporium victoriae. Phytopathology 59:1884–1888.

LITTRELL, R. H., J. D. GAY, and H. D. WELLS. 1969. Chloroneb fungicide for control of Pythium aphanidermatum on several crop plants. Plant Dis. Rept. 53:913–915.

LITZENBERGER, S. C., and H. C. MURPHY. 1947. Methods for determining resistance of oats to Helminthosporium victoriae. Phytopathology 37:790–800.

LOEBENSTEIN, G., MIRIAM ALPER, and S. LEVY. 1970. Field tests with oil sprays for the prevention of aphid-spread viruses in pepper. Phytopathology 60:212–215.

LORENZ, O. A. 1942. Internal breakdown of table beets. Cornell Univ. Agric. Expt. Sta. Memoir 246.

LOVREKOVICH, L., H. LOVREKOVICH, and M. A. STAHMANN. 1968. The importance of peroxidase in the wildfire disease. Phytopathology 58:193–198.

LUKENS, R. J. 1970. Melting-out of Kentucky bluegrass, a low sugar disease. Phytopathology 60:1276–1278.

LUKENS, R. J., and J. G. HORSFALL. 1968. Glycolate oxidase, a target for antisporulants. Phytopathology 58:1671–1676.

LUNN, W. M., D. E. BROWN, J. E. MCMURTREY, and W. W. GARNER. 1939. Tobacco following bare and natural weed fallow. Jour. Agr. Res. 59:829–845.

MAIER, C. R. 1968. Influence of nitrogen nutrition on *Fusarium* root rot of pinto bean and on its suppression by barley straw. Phytopathology 58:620–625.

MARAMOROSCH, K., R. R. GRANADOS, and H. HIRUMI. 1970. Mycoplasma diseases of plant and insects. Adv. in Virus Res. 16:135–193.

MARKS, G. C., J. G. BERBEE, and A. J. RIKER. 1965. Direct penetration of leaves of *Populus tremuloides* by *Colletotrichum gloeosporiodes*. Phytopathology 55:408–412.

MARX, D. H. 1969. The influence of ectotrophic mycorrhizal fungi on the resistance of pine roots to pathogenic infections. I. Antagonisms of mycorrhizal fungi to root pathogenic fungi and soil bacteria. Phytopathology 59:153–163.

MATTHEWS, R. E. F. 1960. Virus inactivation *in vitro* and *in vivo*. In Horsfall and Dimond, 1959–60, vol. II, pp. 461–506.

MAUNDRY, K. W. 1963. Plant virus—host cell relations. Ann. Rev. Phytopath. 1:173–196.

MCCLELLAN, W. D. 1966. Common names for pesticides. Plant Dis. Rept. 50:725–729.

MCGUIRE, J. M., and W. E. COOPER. 1965. Interaction of heat injury and *Diplodia gossypina* and other etiological aspects of collar rot of peanut. Phytopathology 55:231–236.

MCINTOSH, D. L. 1969. A low-volume postharvest spray of benomyl prevents ascospore production in apple leaves infected by *Venturia inaequalis*. Plant Dis. Rept. 53:816–817.

MCNEW, G. L. 1950. Outline of a new approach in teaching plant pathology. Plant Dis. Rept. 34:106–110.

MCONIE, K. C. 1964. Source of inoculum of *Guignardia citricarpa*, the citrus black spot pathogen. Phytopathology 54:64–67.

MERRILL, W. 1967. The oak wilt epidemics in Pennsylvania and West Virginia: an analysis. Phytopathology 57:1206–1210.

MERRILL, W. 1971. Elm disease control programs question of aesthetics vs. cost. Sci. in Agric. 18:6–7.

MIGHELL, R. L. 1958. Oranges do not grow in the north. In 1958 Yearbook of Agriculture, pp.109–113.

MILLER, H. C., S. B. SILVERBORG, and R. J. CAMPANA. 1969. Dutch elm disease: relation of spread and intensification to control by sanitation in Syracuse, New York. Plant Dis. Rept. 53:551–555.

MILLER, P. M., and J. F. AHRENS. 1969. Influence of growing marigolds, weeds, two cover crops and fumigation on subsequent populations of parasitic nematodes and plant growth. Plant Dis. Rept. 53:642–646.

MILLER, P. R. 1959. Plant disease forecasting. In Holton, 1959, pp.557–565.

MILLER, P. R. 1966. International usefulness of an isolation laboratory for plant pathogens, especially viruses and their vectors. Plant Dis. Rept. 50:803–805.

MILLER, P. R., and MURIEL O'BRIEN. 1952. Plant disease forecasting. Botan. Rev. 18:547–601.

MIRCETICH, S. M., H. W. FOGLE, AND J. G. BARRAT. 1968. Further observations on stem pitting in *Prunus*. Plant Dis. Rept. 52:287–291.

MIRCETICH, S. M., H. W. FOGLE, and E. L. CIVEROLO. 1970. Peach stem pitting: transmission and natural spread. Phytopathology 60:1329–1334.

MOLLER, W. J., and J. E. DEVAY. 1968. Carrot as a species-selective isolation medium for *Ceratocystis fimbriata*. Phytopathology 58:123–124.

MONTEITH, J., and E. A. HOLLOWELL. 1929. Pathological symptoms in legumes caused by the potato leaf hopper. Jour. Agr. Res. 38:649–677.

MORRIS, C. L., and D. H. FRAZIER. 1966. Development of a hazard rating for *Fomes annosus* in Virginia. Plant Dis. Rept. 50:510–511.

MUSKETT, A. E. 1967. Plant pathology and the plant pathologist. Ann. Rev. Phytopath. 5:1–16.

NAULT, L. R., M. L. BRIONES, L. E. WILLIAMS, and B. D. BARRY. 1967. Relation of the wheat curl mite to kernel red streak of corn. Phytopathology 57:986–989.

NEELY, D. 1967. Dutch elm disease in Illinois cities. Plant Dis. Rept. 51:511–514.

NITZANY, F. E. 1966. Synergism between *Pythium ultimum* and cucumber mosaic virus. Phytopathology 56:1386–1389.

NITZANY, F. E., H. GEISENBERG, AND B. KOCH. 1964. Tests for the protection of cucumbers from a white fly-borne virus. Phytopathology 54:1059–1061.

NUGENT, T. J. 1950. Three years' experience forecasting late blight in Tidewater Virginia. Plant Dis. Rept. Suppl. 190:9–13.

NYLAND, G., and A. C. GOHEEN. 1969. Heat therapy of virus diseases of perennial plants. Ann. Rev. Phytopath. 7:331–354.

OLIVE, L. S. 1964. Spore discharge mechanism in basidiomycetes. Science 146:542–543.

ORDISH, G., and D. DUFOUR. 1969. Economic bases for protection against plant diseases. Ann. Rev. Phytopath. 7:31–50.

OSTAZESKI, S. 1968. Container effects on birdsfoot trefoil in greenhouse tests. Phytopathology 58:484–485.

OWENS, L. D., R. G. GILBERT, G. E. GRIEBEL, and J. D. MENZIES. 1969. Identification of plant volatiles that stimulate microbial respiration and growth in soil. Phytopathology 59:1468–1472.

PADDOCK, W. C. 1967. Phytopathology in a hungry world. Ann. Rev. Phytopath. 5:375–390.

PAINTER, R. H. 1951. Insect Resistance in Crop Plants. Macmillan, New York.

PAPAVIZAS, G. C. 1966. Suppression of *Aphanomyces* root rot of peas by cruciferous soil amendments. Phytopathology 56:1071–1075.

PARK, D. 1963. The ecology of soil-borne fungal disease. Ann. Rev. Phytopath. 1:241–258.

PARMETER, J. R., R. T. SHERWOOD, and W. D. PLATT. 1969. Anastomosis grouping among isolates of *Thanatephorus curcumeris*. Phytopathology 59:1270–1278.

PATRICK, Z. A., R. M. SAYRE, and H. J. THORPE. 1965. Nematocidal substances selective for plant-parasitic nematodes in extracts of decomposing rye. Phytopathology 55:702–703.

PHELPS, W. R., and R. WEBER. 1969. An evaluation of chemotherapeutants for control of blister rust cankers in eastern white pine. Plant Dis. Rept. 53:514–517.

PIEMEISEL, R. L. 1954. Replacement control; changes in vegetation in relation to control of pests and diseases. Botan. Rev. 20:1–32.

PIEMEISEL, R. L., and E. CARSNER. 1951. Replacement control and biological control. Science 113:14–15.

PIRONE, P. P. 1970. Diseases and Pests of Oranmental Plants, 4th ed. Ronald Press, New York.

POWELL, D. 1967. Night applications for improved effectiveness of streptomycin in preventing fire blight disease. Plant Dis. Rept. 51:605–607.

RANDS, R. D., and E. DOPP. 1938. Pythium root rot of sugarcane. Tech. Bull. 666, U.S. Dept. of Agric.

RAO, A. S. 1968. Biology of *Polymyxa graminis* in relation to soil-borne wheat mosaic virus. Phytopathology 58:1516–1521.

RICH, S. 1960. Fungicidal chemistry. In Horsfall and Dimond, 1959–60, vol. III, pp. 553–602.

RIKER, A. J., and E. M. HILDEBRAND. 1934. Seasonal development of hairy root, crown gall, and wound overgrowth on apple trees in the nursery. Jour. Agr. Res. 48:887–912.

ROMANKO, R. R. 1964. Control of hop mildew by chemical desiccants. Phytopathology 54:1439–1442.

ROTEM, J., and J. PALTI. 1969. Irrigation and plant diseases. Ann. Rev. Phytopath. 7:267–288.

ROWELL, J. B. 1968. Chemical control of the cereal rusts. Ann. Rev. Phytopath. 6:243–262.

RUSSEL, DARRELL A. 1957. Boron and soil fertility. 1957 Yearbook of Agriculture, p.124.

SASSER, J. N., and W. R. JENKINS, eds. 1960. Nematology. North Carolina University Press.

SCHEIFELE, G. L., W. WHITEHEAD, and C. ROWE. 1970. Increased susceptibility to Southern leaf spot (*Helminthosporium maydis*) in inbred lines and hybrids of maize with Texas male-sterile cytoplasm. Plant Dis. Rept. 54:501–503.

SCHEIN, R. D. 1965. Age-correlated changes in susceptibility of bean leaves to *Uromyces phaseoli* and tobacco mosaic virus. Phytopathology 55:454–457.

SCHNATHORST, W. C. 1964. Longevity of *Xanthomonas malvacearum* in dried cotton plants and its significance in dissemination of the pathogen on seed. Phytopathology 54:1009–1011.

SCHNATHORST, W. C., and D. E. MATHRE. 1966. Cross-protection in cotton with strains of *Verticillium albo-atrum*. Phytopathology 56:1204–1209.

SCHOLANDER, P. F., H. T. HAMMEL, EDDA D. BRADSTREET, and E. A. HEMMINGSEN. 1965. Sap pressure in vascular plants. Science 148:339–346.

SCHRÖDTER, H. 1960. Dispersal by air and water—flight and landing. In Horsfall and Dimond, 1959–60, vol. III, pp.169–227.

SCHROTH, M. N., and D. C. HILDEBRAND. 1968. A chemotherapeutic treatment for selectively eradicating crown gall and olive knot neoplasms. Phytopathology 58:848–854.

SCOTT, K. J., and D. J. MACLEAN. 1969. Culturing of rust fungi. Ann. Rev. Phytopath. 7:123–146.

SEMPIO, C. 1959. The host is starved. In Horsfall and Dimond, 1959–60, vol. I, pp. 277–312.

SHAW, D. S. 1967. A method of obtaining single-oospore cultures of *Phytophthora cactorum* using live water snails. Phytopathology 57:454.

SIDDIQUI, W. M., P. M. HALISKY, and S. LUND. 1968. Relationship of clipping frequency to root and crown deterioration in red clover. Phytopathology 58:486–488.

SIDERIS, C. P. 1955. Effects of sea water sprays on pineapple plants. Phytopathology 45:590–595.

SIEGEL, A., and M. ZAITLIN. 1964. Infection process in plant virus diseases. Ann. Rev. Phytopath. 2:179–202.

SIMMONDS, P. M. 1953. Rootrots of cereals II. Botan. Rev. 19:131–146.

SINCLAIR, J. B. 1968. Eradication of citrus canker from Louisiana. Plant Dis. Rept. 52:667–670.

SISLER, H. D., and C. E. COX. 1960. Physiology of fungitoxicity. In Horsfall and Dimond, 1959–60, vol. II, pp. 507–552.

SMITH, A. M., B. A. STYNES, and K. J. MOORE. 1970. Benomyl stimulates growth of a basidiomycete on turf. Plant Dis. Rept. 70:774–775.

SMITH, H. S., Chm. 1933. The efficacy and economic effects of plant quarantines in California. Calif. Agr. Expt. Sta. Bull. 553.

SMITH, P. R., R. N. CAMPBELL, and P. R. FRY. 1969. Root discharge and soil survival of viruses. Phytopathology 59:1678–1687.

SPEARS, J. F. 1968. The golden nematode handbook. USDA Agric. Res. Serv. Handbook 353.

SPEARS, J. F. 1969. Golden nematode found in Delaware. Plant Dis. Rept. 53:243.

STACE-SMITH, R., and F. C. MELLOR. 1968. Eradication of potato viruses X and S by thermotherapy and axillary bud culture. Phytopathology 58:199–203.

STAKMAN, E. C. 1947. Plant diseases are shifty enemies. Amer. Sci. 35:321–350.

STAKMAN, E. C., and J. G. HARRAR. 1957. Principles of Plant Pathology. Ronald Press, New York.

STAKMAN, E. C., M. F. KERNKAMP, W. J. MARTIN, AND T. H. KING. 1943. The inheritance of a white mutant character in *Ustilago zeae*. Phytopathology 33:943–949.

STAKMAN, E. C., M. N. LEVINE, R. U. COTTER, and L. HINES. 1934. Relation of barberry to the origin and persistence of physiologic forms of *Puccinia graminis*. Jour. Agr. Res. 48:953–969.

STANGHELLINI, M. E., and M. ARAGAKI. 1966. Relation of periderm formation and callose deposition to anthracnose resistance in papaya fruit. Phytopathology 56:444–450.

STANLEY, W. M., and C. A. Knight. 1941. The chemical composition of strains of tobacco mosaic virus. Cold Spring Harbor Symp. on Quant. Biol. 9:255–262.

STEVENS, N. E. 1938a. Departures from ordinary methods in controlling plant diseases. Botan. Rev. 4:429–445, 677–678.

STEVENS, N. E. 1938b. Problems involved in control of plant diseases and insects. Econ. Entomol. 31:39–44.

STEVENS, N. E., and R. B. STEVENS. 1952. Disease in Plants. Chronica Botanica, Waltham, Mass.

STEVENS, R. B. 1949. Replanting "discarded" varieties as a means of disease control. Science 110:49.

STODDARD, E. M. 1947. X-disease of peach and its chemotherapy. Conn. Agr. Expt. Sta. Bull. 506.

STOUFFER, R. F., and F. H. LEWIS. 1969. The present status of peach stem pitting in Pennsylvania. Plant Dis. Rept. 53:429–434.

STOUFFER, R. F., F. H. LEWIS, and D. M. SOULEN. 1969. Stem pitting in commercial cherry and plum orchards in Pennsylvania. Plant Dis. Rept. 53:434–438.

STRETCH, A. W., and J. K. SPRINGER. 1966. The "ground effect" machine as a vehicle for applying pesticides on cranberry. Plant Dis. Rept. 50:715–717.

SWENSON, K. G. 1968. Role of aphids in the ecology of plant viruses. Ann. Rev. Phytopath. 6:351–374.

TAYLOR, A. L. 1946. Costs cut for root-knot control. Florida Grower 55:6.

TAYLOR, A. L. 1967. Introduction to Research on Plant Nematology—an FAO Guide to the Study and Control of Plant-Parasitic Nematodes. Food and Agriculture Organization of the United Nations, Rome.

THEIS, T., and L. CALPOUZOS. 1957. A seven-day instrument for recording periods of rainfall and dew. Phytopathology 47:746–747.

TOWER, W. L. 1906. An investigation of evolution in Chrysomelid beetles of the genus *Leptinotarsa*. Carnegie Inst. Wash. Publ. 48.

Troutman, J. L, and W. H. Wills. 1964. Electrotaxis of *Phytophthora parasitica* zoospores and its possible role in infection of tobacco by the fungus. Phytopathology 54:225–228.

TU, J. C., and J. W. HENDRIX. 1970. The summer biology of *Puccinia striiformis* in southeastern Washington II. Natural infection during the summer. Plant Dis. Rept. 54:384–386.

ULLSTRUP, A. J. 1969. "Buggy-whip" of corn and its relation to the incidence of common smut. Plant Dis. Rept. 53:250–252.

ULRICH, R. 1958. Postharvest physiology of fruits. Ann. Rev. Plant Physiol. 9:385–416.

VALLEAU, W. D. 1953. Suggestions for more complete control of downy mildew or blue mold of tobacco. Phytopathology 43:616–618.

VALLEAU, W. D., E. M. JOHNSON, and S. DIACHUN. 1942. Tobacco diseases. Ky. Agric. Expt. Sta. Bull. 437.

VAN ARSDEL, E. P. 1967. The nocturnal diffusion and transport of spores. Phytopathology 57:1221–1229.

VAN DER PLANK, J. E. 1959. Some epidemiological consequences of systemic infection. In Holton, 1959, pp. 566–573.

VAN DER PLANK, J. E. 1960. Analysis of epidemics. In Horsfall and Dimond, 1959–60, vol. III, pp. 229–289.

VAN DER PLANK, J. E. 1963. Plant Diseases; Epidemics and Control. Academic Press, New York.

VAN DER ZWET, T. 1968. Recent spread and present distribution of fire blight in the world. Plant Dis. Rept. 52:698–702.

VAUGHAN, E. K. 1956. A method for eliminating the red-stele fungus from valuable strawberry stocks. Phytopathology 46:235–236.

VAVILOV, N. I. 1949–50. Phytogeographic basis of plant breeding. In The Origin, Variation, Immunity and Breeding of Cultivated Plants. Ronald Press, New York, pp.13–54. (Translated from the Russian by K. S. Chester.)

VIRGINIA POLYTECHNIC INSTITUTE. 1966. A Handbook of Agronomy. VPI Bull. 97.

WAGENER, W. W., and R. W. Davidson. 1954. Heart rots in living trees. Botan. Rev. 20:61–134.

WAGGONER, P. E. 1960. Forecasting epidemics. In Horsfall and Dimond, 1959–60, vol. III, p.291–321.

WAGGONER, P. E. 1965. Microclimate and plant disease. Ann. Rev. Phytopath. 3:103–126.

WALKER, J. C. 1923. Disease resistance in onion smudge. Jour. Agr. Res. 24:1019–1039.

WALKER, J. C., and P. N. PATEL. 1964. Splash dispersal and wind as factors in epidemiology of halo blight of bean. Phytopathology 54:140–141.

WEDDERBURN, A. J. 1948. Photography in science. Sci. Monthly 66:9–16.

WEIDENSAUL, T. C., and N. H. PLAUGHER. 1966. An evaluation of three stump treatment chemicals for preventing surface infection by *Fomes annosus*. Plant Dis. Rept. 50:22–25.

WEINHOLD, A. R., T. Bowman, and R. L. Dodman. 1969. Virulence of *Rhizoctonia solani* as affected by nutrition of the pathogen. Phytopathology 59:1601–1605.

WEISS. P. 1962. Renewable Resources—A Report to the Committee on Natural Resources. Natl. Acad. Sci. Publ. 1000-A.

WELLMAN, F. L. 1935. Dissemination of southern celery-mosaic virus on vegetable crops in Florida. Phytopathology 25:289–308.

WELLMAN, F. L. 1964. Parasitism among neotropical phanerogams. Ann. Rev. Phytopath. 2:43–56.

WELLMAN, F. L. 1970a. *Hemileia* coffee rust in South America. Phytopathology News 4:1.

WELLMAN, F. L. 1970b. The rust *Hemileia vastatrix* now firmly established in coffee in Brazil. Plant Dis. Rept. 54:539–541.

WELLMAN, R. H. 1959. Commercial development of fungicides. In Holton, 1959, pp. 239–245.

WENT, F. W. 1957. The Experimental Control of Plant Growth. Ronald Press, New York.

WHETZEL, H. H., and V. B. Stewart. 1909. Fire blight of pears, apples, quinces, etc. Cornell Univ. Exp. Sta. Bull. 272.

WHIPPLE, O. C. 1941. Injury to tomatoes by lightning. Phytopathology 31:1017–1022.

WHITCOMB, R. F., and R. E. Davis. 1970. *Mycoplasma* and phytarboviruses as plant pathogens persistently transmitted by insects. Ann. Rev. Entomol. 15:405–464.

WHITMAN, V. E. 1926. Studies in the electrification of dust clouds. Physical Review 28:1287–1301.

WICKER, E. F. 1967. Appraisal of biological control of *Arceuthobium campylopodum* f. *campylopodum* by *Colletotrichum gloeosporioides*. Plant Dis. Rept. 51:311–313.

WILHELM, S. 1966. Chemical treatments and inoculum potential of soil. Ann. Rev. Phytopath. 4:53–78.

WILLIAMS, P. G., K. J. Scott, JOY L. KUHL, and D. J. MACLEAN. 1967. Sporulation and pathogenicity of *Puccinia graminis* f sp. *tritici* grown on an artificial medium. Phytopathology 57:326–327.

WILLIAMS, P. H., and N. T. KEEN. 1967. Relation of cell permeability alterations to water congestion in cucumber angular leaf spot. Phytopathology 57:1378–1385.

Wilson, H. F., R. J. JANES, and E. J. CAMPAU. 1944. Electrostatic charge effects produced by insecticidal dusts. Jour. Econ. Entomol. 37:651–655.

WINSLOW, R. D. 1960. Some aspects of the ecology of free-living and plant-parasitic nematodes. In Sasser and Jenkins, 1960, pp. 341–415.

WOODBRIDGE, C. G. 1950. The role of boron in the agricultural regions of the Pacific Northwest. Sci. Monthly 70:97–104.

WOODCOCK, E. 1959. The relation of chemical structure to fungicidal activity. In Holton, 1959, pp. 267–279.

YARWOOD, C. E. 1956. Obligate parasitism. Ann. Rev. Plant Physiol. 7:115–142.

YARWOOD, C. E. 1959. Predisposition. In Horsfall and Dimond, 1959, pp. 521–562.

YARWOOD, C. E. 1964. Adaptation and sensitization of bean leaves to rust. Phytopathology 54:936–940.

YARWOOD, C. E. 1965. Predisposition to mildew by rust infection, heat, abrasion, and pressure. Phytopathology 55:1372.

YIRGOU, D., and R. M. CALDWELL. 1963. Stomatal penetration of wheat seedlings by stem and leaf rust: effect of light and carbon dioxide. Science 141:272–273.

ZAUMEYER, W. J., and H. R. THOMAS. 1948. Inheritance of symptom expression of bean mosaic virus 4. Jour. Agr. Res. 77:295–300.

ZEHR, E. I. 1968. Selected organic fungicides and dimethyl sulfoxide as supplements to streptomycin for fire blight control on bartlett pear. Phytopathology 58:1624–1629.

Index